I0021118

Cocos2d for iPhone 1 Game Development Cookbook

Over 90 recipes for iOS 2D game development using cocos2d

Nathan Burba

PUBLISHING

BIRMINGHAM - MUMBAI

Cocos2d for iPhone 1 Game Development Cookbook

Copyright © 2011 Packt Publishing

All rights reserved. No part of this book may be reproduced, stored in a retrieval system, or transmitted in any form or by any means, without the prior written permission of the publisher, except in the case of brief quotations embedded in critical articles or reviews.

Every effort has been made in the preparation of this book to ensure the accuracy of the information presented. However, the information contained in this book is sold without warranty, either express or implied. Neither the author, nor Packt Publishing, and its dealers and distributors will be held liable for any damages caused or alleged to be caused directly or indirectly by this book.

Packt Publishing has endeavored to provide trademark information about all of the companies and products mentioned in this book by the appropriate use of capitals. However, Packt Publishing cannot guarantee the accuracy of this information.

First published: December 2011

Production Reference: 1081211

Published by Packt Publishing Ltd.
Livery Place
35 Livery Street
Birmingham B3 2PB, UK.

ISBN 978-1-84951-400-2

www.packtpub.com

Cover Image by Vinayak Chittar (vinayak.chittar@gmail.com)

Credits

Author

Nathan Burba

Reviewers

Chris Cockcroft

Hai "EvilJack" Nguyen

Senior Acquisition Editor

Usha Iyer

Development Editor

Susmita Panda

Technical Editors

Priyanka Shah

Naheed Shaikh

Project Coordinator

Jovita Pinto

Proofreader

Aaron Nash

Indexer

Monica Ajmera Mehta

Production Coordinator

Arvindkumar Gupta

Cover Work

Arvindkumar Gupta

About the Author

Nathan Burba is a game developer, student, producer, and entrepreneur. He graduated from Ithaca College with a BA in Computer Science in 2008 and began working toward an MFA in Interactive Media at the University of Southern California School of Cinematic Arts in 2011. He founded Logical Extreme Studios LLC in 2011 and plans to release his first iOS game, Golden Age Baseball, in early 2012.

I would like to thank my family and friends for their constant support. In particular, I would like to thank my loving girlfriend Julie for her exuberant encouragement and unending patience. I would also like to thank my Computer Science peers and mentors throughout the years including, but not limited to, Zander Li, Joseph Blass, Alex Martinez, Ali Erkan, John Barr, Chris Ledet, George Smith, and Jared Combs. This book is a collection of recipes that hundreds of dedicated individuals have contributed to in one way or another. I'd like to thank Ricardo Quesada and those who've contributed directly to Cocos2d, Erin Catto and those who've contributed to Box2d, Cocos2d forum members: ascorbin, manucorporat, asinesio, Blue Ether, jbarron, Joao Caxaria, and BrandonReynolds, programmers: John W. Ratcliff, Ray Wenderlich, Gus Mueller, and Alex Eckermann, and Open Game Art contributors: artisticdude, p0ss, mrpoly and Bart K.

About the Reviewers

Chris Cockcroft has over 12 years of experience in the graphic design and illustration industry. He has more recently become involved in iOS interactive entertainment in both design and development roles. In addition to self-publishing several titles built around the Cocos2D frameworks, Chris also worked with developer Andreas Ehnbom on the visual design of the popular Cocos2D-driven (and Apple-featured) title, Fuji Leaves. Chris' work can be viewed at www.chriscockcroft.com.

Hai "EvilJack" Nguyen fits your typical engineering stereotype: scrawny, loves to program, and scared to death of women. He spends his free time tinkering with gadgets and updating his Facebook status.

After finishing graduate school at the University of Florida, Jack moved to Taiwan in mid 2003. Shortly thereafter SARS hit the Asia Pacific region (unrelated to Jack's arrival, of course). He then joined a software company that worked on mobile phones (Aplix) and got a chance to play with all the latest phones and gadgets.

Eventually, he left that awesome job and moved to Korea a few years later (to chase a girl) and spent the better part of a year studying Korean. Shortly after moving there, North Korea began conducting tests of their nuclear stockpile (unrelated to jack's arrival, of course).

Eventually, he moved back to the USA and began working for a voice over IP startup creating mobile applications for them. Shortly after moving back to the US (2007), the greatest financial crisis in almost a century occurred (unrelated to Jack's arrival, of course).

Jack currently splits his time between California and Florida while trying to avoid getting kicked out of (yet) another country. He is currently hiding away in his mother's basement writing iPhone apps.

www.PacktPub.com

Support files, eBooks, discount offers and more

You might want to visit www.PacktPub.com for support files and downloads related to your book.

Did you know that Packt offers eBook versions of every book published, with PDF and ePub files available? You can upgrade to the eBook version at www.PacktPub.com and as a print book customer, you are entitled to a discount on the eBook copy. Get in touch with us at service@packtpub.com for more details.

At www.PacktPub.com, you can also read a collection of free technical articles, sign up for a range of free newsletters and receive exclusive discounts and offers on Packt books and eBooks.

http://PacktLib.PacktPub.com

Do you need instant solutions to your IT questions? PacktLib is Packt's online digital book library. Here, you can access, read and search across Packt's entire library of books.

Why Subscribe?

- ▸ Fully searchable across every book published by Packt
- ▸ Copy and paste, print and bookmark content
- ▸ On demand and accessible via web browser

Free Access for Packt account holders

If you have an account with Packt at www.PacktPub.com, you can use this to access PacktLib today and view nine entirely free books. Simply use your login credentials for immediate access.

Table of Contents

Preface

Cocos2d for iPhone is a robust but simple to use 2D game framework for iPhone. It is fast, flexible, free, and App Store approved. More than 2500 App Store games already use it, including many best-selling games. Do you want to take your Cocos2d game development skills to the next level and become more professional in Cocos2d game design?

Cocos2d for iPhone 1 Game Development Cookbook will help you reach that next level. You will find over 90 recipes here that explain everything from the drawing of a single sprite to AI pathfinding and advanced networking. Full working examples are emphasized.

Starting with the first chapter, *Graphics*, you will be taken through every major topic of game development. You will find both simple and complex recipes in the book.

Each recipe is either a solution to a common problem (playing video files, accelerometer steering) or a cool advanced technique (3D rendering, textured polygons).

This cookbook will have you creating professional quality iOS games quickly with its breadth of working example code.

What this book covers

Chapter 1, Graphics, covers a wide array of topics. It starts by taking a look at the basic uses of sprites. From there it provides examples for 2D and 3D primitive drawing, video playing, particle effects, ease actions, texture filled polygons, palette swapping, lighting, parallaxing, and more.

Chapter 2, User Input, provides examples of different styles of input typically used in iOS game development. This includes tapping, holding, dragging, buttons, directional pad, analog stick, accelerometer, pinch zooming, and gestures.

Chapter 3, Files and Data, discusses techniques for persisting data. These include PLIST files, JSON files, XML files, NSUserDefaults, archive objects, SQLite, and Core Data.

Chapter 4, Physics, covers a large number of uses of the Box2D physics engine. Examples include debug drawing, collision response, different shapes, dragging, physical properties, impulses, forces, asynchronous body destruction, joints, vehicles, character movement, bullets, ropes, and finally creating a top-down isometric game engine.

Chapter 5, Scenes and Menus, provides examples of user interface implementations. It starts with examples involving scene management then moves to typical UI elements like labels, menus, alert dialogs, and UIKit wrapping. From there it moves into more advanced techniques like draggable menu windows, scrolling menus, sliding menus, loading screens, and a minimap.

Chapter 6, Audio, covers a wide range of audio topics which vary in difficulty. These include sounds, music, audio properties, fading audio, in-game examples, positional audio, metering music and dialogue, recording, streaming, playing iPod music, creating a MIDI synthesizer, speech recognition, and text to speech.

Chapter 7, AI and Logic, discusses techniques for adding intelligent AI actors into your games. These include processing waypoints, firing projectiles at moving targets, line of sight, and flocking behavior using Boids. The pathfinding problem is tackled in four separate recipes: A* pathfinding in a grid, a Box2D world, a TMX tilemap, and a side-scroller. Finally, the chapter discusses adding Lua scripting support, dynamically loading scripts, and using Lua for dialogue trees.

Chapter 8, Tips, Tools, and Ports, provides example uses of commonly-used tools including the Cocos2d-iPhone testbed, Zwoptex, Tiled, JSONWorldBuilder, and CocosBuilder. It also discusses porting a Cocos2d project to C++ using Cocos2d-X and using Cocos3d to develop a 3D iOS game. Finally, it discusses the process of releasing your app on the Apple App Store.

What you need for this book

This book includes projects that contain fully functioning example code. You'll need the following to run the example code:

- An Intel-based Macintosh running Snow Leopard (OSX 10.6 or later).
- XCode (4.0 or later recommended).
- You must be enrolled as an iPhone developer in order to test the example projects on a device. They can be run in the iPhone Simulator without the aforementioned enrollment.

Who this book is for

If you want to elevate your basic Cocos2d project to the next level, then this is the book for you. Some understanding of Objective-C and Cocos2d is recommended. People with some programming experience may also find this book useful.

Conventions

In this book, you will find a number of styles of text that distinguish between different kinds of information. Here are some examples of these styles, and an explanation of their meaning.

Code words in text are shown as follows: "In this recipe we will cover drawing sprites using CCSprite, spritesheets, CCSpriteFrameCache, and CCSpriteBatchNode."

A block of code is set as follows:

```
@implementation Ch1_DrawingSprites
-(CCLayer*) runRecipe {
/*** Draw a sprite using CCSprite ***/
CCSprite *tree1 = [CCSprite spriteWithFile:@"tree.png"];
```

Any command-line input or output is written as follows:

```
afconvert -f caff -d ima4 mysound.wav
```

New terms and **important words** are shown in bold. Words that you see on the screen, in menus or dialog boxes for example, appear in the text like this: "Right-click your project under **Groups & Files**."

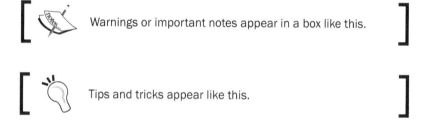

Warnings or important notes appear in a box like this.

Tips and tricks appear like this.

Reader feedback

Feedback from our readers is always welcome. Let us know what you think about this book— what you liked or may have disliked. Reader feedback is important for us to develop titles that you really get the most out of.

To send us general feedback, simply send an e-mail to feedback@packtpub.com, and mention the book title via the subject of your message.

If there is a book that you need and would like to see us publish, please send us a note in the **SUGGEST A TITLE** form on www.packtpub.com or e-mail suggest@packtpub.com.

If there is a topic that you have expertise in and you are interested in either writing or contributing to a book, see our author guide on www.packtpub.com/authors.

Customer support

Now that you are the proud owner of a Packt book, we have a number of things to help you to get the most from your purchase.

For more information on Cocos2d or for any questions, you can log on to `www.Cocos2dCookbook.com`.

Downloading the example code

You can download the example code files for all Packt books you have purchased from your account at `http://www.PacktPub.com`. If you purchased this book elsewhere, you can visit `http://www.PacktPub.com/support` and register to have the files e-mailed directly to you.

Errata

Although we have taken every care to ensure the accuracy of our content, mistakes do happen. If you find a mistake in one of our books—maybe a mistake in the text or the code—we would be grateful if you would report this to us. By doing so, you can save other readers from frustration and help us improve subsequent versions of this book. If you find any errata, please report them by visiting `http://www.packtpub.com/support`, selecting your book, clicking on the **errata submission form** link, and entering the details of your errata. Once your errata are verified, your submission will be accepted and the errata will be uploaded on our website, or added to any list of existing errata, under the Errata section of that title. Any existing errata can be viewed by selecting your title from `http://www.packtpub.com/support`.

Piracy

Piracy of copyright material on the Internet is an ongoing problem across all media. At Packt, we take the protection of our copyright and licenses very seriously. If you come across any illegal copies of our works, in any form, on the Internet, please provide us with the location address or website name immediately so that we can pursue a remedy.

Please contact us at `copyright@packtpub.com` with a link to the suspected pirated material.

We appreciate your help in protecting our authors, and our ability to bring you valuable content.

Questions

You can contact us at `questions@packtpub.com` if you are having a problem with any aspect of the book, and we will do our best to address it.

1
Graphics

In this chapter, we will cover the following topics:

- ▸ Introduction
- ▸ Drawing sprites
- ▸ Coloring sprites
- ▸ Animating sprites
- ▸ Drawing OpenGL primitives
- ▸ Playing video files
- ▸ Grid, particle, and motion streak effects
- ▸ Using Retina Display mode
- ▸ 1D and 2D Ease Actions
- ▸ Rendering and texturing 3D Cubes
- ▸ Rendering a texture filled polygon
- ▸ Animating a texture filled polygon
- ▸ Swapping palettes using layers
- ▸ Swapping palettes using CCTexture2DMutable
- ▸ Using AWTextureFilter for blur and font shadows
- ▸ Taking and using screenshots
- ▸ Using CCParallaxNode
- ▸ Lighting using glColorMask

Introduction

Cocos2d is first and foremost a rich graphical API which allows a game developer easy access to a broad range of functionality. In this chapter we will go over some more advanced features of Cocos2d and how you can use these features to serve a variety of different purposes. We'll also explain advanced techniques that are not yet part of the Cocos2d source.

For the purposes of this chapter **Graphics** can be considered an umbrella term. We will also go over advanced techniques using **Actions** and **Particles**.

Drawing sprites

The most fundamental task in 2D game development is drawing a **sprite**. Cocos2d provides the user with a lot of flexibility in this area. In this recipe we will cover drawing sprites using `CCSprite`, spritesheets, `CCSpriteFrameCache`, and `CCSpriteBatchNode`. We will also go over **mipmapping**. To keep things fun and interesting, many recipes in this book will have a distinct theme. In this recipe we see a scene with Alice from Through The Looking Glass.

 You can download the example code files for all Packt books you have purchased from your account at `http://www.PacktPub.com`. If you purchased this book elsewhere, you can visit `http://www.PacktPub.com/support` and register to have the files e-mailed directly to you.

Getting ready

Please refer to the project `RecipeCollection01` for the full working code of this recipe.

How to do it...

Execute the following code:

```
@implementation Ch1_DrawingSprites
-(CCLayer*) runRecipe {
  /*** Draw a sprite using CCSprite ***/
  CCSprite *tree1 = [CCSprite spriteWithFile:@"tree.png"];

  //Position the sprite using the tree base as a guide (y anchor point
= 0)
[tree1 setPosition:ccp(20,20)];
  tree1.anchorPoint = ccp(0.5f,0);
  [tree1 setScale:1.5f];
  [self addChild:tree1 z:2 tag:TAG_TREE_SPRITE_1];

  /*** Load a set of spriteframes from a PLIST file and draw one by
name ***/

  //Get the sprite frame cache singleton
  CCSpriteFrameCache *cache = [CCSpriteFrameCache
sharedSpriteFrameCache];

  //Load our scene sprites from a spritesheet
  [cache addSpriteFramesWithFile:@"alice_scene_sheet.plist"];

  //Specify the sprite frame and load it into a CCSprite
  CCSprite *alice = [CCSprite spriteWithSpriteFrameName:@"alice.png"];

  //Generate Mip Maps for the sprite
  [alice.texture generateMipmap];
  ccTexParams texParams = { GL_LINEAR_MIPMAP_LINEAR, GL_LINEAR, GL_
CLAMP_TO_EDGE, GL_CLAMP_TO_EDGE };
  [alice.texture setTexParameters:&texParams];

  //Set other information.
  [alice setPosition:ccp(120,20)];
  [alice setScale:0.4f];
  alice.anchorPoint = ccp(0.5f,0);

  //Add Alice with a zOrder of 2 so she appears in front of other
sprites
  [self addChild:alice z:2 tag:TAG_ALICE_SPRITE];

  //Make Alice grow and shrink.
  [alice runAction: [CCRepeatForever actionWithAction:
    [CCSequence actions:[CCScaleTo actionWithDuration:4.0f
scale:0.7f], [CCScaleTo actionWithDuration:4.0f scale:0.1f], nil] ] ];

  /*** Draw a sprite CGImageRef ***/
```

```objc
    UIImage *uiImage = [UIImage imageNamed: @"cheshire_cat.png"];
    CGImageRef imageRef = [uiImage CGImage];
    CCSprite *cat = [CCSprite spriteWithCGImage:imageRef key:@"cheshire_
cat.png"];
    [cat setPosition:ccp(250,180)];
    [cat setScale:0.4f];
    [self addChild:cat z:3 tag:TAG_CAT_SPRITE];

    /*** Draw a sprite using CCTexture2D ***/
    CCTexture2D *texture = [[CCTextureCache sharedTextureCache]
addImage:@"tree.png"];
    CCSprite *tree2 = [CCSprite spriteWithTexture:texture];
    [tree2 setPosition:ccp(300,20)];
    tree2.anchorPoint = ccp(0.5f,0);
    [tree2 setScale:2.0f];
    [self addChild:tree2 z:2 tag:TAG_TREE_SPRITE_2];

    /*** Draw a sprite using CCSpriteFrameCache and CCTexture2D ***/
    CCSpriteFrame *frame = [CCSpriteFrame frameWithTexture:texture
rect:tree2.textureRect];
    [[CCSpriteFrameCache sharedSpriteFrameCache] addSpriteFrame:frame
name:@"tree.png"];
    CCSprite *tree3 = [CCSprite spriteWithSpriteFrame:[[CCSpriteFrameCac
he sharedSpriteFrameCache] spriteFrameByName:@"tree.png"]];
    [tree3 setPosition:ccp(400,20)];
    tree3.anchorPoint = ccp(0.5f,0);
    [tree3 setScale:1.25f];
    [self addChild:tree3 z:2 tag:TAG_TREE_SPRITE_3];

    /*** Draw sprites using CCBatchSpriteNode ***/

    //Clouds
    CCSpriteBatchNode *cloudBatch = [CCSpriteBatchNode
batchNodeWithFile:@"cloud_01.png" capacity:10];
    [self addChild:cloudBatch z:1 tag:TAG_CLOUD_BATCH];
    for(int x=0; x<10; x++){
        CCSprite *s = [CCSprite spriteWithBatchNode:cloudBatch
rect:CGRectMake(0,0,64,64)];
        [s setOpacity:100];
        [cloudBatch addChild:s];
        [s setPosition:ccp(arc4random()%500-50, arc4random()%150+200)];
    }

    //Middleground Grass
    int capacity = 10;
    CCSpriteBatchNode *grassBatch1 = [CCSpriteBatchNode
batchNodeWithFile:@"grass_01.png" capacity:capacity];
    [self addChild:grassBatch1 z:1 tag:TAG_GRASS_BATCH_1];
    for(int x=0; x<capacity; x++){
```

```
    CCSprite *s = [CCSprite spriteWithBatchNode:grassBatch1
rect:CGRectMake(0,0,64,64)];
    [s setOpacity:255];
    [grassBatch1 addChild:s];
    [s setPosition:ccp(arc4random()%500-50, arc4random()%20+70)];
  }

  //Foreground Grass
  CCSpriteBatchNode *grassBatch2 = [CCSpriteBatchNode
batchNodeWithFile:@"grass_01.png" capacity:10];
  [self addChild:grassBatch2 z:3 tag:TAG_GRASS_BATCH_2];
  for(int x=0; x<30; x++){
    CCSprite *s = [CCSprite spriteWithBatchNode:grassBatch2
rect:CGRectMake(0,0,64,64)];
    [s setOpacity:255];
    [grassBatch2 addChild:s];
    [s setPosition:ccp(arc4random()%500-50, arc4random()%40-10)];
  }

  /*** Draw colored rectangles using a 1px x 1px white texture ***/

  //Draw the sky using blank.png
  [self drawColoredSpriteAt:ccp(240,190) withRect:CGRectMa
ke(0,0,480,260) withColor:ccc3(150,200,200) withZ:0];

  //Draw the ground using blank.png
  [self drawColoredSpriteAt:ccp(240,30)
withRect:CGRectMake(0,0,480,60) withColor:ccc3(80,50,25) withZ:0];

  return self;
}

-(void) drawColoredSpriteAt:(CGPoint)position withRect:(CGRect)rect
withColor:(ccColor3B)color withZ:(float)z {
  CCSprite *sprite = [CCSprite spriteWithFile:@"blank.png"];
  [sprite setPosition:position];
  [sprite setTextureRect:rect];
  [sprite setColor:color];
  [self addChild:sprite];

  //Set Z Order
  [self reorderChild:sprite z:z];
}

@end
```

How it works...

This recipe takes us through most of the common ways of drawing sprites:

- Creating a CCSprite from a file:

  First, we have the simplest way to draw a sprite. This involves using the CCSprite class method as follows:

  ```
  +(id)spriteWithFile:(NSString*)filename;
  ```

  This is the most straightforward way to initialize a sprite and is adequate for many situations.

- Other ways to load a sprite from a file:

  After this, we will see examples of CCSprite creation using UIImage/CGImageRef, CCTexture2D, and a CCSpriteFrame instantiated using a CCTexture2D object. CGImageRef support allows you to tie Cocos2d into other frameworks and toolsets. CCTexture2D is the underlying mechanism for texture creation.

- Loading spritesheets using CCSpriteFrameCache:

  Next, we will see the most powerful way to use sprites, the CCSpriteFrameCache class. Introduced in Cocos2d-iPhone v0.99, the CCSpriteFrameCache singleton is a cache of all sprite frames. Using a **spritesheet** and its associated PLIST file (created using **Zwoptex**, more on this later) we can load multiple sprites into the cache. From here we can create CCSprite objects with sprites from the cache:

  ```
  +(id)spriteWithSpriteFrameName:(NSString*)filename;
  ```

- **Mipmapping**:

  Mipmapping allows you to scale a texture or to zoom in or out of a scene without aliasing your sprites. When we scale Alice down to a small size, aliasing will inevitably occur. With mipmapping turned on, Cocos2d dynamically generates lower resolution textures to smooth out any pixelation at smaller scales. Go ahead and comment out the following lines:

  ```
  [alice.texture generateMipmap];
    ccTexParams texParams = { GL_LINEAR_MIPMAP_LINEAR, GL_LINEAR,
  GL_CLAMP_TO_EDGE, GL_CLAMP_TO_EDGE };
    [alice.texture setTexParameters:&texParams];
  ```

  Now you should see this pixelation as Alice gets smaller.

- Drawing many derivative sprites with CCSpriteBatchNode:

  The CCSpriteBatchNode class, added in v0.99.5, introduces an efficient way to draw and re-draw the same sprite over and over again. A batch node is created with the following method:

```
CCSpriteBatchNode *cloudBatch = [CCSpriteBatchNode
batchNodeWithFile:@"cloud_01.png" capacity:10];
```

Then, you create as many sprites as you want using the follow code:

```
CCSprite *s = [CCSprite spriteWithBatchNode:cloudBatch
rect:CGRectMake(0,0,64,64)];
   [cloudBatch addChild:s];
```

Setting the capacity to the number of sprites you plan to draw tells Cocos2d to allocate that much space. This is yet another tweak for extra efficiency, though it is not absolutely necessary that you do this. In these three examples we draw 10 randomly placed clouds and 60 randomly placed bits of grass.

► Drawing colored rectangles:

Finally, we have a fairly simple technique that has a variety of uses. By drawing a sprite with a blank 1px by 1px white texture and then coloring it and setting its textureRect property we can create very useful colored bars:

```
CCSprite *sprite = [CCSprite spriteWithFile:@"blank.png"];
[sprite setTextureRect:CGRectMake(0,0,480,320)];
[sprite setColor:ccc3(255,128,0)];
```

In this example we have used this technique to create very simple ground and sky backgrounds.

Coloring sprites

In the previous recipe we used colored rectangles to draw both the ground and the sky. The ability to set texture color and opacity are simple tools which, if used properly, can create very cool effects. In this recipe we will create a cinematic scene where two samurai face each other with glowing swords.

Getting ready

Please refer to the project `RecipeCollection01` for full working code of this recipe. Also, note that some code has been omitted for brevity.

How to do it...

Execute the following code:

```
#import "CCGradientLayer.h"

@implementation Ch1_ColoringSprites

-(CCLayer*) runRecipe {
  [self initButtons];

  //The Fade Scene Sprite
  CCSprite *fadeSprite = [CCSprite spriteWithFile:@"blank.png"];
  [fadeSprite setOpacity:0];
  [fadeSprite setPosition:ccp(240,160)];
  [fadeSprite setTextureRect:CGRectMake(0,0,480,320)];
  [self addChild:fadeSprite z:3 tag:TAG_FADE_SPRITE];

  //Add a gradient below the mountains
//CCGradientDirectionT_B is an enum provided by CCGradientLayer
  CCGradientLayer *gradientLayer = [CCGradientLayer layerWithColor:
ccc4(61,33,62,255) toColor:ccc4(65,89,54,255) withDirection:CCGradient
DirectionT_B width:480 height:100];
  [gradientLayer setPosition:ccp(0,50)];
  [self addChild:gradientLayer z:0 tag:TAG_GROUND_GRADIENT];

  //Add a sinister red glow gradient behind the evil samurai
  CCGradientLayer *redGradient = [CCGradientLayer
layerWithColor:ccc4(0,0,0,0) toColor:ccc4(255,0,0,100) withDirection:C
CGradientDirectionT_B width:200 height:200];
  [redGradient setPosition:ccp(280,60)];
  [redGradient setRotation:-90];
  [self addChild:redGradient z:2 tag:TAG_RED_GRADIENT];

  // Make the swords glow
  [self glowAt:ccp(230,280) withScale:CGSizeMake(3.0f, 11.0f)
withColor:ccc3(0,230,255) withRotation:45.0f withSprite:goodSamurai];
  [self glowAt:ccp(70,280) withScale:CGSizeMake(3.0f, 11.0f)
withColor:ccc3(255,200,2) withRotation:-45.0f withSprite:evilSamurai];

  return self;
}

 -(void) initButtons {
```

```
    [CCMenuItemFont setFontSize:16];

    //'Fade To Black' button
    CCMenuItemFont* fadeToBlack = [CCMenuItemFont itemFromString:@"FADE
TO BLACK" target:self selector:@selector(fadeToBlackCallback:)];
    CCMenu *fadeToBlackMenu = [CCMenu menuWithItems:fadeToBlack, nil];
      fadeToBlackMenu.position = ccp( 180 , 20 );
      [self addChild:fadeToBlackMenu z:4 tag:TAG_FADE_TO_BLACK];
}


/* Fade the scene to black */
-(void) fadeToBlackCallback:(id)sender {
    CCSprite *fadeSprite = [self getChildByTag:TAG_FADE_SPRITE];
    [fadeSprite stopAllActions];
    [fadeSprite setColor:ccc3(0,0,0)];
    [fadeSprite setOpacity:0.0f];
    [fadeSprite runAction:
    [CCSequence actions:[CCFadeIn actionWithDuration:2.0f], [CCFadeOut
actionWithDuration:2.0f], nil] ];
}


/* Create a glow effect */
-(void) glowAt:(CGPoint)position withScale:(CGSize)size
withColor:(ccColor3B)color withRotation:(float)rotation
withSprite:(CCSprite*)sprite {
    CCSprite *glowSprite = [CCSprite spriteWithFile:@"fire.png"];
    [glowSprite setColor:color];
    [glowSprite setPosition:position];
    [glowSprite setRotation:rotation];
    [glowSprite setBlendFunc: (ccBlendFunc) { GL_ONE, GL_ONE }];
    [glowSprite runAction: [CCRepeatForever actionWithAction:
      [CCSequence actions:[CCScaleTo actionWithDuration:0.9f
scaleX:size.width scaleY:size.height], [CCScaleTo
actionWithDuration:0.9f scaleX:size.width*0.75f scaleY:size.
height*0.75f], nil] ] ];
    [glowSprite runAction: [CCRepeatForever actionWithAction:
      [CCSequence actions:[CCFadeTo actionWithDuration:0.9f
opacity:150], [CCFadeTo actionWithDuration:0.9f opacity:255], nil] ]
];

    [sprite addChild:glowSprite];
}

@end
```

How it works...

This recipe shows a number of color based techniques.

▸ Setting sprite color:

The simplest use of color involves setting the color of a sprite using the following method:

```
-(void) setColor:(ccColor3B)color;
```

Setting sprite color effectively reduces the color you can display but it allows some programmatic flexibility in drawing. In this recipe we use setColor for a number of things, including drawing a blue sky, a yellow sun, black "dramatic movie bars", and more.

ccColor3B is a C struct which contains three GLubyte variables. Use the following helper macro to create ccColor3B structures:

```
ccColor3B ccc3(const GLubyte r, const GLubyte g, const GLubyte
b);
```

Cocos2d also specifies a number of pre-defined colors as constants. These include the following:

```
ccWHITE, ccYELLOW, ccBLUE, ccGREEN, ccRED,
ccMAGENTA, ccBLACK, ccORANGE, ccGRAY
```

▸ Fading to a color:

To fade a scene to a specific color we use the blank.png technique we went over in the last recipe. We first draw a sprite as large as the screen, then color the sprite to the color we want to fade to, and then finally run a CCFadeIn action on the sprite to fade to that color:

```
[fadeSprite setColor:ccc3(255,255,255)];
[fadeSprite setOpacity:0.0f];
[fadeSprite runAction: [CCFadeIn actionWithDuration:2.0f] ];
```

▸ Using CCGradientLayer:

Using the CCGradientLayer class we can programmatically create gradients. To make the mountains in the background fade into the ground the two samurai are standing on we created a gradient using this method:

```
    CCGradientLayer *gradientLayer = [CCGradientLayer layerWithColor
:ccc4(61,33,62,255) toColor:ccc4(65,89,54,255) withDirection:CCGra
dientDirectionT_B width:480 height:100];
    [gradientLayer setPosition:ccp(0,50)];
    [self addChild:gradientLayer z:0 tag:TAG_GROUND_GRADIENT];
```

Because CCGradientLayer lets you control opacity as well as color, it has many uses. As you can see there is also a sinister red glow behind the evil samurai.

> ▶ Making a sprite glow:

To make the swords in the demo glow we use subtle color manipulation, additive blending and fading and scaling actions. First we load the **fire.png** sprite supplied by Cocos2d. By changing its X and Y scale independently we can make it thinner or fatter. Once you have the desired scale ratio (in this demo we use x:y 3:11 because the sword is so thin) you can constantly scale and fade the sprite in and out to give some life to the effect. You also need to set the blend function to { `GL_ONE, GL_ ONE` } for additive blending. Finally this effect sprite is added to the actual sprite to make it seem like it glows.

```
CCSprite *glowSprite = [CCSprite spriteWithFile:@"fire.png"];
    [glowSprite setColor:color];
    [glowSprite setPosition:position];
    [glowSprite setRotation:rotation];
    [glowSprite setBlendFunc: (ccBlendFunc) { GL_ONE, GL_ONE }];
    [glowSprite runAction: [CCRepeatForever actionWithAction:
    [CCSequence actions:[CCScaleTo actionWithDuration:0.9f
scaleX:size.width scaleY:size.height], [CCScaleTo
actionWithDuration:0.9f scaleX:size.width*0.75f scaleY:size.
height*0.75f], nil] ] ];
    [glowSprite runAction: [CCRepeatForever actionWithAction:
    [CCSequence actions:[CCFadeTo actionWithDuration:0.9f
opacity:150], [CCFadeTo actionWithDuration:0.9f opacity:255], nil]
] ];
    [sprite addChild:glowSprite];
```

Animating sprites

Now it is time to add some animation to our sprites. One thing that should be stressed about animation is that it is only as complicated as you make it. In this recipe we will use very simple animation to create a compelling effect. We will create a scene where bats fly around a creepy looking castle. I've also added a cool lightning effect based on the technique used to make the swords glow in the previous recipe.

Getting ready

Please refer to the project `RecipeCollection01` for full working code of this recipe. Also note that some code has been omitted for brevity.

How to do it...

Execute the following code:

```
//SimpleAnimObject.h
@interface SimpleAnimObject : CCSprite {
  int animationType;
  CGPoint velocity;
}


@interface Ch1_AnimatingSprites {
  NSMutableArray *bats;
  CCAnimation *batFlyUp;
  CCAnimation *batGlideDown;
  CCSprite *lightningBolt;
  CCSprite *lightningGlow;
  int lightningRemoveCount;
}


-(CCLayer*) runRecipe {
  //Add our PLIST to the SpriteFrameCache
  [[CCSpriteFrameCache sharedSpriteFrameCache] addSpriteFramesWithFile
:@"simple_bat.plist"];

  //Add a lightning bolt
  lightningBolt = [CCSprite spriteWithFile:@"lightning_bolt.png"];
  [lightningBolt setPosition:ccp(240,160)];
  [lightningBolt setOpacity:64];
  [lightningBolt retain];

  //Add a sprite to make it light up other areas.
  lightningGlow = [CCSprite spriteWithFile:@"lightning_glow.png"];
  [lightningGlow setColor:ccc3(255,255,0)];
  [lightningGlow setPosition:ccp(240,160)];
  [lightningGlow setOpacity:100];
  [lightningGlow setBlendFunc: (ccBlendFunc) { GL_ONE, GL_ONE }];
  [lightningBolt addChild:lightningGlow];

  //Set a counter for lightning duration randomization
```

```
   lightningRemoveCount = 0;

   //Bats Array Initialization
   bats = [[NSMutableArray alloc] init];

   //Add bats using a batch node.
   CCSpriteBatchNode *batch1 = [CCSpriteBatchNode
batchNodeWithFile:@"simple_bat.png" capacity:10];
   [self addChild:batch1 z:2 tag:TAG_BATS];

   //Make them start flying up.
   for(int x=0; x<10; x++){
     //Create SimpleAnimObject of bat
     SimpleAnimObject *bat = [SimpleAnimObject
spriteWithBatchNode:batch1 rect:CGRectMake(0,0,48,48)];
     [batch1 addChild:bat];
     [bat setPosition:ccp(arc4random()%400+40, arc4random()%150+150)];

     //Make the bat fly up. Get the animation delay (flappingSpeed).
     float flappingSpeed = [self makeBatFlyUp:bat];

     //Base y velocity on flappingSpeed.
     bat.velocity = ccp((arc4random()%1000)/500 + 0.2f, 0.1f/
flappingSpeed);

     //Add a pointer to this bat object to the NSMutableArray
     [bats addObject:[NSValue valueWithPointer:bat]];
     [bat retain];

     //Set the bat's direction based on x velocity.
     if(bat.velocity.x > 0){
       bat.flipX = YES;
     }
   }

   //Schedule physics updates
   [self schedule:@selector(step:)];

   return self;
}

-(float)makeBatFlyUp:(SimpleAnimObject*)bat {
   CCSpriteFrameCache * cache = [CCSpriteFrameCache
sharedSpriteFrameCache];
```

```objc
  //Randomize animation speed.
  float delay = (float)(arc4random()%5+5)/80;
  CCAnimation *animation = [[CCAnimation alloc] initWithName:@"simply_
bat_fly" delay:delay];


  //Randomize animation frame order.
  int num = arc4random()%4+1;
  for(int i=1; i<=4; i+=1){
    [animation addFrame:[cache spriteFrameByName:[NSString
stringWithFormat:@"simple_bat_0%i.png",num]]];
    num++;
    if(num > 4){ num = 1; }
  }


  //Stop any running animations and apply this one.
  [bat stopAllActions];
  [bat runAction:[CCRepeatForever actionWithAction: [CCAnimate actionW
ithAnimation:animation]]];


  //Keep track of which animation is running.
  bat.animationType = BAT_FLYING_UP;


  return delay;  //We return how fast the bat is flapping.
}


-(void)makeBatGlideDown:(SimpleAnimObject*)bat {
  CCSpriteFrameCache * cache = [CCSpriteFrameCache
sharedSpriteFrameCache];


  //Apply a simple single frame gliding animation.
  CCAnimation *animation = [[CCAnimation alloc] initWithName:@"simple_
bat_glide" delay:100.0f];
  [animation addFrame:[cache spriteFrameByName:@"simple_bat_01.png"]];


  //Stop any running animations and apply this one.
  [bat stopAllActions];
  [bat runAction:[CCRepeatForever actionWithAction: [CCAnimate actionW
ithAnimation:animation]]];


  //Keep track of which animation is running.
  bat.animationType = BAT_GLIDING_DOWN;
}


-(void)step:(ccTime)delta {
  CGSize s = [[CCDirector sharedDirector] winSize];
```

```
    for(id key in bats){
      //Get SimpleAnimObject out of NSArray of NSValue objects.
      SimpleAnimObject *bat = [key pointerValue];

      //Make sure bats don't fly off the screen
      if(bat.position.x > s.width){
        bat.velocity = ccp(-bat.velocity.x, bat.velocity.y);
        bat.flipX = NO;
      }else if(bat.position.x < 0){
        bat.velocity = ccp(-bat.velocity.x, bat.velocity.y);
        bat.flipX = YES;
      }else if(bat.position.y > s.height){
        bat.velocity = ccp(bat.velocity.x, -bat.velocity.y);
        [self makeBatGlideDown:bat];
      }else if(bat.position.y < 0){
        bat.velocity = ccp(bat.velocity.x, -bat.velocity.y);
        [self makeBatFlyUp:bat];
      }

      //Randomly make them fly back up
      if(arc4random()%100 == 7){
        if(bat.animationType == BAT_GLIDING_DOWN){ [self
makeBatFlyUp:bat]; bat.velocity = ccp(bat.velocity.x, -bat.
velocity.y); }
        else if(bat.animationType == BAT_FLYING_UP){ [self
makeBatGlideDown:bat]; bat.velocity = ccp(bat.velocity.x, -bat.
velocity.y); }
      }

      //Update bat position based on direction
      bat.position = ccp(bat.position.x + bat.velocity.x, bat.position.y
+ bat.velocity.y);
    }

    //Randomly make lightning strike
    if(arc4random()%70 == 7){
      if(lightningRemoveCount < 0){
        [self addChild:lightningBolt z:1 tag:TAG_LIGHTNING_BOLT];
        lightningRemoveCount = arc4random()%5+5;
      }
    }

    //Count down
    lightningRemoveCount -= 1;
```

```
    //Clean up any old lightning bolts
    if(lightningRemoveCount == 0){
      [self removeChildByTag:TAG_LIGHTNING_BOLT cleanup:NO];
    }
  }
}

@end
```

How it works...

This recipe shows us how to structure animation based classes through the use of `SimpleAnimObject`:

►   Animated object class structure:

When switching from one animation to another it is often important to keep track of what state the animated object is in. In our example we use `SimpleAnimObject`, which keeps an arbitrary `animationType` variable. We also maintain a velocity variable that has a Y scalar value that is inversely proportional to the animation frame delay:

```
@interface SimpleAnimObject : CCSprite {
  int animationType;
  CGPoint velocity;
}
```

Depending on how in-depth you want your animation system to be you should maintain more information such as, for example, a pointer to the running `CCAnimation` instance, frame information, and physical bodies.

There's more...

As you get more involved with Cocos2d game development you will become more and more tempted to use **asynchronous actions** for gameplay logic and AI. Derived from the CCAction class, these actions can be used for everything from moving a CCNode using CCMoveBy to animating a CCSprite using CCAnimate. When an action is run, an asynchronous timing mechanism is maintained in the background. First time game programmers often over-rely on this feature. The extra overhead required by this technique can multiply quickly when multiple actions are being run. In the following example we have used a simple integer timer that allows us to regulate how long lightning lasts onscreen:

```
    //Randomly make lightning strike
    if(arc4random()%70 == 7){
      if(lightningRemoveCount < 0){
        [self addChild:lightningBolt z:1 tag:TAG_LIGHTNING_BOLT];
        lightningRemoveCount = arc4random()%5+5;
```

```
    }
  }

  //Count down
  lightningRemoveCount -= 1;

  //Clean up any old lightning bolts
  if(lightningRemoveCount == 0){
    [self removeChildByTag:TAG_LIGHTNING_BOLT cleanup:NO];
  }
```

Synchronous timers like the one shown in the preceding code snippet are often, but not always, preferable to asynchronous actions. Keep this in mind as your games grow in size and scope.

Drawing OpenGL primitives

Sometimes in 2D game development we need to make use of good old-fashioned **OpenGL primitives**. With these we can make minimaps, heads up displays, and special effects like bullet tracers and lightning blasts to name a few. In the following scene I've created a simple figure using all of the primitive drawing functions supplied by Cocos2d as well as one I've tweaked and added.

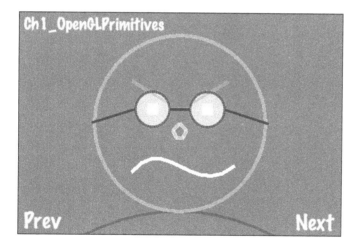

Getting ready

Please refer to the project `RecipeCollection01` for full working code of this recipe.

How to do it...

Execute the following code:

```
/* Create a solid circle */
void ccDrawSolidCircle( CGPoint center, float r, float a, NSUInteger
segs, BOOL drawLineToCenter)
{
  //Check to see if  we need to draw a line to the center
  int additionalSegment = 1;
  if (drawLineToCenter)
    additionalSegment++;

  const float coef = 2.0f * (float)M_PI/segs;

  GLfloat *vertices = calloc( sizeof(GLfloat)*2*(segs+2), 1);
  if( ! vertices )
    return;

  //Calculate line segments
  for(NSUInteger i=0;i<=segs;i++)
  {
    float rads = i*coef;
    GLfloat j = r * cosf(rads + a) + center.x;
    GLfloat k = r * sinf(rads + a) + center.y;

    vertices[i*2] = j * CC_CONTENT_SCALE_FACTOR();
    vertices[i*2+1] =k * CC_CONTENT_SCALE_FACTOR();
  }
  vertices[(segs+1)*2] = center.x * CC_CONTENT_SCALE_FACTOR();
  vertices[(segs+1)*2+1] = center.y * CC_CONTENT_SCALE_FACTOR();

  //Draw our solid polygon
  glDisable(GL_TEXTURE_2D);
  glDisableClientState(GL_TEXTURE_COORD_ARRAY);
  glDisableClientState(GL_COLOR_ARRAY);

  glVertexPointer(2, GL_FLOAT, 0, vertices);
  glDrawArrays(GL_TRIANGLE_FAN, 0, segs+additionalSegment);

  glEnableClientState(GL_COLOR_ARRAY);
  glEnableClientState(GL_TEXTURE_COORD_ARRAY);
  glEnable(GL_TEXTURE_2D);
```

```
  //Free up memory
  free( vertices );
}

@implementation ShapeLayer

-(void) draw {
  //Set line width.
  glLineWidth(4.0f);

  //Set point size
  glPointSize(16);

  //Enable line smoothing
  glEnable(GL_LINE_SMOOTH);

  //Draw a blue quadratic bezier curve
  glColor4ub(0, 0, 255, 255);
  ccDrawQuadBezier(ccp(100,0), ccp(240,70), ccp(380,0), 10);

  //Draw a hollow purple circle
  glColor4ub(255, 0, 255, 255);
  ccDrawCircle(ccp(240,160), 125.0f, 0.0f, 100, NO);

  //Draw a solid red lines
  glColor4ub(255, 0, 0, 255);
  ccDrawLine(ccp(170,220), ccp(220,190));
  ccDrawLine(ccp(260,190), ccp(310,220));

  //Draw a green point
  glColor4ub(0, 255, 0, 255);
  ccDrawPoint(ccp(200,180));
  ccDrawPoint(ccp(280,180));

  //Draw a turquoise solid circle
  glColor4ub(0, 128, 255, 50);
  ccDrawSolidCircle(ccp(200,180), 25.0f, 0.0f, 20, NO);
  ccDrawSolidCircle(ccp(280,180), 25.0f, 0.0f, 20, NO);

  //Draw a brown hollow circle
  glColor4ub(64,32, 0, 255);
  ccDrawCircle(ccp(200,180), 25.0f, 0.0f, 100, NO);
  ccDrawCircle(ccp(280,180), 25.0f, 0.0f, 100, NO);
```

```
//Draw brown lines
glColor4ub(64,32, 0, 255);
ccDrawLine(ccp(225,180), ccp(255,180));
ccDrawLine(ccp(305,180), ccp(370,160));
ccDrawLine(ccp(175,180), ccp(110,160));

//Draw an orange polygon
glColor4ub(255, 128, 0, 255);
CGPoint vertices[5]={ ccp(230,150),ccp(240,160),ccp(250,150),ccp(245
,140),ccp(235,140) };
ccDrawPoly(vertices, 5, YES);

//Draw a yellow cubic bezier curve
glColor4ub(255, 255, 0, 255);
ccDrawCubicBezier(ccp(170,90), ccp(220,150), ccp(260,50),
ccp(320,100), 10);

//Restore original values
glLineWidth(1);
glDisable(GL_LINE_SMOOTH);
glColor4ub(255,255,255,255);
glPointSize(1);
}

@end

-(CCLayer*) runRecipe {
  ShapeLayer *layer = [[ShapeLayer alloc] init];
  [layer setPosition:ccp(0,0)];
  [self addChild:layer z:2 tag:0];

  return self;
}
```

How it works...

This recipe shows us how to use each primitive drawing function:

▶ Overriding the `draw` method:

In order to use OpenGL drawing routines we must override the following method of a CCNode:

```
-(void) draw;
```

As stated in `CCNode.h`, overriding this method gives us control of underlying OpenGL drawing routines. The following OpenGL statements are implicit:

```
glEnableClientState(GL_VERTEX_ARRAY);
  glEnableClientState(GL_COLOR_ARRAY);
  glEnableClientState(GL_TEXTURE_COORD_ARRAY);
  glEnable(GL_TEXTURE_2D);
```

To overload this method we create a class named `ShapeLayer` which inherits from `CCLayer`, and therefore from `CCNode`. Once attached to the scene this overridden `draw` method will be called once every cycle.

▶ Primitive drawing functions:

The following primitive drawing functions are available in Cocos2d:

```
    void ccDrawPoint( CGPoint point );
    void ccDrawPoints( const CGPoint *points, NSUInteger
    numberOfPoints );
    void ccDrawLine( CGPoint origin, CGPoint destination );
    void ccDrawPoly( const CGPoint *vertices, NSUInteger
    numOfVertices, BOOL closePolygon );
    void ccDrawCircle( CGPoint center, float radius, float angle,
    NSUInteger segments, BOOL drawLineToCenter);
    void ccDrawQuadBezier(CGPoint origin, CGPoint control, CGPoint
    destination, NSUInteger segments);
    void ccDrawCubicBezier(CGPoint origin, CGPoint control1, CGPoint
    control2, CGPoint destination, NSUInteger segments);
```

On top of all this we have tweaked `ccDrawCircle` to create `ccDrawSolidCircle` as follows:

```
    void ccDrawSolidCircle( CGPoint center, float r, float a,
    NSUInteger segs, BOOL drawLineToCenter);
```

Because we are controlling these OpenGL render calls for each frame this technique works well when used in a real-time minimap. We will explore this in a later recipe.

There's more...

If you are planning to use primitive drawing extensively you may want to consider using the **Vertex Buffer Object** OpenGL extension. Using the GL functions `glGenBuffers`, `glBindBuffer`, and `glBufferData` you can put vertex and other information into video memory rather than system memory. This can drastically improve performance depending on the situation. For more information view the section *Best Practices for Working with Vertex Data* in the Apple Developer document *OpenGL ES Programming Guide for iOS* located at `http://developer.apple.com/library/ios/#documentation/3DDrawing/ Conceptual/OpenGLES_ProgrammingGuide/TechniquesforWorkingwithVertexData/TechniquesforWorkingwithVertexData.html`.

Playing video files

The **cutscene** is a concept that has existed since the early days of video games. Cutscenes are usually interspersed in between gameplay segments or shown when a game is loading. For more complex cutscenes it is often advantageous to use full motion video. In this recipe we will see how to insert a video into our game.

Getting ready

Please refer to the project RecipeCollection01 for full working code of this recipe.

How to do it...

This recipe requires the extra step of linking the **MediaPlayer iOS framework** to our project:

1. Right-click your project under **Groups & Files**.
2. Click **Add | Existing Frameworks**
3. Under **iOS SDK** select **MediaPlayer.framework**

Keep in mind that RecipeCollection01 already has this library linked.

Now, execute the following code:

```
#import <MediaPlayer/MediaPlayer.h>

@interface Ch1_PlayingVideoFiles {
  MPMoviePlayerController *moviePlayer;
}

@implementation Ch1_PlayingVideoFiles

-(CCLayer*) runRecipe {
  //Load our video file
  NSURL *url = [NSURL fileURLWithPath:[[NSBundle mainBundle]
pathForResource:@"example_vid" ofType:@"mov"]];

  //Create a MPMoviePlayerController object
  moviePlayer = [[MPMoviePlayerController alloc]
initWithContentURL:url];

  //Register to receive a notification when the movie has finished
playing.
  [[NSNotificationCenter defaultCenter] addObserver:self
    selector:@selector(moviePlayBackDidFinish:)
    name:MPMoviePlayerPlaybackDidFinishNotification
    object:moviePlayer];

  //Set the movie's control style and whether or not it should
automatically play.
  if ([moviePlayer respondsToSelector:@selector(setFullscreen:animat
ed:)]) {
    //Use the new 3.2 style API.
    moviePlayer.controlStyle = MPMovieControlStyleNone;
    moviePlayer.shouldAutoplay = YES;

    CGSize winSize = [[CCDirector sharedDirector] winSize];
    moviePlayer.view.frame = CGRectMake(45, 50, winSize.width-90,
winSize.height-100);
    [[[CCDirector sharedDirector] openGLView] addSubview:moviePlayer.
view];
  } else {
    //Use the old 2.0 style API.
    moviePlayer.movieControlMode = MPMovieControlModeHidden;
    [self playMovie];
  }

  return self;
}

-(void)moviePlayBackDidFinish:(NSNotification*)notification {
  //If playback is finished we stop the movie.
```

```
    [self stopMovie];
}

-(void)playMovie {
  //We do not play the movie if it is already playing.
  MPMoviePlaybackState state = moviePlayer.playbackState;
  if(state == MPMoviePlaybackStatePlaying) {
    NSLog(@"Movie is already playing.");
    return;
  }

  [moviePlayer play];
}

-(void)stopMovie {
  //We do not stop the movie if it is already stopped.
  MPMoviePlaybackState state = moviePlayer.playbackState;
  if(state == MPMoviePlaybackStateStopped) {
    NSLog(@"Movie is already stopped.");
    return;
  }

  //Since playback has finished we remove the observer.
  [[NSNotificationCenter defaultCenter] removeObserver:self
    name:MPMoviePlayerPlaybackDidFinishNotification
      object:moviePlayer];

  //If the moviePlayer.view was added to the openGL view, it needs to
be removed.
  if ([moviePlayer respondsToSelector:@selector(setFullscreen:animat
ed:)]) {
    [moviePlayer.view removeFromSuperview];
  }
}

-(void)cleanRecipe {
  [super cleanRecipe];
  [self stopMovie];
  [moviePlayer release];
}

@end
```

How it works...

This recipe shows us how to load, play, and stop a movie.

- Using MPMoviePlayerController:

  This recipe is merely the tip of the iceberg regarding movie playback. Movies can also be played back in fullscreen mode, in portrait mode, and using a variety of other options. Please refer to official Apple documentation when customizing and/or adding to this technique.

- Using `Objective-C` observers:

  The **observer pattern** is not used very often while doing Cocos2d programming, but it is a powerful mechanism and it is the recommended way of knowing when your video has finished playback. You can read more about observers by referring to the official `Objective-C` documentation.

- Movie file format:

  According to Apple documentation it is recommended that you compress your movies using `H.264/MPEG-4` for video, `AAC` audio and one of the following file formats: `MOV`, `MP4`, `MPV`, `3GP`.

  It is also recommended that your movies be no larger than `640x480` and run no faster than `30 FPS`.

  The movie used in the recipe was created and encoded using Apple's iMovie software.

  For more information please consult official Apple iOS SDK documentation.

Grid, particle, and motion streak effects

Cocos2d comes equipped with a variety of easy to use special effects. Here, we will only briefly go over all of the effects as they are fairly straightforward and are well covered in other texts.

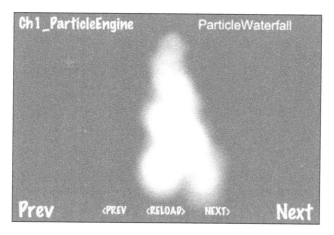

Please refer to the project `RecipeCollection01` for full working code of this recipe.

To get grid effects to show up properly in your game you first need to set the `EAGLView` `pixelFormat` to `kEAGLColorFormatRGBA8` (it is set to `kEAGLColorFormatRGB565` by default).

Do this by going into your project file's `${PROJECT_NAME}AppDelegate.m` file and changing the following code:

```
EAGLView *glView = [EAGLView viewWithFrame:[window bounds]
                 pixelFormat: kEAGLColorFormatRGB565
                 depthFormat:0
        ];
```

Change it to this:

```
EAGLView *glView = [EAGLView viewWithFrame:[window bounds]
                 pixelFormat: kEAGLColorFormatRGBA8
                 depthFormat:0
        ];
```

Then, execute the following code:

```
//Custom particle effect
@implementation ParticleWaterfall

-(id)init {
  return [self initWithTotalParticles:400];
}
-(id)initWithTotalParticles:(int)p {
  if(self != [super initWithTotalParticles: p])
    return nil;

  //Angle
  angle = 270;
  angleVar = 12;

  //Emitter position
  self.position = ccp(160, 60);
  posVar = ccp(16, 4);

  //Life of particles
```

```
  life = 2;
  lifeVar = 0.25f;

  //Speed of particles
  self.speed = 100;
  self.speedVar = 20;
  self.gravity = ccp(self.gravity.x, -5);

  //Size of particles
  startSize = 35.0f;
  endSize = 100.0f;

  //Color of particles
  startColor = ccc4(0.4f, 0.4f, 1.0f, 0.6f);
  startColorVar = ccc4(0,0,0,0);
  endColor = ccc4(0.5f, 0.5f, 0.5f, 0);
  endColorVar = ccc4(0,0,0,0);

  //Additive
  self.blendAdditive = NO;

  return self;
}

@end

@interface Ch1_GridParticleMotionEffects
{
  //Variables for motion streak effect
  CCSprite *rocket;
  CCMotionStreak *streak;
  CGPoint rocketDirection;
}

@implementation Ch1_GridParticleMotionEffects

-(CCLayer*) runRecipe {
  CGSize s = [[CCDirector sharedDirector] winSize];

  /*** Grid effect demo ***/

  //Create a CCSprite
  CCSprite *sprite = [CCSprite spriteWithFile:@"colorable_sprite.
png"];
```

```
      [sprite setPosition:ccp(240,160)];
      [self addChild:sprite z:1 tag:TAG_SPRITE];

      //Create a grid effect
      CCAction *gridEffect = [CCShaky3D actionWithRange:5 shakeZ:YES
   grid:ccg(15,10) duration:10];

      //Run the effect
      [sprite runAction:gridEffect];

      /*** Particle effect demo ***/

   //Create a simple fire particle effect
   CCNode *fireEffect = [CCParticleFire node];
   [self addChild:fireEffect z:1 tag:TAG_FIRE_EFFECT];

      //Create a waterfall particle effect
      CCNode *waterfallEffect = [ParticleWaterfall node];
      [self addChild:waterfallEffect z:1 tag:TAG_WATERFALL_EFFECT];

      /*** Motion streak demo ***/

      //Set the rocket initially in a random direction.
      rocketDirection = ccp(arc4random()%4+1,arc4random()%4+1);

      //Add the rocket sprite.
      rocket = [CCSprite spriteWithFile:@"rocket.png"];
      [rocket setPosition:ccp(s.width/2, s.height/2)];
      [rocket setScale:0.5f];
      [self addChild:rocket];

      //Create the streak object and add it to the scene.
      streak = [CCMotionStreak streakWithFade:1 minSeg:1 image:@"streak.
   png" width:32 length:32 color:ccc4(255,255,255,255)];
      [self addChild:streak];

      streak.position = ccp(s.width/2, s.height/2);

      [self schedule:@selector(step:)];

      return self;
   }

   -(void)step:(ccTime)delta {
```

```
CGSize s = [[CCDirector sharedDirector] winSize];

//Make rocket bounce off walls
if(rocket.position.x > s.width || rocket.position.x < 0){
  rocketDirection = ccp(-rocketDirection.x, rocketDirection.y);
}
else if(rocket.position.y > s.height || rocket.position.y < 0){
  rocketDirection = ccp(rocketDirection.x, -rocketDirection.y);
}

//Slowly turn the rocket
rocketDirection = ccp(rocketDirection.x, rocketDirection.y+0.05f);

//Update rocket position based on direction
rocket.position = ccp(rocket.position.x + rocketDirection.x, rocket.
position.y + rocketDirection.y);
  [streak setPosition:rocket.position];

//Set the rocket's rotation
  [rocket setRotation: radiansToDegrees(vectorToRadians(rocketDirecti
on))];
}

@end
```

How it works...

In this recipe we see a number of things. For the sake of brevity I've only included one grid effect and two particle effects in the book. Every stock grid and particle effect is viewable in `RecipeCollection01`, along with some customized particle effects like `Waterfall` and `WaterSplash`.

▶ Custom Particles:

Cocos2d particles have many variables and it is most often advantageous to sub-class a built-in particle to help create your own. Here is a list of the built-in Cocos2d particles:

CCParticleExplosion, CCParticleFire, CCParticleFireworks, CCParticleFlower, CCParticleGalaxy, CCParticleMeteor, CCParticleRain, CCParticleSmoke, CCParticleSnow, CCParticleSpiral, CCParticleSun

► Using CCMotionStreak:

A motion streak is a great way to add a dynamic element a `CCNode`. These can often be combined with particles for a great effect.

One thing to keep in mind when creating a motion streak is that the texture needs to look good when it bends in on itself. **Vertical textures** with **transparent gradient edges** usually look the best.

Using Retina Display mode

Both the iPhone 4 and the iPad support Apple's **Retina Display** mode. On the iPhone 4 this doubles the resolution to `960x640`.

The creators of Cocos2d have taken a lot of care in integrating this feature into the framework. Retina display can be turned on with the flick of a switch. Getting your game to run similarly in both hi-definition and standard-definition can be tricky though. Luckily they have taken this into consideration as well. In this recipe we will enable Retina Display and then display a hi-resolution image, as shown in the following screenshot:

Getting ready

To properly see Retina Display you need a retina display device. In the simulator you need to do the following to switch to an **iPhone Retina** simulation:

1. Go to the iOS simulator.
2. In the file menu click on **Hardware | Device | iPhone (Retina)**.

You may also of course use a real iPhone 4 or iPad device.

How to do it...

First you must enable **Retina Display** in your application. Go into `${PROJECT_NAME}` `AppDelegate.m` and *uncomment* the following lines:

```
if( ! [director enableRetinaDisplay:YES] )
  CCLOG(@"Retina Display Not supported");
```

Retina Display will now be turned on for devices that support it and turned off for devices that do not.

Now, execute the following code:

```
-(CCLayer*) runRecipe {
  //Switch to Retina mode to see the difference
  CCSprite *sprite = [CCSprite spriteWithFile:@"cocos2d_beginner.
png"];
  [sprite setPosition:ccp(240,160)];
  [sprite setScale:1.0f];
  [self addChild:sprite];

  return self;
}
```

How it works...

▸ One sprite for the price of two:

As you can see the sprite we created is now very large and detailed. If you turn Retina Display off or run this on a device that does not support it you will see a smaller blurrier sprite. This happens because Retina Display chooses the higher resolution version of every sprite if there is one available. We specify the higher resolution version with the `-hd` suffix. So, in Retina Display mode Cocos2d automatically displays `cocos2d_beginner-hd.png` instead of `cocos2d_beginner.png`.

▸ Position, sizing, and so on:

Supposedly Cocos2d will convert all coordinate positions, size ratios, and anything else accordingly. The only thing you should have to change is adding the high resolution imagery.

It is recomended that a number of caveats are practiced with this. Lower level OpenGL hacking often doesn't display as you would want it to. Be wary of this and be sure to test any complex techniques in Retina Display mode before thinking about supporting both modes.

> ▸ The downside of Retina Display:

> The major downside of Retina Display is simply the amount of disk space it takes up. Including all of the HD images will more than double the space all of your art assets take up. Also, the higher resolution images take up more memory at runtime.

> ▸ The upside of Retina Display.

> On the other hand Apple keeps increasing app size limits and device memory. With newer hardware coming out and the ability to make desktop applications, increased resolution is a must for triple-A game titles.

1D and 2D Ease Actions

Ease Actions allow you to fine tune the actions used in your game using a number of formulae. They can be applied to any action: moving, scaling, fading, and so on. Regarding movement specifically, a small tweak can be applied to allow for independent *Easing* on both the X and the Y axis. This can be used to create a number of cool effects.

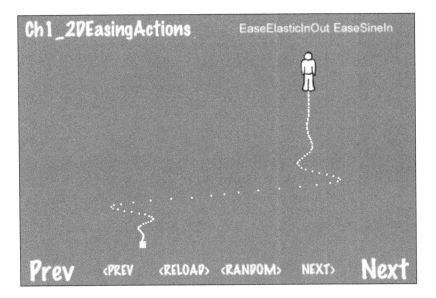

Getting ready

Please refer to the project `RecipeCollection01` for full working code of this recipe.

How to do it...

Execute the following code:

```
@interface CCMoveByCustom : CCMoveBy
{}
-(void) update: (ccTime) t;
@end

@implementation CCMoveByCustom
-(void) update: (ccTime) t {
  //Here we neglect to change something with a zero delta.
  if(delta.x == 0){
    [target_ setPosition:ccp( [(CCNode*)target_ position].x,
(startPosition.y + delta.y*t ) )];
  }else if(delta.y == 0){
    [target_ setPosition:ccp( (startPosition.x + delta.x*t ),
[(CCNode*)target_ position].y )];
  }else{
    [target_ setPosition:ccp( (startPosition.x + delta.x*t ),
(startPosition.y + delta.y * t ) )];
  }
}
@end

@implementation Ch1_EasingActions

-(CCLayer*) runRecipe {
  /*** 1D Movement Ease Action ***/

  //Create the basic action to move by a certain X and Y vector
  CCActionInterval *action1D = [CCMoveBy actionWithDuration:2
position:ccp(200,200)];

  //Create a sprite to move
  CCSprite *spriteEase1D = [CCSprite spriteWithFile:@"colorable_
sprite.png"];
  [spriteEase1D setPosition:ccp(150,50)];
  [self addChild:spriteEase1D z:1 tag:TAG_SPRITE_EASE_1D];

  //Create an 'eased' movement action with a CCEase class
  CCActionInterval *easeAction1D = [CCEaseInOut
actionWithAction:action1D rate:2];

  //Run the action
```

```
[spriteEase1D runAction:easeAction1D];

  /*** 2D Movement Ease Action ***/

  //Create two movement actions, one in each dimension
  CCActionInterval *action2DX = [CCMoveByCustom actionWithDuration:2
position:ccp(200,0)];
  CCActionInterval *action2DY = [CCMoveByCustom actionWithDuration:2
position:ccp(0,200)];

  //Create a sprite to move
  CCSprite *spriteEase2D = [CCSprite spriteWithFile:@"colorable_
sprite.png"];
  [spriteEase2D setPosition:ccp(150,50)];
  [self addChild:spriteEase2D z:1 tag:TAG_SPRITE_EASE_2D];

  //Create two 'eased' movement actions, one on each dimension
  CCActionInterval *easeAction2DX = [CCEaseSineIn
actionWithAction:action2DX];
  CCActionInterval *easeAction2DY = [CCEaseBounceIn
actionWithAction:action2DY];

  //Run both actions
  [spriteEase2D runAction:easeAction2DX];
  [spriteEase2D runAction:easeAction2DY];

  return self;
}

@end
```

How it works...

Upon executing this code you should see one character moving in a straight line toward the destination while the other moves there in a seemly erratic yet calculated way.

- ▶ Uses of 2D eased movement actions:

  While creating the iOS game *GoldenAgeBaseball* this summer I used `CCMoveByCustom` to simulate different pitches. A slider moved down and away, a cutter only away and a sinker only down. This variation of pitch styles was crucial to the development of the pitching/batting gameplay mechanic.

  Overall, Ease Actions give your game a polished and professional feel. Whether you are smoothing out a camera movement or simulating a baseball pitch, Ease Actions are a fine tool to help tweak your game to perfection.

Rendering and texturing 3D shapes

As odd as it sounds, sometimes in a 2D game you simply just want to add some simple **3D graphics**. Whether you are creating a cool 2D/3D hybrid or a simple 3D game with a 2D HUD, 3D graphics are no easy thing to produce. The complexities of a third dimension often conflict with 2D programming paradigms.

For the sake of simplicity, this recipe will show you how to create a **simple colored cube** and a **simple textured cube**. The uses of simple geometry are varied even when making a 2D game. However, more examples including **shaders** and **3D models** are beyond the scope of this book.

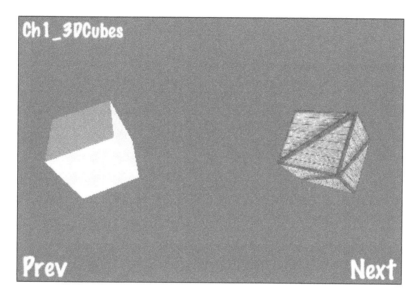

Getting ready

Please refer to the project `RecipeCollection01` for full working code of this recipe.

How to do it...

Execute the following code:

```
#import "Vector3D.h"

@interface Cube3D : CCSprite
{
  Vector3D *translation3D;
  Vector3D *rotation3DAxis;
```

```
    GLfloat rotation3DAngle;
    bool drawTextured;
}
@property (readwrite, assign) Vector3D *translation3D;
@property (readwrite, assign) Vector3D *rotation3DAxis;
@property (readwrite, assign) GLfloat rotation3DAngle;
@property (readwrite, assign) bool drawTextured;
-(void) draw;
@end

@implementation Cube3D
@synthesize translation3D,rotation3DAxis,rotation3DAngle,drawTextured;

-(void) draw {
  //Vertices for each side of the cube
  const GLfloat frontVertices[]={ -0.5f,-0.5f,0.5f, 0.5f,-0.5f,0.5f,
-0.5f,0.5f,0.5f, 0.5f,0.5f,0.5f};
  const GLfloat backVertices[] = { -0.5f,-0.5f,-0.5f, -0.5f,0.5f,-
0.5f, 0.5f,-0.5f,-0.5f, 0.5f,0.5f,-0.5f };
  const GLfloat leftVertices[] = { -0.5f,-0.5f,0.5f, -0.5f,0.5f,0.5f,
-0.5f,-0.5f,-0.5f, -0.5f,0.5f,-0.5f };
  const GLfloat rightVertices[] = { 0.5f,-0.5f,-0.5f, 0.5f,0.5f,-0.5f,
0.5f,-0.5f,0.5f, 0.5f,0.5f,0.5f };
  const GLfloat topVertices[] = { -0.5f,0.5f,0.5f, 0.5f,0.5f,0.5f,
-0.5f,0.5f,-0.5f, 0.5f,0.5f,-0.5f };
  const GLfloat bottomVertices[] = {-0.5f,-0.5f,0.5f,-0.5f,-0.5f,-
0.5f,0.5f,-0.5f,0.5f, 0.5f,-0.5f,-0.5f  };

  //Coordinates for our texture to map it to a cube side
  const GLfloat textureCoordinates[] = { 0,0, 1,0, 0,1, 1,1,};

  //We enable back face culling to properly set the depth buffer
  glEnable(GL_CULL_FACE);
  glCullFace(GL_BACK);

  //We are not using GL_COLOR_ARRAY
  glDisableClientState(GL_COLOR_ARRAY);

  //We disable GL_TEXTURE_COORD_ARRAY if not using a texture
  if(!drawTextured){
    glDisableClientState(GL_TEXTURE_COORD_ARRAY);
  }

  //Replace the current matrix with the identity matrix
  glLoadIdentity();
  //Translate and rotate
  glTranslatef(translation3D.x, translation3D.y, translation3D.z);
```

```
    glRotatef(rotation3DAngle, rotation3DAxis.x, rotation3DAxis.y,
rotation3DAxis.z);

    //Bind our texture if neccessary
    if(drawTextured){
      glBindTexture(GL_TEXTURE_2D, texture_.name);
    }

    //Here we define our vertices, set our textures or colors and
finally draw the cube sides
        glVertexPointer(3, GL_FLOAT, 0, frontVertices);
    if(drawTextured){ glTexCoordPointer(2, GL_FLOAT, 0,
textureCoordinates); }
    else{ glColor4f(1.0f, 0.0f, 0.0f, 1.0f); }
    glDrawArrays(GL_TRIANGLE_STRIP, 0, 4);

        glVertexPointer(3, GL_FLOAT, 0, backVertices);
    if(drawTextured){ glTexCoordPointer(2, GL_FLOAT, 0,
textureCoordinates); }
    else{ glColor4f(1.0f, 1.0f, 0.0f, 1.0f); }
    glDrawArrays(GL_TRIANGLE_STRIP, 0, 4);

        glVertexPointer(3, GL_FLOAT, 0, leftVertices);
    if(drawTextured){ glTexCoordPointer(2, GL_FLOAT, 0,
textureCoordinates); }
    else{ glColor4f(1.0f, 0.0f, 1.0f, 1.0f); }
    glDrawArrays(GL_TRIANGLE_STRIP, 0, 4);

        glVertexPointer(3, GL_FLOAT, 0, rightVertices);
    if(drawTextured){ glTexCoordPointer(2, GL_FLOAT, 0,
textureCoordinates); }
    else{ glColor4f(0.0f, 1.0f, 1.0f, 1.0f); }
    glDrawArrays(GL_TRIANGLE_STRIP, 0, 4);

        glVertexPointer(3, GL_FLOAT, 0, topVertices);
    if(drawTextured){ glTexCoordPointer(2, GL_FLOAT, 0,
textureCoordinates); }
    else{ glColor4f(0.0f, 1.0f, 0.0f, 1.0f); }
    glDrawArrays(GL_TRIANGLE_STRIP, 0, 4);

        glVertexPointer(3, GL_FLOAT, 0, bottomVertices);
    if(drawTextured){ glTexCoordPointer(2, GL_FLOAT, 0,
textureCoordinates); }
    else{ glColor4f(0.0f, 0.0f, 1.0f, 1.0f); }
    glDrawArrays(GL_TRIANGLE_STRIP, 0, 4);

    //We re-enable the default render state
```

```
    glEnableClientState(GL_COLOR_ARRAY);
    glEnableClientState(GL_TEXTURE_COORD_ARRAY);
    glDisable(GL_CULL_FACE);
    glColor4f(1.0f, 1.0f, 1.0f, 1.0f);
  }
  @end


  @interface Ch1_3DCubes {
    Cube3D *cube3d1;
    Cube3D *cube3d2;
  }

  @implementation Ch1_3DCubes

  -(CCLayer*) runRecipe {
    //Load a textured cube and set initial variables
    cube3d1 = [Cube3D spriteWithFile:@"crate.jpg"];
    cube3d1.translation3D = [Vector3D x:2.0f y:0.0f z:-4.0f];
    cube3d1.rotation3DAxis = [Vector3D x:2.0f y:2.0f z:4.0f];
    cube3d1.rotation3DAngle = 0.0f;
    cube3d1.drawTextured = YES;
    [self addChild:cube3d1 z:3 tag:0];

    //Load a colored cube and set initial variables
    cube3d2 = [Cube3D spriteWithFile:@"blank.png"];
    cube3d2.translation3D = [Vector3D x:-2.0f y:0.0f z:-4.0f];
    cube3d2.rotation3DAxis = [Vector3D x:2.0f y:2.0f z:4.0f];
    cube3d2.rotation3DAngle = 0.0f;
    cube3d2.drawTextured = NO;
    [self addChild:cube3d2 z:1 tag:1];

    //Schedule cube rotation
    [self schedule:@selector(step:)];

    return self;
  }

  -(void) step:(ccTime)delta {
    cube3d1.rotation3DAngle += 0.5f;
    cube3d2.rotation3DAngle -= 0.5f;
  }

  @end
```

How it works...

What we see here is a crash course in OpenGL ES cube rendering with a Cocos2d twist. Like when we drew OpenGL primitives, here we create another `CCNode` and override its draw method to create more complex OpenGL geometry.

- ▸ Texturing:

  We harness a `CCSprite` method to load a texture into memory to allow us to bind that texture for 3D drawing. This process is fairly straightforward.

- ▸ Depth testing, sizing, and translation:

  Thanks to Cocos2d's built-in depth testing, cubes will be properly ordered based on the Z property. The `translation3D.z` value affects the actual size of the cube while its `translation3D.x` and `translation3D.y` values affect where it is on the screen proportional to `translation3D.z`.

There's more...

For more information about 3D graphics, please refer to the recipe *Using Cocos3d* in *Chapter 8, Tips, Tools, and Ports*.

Rendering a texture-filled polygon

When creating games with large levels it is often easy to run into memory limitations. Large maps also contain repetitive drawing of things like grass, trees, mountains, and so on. This recipe will show you how to efficiently render a **polygon** that is filled in with a **repeated texture**. These can be drawn at any size and still only use a small amount of memory and CPU time.

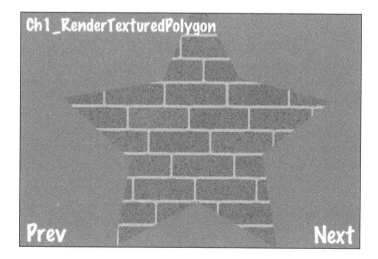

Please refer to the project `RecipeCollection01` for full working code of this recipe.

Execute the following code:

```
#import "Vector3D.h"

//Included for CPP polygon triangulation
#import "triangulate.h"
#include <stdio.h>
#include <stdlib.h>
#include <string.h>
#include <assert.h>

@implementation TexturedPolygon
@synthesize vertices, triangles;

+(id) createWithFile:(NSString*)file withVertices:(NSArray*)verts {
  /*** Create a TexturedPolygon with vertices only. ***/
  /*** Perform polygon trianglulation to get triangles. ***/

  //Initialization
  TexturedPolygon *tp = [TexturedPolygon spriteWithFile:file];
  tp.vertices = [[NSMutableArray alloc] init];
  tp.triangles = [[NSMutableArray alloc] init];

  //Polygon Triangulation
  Vector2dVector a;

  for(int i=0; i<[verts count];i+=1){
    //Add polygon vertices
    [tp.vertices addObject:[verts objectAtIndex:i]];

    //Add polygon vertices to triangulation container
    CGPoint vert = [[verts objectAtIndex:i] CGPointValue];
    a.push_back( Vector2d(vert.x, vert.y) );
  }

  //Run triangulation algorithm
  Vector2dVector result;
```

```
  Triangulate::Process(a,result);

  //Gather all triangles from result container
  int tcount = result.size()/3;
  for (int i=0; i<tcount; i++) {
    const Vector2d &p1 = result[i*3+0];
    const Vector2d &p2 = result[i*3+1];
    const Vector2d &p3 = result[i*3+2];

    //Add triangle index
    [tp.triangles addObject: [tp getTriangleIndicesFromPoint1:ccp
(p1.GetX(),p1.GetY()) point2:ccp(p2.GetX(),p2.GetY()) point3:ccp(p3.
GetX(), p3.GetY())] ];
  }

  //Set texture coordinate information
  [tp setCoordInfo];

  return tp;
}


+(id) createWithFile:(NSString*)file withVertices:(NSArray*)verts
withTriangles:(NSArray*)tris {
  /*** Create a TexturedPolygon with vertices and triangles given.
***/

  //Initialization
  TexturedPolygon *tp = [TexturedPolygon spriteWithFile:file];
  tp.vertices = [[NSMutableArray alloc] init];
  tp.triangles = [[NSMutableArray alloc] init];

  //Set polygon vertices
  for(int i=0; i<[verts count];i+=1){
    [tp.vertices addObject:[verts objectAtIndex:i]];
  }

  //Set triangle indices
  for(int i=0; i<[tris count];i+=1){
    [tp.triangles addObject:[tris objectAtIndex:i]];
  }

  //Set texture coordinate information
  [tp setCoordInfo];

  return tp;
```

```
}

-(Vector3D*) getTriangleIndicesFromPoint1:(CGPoint)p1 point2:(CGPoint)
p2 point3:(CGPoint)p3 {
  /*** Convert three polygon vertices to triangle indices ***/

  Vector3D* indices = [Vector3D x:-1 y:-1 z:-1];

  for(int i=0; i< [vertices count]; i++){
    CGPoint vert = [[vertices objectAtIndex:i] CGPointValue];
    if(p1.x == vert.x and p1.y == vert.y){
      indices.x = i;
    }else if(p2.x == vert.x and p2.y == vert.y){
      indices.y = i;
    }else if(p3.x == vert.x and p3.y == vert.y){
      indices.z = i;
    }
  }

  return indices;
}

-(void) addAnimFrameWithFile:(NSString*)file toArray:(NSMutableArray*)
arr {
  /*** For textured polygon animation ***/

  ccTexParams params = {GL_NEAREST,GL_NEAREST_MIPMAP_NEAREST,GL_
REPEAT,GL_REPEAT};
  CCTexture2D *frameTexture = [[CCTextureCache sharedTextureCache]
addImage:file];
  [frameTexture setTexParameters:&params];
  CCSpriteFrame *frame = [CCSpriteFrame frameWithTexture:frameTexture
rect:self.textureRect];
  [[CCSpriteFrameCache sharedSpriteFrameCache]
addSpriteFrame:frameTexture name:file];
  [arr addObject:frame];
}

-(void) setCoordInfo {
  /*** Set texture coordinates for each vertex ***/

  if(coords){ free(coords); }
  coords = (ccV2F_T2F*)malloc(sizeof(ccV2F_T2F)*[vertices count]);

  for(int i=0;i<[vertices count];i++) {
```

```
    coords[i].vertices.x = [[vertices objectAtIndex:i]
CGPointValue].x;
    coords[i].vertices.y = [[vertices objectAtIndex:i]
CGPointValue].y;

    float atlasWidth = texture_.pixelsWide;
    float atlasHeight = texture_.pixelsHigh;

    coords[i].texCoords.u = (coords[i].vertices.x + rect_.origin.x)/
atlasWidth;
    coords[i].texCoords.v = (contentSize_.height - coords[i].
vertices.y + rect_.origin.y)/ atlasHeight ;
  }
}

-(void) dealloc
{
  //Release texture coordinates if necessary
  if(coords) free(coords);
  [super dealloc];
}

-(void) draw
{
  /*** This is where the magic happens. Texture and draw all
triangles. ***/

  glDisableClientState(GL_COLOR_ARRAY);

  glColor4ub( color_.r, color_.g, color_.b, quad_.bl.colors.a);

  BOOL newBlend = NO;
  if( blendFunc_.src != CC_BLEND_SRC || blendFunc_.dst != CC_BLEND_DST
) {
    newBlend = YES;
    glBlendFunc( blendFunc_.src, blendFunc_.dst );
  }

  glBindTexture(GL_TEXTURE_2D, texture_.name);

  unsigned int offset = (unsigned int)coords;
  unsigned int diff = offsetof( ccV2F_T2F, vertices);
  glVertexPointer(2, GL_FLOAT, sizeof(ccV2F_T2F), (void*)(offset +
diff));
  diff = offsetof( ccV2F_T2F, texCoords);
```

```
    glTexCoordPointer(2, GL_FLOAT, sizeof(ccV2F_T2F), (void*) (offset +
diff));

    for(int i=0;i<[triangles count];i++){
      Vector3D *tri = [triangles objectAtIndex:i];
      short indices[] = {tri.x, tri.y, tri.z};
      glDrawElements(GL_TRIANGLE_STRIP, 3, GL_UNSIGNED_SHORT, indices);
    }

    if(newBlend) { glBlendFunc(CC_BLEND_SRC, CC_BLEND_DST); }

    glColor4ub( 255, 255, 255, 255);

    glEnableClientState(GL_COLOR_ARRAY);
}
@end


@implementation Ch1_RenderTexturedPolygon

-(CCLayer*) runRecipe {
  CGSize s = [[CCDirector sharedDirector] winSize];

  //Set polygon vertices
  CGPoint vertexArr[] = { ccp(248,340), ccp(200,226), ccp(62,202),
ccp(156,120), ccp(134,2), ccp(250,64), ccp(360,0), ccp(338,128),
ccp(434,200), ccp(306,230) };
  int numVerts = 10;

  NSMutableArray *vertices = [[NSMutableArray alloc] init];

  //Add vertices to array
  for(int i=0; i<numVerts; i++){
    [vertices addObject:[NSValue valueWithCGPoint:vertexArr[i]]];
  }

  //Note: Your texture size MUST be a product of 2 for this to work.
  //Set texture parameters to repeat
ccTexParams params = {GL_NEAREST,GL_NEAREST_MIPMAP_NEAREST,GL_
REPEAT,GL_REPEAT};

  //Create textured polygon
TexturedPolygon *texturedPoly = [TexturedPolygon
createWithFile:@"bricks.jpg" withVertices:vertices];
  [texturedPoly.texture setTexParameters:&params];
```

```
texturedPoly.position = ccp(128,128);

//Add textured polygon to scene
[self addChild:texturedPoly z:1 tag:0];

return self;
}

@end
```

How it works...

`TexturedPolygon` takes a given set of **vertices** and uses a **polygon triangulation algorithm** to find all triangles contained within the polygon. It then textures and draws these triangles using OpenGL triangles strips.

 ▸ Triangulation:

   Triangulation, depending on the polygon, can be a complex process. This is often performed while a map is loading. For very complex polygons it can be advantageous to perform polygon triangulation during level creation and store triangle **indices** along with the polygon vertices. This can speed up level load times.

 ▸ Uses:

   Textured polygons have many uses including static map textures and background textures.

 ▸ Performance:

   Using this technique you can efficiently draw polygons of virtually any size. Space requirements rely on the size of each texture used rather that the size of each polygon. To use less space, modify `TexturedPolygon` to re-use pre-initialized textures.

 ▸ Caveats:

   This technique has a few caveats. The textures used must be square and each side's size must be equal to 2n (16x16, 32x32, 64x64, and so on). Also, textures can only be single files, not sprite frames.

There's more...

This recipe may be your first foray into combining `Objective-C` and `C++` code. This is commonly referred to as `Objective-C++`. For more information please refer to Apple's official developer documentation *Using C++ With Objective-C* at `http://developer.apple.com/library/mac/#documentation/Cocoa/Conceptual/ObjectiveC/Articles/ocCPlusPlus.html`.

Animating a texture-filled polygon

The TexturedPolygon can also be easily animated. This is useful for animated crowds, ocean waves, bubbling lava pits, and so on. In the example we see an animated field of wheat.

Getting ready

Please refer to the project RecipeCollection01 for full working code of this recipe.

How to do it...

Execute the following code:

```
#import "Vector3D.h"
#import "TexturedPolygon.h"

@implementation Ch1_AnimateTexturedPolygon

-(CCLayer*) runRecipe {
  CGSize s = [[CCDirector sharedDirector] winSize];

  ccTexParams params = {GL_NEAREST, GL_NEAREST_MIPMAP_NEAREST, GL_
REPEAT,GL_REPEAT};

  //Create grass animated textured polygon
  CGPoint grassVertexArr[] = { ccp(0,0), ccp(480,0), ccp(480,320),
ccp(0,320) };
```

```
    int grassNumVerts = 4;
    NSMutableArray *grassVertices = [[NSMutableArray alloc] init];
    for(int i=0; i<grassNumVerts; i++){
        [grassVertices addObject:[NSValue valueWithCGPoint:ccp(grassVertex
Arr[i].x*1, grassVertexArr[i].y*1)]];
    }


    TexturedPolygon *grassPoly = [TexturedPolygon
createWithFile:@"grass_tile_01.png" withVertices:grassVertices];
    [grassPoly.texture setTexParameters:&params];
    grassPoly.position = ccp(32,32);
    [self addChild:grassPoly z:1 tag:1];


    //Create swaying grass animation
    NSMutableArray *grassAnimFrames = [NSMutableArray array];


    //This is a two part animation with 'back' and 'forth' frames
    for(int i=0; i<=6; i++){
        [grassPoly addAnimFrameWithFile:[NSString
stringWithFormat:@"grass_tile_0%d.png",i] toArray:grassAnimFrames];
    }
    for(int i=5; i>0; i--){
        [grassPoly addAnimFrameWithFile:[NSString
stringWithFormat:@"grass_tile_0%d.png",i] toArray:grassAnimFrames];
    }


    CCAnimation *grassAnimation = [[CCAnimation alloc]
initWithName:@"grass_tile_anim" delay:0.1f];
    for(int i=0; i<[grassAnimFrames count]; i++){
        [grassAnimation addFrame:[grassAnimFrames objectAtIndex:i]];
    }


    CCActionInterval *grassAnimate = [CCSequence actions: [CCAnimate act
ionWithAnimation:grassAnimation restoreOriginalFrame:NO],
        [CCDelayTime actionWithDuration:0.0f], nil];
    CCActionInterval *grassRepeatAnimation = [CCRepeatForever
actionWithAction:grassAnimate];
    [grassPoly runAction:grassRepeatAnimation];


    return self;
}

@end
```

How it works...

By dynamically changing the texture using `CCAnimation` we can create very simple tiled animation. The only extra cost of this operation is the extra space allocated for each frame of the animation.

Swapping palettes using layers

A vital tool in any game developer's repertoire is the ability to swap color palettes. From *The Legend of Zelda* on *NES* to *Halo* on the *Xbox*, palette swapping is a simple yet effective visual cue that can stretch a limited amount of art.

In the following example you learn how to palette swap using layers. We are using an animated baseball player for this example.

Getting ready

Please refer to the project `RecipeCollection01` for full working code of this recipe.

For this recipe you will need an image manipulation program. I recommend the free and easy to use *GIMP*.

How to do it...

The first thing we will do is draw the sprite and the colorable areas:

1. Draw your texture with all dynamically colorable areas left blank. In your image editing program your texture should look something like the following:

2. Create a new layer and color a specific area white. In this example we are coloring his uniform (legs and shirt) white:

3. Hide the other layer and save that white-only layer as a separate texture.
4. Repeat this for any other separately colored sections.

5. Once we have our textures we can write some code:

```
@implementation Ch1_PaletteSwapping

-(CCLayer*) runRecipe {
  //Create a nice looking background
  CCSprite *bg = [CCSprite spriteWithFile:@"baseball_bg_02.png"];
  [bg setPosition:ccp(240,160)];
  bg.opacity = 100;
  [self addChild:bg z:0 tag:0];

  /*** Animate 4 different fielders with different color
combinations ***/

  //Set color arrays
  ccColor3B colors1[] = {
      ccc3(255,217,161), ccc3(225,225,225), ccc3(0,0,150),
ccc3(255,255,255) };
  ccColor3B colors2[] = {
     ccc3(140,100,46), ccc3(150,150,150), ccc3(255,0,0),
ccc3(255,255,255) };
  ccColor3B colors3[] = {
      ccc3(255,217,161), ccc3(115,170,115), ccc3(115,170,115),
ccc3(255,255,255) };
  ccColor3B colors4[] = {
     ccc3(140,100,46),   ccc3(50,50,50), ccc3(255,255,0),
ccc3(255,255,255) };

  //Animate fielders with colors
  [self animateFielderWithColors:colors1
withPosition:ccp(150,70)];
  [self animateFielderWithColors:colors2
withPosition:ccp(150,200)];
  [self animateFielderWithColors:colors3
withPosition:ccp(300,200)];
  [self animateFielderWithColors:colors4
withPosition:ccp(300,70)];

  return self;
}

-(void) animateFielderWithColors:(ccColor3B[])colors
withPosition:(CGPoint)pos {
  //The names of our layers
```

```
    NSString *layers[] = { @"skin", @"uniform", @"trim", @"black_
lines" };

  //Number of layers
  int numLayers = 4;

  for(int i=0; i<numLayers; i+=1){
    NSString *layerName = layers[i];
    ccColor3B color = colors[i];

    //We need each plist, the first frame name and finally a name
for the animation
    NSString *plistName = [NSString stringWithFormat:@"fielder_
run_%@.plist", layerName];
    NSString *firstFrameName = [NSString
stringWithFormat:@"fielder_run_%@_01.png", layerName];
    NSString *animationName = [NSString
stringWithFormat:@"fielder_run_%@", layerName];

    //Add plist frames to the SpriteFrameCache
    [[CCSpriteFrameCache sharedSpriteFrameCache] addSpriteFramesWi
thFile:plistName];

    //Get the first sprite frame
    CCSpriteFrame *firstFrame = [[CCSpriteFrameCache
sharedSpriteFrameCache] spriteFrameByName:firstFrameName];

    //Create our sprite
    CCSprite *sprite = [CCSprite spriteWithSpriteFrame:firstFrame]
;

    //Set color and position
    sprite.position = pos;
    sprite.color = color;

    //Create the animation and add frames
    CCAnimation *animation = [[CCAnimation alloc]
initWithName:animationName delay:0.15f];
    for(int i=1; i<=8; i+=1){
      CCSpriteFrame *frame = [[CCSpriteFrameCache
sharedSpriteFrameCache] spriteFrameByName:[NSString
stringWithFormat:@"fielder_run_%@_0%i.png",layerName,i]];
      [animation addFrame:frame];
    }
```

```
        //Run the repeating animation
        [sprite runAction:[CCRepeatForever actionWithAction:
    [CCAnimate actionWithAnimation:animation]]];

        //Finally, add the sprite
        [self addChild:sprite];
    }
}

@end
```

How it works...

By drawing the swappable layers under the main layer (the black outline) we cover up any imprecision in the coloring. This technique is slightly more difficult for art that doesn't use a thick black outline like the drawings shown in the preceding section.

- ► Efficiency—Disk Space:

  Keeping your iOS app below a certain size on the disk is always a good idea. This technique is fairly easy on your disk space as the swappable textures take up only a small amount of space due to easy PNG compression of simplistic textures.

- ► Efficiency—Memory Usage:

  Unfortunately the size of a texture in memory is determined by its pixel size. So, if you are palette swapping large animated textures you might run into memory consumption issues. Memory consumption for a palette swapped texture equals the normal memory size times the number of palettes to swap.

- ► Efficiency—CPU:

  When animating a palette swapped texture the CPU time used by the animation routine will also be multiplied by the number of swappable layers. This is usually fairly inconsequential as animation takes up very little CPU time as it is.

Swapping palettes using CCTexture2DMutable

Another way to palette swap involves **sentinel colors** and the ability to modify a texture pixel by pixel. This method can help reclaim some extra space on the disk and in memory but it tends to take a lot of CPU time. It is also messier than the previous technique when used with anti-aliased or blended textures.

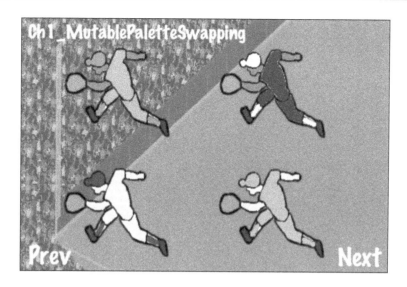

Getting ready

Please refer to the project `RecipeCollection01` for full working code of this recipe. Also note the included library `CCTexture2DMutable` that is not included in the book itself.

For this recipe you will need an image manipulation program. Once again I recommend the free and easy to use *GIMP*.

How to do it...

The first thing we will do is draw a sprite that contains colorable areas defined by sentinel colors. A sentinel color is usually a primary color that is easily recognizable and can be replaced programmatically. In this case we will use red, blue, and green:

It is best to avoid aliasing and blending as much as possible when using this technique. Adjusting your coloring algorithm's tolerance according to your texture can be tricky.

Now, execute the following code:

```
#import "CCTexture2DMutable.h"

@implementation Ch1_MutablePaletteSwapping

-(CCLayer*) runRecipe {
  //Create a nice looking background
  CCSprite *bg = [CCSprite spriteWithFile:@"baseball_bg_01.png"];
  [bg setPosition:ccp(240,160)];
  bg.opacity = 100;
  [self addChild:bg z:0 tag:0];

  /*** Animate 4 different fielders with different color combinations
***/

  //Set color arrays
  ccColor4B colors1[] = { ccc4(255,217,161,255),
ccc4(225,225,225,255), ccc4(0,0,150,255) };
  ccColor4B colors2[] = { ccc4(140,100,46,255), ccc4(150,150,150,255),
ccc4(255,0,0,255) };
  ccColor4B colors3[] = { ccc4(255,217,161,255),
ccc4(115,170,115,255), ccc4(115,170,115,255) };
  ccColor4B colors4[] = { ccc4(140,100,46,255),   ccc4(50,50,50,255),
ccc4(255,255,0,255) };

  //Create texture copy to use as an immutable guide.
  CCTexture2DMutable* textureCopy = [[[CCTexture2DMutable alloc]
initWithImage:[UIImage imageNamed:@"fielder_run_sentinel_colors.png"]]
autorelease];

  //Create our sprites using mutable textures.
  CCSprite *sprite1 = [CCSprite spriteWithTexture:[[[CCTexture2DMuta
ble alloc] initWithImage:[UIImage imageNamed:@"fielder_run_sentinel_
colors.png"]] autorelease]];
  CCSprite *sprite2 = [CCSprite spriteWithTexture:[[[CCTexture2DMuta
ble alloc] initWithImage:[UIImage imageNamed:@"fielder_run_sentinel_
colors.png"]] autorelease]];
  CCSprite *sprite3 = [CCSprite spriteWithTexture:[[[CCTexture2DMuta
ble alloc] initWithImage:[UIImage imageNamed:@"fielder_run_sentinel_
colors.png"]] autorelease]];
  CCSprite *sprite4 = [CCSprite spriteWithTexture:[[[CCTexture2DMuta
ble alloc] initWithImage:[UIImage imageNamed:@"fielder_run_sentinel_
colors.png"]] autorelease]];

  //Set sprite positions
```

```
    [sprite1 setPosition:ccp(125,75)];
    [sprite2 setPosition:ccp(125,225)];
    [sprite3 setPosition:ccp(325,75)];
    [sprite4 setPosition:ccp(325,225)];


    //Swap colors in each sprite mutable texture and apply the changes.
    [self swapColor:ccc4(0,0,255,255) withColor:colors1[0]
inTexture:sprite1.texture withCopy:textureCopy];
    [self swapColor:ccc4(0,255,0,255) withColor:colors1[1]
inTexture:sprite1.texture withCopy:textureCopy];
    [self swapColor:ccc4(255,0,0,255) withColor:colors1[2]
inTexture:sprite1.texture withCopy:textureCopy];
    [sprite1.texture apply];


    /* CODE OMITTED */


    //Finally, add the sprites to the scene.
    [self addChild:sprite1 z:0 tag:0];
    [self addChild:sprite2 z:0 tag:1];
    [self addChild:sprite3 z:0 tag:2];
    [self addChild:sprite4 z:0 tag:3];


    return self;
}


-(void) swapColor:(ccColor4B)color1 withColor:(ccColor4B)color2
inTexture:(CCTexture2DMutable*)texture withCopy:(CCTexture2DMutable*)
copy {
    //Look through the texture, find all pixels of the specified color
and change them.
    //We use a tolerance of 200 here.
    for(int x=0; x<texture.pixelsWide; x++){
        for(int y=0; y<texture.pixelsHigh; y++){
            if( [self isColor:[copy pixelAt:ccp(x,y)] equalTo:color1
withTolerance:200] ){
                [texture setPixelAt:ccp(x,y) rgba:color2];
            }
        }
    }
}


-(bool) isColor:(ccColor4B)color1 equalTo:(ccColor4B)color2
withTolerance:(int)tolerance {
    //If the colors are equal within a tolerance we change them.
    bool equal = YES;
```

```
    if ( abs(color1.r - color2.r) + abs(color1.g - color2.g) +
      abs(color1.b - color2.b) + abs(color1.a - color2.a) > tolerance ){
        equal = NO;
    }
    return equal;
}

@end
```

How it works...

For better or worse this technique works the same way color selection and replacement works in *Adobe Photoshop*, and similar drawing programs. Using `CCTexture2DMutable` can often be a slow process and this technique is only recommended for games that require pixel-perfect graphics or have very strict space/memory requirements.

Using AWTextureFilter for blur and font shadows

By harnessing `CCTexture2DMutable` the class `AWTextureFilter` can be used to create some cool effects. These include **Gaussian Blur**, selective Gaussian Blur, and dynamically generated font shadows as shown in the following scene:

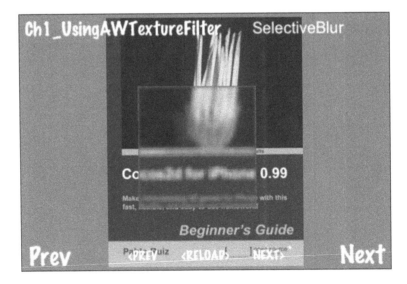

Getting ready

Please refer to the project `RecipeCollection01` for full working code of this recipe.

How to do it...

Execute the following code:

```
#import "CCTexture2DMutable.h"
#import "AWTextureFilter.h"

@implementation Ch1_UsingAWTextureFilter

-(CCLayer*) runRecipe {
  CGSize winSize = [[CCDirector sharedDirector] winSize];

//Pixel Format RGBA8888 is required for blur effects
  [CCTexture2D setDefaultAlphaPixelFormat:kCCTexture2DPixelFormat_
RGBA8888];

  /*** Display a blurred texture ***/

  //Create the blur mutable texture
  CCTexture2DMutable *mutableBlurTexture = [[[CCTexture2DMutable
alloc] initWithImage:[UIImage imageNamed:@"cocos2d_beginner.png"]]
autorelease];

  //Apply blur to the mutable texture
  [AWTextureFilter blur:mutableBlurTexture radius:3];

  //Create a sprite to show the blur
  CCSprite *blurSprite = [CCSprite spriteWithTexture:mutableBlurTextu
re];
  [blurSprite setPosition:ccp(winSize.width/2+blur.contentSize.
width/2+1, winSize.height/2)];

  //Add sprite to the scene
[self addChild:blurSprite z:0 tag:0];

/*** Display a selectively blurred texture ***/

  //Create the mutable texture to selectively blur
```

```
   CCTexture2DMutable *mutableSelectiveBlurTexture =
[[[CCTexture2DMutable alloc] initWithImage:[UIImage
imageNamed:@"cocos2d_beginner.png"]] autorelease];

  //Apply selective blur to the mutable texture
  [AWTextureFilter blur:mutableSelectiveBlurTexture radius:8
rect:CGRectMake(240-200, (winSize.height-160)-75, 150, 150)];

  //Create a sprite to show the selective blur
  CCSprite *selectiveBlurSprite = [CCSprite spriteWithTexture:mutableS
electiveBlurTexture];
  [selectiveBlurSprite setPosition:ccp(winSize.width/2, winSize.
height/2)];

  //Add sprite to the scene
[self addChild:selectiveBlurSprite z:0 tag:1];

/*** Display dynamic font shadow effect ***/

  //Create a background so we can see the shadow
  CCLayerColor *background = [CCLayerColor layerWithColor:ccc4(200,
100, 100, 255) width:300 height:50];
  [background setIsRelativeAnchorPoint:YES];
  [background setAnchorPoint:ccp(0.5f, 0.5f)];
  [background setPosition:ccp(winSize.width/2, winSize.height/2)];

  //Create a sprite for the font label
  CCSprite* labelSprite = [CCSprite node];
  [labelSprite setPosition:ccp(winSize.width/2, winSize.height/2)];

  //Create a sprite for the shadow
  CCSprite* shadowSprite = [CCSprite node];
  [shadowSprite setPosition:ccp(winSize.width/2+1, winSize.
height/2+1)];

  //Color it black
  [shadowSprite setColor:ccBLACK];

  //Add sprites to a node and the node to the scene
  CCNode* node = [[CCNode alloc] init];
  [node addChild:background z:-1];
  [node addChild:shadowSprite z:0];
  [node addChild:labelSprite z:1];
  [self addChild:node z:-1 tag:2];
```

```
    //Create a mutable texture with a string
    CCTexture2DMutable *shadowTexture = [[[CCTexture2DMutable alloc]
initWithString:@"Shadowed Text" fontName:@"Arial" fontSize:28]
autorelease];

    //Copy the mutable texture as non mutable texture
    CCTexture2D *labelTexture = [[shadowTexture copyMutable:NO]
autorelease];

    //Set the label texture
    [labelSprite setTexture:labelTexture];
    [labelSprite setTextureRect:CGRectMake(0, 0, shadowTexture.
contentSize.width, shadowTexture.contentSize.height)];

    //Apply blur to the shadow texture
    [AWTextureFilter blur:shadowTexture radius:4];

    //Set the shadow texture
    [shadowSprite setTexture:shadowTexture];
    [shadowSprite setTextureRect:CGRectMake(0, 0, shadowTexture.
contentSize.width, shadowTexture.contentSize.height)];

    return self;
}
```

How it works...

AWTextureFilter uses CCTexture2DMutable to achieve a compelling Gaussian Blur effect. This is one example of complex pixel manipulation.

Font shadows:

CCTexture2DMutable inherits from CCTexture2D. This allows us to use the following method:

```
    - (id) initWithString:(NSString*)string fontName:(NSString*)name
    fontSize:(CGFloat)size;
```

This creates a label texture that we can then use to create a blurred font shadow effect by creating a similar texture that we offset, darken, blur, and finally draw behind the original label texture.

There's more...

Here are a few other suggestions for the use of this blurring technique:

- Blurring a screenshot as a background for the pause menu (see the next recipe in this chapter, *Taking and using screenshots*)
- Combine with a color effect for a cool glow effect
- Increase or decrease blur radius for reveal-based puzzle and trivia games

Taking and using screenshots

As hinted in the last recipe, in-game screenshots can be taken and used in-game to create cool effects like a blurred background for a pause menu. For an example of this in a published app, take a look at the pause menu in *2K Sports NHL 2K11*.

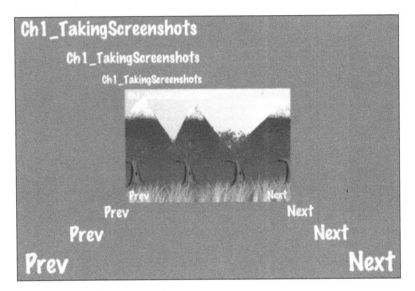

Getting ready

Please refer to the project `RecipeCollection01` for full working code of this recipe. Also note the included library `Screenshot` that is not included in the book itself.

How to do it...

Execute the following code:

```
#import "Screenshot.h"

@implementation Ch1_TakingScreenshots

-(CCLayer*) runRecipe {
CCSprite* sprite = [CCSprite spriteWithTexture:[Screenshot
takeAsTexture2D]];
[sprite setPosition:ccp(240,160)];
[sprite setScale:0.75f];

[self addChild:sprite z:0 tag:0];

   return self;
}
```

How it works...

The included `Screenshot` library uses some complex iOS techniques that are beyond the scope of this book. The library is included in `RecipeCollection01`. You can take a look at it there.

Simply put, `Screenshot` takes a capture of what's currently on the screen and shoves that into a `CCTexture2D` for you to manipulate.

There's more...

Live screenshots can be used for a wide variety of things such as the following:

- Screenshot highlights and recaps of interesting moments of gameplay at the end of a match or level
- Considering the fact that you can analyze exactly what the player is currently seeing you could "break the fourth wall" (think *Psycho Mantis* in *Metal Gear Solid* for *Sony PlayStation*)
- An in-game user controlled camera like in *Pokemon Snap* for *Nintentdo 64*

Using CCParallaxNode

Parallaxing is a staple of 2D side-scrolling video games. A competent developer would be remiss if he didn't include a nice parallaxed background in a 2D side-scroller. Cocos2d makes parallaxing easy with CCParallaxNode.

Getting ready

Please refer to the project `RecipeCollection01` for full working code of this recipe.

How to do it...

Execute the following code:

```
@implementation Ch1_UsingCCParallaxNode

-(CCLayer*) runRecipe {
  //Create four parallax sprites, one for each layer
  CCSprite* parallaxLayer01 = [CCSprite spriteWithFile:@"parallax_
layer_01.png"];
  CCSprite* parallaxLayer02 = [CCSprite spriteWithFile:@"parallax_
layer_02.png"];
  CCSprite* parallaxLayer03 = [CCSprite spriteWithFile:@"parallax_
layer_03.png"];
  CCSprite* parallaxLayer04 = [CCSprite spriteWithFile:@"parallax_
layer_04.png"];

  //Create a parallax node and add all four sprites
```

```
CCParallaxNode* parallaxNode = [CCParallaxNode node];
[parallaxNode setPosition:ccp(0,0)];
[parallaxNode addChild:parallaxLayer01 z:1 parallaxRatio:ccp(0, 0)
positionOffset:ccp(240,200)];
[parallaxNode addChild:parallaxLayer02 z:2 parallaxRatio:ccp(1, 0)
positionOffset:ccp(240,100)];
[parallaxNode addChild:parallaxLayer03 z:3 parallaxRatio:ccp(2, 0)
positionOffset:ccp(240,100)];
[parallaxNode addChild:parallaxLayer04 z:4 parallaxRatio:ccp(3, 0)
positionOffset:ccp(240,20)];
[self addChild:parallaxNode z:0 tag:1];

//Move the node to the left then the right
//This creates the effect that we are moving to the right then the
left
CCMoveBy* moveRight = [CCMoveBy actionWithDuration:5.0f
position:ccp(-80, 0)];
CCMoveBy* moveLeft = [CCMoveBy actionWithDuration:2.5f
position:ccp(80, 0)];
CCSequence* sequence = [CCSequence actions:moveRight, moveLeft,
nil];
CCRepeatForever* repeat = [CCRepeatForever
actionWithAction:sequence];
[parallaxNode runAction:repeat];

return self;
}

@end
```

How it works...

Cocos2d makes it very easy to create a professional looking scrolling background. `CCParallaxNode` breaks the concept of parallaxing down to its key components. In the following example we attach four sprites to an instance of `CCParallaxNode`. Keep in mind that you can attach any `CCNode` to a `CCParallaxNode`. We then set `parallaxRatio` and `parallaxOffset` to create the desired effect.

▶ **Parallax Ratio**:

This ratio determines how real game coordinates affect the coordinates of this particular parallaxed layer. A ratio of `ccp(2,0)` means the sprite will scroll twice as fast on the X and not at all on the Y. Higher (faster) ratios are typically drawn closer to the camera.

▶ **Position Offset**:

The position offset of each child node represents where it will be drawn when its parent (the `CCParallaxNode`) is at the origin or `ccp(0,0)`. Once the main `CCParallaxNode` instance moves the children will move with the proper ratio.

There's more...

There are a number of ways to loop a parallaxed background. One involves checking the `parallaxNode` position at every step and adjusting all the child position offsets based on the integer value of the parallax node X position divided by the screen size:

```
parallaxNodeChildXOffset = baseXOffset + ((int) (self.position.x /
winSize.width)) * winSize.width;
```

This effectively resets the child positions after the `parallaxNode` has moved one full screen width.

Lighting using glColorMask

Lighting is a fundamental part of most 3D video games. 2D games do not naturally lend themselves to lighting effects, but with the right technique we can create a 2D experience where lighting plays a vital role. This adds suspense to our 2D scene.

In this recipe we see a monk walking through a dark cave carrying a lantern. The monk's lantern gives off light in a circular shape that illuminates dark parts of the scene. As the monk moves through the cave a colony of bats becomes visible.

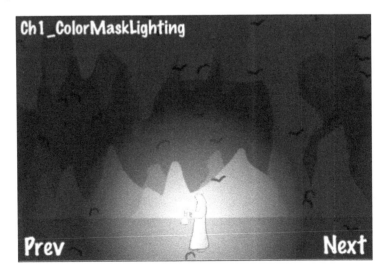

Please refer to the project `RecipeCollection01` for full working code of this recipe. Also note that code used to create the 'flying bats' effect has been omitted as that was covered in a previous recipe.

Execute the following code:

```
@interface Ch1_ColorMaskLighting : Recipe
{
   SimpleAnimObject *burnSprite;
   SimpleAnimObject *lightSprite;
   SimpleAnimObject *monkSprite;
   CCRenderTexture *darknessLayer;

   NSMutableArray *bats;
   CCAnimation *batFlyUp;
   CCAnimation *batGlideDown;
}

@end

@implementation Ch1_ColorMaskLighting

-(CCLayer*) runRecipe {
   //Add our PLISTs to the SpriteFrameCache singleton
   CCSpriteFrameCache * cache = [CCSpriteFrameCache
sharedSpriteFrameCache];
   [cache addSpriteFramesWithFile:@"simple_bat.plist"];
   [cache addSpriteFramesWithFile:@"monk_lantern.plist"];

   //Add cave background
   CCSprite *caveBg = [CCSprite spriteWithFile:@"cave.png"];
   [caveBg setPosition:ccp(240,160)];
   [self addChild: caveBg z:0 tag:TAG_CAVE_BG];

   //Set up the burn sprite that will "knock out" parts of the darkness
layer depending on the alpha value of the pixels in the image.
   burnSprite = [SimpleAnimObject spriteWithFile:@"fire.png"];
   burnSprite.position = ccp(50,50);
   burnSprite.scale = 10.0f;
```

```
  [burnSprite setBlendFunc: (ccBlendFunc) { GL_ZERO, GL_ONE_MINUS_SRC_
ALPHA }];
  [burnSprite retain];
  burnSprite.velocity = ccp(1,0);


  //Add a 'light' sprite which additively blends onto the scene. This
represents the cone of light created by the monk's candle.
  lightSprite = [SimpleAnimObject spriteWithFile:@"fire.png"];
  lightSprite.position = ccp(50,50);
  lightSprite.scale = 10.0f;
  [lightSprite setColor:ccc3(100,100,50)];
  [lightSprite setBlendFunc: (ccBlendFunc) { GL_ONE, GL_ONE }];
  lightSprite.velocity = ccp(1,0);
  [self addChild:lightSprite z:4 tag:TAG_LIGHT_SPRITE];


  //Add the monk
  monkSprite = [[SimpleAnimObject alloc] init];
  monkSprite.position = ccp(50,50);
  monkSprite.velocity = ccp(1,0);
  [self addChild:monkSprite z:1 tag:TAG_MONK];


  //Animate the monk to simulate walking.
  CCAnimation *animation = [[CCAnimation alloc] initWithName:@"monk_
lantern_walk" delay:0.1f];
  for(int i=1; i<=5; i+=1){
    [animation addFrame:[cache spriteFrameByName:[NSString
stringWithFormat:@"monk_lantern_0%i.png",i]]];
  }
  for(int i=4; i>=2; i-=1){
    [animation addFrame:[cache spriteFrameByName:[NSString
stringWithFormat:@"monk_lantern_0%i.png",i]]];
  }
  [monkSprite runAction:[CCRepeatForever actionWithAction: [CCAnimate
actionWithAnimation:animation]]];


  //Add the 'darkness' layer. This simulates darkness in the cave.
  darknessLayer = [CCRenderTexture renderTextureWithWidth:480
height:320];
  darknessLayer.position =  ccp(240,160);
  [self addChild:darknessLayer z:0 tag:TAG_DARKNESS_LAYER];


  //Schedule physics updates
  [self schedule:@selector(step:)];


  return self;
```

```
}

-(void)step:(ccTime)delta {
  CGSize s = [[CCDirector sharedDirector] winSize];

  //Clear the darkness layer for redrawing. Here we clear it to BLACK
with 90% opacity.
  [darknessLayer clear:0.0f g:0.0f b:0.0f a:0.9f];

  //Begin the darkness layer drawing routine. This transforms to the
proper location, among other things.
  [darknessLayer begin];

  //Limit drawing to the alpha channel.
  glColorMask(0.0f, 0.0f, 0.0f, 1.0f);

  //Draw the burn sprite only on the alpha channel.
  [burnSprite visit];

  //Reset glColorMask to allow drawing of colors.
  glColorMask(1.0f, 1.0f, 1.0f, 1.0f);

  //Finish transformation.
  [darknessLayer end];

  //Make the monk walk back and forth.
  if(monkSprite.position.x > 480){
    monkSprite.flipX = YES;
    burnSprite.velocity = ccp(-1,0);
    lightSprite.velocity = ccp(-1,0);
    monkSprite.velocity = ccp(-1,0);
  }else if(monkSprite.position.x < 0){
    monkSprite.flipX = NO;
    burnSprite.velocity = ccp(1,0);
    lightSprite.velocity = ccp(1,0);
    monkSprite.velocity = ccp(1,0);
  }

  //Update our SimpleAnimObjects
  [burnSprite update:delta];
  [lightSprite update:delta];
  [monkSprite update:delta];
}

@end
```

How it works...

Cocos2d exposes just the right amount of OpenGL drawing logic to make complex manipulations of rendering order look easy. To achieve this effect we use `CCRenderTexture`. First, we clear the screen using the following call:

```
[darknessLayer clear:0.0f g:0.0f b:0.0f a:0.9f];
```

We then limit drawing to only the **alpha channel** using a `glColorMask` call. This, in effect, tells OpenGL to modify the opacity (only the opacity, not the color) of the graphics buffer based on what we render. So, we render the `fire.png` texture to simulate light that is 2D and diffuses in a circle.

Finally, we additively draw another `fire.png` texture over this one to simulate the brightness and color of the light.

The node `darknessLayer` is only rendered within the screen's viewing area while `burnSprite` and `lightSprite` are rendered at the lantern's position.

There's more...

Using a similar technique lights can be created in all shapes, sizes, and colors. These can include animated lights like torches, shaped lights like a car's headlights, or short, quick lighting effects like a bright flash from an explosion.

Most importantly, this effect gives us the ability to tease the player with what may or may not lurk in the shadows of the game world.

2
User Input

In this chapter, we will cover the following points:

- ▸ Tap, hold, and drag input
- ▸ Depth testing input
- ▸ Creating buttons
- ▸ Creating a directional pad
- ▸ Creating an analog stick
- ▸ Using the accelerometer for steering
- ▸ Using the accelerometer for 3D rotation
- ▸ Pinch zooming
- ▸ Performing gestures

Introduction

Without user input a video game is merely a tech demo. iOS touch devices allow limitless customization of user input. In this chapter, we will cover the most common input methods using both the **touch screen** and the **accelerometer**.

Tap, hold, and drag input

Tapping, **holding**, and **dragging** are the most commonly used input techniques. They form the basic building blocks of input for user interfaces as well as for interacting with game objects. In this recipe, we subclass `CCSprite` in order to create a sprite which can process touch events and maintain some custom state information. This, plus some logic, allows us to touch, hold, and drag this sprite.

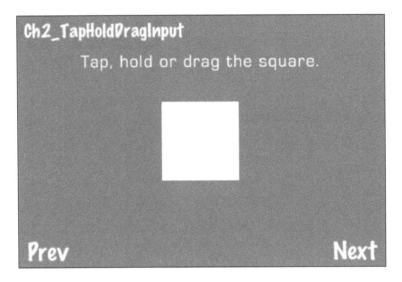

Getting ready

Please refer to the project *RecipeCollection01* for full working code of this recipe.

How to do it...

Execute the following code:

```
//ColorTouchSprite.h

enum { TS_NONE, TS_TAP, TS_HOLD, TS_DRAG };

@interface ColorTouchSprite : CCSprite
{
  @public
    float holdTime;        //How long have we held down on this?
    int touchedState;       //Current touched state
    bool isTouched;        //Are we touching this currently?
```

```
    float lastMoved;          //How long has it been since we moved
this?
    CGPoint lastTouchedPoint;  //Where did we last touch?
  const float releaseThreshold = 1.0f; //How long before we recognize
a release
    const float holdThreshold = 0.2f; //How long before a tap turns
into a hold
    const float lastMovedThreshold = 0.5f; //How long before we
consider you to be 'not moving'
  const int dragThreshold = 3; //We have a drag threshold of 3 pixels.
}

@end

@implementation ColorTouchSprite

@synthesize touchedState;

-(id) init {
  holdTime = 0;  lastMoved = 0; touchedState = TS_NONE;
  isTouched = NO; lastTouchedPoint = ccp(0,0);

  [self schedule:@selector(step:)];

  return [super init];
}

-(void) step:(ccTime)dt {
  //We use holdTime to determine the difference between a tap and a
hold
  if(isTouched){
    holdTime += dt; lastMoved += dt;
  }else{
    holdTime += dt;
    if(holdTime > releaseThreshold){
      touchedState = TS_NONE;
    }
  }

  //If you are holding and you haven't moved in a while change the
state
  if(holdTime > holdThreshold && isTouched && lastMoved >
lastMovedThreshold){
    touchedState = TS_HOLD;
  }
```

```
  }

  /* Used to determine whether or not we touched this object */
  - (CGRect) rect {
    float scaleMod = 1.0f;
    float w = [self contentSize].width * [self scale] * scaleMod;
    float h = [self contentSize].height * [self scale] * scaleMod;
    CGPoint point = CGPointMake([self position].x - (w/2), [self
position].y - (h/2));

    return CGRectMake(point.x, point.y, w, h);
  }

  /* Process touches */
  -(void) ccTouchesBegan:(NSSet *)touches withEvent:(UIEvent *)event {
    UITouch *touch = [touches anyObject];
CGPoint point = [touch locationInView: [touch view]];
    point = [[CCDirector sharedDirector] convertToGL: point];

    isTouched = YES;       holdTime = 0; touchedState = TS_NONE;

    lastTouchedPoint = point;
  }
  -(void) ccTouchesMoved:(NSSet *)touches withEvent:(UIEvent *)event {
    if(!isTouched){ return; }

    UITouch *touch = [touches anyObject];
CGPoint point = [touch locationInView: [touch view]];
    point = [[CCDirector sharedDirector] convertToGL: point];

    if(touchedState == TS_DRAG || distanceBetweenPoints(lastTouchedPoi
nt, point) > dragThreshold){
      touchedState = TS_DRAG;
      self.position = point;
      lastMoved = 0;
    }
    lastTouchedPoint = point;
  }
  -(void) ccTouchesEnded:(NSSet *)touches withEvent:(UIEvent *)event {
    if(!isTouched){ return; }

    UITouch *touch = [touches anyObject];
CGPoint point = [touch locationInView: [touch view]];
    point = [[CCDirector sharedDirector] convertToGL: point];
```

```
  //A short hold time after a touch ended means a tap.
  if(holdTime < 10){
    touchedState = TS_TAP;
  }
  holdTime = 0;
  isTouched = NO;

  lastTouchedPoint = point;
}

@end

#import "Helpers.h"

@implementation Ch2_TapHoldDragInput

-(CCLayer*) runRecipe {
  self.isTouchEnabled = YES;

  //Our message sprite
  message = [CCLabelBMFont labelWithString:@"Tap, hold or drag the
square." fntFile:@"eurostile_30.fnt"];
  message.position = ccp(240,260);
  message.scale = 0.75f;
  [self addChild:message];

  //Init the ColorTouchSprite
  colorTouchSprite = [ColorTouchSprite spriteWithFile:@"blank.png"];
  colorTouchSprite.position = ccp(240,160);
  [colorTouchSprite setTextureRect:CGRectMake(0,0,100,100)];
  [self addChild:colorTouchSprite];

  [self schedule:@selector(step)];

  return self;
}

/* Process touch events */
-(void) ccTouchesBegan:(NSSet *)touches withEvent:(UIEvent *)event {
  UITouch *touch = [touches anyObject];
CGPoint point = [touch locationInView: [touch view]];
  point = [[CCDirector sharedDirector] convertToGL: point];

  //Helper function 'pointIsInRect' is defined in Helpers.h
```

```
    if(pointIsInRect(point, [colorTouchSprite rect])){
      [colorTouchSprite ccTouchesBegan:touches withEvent:event];
    }
  }
}
-(void) ccTouchesMoved:(NSSet *)touches withEvent:(UIEvent *)event {
  /* CODE OMITTED */
}
-(void) ccTouchesEnded:(NSSet *)touches withEvent:(UIEvent *)event {
  /* CODE OMITTED */
}

@end
```

How it works...

First, we create the `ColorTouchSprite` class by sub-classing `CCSprite`. Here is where we maintain state variables to let us differentiate between a tap, a hold, and a drag. We also specify a `(CGRect)rect` method. This is used to determine whether or not the sprite was touched. The main recipe layer passes touch event information to this sprite using the following three methods:

```
-(void) ccTouchesBegan:(NSSet *)touches withEvent:(UIEvent *)event;
-(void) ccTouchesMoved:(NSSet *)touches withEvent:(UIEvent *)event;
-(void) ccTouchesEnded:(NSSet *)touches withEvent:(UIEvent *)event;
```

These methods are fairly straightforward. Whenever we touch the layer we call `ccTouchesBegan`. When we move we call `ccTouchesMoved`. Finally, when we lift a finger up we call `ccTouchesEnded`. Each method does a `pointIsInRect` check and then calls the requisite touches method on the sprite. Finally, the sprite runs some simple logic to determine state and to allow dragging of the sprite.

There's more...

The technique used previously is not the only way to capture input. Cocos2d also provides the `CCTouchDispatcher` class. With this you can implement methods in the `CCTargetedTouchDelegate` protocol and assign a delegate object to automatically handle your touch input.

See also...

For more information on this method please consult the official Cocos2d documentation and the Cocos2d forum.

Depth testing input

Handling input manually like in the previous recipe gives us the opportunity to manage touchable objects at a high level. Using an array of sprites sorted by Z order we can "swallow the input" so that background sprites aren't affected.

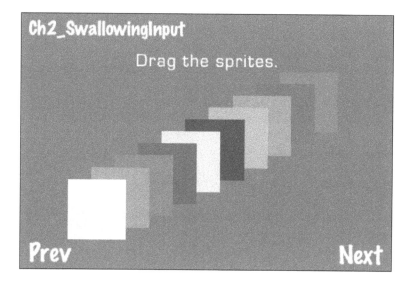

Getting ready

Please refer to the project *RecipeCollection01* for full working code of this recipe.

How to do it...

Execute the following code:

```
#import "ColorTouchSprite.h"

@implementation Ch2_DepthTestingInput

-(CCLayer*) runRecipe {
  //Init the ColorTouchSprites
  [self initSprites];

  return self;
}

-(void) initSprites {
```

```
    sprites = [[NSMutableArray alloc] init];

    //We add 10 randomly colored sprites
    for(int x=0; x<10; x++){
      CCSprite *sprite = [ColorTouchSprite spriteWithFile:@"blank.png"];
      /* CODE OMITTED */
    }
}

/* Process touch events */
-(void) ccTouchesBegan:(NSSet *)touches withEvent:(UIEvent *)event {
  UITouch *touch = [touches anyObject];
  CGPoint point = [touch locationInView: [touch view]];
  point = [[CCDirector sharedDirector] convertToGL: point];

  //Process input for all sprites
  for(id sprite in sprites){
    if(pointIsInRect(point, [sprite rect])){
      //Swallow the input
      [sprite ccTouchesBegan:touches withEvent:event];
      return;
    }
  }
}
-(void) ccTouchesMoved:(NSSet *)touches withEvent:(UIEvent *)event {
  /* CODE OMITTED */

  //Process input for all sprites
  for(id sprite in sprites){
    if(pointIsInRect(point, [sprite rect])){
      [sprite ccTouchesMoved:touches withEvent:event];
    }
  }
}
-(void) ccTouchesEnded:(NSSet *)touches withEvent:(UIEvent *)event {
  /* CODE OMITTED */

  //Process input for all sprites
  for(id sprite in sprites){
    //End all input when you lift up your finger
    [sprite ccTouchesEnded:touches withEvent:event];
  }
}

@end
```

How it works...

Our array of sprites has a **node order** which corresponds directly to their **Z order**. So, looping through these sprites does implicit **depth testing**. When a sprite touch begins we swallow the input allowing only that sprite to be touched.

▶   Caveats:

The only caveat to this technique is that input depth testing is tied to sprite array order. Any modification of sprite **Z** order requires a **re-sorting** of nodes in the array.

Creating buttons

Buttons in one form or another are used in most games. It is easy to implement a simple button solution using Cocos2d but creating one that supports **multiple simultaneous button touches** is more difficult. In this recipe, we will implement a simple but effective solution to this problem.

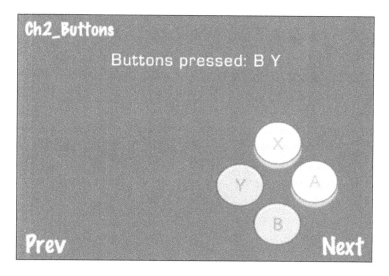

Getting ready

Please refer to the project *RecipeCollection01* for full working code of this recipe.

How to do it...

Execute the following code:

```
//TouchableSprite.h
@interface TouchableSprite : CCSprite
{
  @public
    bool pressed;        //Is this sprite pressed
    NSUInteger touchHash;  //Used to identify individual touches
}

@end

@implementation TouchableSprite

- (bool)checkTouchWithPoint:(CGPoint)point {
  if(pointIsInRect(point, [self rect])){
    return YES;
  }else{
    return NO;
  }
}

- (CGRect) rect {
  //We set our scale mod to make sprite easier to press.
  //This also lets us press 2 sprites with 1 touch if they are
sufficiently close.
  float scaleMod = 1.5f;
  float w = [self contentSize].width * [self scale] * scaleMod;
  float h = [self contentSize].height * [self scale] * scaleMod;
  CGPoint point = CGPointMake([self position].x - (w/2), [self
position].y - (h/2));

  return CGRectMake(point.x, point.y, w, h);
}

- (void)ccTouchesBegan:(NSSet *)touches withEvent:(UIEvent *)event {
  UITouch *touch = [touches anyObject];
CGPoint point = [touch locationInView: [touch view]];
  point = [[CCDirector sharedDirector] convertToGL: point];

  //We use circle collision for our buttons
  if(pointIsInCircle(point, self.position, self.rect.size.width/2)){
    touchHash = [touch hash];
    [self processTouch:point];
  }
```

```
  }

- (void)ccTouchesMoved:(NSSet *)touches withEvent:(UIEvent *)event {
  /* CODE OMITTED */

  if(pointIsInCircle(point, self.position, self.rect.size.width/2)){
    if(touchHash == [touch hash]){    //If we moved on this sprite
      [self processTouch:point];
    }else if(!pressed){            //If a new touch moves onto this
sprite
      touchHash = [touch hash];
      [self processTouch:point];
    }
  }else if(touchHash == [touch hash]){  //If we moved off of this
sprite
    [self processRelease];
  }
}

- (void)ccTouchesEnded:(NSSet *)touches withEvent:(UIEvent *)event {
  /* CODE OMITTED */

  if(touchHash == [touch hash]){  //If the touch which pressed this
sprite ended we release
    [self processRelease];
  }
}

- (void)processTouch:(CGPoint)point {
  pressed = YES;
}

- (void)processRelease {
  pressed = NO;
}

@end

//GameButton.h
@interface GameButton : TouchableSprite {
  @public
    NSString* upSpriteFrame;
    NSString* downSpriteFrame;
    NSString* name;
}
```

```
@end

@implementation GameButton

- (void)processTouch:(CGPoint)point {
  CCSpriteFrameCache *cache = [CCSpriteFrameCache
sharedSpriteFrameCache];
  [self setDisplayFrame:[cache spriteFrameByName:downSpriteFrame]];
  pressed = true;
  [self setColor:ccc3(255,200,200)];
}

- (void)processRelease {
  CCSpriteFrameCache *cache = [CCSpriteFrameCache
sharedSpriteFrameCache];
  [self setDisplayFrame:[cache spriteFrameByName:upSpriteFrame]];
  pressed = false;
  [self setColor:ccc3(255,255,255)];
}

@end

@implementation Ch2_Buttons

-(CCLayer*) runRecipe {
  //Init buttons data structure
  buttons = [[NSMutableArray alloc] init];

  //Create buttons
  CCSpriteFrameCache *cache = [CCSpriteFrameCache
sharedSpriteFrameCache];
  [cache addSpriteFramesWithFile:@"dpad_buttons.plist"];

  [self createButtonWithPosition:ccp(350,50) withUpFrame:@"b_button_
up.png" withDownFrame:@"b_button_down.png" withName:@"B"];
  /* CODE OMITTED */

  //Schedule step method
  [self schedule:@selector(step)];

  return self;
}

/* Display pressed buttons */
-(void) step {
  [message setString:@"Buttons pressed:"];
  for(GameButton *b in buttons){
```

```
    if(b.pressed){
       [message setString:[NSString stringWithFormat:@"%@ %@",message.
string,b.name]];
    }
  }
}

/* Button creation shortcut method */
-(void) createButtonWithPosition:(CGPoint)position
withUpFrame:(NSString*)upFrame withDownFrame:(NSString*)downFrame
withName:(NSString*)name {
  CCSpriteFrameCache *cache = [CCSpriteFrameCache
sharedSpriteFrameCache];

  GameButton *button = [[GameButton alloc] init];
  button.position = position;
  [button setUpSpriteFrame:upFrame];
  [button setDownSpriteFrame:downFrame];
  [button setDisplayFrame:[cache spriteFrameByName:[button
upSpriteFrame]]];
  button.name = name;
  [self addChild:button];
  [buttons addObject:button];
}
-(void) ccTouchesBegan:(NSSet *)touches withEvent:(UIEvent *)event {
  UITouch *touch = [touches anyObject];
CGPoint point = [touch locationInView: [touch view]];
  point = [[CCDirector sharedDirector] convertToGL: point];

  //Pass all touchesBegan events to GameButton instances
  for(GameButton *b in buttons){
    [b ccTouchesBegan:touches withEvent:event];
  }
}
-(void) ccTouchesMoved:(NSSet *)touches withEvent:(UIEvent *)event {
  /* CODE OMITTED */
}
-(void) ccTouchesEnded:(NSSet *)touches withEvent:(UIEvent *)event {
  /* CODE OMITTED */
}

@end
```

How it works...

This recipe uses a couple of different classes, all derived from `CCSprite`, to create realistic buttons. These buttons can all be touched independently.

▶ Touching multiple buttons independently:

To get multiple-button touching working, first we call the following method on our main `UIWindow` in our `AppDelegate` file:

`[window setMultipleTouchEnabled:YES];`

Then our `TouchableSprite` class uses the `hash` variable that uniquely identifies each `UITouch` object that passes through a `ccTouches` method. This way we can keep track of each unique touch. A touch can even be used to touch two buttons at once.

▶ Touching two buttons with one touch:

Our `(CGRect)rect` method uses a `scaleMod` of `1.5f`. This, along with using `pointInCircle` for touch detection, allows us to press two buttons with one well placed touch. This is vital for many games. For example, the original Super Mario Brothers required the user to hold down the *B* button to run while pressing the *A* button to jump. This technique allows a similar use of the *Y* and *A* buttons.

Creating a directional pad

Another fundamental form of video game input is the **directional pad**. In this recipe, you will see how to create a convincing 3D-ish directional pad and you will see how to properly process directional pad information in a game situation.

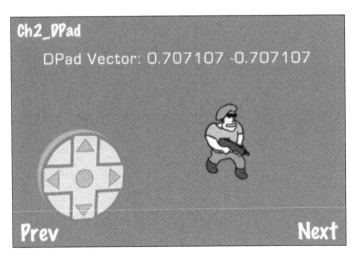

Getting ready

Please refer to the project *RecipeCollection01* for full working code of this recipe. Also, note that some code has been omitted for brevity.

How to do it...

Execute the following code:

```
#import "TouchableSprite.h"
@interface DPad : TouchableSprite {
  @public
    CGPoint pressedVector;
    int direction;
}

@end

@implementation DPad

-(id)init {
    self = [super init];
    if (self != nil) {
  pressedVector = ccp(0,0);
  direction = DPAD_NO_DIRECTION;

  CCSpriteFrameCache *cache = [CCSpriteFrameCache
sharedSpriteFrameCache];
  [cache addSpriteFramesWithFile:@"dpad_buttons.plist"];

  //Set the sprite display frame
  [self setDisplayFrame:[cache spriteFrameByName:@"d_pad_normal.
png"]];
    }
    return self;
}

/* Process DPad touch */
- (void)processTouch:(CGPoint)point {
  CCSpriteFrameCache *cache = [CCSpriteFrameCache
sharedSpriteFrameCache];

  //Set a color visual cue if pressed
  [self setColor:ccc3(255,200,200)];
```

```
    pressed = true;

    CGPoint center = CGPointMake( self.rect.origin.x+self.rect.size.
width/2, self.rect.origin.y+self.rect.size.height/2 );

    //Process center dead zone
    if(distanceBetweenPoints(point, center) < self.rect.size.width/10){
      [self setDisplayFrame:[cache spriteFrameByName:@"d_pad_normal.
png"]];
      self.rotation = 0;
      pressedVector = ccp(0,0);
      direction = DPAD_NO_DIRECTION;
      return;
    }

    //Process direction
    float radians = vectorToRadians( CGPointMake(point.x-center.x,
point.y-center.y) );
    float degrees = radiansToDegrees(radians) + 90;

    float sin45 = 0.7071067812f;

    if(degrees >= 337.5 || degrees < 22.5){
      [self setDisplayFrame:[cache spriteFrameByName:@"d_pad_horizontal.
png"]];
      self.rotation = 180; pressedVector = ccp(-1,0); direction = DPAD_
LEFT;
    }else if(degrees >= 22.5 && degrees < 67.5){
      [self setDisplayFrame:[cache spriteFrameByName:@"d_pad_diagonal.
png"]];
      self.rotation = -90; pressedVector = ccp(-sin45,sin45); direction
= DPAD_UP_LEFT;
    }/* CODE OMITTED */
}

/* Process DPad release */
- (void)processRelease {
  [self setColor:ccc3(255,255,255)];

  CCSpriteFrameCache *cache = [CCSpriteFrameCache
sharedSpriteFrameCache];
  [self setDisplayFrame:[cache spriteFrameByName:@"d_pad_normal.
png"]];
  self.rotation = 0;
  pressed = false;
```

```
    pressedVector = ccp(0,0);
    direction = DPAD_NO_DIRECTION;
  }

@end

@implementation Ch2_DPad

-(CCLayer*) runRecipe {
  //Add gunman sprites
  CCSpriteFrameCache *cache = [CCSpriteFrameCache
sharedSpriteFrameCache];
  [cache addSpriteFramesWithFile:@"gunman.plist"];

  //Initialize gunman
  gunman = [SimpleAnimObject spriteWithSpriteFrame:[cache
spriteFrameByName:@"gunman_stand_down.png"]];
  gunman.position = ccp(240,160);
  [self addChild:gunman];
  gunmanDirection = DPAD_DOWN;

  //Initialize DPad
  [cache addSpriteFramesWithFile:@"dpad_buttons.plist"];
  dPad = [[DPad alloc] init];
  dPad.position = ccp(100,100);
  [self addChild:dPad];

  [self schedule:@selector(step:)];

  return self;
}

-(void) step:(ccTime)delta {
  //We reset the animation if the gunman changes direction
  if(dPad.direction != DPAD_NO_DIRECTION){
    if(gunmanDirection != dPad.direction){
      resetAnimation = YES;
      gunmanDirection = dPad.direction;
    }
  }
  if(gunman.velocity.x != dPad.pressedVector.x*2 || gunman.velocity.y
!= dPad.pressedVector.y*2){
    gunman.velocity = ccp(dPad.pressedVector.x*2, dPad.
pressedVector.y*2);
    resetAnimation = YES;
```

```
    }

    //Update gunman position
    [gunman update:delta];

    //Re-animate if necessary
    if(resetAnimation){
      [self animateGunman];
    }
}
-(void) animateGunman {
    CCSpriteFrameCache *cache = [CCSpriteFrameCache
sharedSpriteFrameCache];

    /* Animate our gunman */
    CCAnimation *animation = [[CCAnimation alloc] initWithName:@"gunman_
anim" delay:0.15f];

    NSString *direction;
    bool flipX = NO;
    bool moving = YES;
    if(gunman.velocity.x == 0 && gunman.velocity.y == 0){ moving = NO; }

    if(gunmanDirection == DPAD_LEFT){ direction = @"right"; flipX = YES;
}
    else if(gunmanDirection == DPAD_UP_LEFT){ direction = @"up_right";
flipX = YES; }
    /* CODE OMITTED */

    //Our simple running loop
    if(moving){
      [animation addFrame:[cache spriteFrameByName:[NSString
stringWithFormat:@"gunman_run_%@_01.png",direction]]];
      /* CODE OMITTED */
    }

    gunman.flipX = flipX;
    [gunman runAction:[CCRepeatForever actionWithAction: [CCAnimate acti
onWithAnimation:animation]]];
}

/* Process touches */
-(void) ccTouchesBegan:(NSSet *)touches withEvent:(UIEvent *)event {
    UITouch *touch = [touches anyObject];
        CGPoint point = [touch locationInView: [touch view]];
```

```
    point = [[CCDirector sharedDirector] convertToGL: point];

    [dPad ccTouchesBegan:touches withEvent:event];
}
-(void) ccTouchesMoved:(NSSet *)touches withEvent:(UIEvent *)event {
    /* CODE OMITTED */
}
-(void) ccTouchesEnded:(NSSet *)touches withEvent:(UIEvent *)event {
    /* CODE OMITTED */
}

@end
```

How it works...

This recipe uses a few simple tricks to make a compelling directional pad effect. First, we must look at the DPad class.

▶ The DPad class:

   The DPad class determines touch direction by first creating a 2D vector from the center of the DPad image to the point where it is touched. It then divides the image into eight directional slices. Each direction corresponds to a different sprite frame. When everything is put together we get a nice looking pseudo-3D effect.

▶ Processing DPad state and pressedVector:

   The DPad class maintains both a direction enumeration and a direction vector. This allows us to determine which of the eight directions our "gunman" sprite should be facing and how we should set his velocity variable to instigate movement.

▶ DPad dead zone:

   Our DPad has a roughly 10 percent **dead zone** right in the middle. This makes the control feel a little more natural to the user. We do this because, on a real directional pad, pressing directly in the middle results in no movement.

Creating an analog stick

By building on the last recipe, we can create a more sophisticated virtual analog stick. This input method measures vector magnitude as well as direction. We've also created a cool looking visual effect for the analog stick.

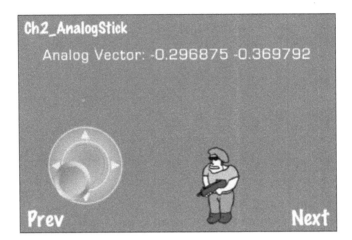

Getting ready

Please refer to the project *RecipeCollection01* for full working code of this recipe.

How to do it...

Execute the following code:

```
#import "TouchableSprite.h"
//AnalogStick.h
@interface AnalogStick : TouchableSprite {
  @public
    CGPoint _pressedVector;  //Internal _pressedVector with no outer
dead zone
    CCSprite *nub;
    CCSprite *bar;
    int direction;
}

@property (readonly) CGPoint pressedVector;  //External pressedVector
with a dead zone
```

```objc
@end

@implementation AnalogStick

-(id)init {
    self = [super init];
    if (self != nil) {
    self.scale = 0.5f;

    _pressedVector = ccp(0,0);

    CCSpriteFrameCache *cache = [CCSpriteFrameCache
sharedSpriteFrameCache];
    [cache addSpriteFramesWithFile:@"analog_stick.plist"];

    //Set the sprite display frame
    [self setDisplayFrame:[cache spriteFrameByName:@"analog_pad.
png"]];

    //Init the bar, set position and display frame
    bar = [[CCSprite alloc] init];
    [bar setDisplayFrame:[cache spriteFrameByName:@"analog_bar.png"]];
    [self repositionBarWithPoint:self.position];
    [self addChild:bar];

    //Init the nub, set position and display frame
    nub = [[CCSprite alloc] init];
    [self repositionNub];
    [nub setDisplayFrame:[cache spriteFrameByName:@"analog_nub.png"]];
    [self addChild:nub];
  }
    return self;
}

-(void)dealloc {
  [nub release];
  [bar release];
  [super dealloc];
}

/* Process analog stick touch */
-(void)processTouch:(CGPoint)point {
  self.pressed = YES;
```

```
   [self setColor:ccc3(255,200,200)]; [nub setColor:ccc3(255,200,200)];
[bar setColor:ccc3(255,200,200)];

   CGPoint center = CGPointMake( self.rect.origin.x+self.rect.size.
width/2, self.rect.origin.y+self.rect.size.height/2 );
   _pressedVector = CGPointMake((point.x-center.x)/(self.rect.size.
width/2), (point.y-center.y)/(self.rect.size.height/2));

   [self repositionNub];
   [self repositionBarWithPoint:point];
   [self resetDirection];
}

/* Process analog stick release */
-(void)processRelease {
   [self setColor:ccc3(255,255,255)]; [nub setColor:ccc3(255,255,255)];
[bar setColor:ccc3(255,255,255)];

   self.pressed = NO;
   _pressedVector = ccp(0,0);
   [self repositionNub];
   [self repositionBarWithPoint:self.position];
}

/* Reposition the nub according to the pressedVector */
-(void)repositionNub {
   float width = ([self contentSize].width);
   float height = ([self contentSize].height);

   nub.position = ccp(_pressedVector.x*(width/2)+width/2,
      _pressedVector.y*(height/2)+height/2);
}

/* Reposition the bar according to a pressed point */
-(void)repositionBarWithPoint:(CGPoint)point {
   float width = ([self contentSize].width);
   float height = ([self contentSize].height);

   //Rotation
   float radians = vectorToRadians( _pressedVector );
   float degrees = radiansToDegrees(radians);
   bar.rotation = degrees;

   //Set the display frame of the bar
```

```
    CCSpriteFrameCache *cache = [CCSpriteFrameCache
  sharedSpriteFrameCache];
    [bar setDisplayFrame:[cache spriteFrameByName:@"analog_bar.png"]];

    //Calculate bar position
    float distFromCenter = distanceBetweenPoints(point, self.position);
    float sizeMod = distFromCenter / [self contentSize].width;
    float oldHeight = bar.textureRect.size.height;
    float newHeight = oldHeight * sizeMod * 5;

    //Custom fixes
    if(newHeight < 100){ newHeight = 100.0f; }
    if(distFromCenter < 3){ newHeight = 0.0f; }

    bar.textureRect = CGRectMake(bar.textureRect.origin.x,bar.
  textureRect.origin.y+ (oldHeight-newHeight),
    bar.textureRect.size.width,newHeight );

    bar.anchorPoint = ccp(0.5f,0);
    CGPoint directionVector = radiansToVector(radians-PI/2);
    bar.position = ccp(width/2 + directionVector.x*width/4, height/2 +
  directionVector.y*height/4);
  }

  /* Reset the direction based on the pressedVector */
  -(void) resetDirection {
    if(_pressedVector.x == 0 && _pressedVector.y == 0){
      direction = AS_NO_DIRECTION;
      return;
    }

    float radians = vectorToRadians(_pressedVector);
    float degrees = radiansToDegrees(radians) + 90;

    if(degrees >= 337.5 || degrees < 22.5){
      direction = AS_LEFT;
    }else if(degrees >= 22.5 && degrees < 67.5){
      direction = AS_UP_LEFT;
    }/* CODE OMITTED */
  }

  -(float) magnitude {
    float m = sqrt( pow(_pressedVector.x,2) + pow(_pressedVector.y,2) );
```

```
    //25% end deadzone to make it easier to hold highest magnitude
    m += 0.25f;
    if(m > 1.0f){ m = 1.0f; }

    return m;
}

-(CGPoint) pressedVector {
    float m = sqrt( pow(_pressedVector.x,2) + pow(_pressedVector.y,2) );
    m += 0.25f;

    CGPoint pv = ccp(_pressedVector.x*1.25f, _pressedVector.y*1.25f);

    //25% end deadzone to make it easier to hold highest magnitude
    if(m > 1){
      float radians = vectorToRadians(_pressedVector);
      pv = radiansToVector(radians + PI/2);
    }

    return pv;
}

@end

@implementation Ch2_AnalogStick

-(CCLayer*) runRecipe {
    self.isTouchEnabled = YES;

    CCSpriteFrameCache *cache = [CCSpriteFrameCache
sharedSpriteFrameCache];
    [cache addSpriteFramesWithFile:@"gunman.plist"];

    //Initialize gunman
    gunman = [SimpleAnimObject spriteWithSpriteFrame:[cache
spriteFrameByName:@"gunman_stand_down.png"]];
    gunman.position = ccp(240,160);
    [self addChild:gunman];
    gunman.velocity = ccp(0,0);
    gunmanDirection = AS_DOWN;

    //Initialize analog stick
    [cache addSpriteFramesWithFile:@"analog_stick.plist"];
    analogStick = [[AnalogStick alloc] init];
```

```
  analogStick.position = ccp(100,100);
  [self addChild:analogStick];

  [self schedule:@selector(step:)];

  //This sets off a chain reaction.
  [self animateGunman];

  return self;
}

-(void) step:(ccTime)delta {
  //Set gunman velocity and animate if necessary
  if(analogStick.direction != AS_NO_DIRECTION){
    if(analogStick.direction != gunmanDirection){
      [gunman stopAllActions];
      gunmanDirection = analogStick.direction;
      [self animateGunman];
    }
  }
  gunman.velocity = ccp(analogStick.pressedVector.x*4, analogStick.
pressedVector.y*4);

  [gunman update:delta];
}

-(void) animateGunman {
  CCSpriteFrameCache *cache = [CCSpriteFrameCache
sharedSpriteFrameCache];

  float speed = [analogStick magnitude];

  //Animation delay is inverse speed
  float delay = 0.075f/speed;
  if(delay > 0.5f){ delay = 0.5f; }
  CCAnimation *animation = [[CCAnimation alloc] initWithName:@"gunman_
anim" delay:delay];

  NSString *direction;
  bool flipX = NO;
  bool moving = YES;
  if(gunman.velocity.x == 0 && gunman.velocity.y == 0){ moving = NO; }

  if(gunmanDirection == AS_LEFT){ direction = @"right"; flipX = YES; }
```

```objc
  else if(gunmanDirection == AS_UP_LEFT){ direction = @"up_right";
flipX = YES; }
  /* CODE OMITTED */

  //Our simple animation loop
  if(moving){
    [animation addFrame:[cache spriteFrameByName:[NSString
stringWithFormat:@"gunman_run_%@_01.png",direction]]];
    /* CODE OMITTED */
  }

  gunman.flipX = flipX;

  //animateGunman calls itself indefinitely
  [gunman runAction:[CCSequence actions: [CCAnimate
actionWithAnimation:animation],
    [CCCallFunc actionWithTarget:self selector:@
selector(animateGunman)], nil ]];
}

/* Process touches */
-(void) ccTouchesBegan:(NSSet *)touches withEvent:(UIEvent *)event {
  UITouch *touch = [touches anyObject];
CGPoint point = [touch locationInView: [touch view]];
  point = [[CCDirector sharedDirector] convertToGL: point];

  [analogStick ccTouchesBegan:touches withEvent:event];
}
-(void) ccTouchesMoved:(NSSet *)touches withEvent:(UIEvent *)event {
  /* CODE OMITTED */
}
-(void) ccTouchesEnded:(NSSet *)touches withEvent:(UIEvent *)event {
  /* CODE OMITTED */
}

@end
```

How it works...

Using the `AnalogStick` class provides the user with more precise control.

▸ The `AnalogStick` class:

Like the `DPad` class the `AnalogStick` class determines direction. Unlike `DPad` it also determines **magnitude** using the following lines:

```
CGPoint center = CGPointMake( self.rect.origin.x+self.rect.size.
width/2, self.rect.origin.y+self.rect.size.height/2 );
  _pressedVector = CGPointMake((point.x-center.x)/(self.rect.size.
width/2), (point.y-center.y)/(self.rect.size.height/2));
```

This touched position also determines the position and orientation of the "nub" and the "bar". Without going into too much detail, this creates a nice analog stick visual effect. Like our `DPad` class from the previous recipe, our `AnalogStick` class also includes a dead zone.

▸ `AnalogStick` dead zone:

This time, the dead zone involves making the outer 25 percent of the touchable area max out the vector's magnitude. To achieve this we store an internal `_pressedVector` variable and give `readonly` access to a `pressedVector` property. This points to a method that does the proper calculations. The reason we provide this zone is so the user can comfortably make the 'gunman' run at top-speed.

Using the accelerometer for steering

iOS applications also have another form of input: the **accelerometer**. This measures the **orientation** of the iOS device on the **X, Y,** and **Z planes**. Device orientation is a dynamic (if slightly delayed) input mechanism with a variety of uses. One of these uses is steering in racing video games.

Getting ready

Please refer to the project *RecipeCollection01* for full working code of this recipe.

How to do it...

Execute the following code:

```
@implementation Ch2_AccelerometerSteering

-(CCLayer*) runRecipe {
  //Enable the accelerometer and set its updateInterval
  self.isAccelerometerEnabled = YES;
  [[UIAccelerometer sharedAccelerometer] setUpdateInterval:(1.0 /
60)];

  //Init car background
  CCSprite *bg = [CCSprite spriteWithFile:@"car_dash.jpg"];
  bg.position = ccp(240,160);
  bg.opacity = 200;
  [self addChild:bg z:0];

  //Init steeringWheel sprite
  steeringWheel = [CCSprite spriteWithFile:@"car_steering_wheel.png"];
  steeringWheel.position = ccp(230,170);
  [self addChild:steeringWheel z:1];

  return self;
}

/* Handle accelerometer input */
- (void)accelerometer:(UIAccelerometer*)accelerometer
didAccelerate:(UIAcceleration*)acceleration{
  //Set steeringWheel rotation based on Y plane rotation
  steeringWheel.rotation = -acceleration.y * 180;
}

@end
```

How it works...

Rotating your iPhone left or right while looking directly at the screen will result in seeing the steering wheel rotate. The 3D vector contained within the `UIAcceleration` variable goes up or down by 1 for every 90 degrees the iOS device rotates. So, by multiplying this rotation by 180 degrees, we equate a 45-degree tilt with a 90-degree turn of the steering wheel.

▶ Accelerometer delay:

Mechanically the accelerometer has a slight delay compared to the touch screen. This makes its application impractical for some gametypes where absolute split second control is required.

Using the accelerometer for 3D rotation

Using multiple accelerometer values at once can allow the user to manipulate the rotation of a 3D object in space. This is used to great effect in the Super Monkey Ball series of iOS games.

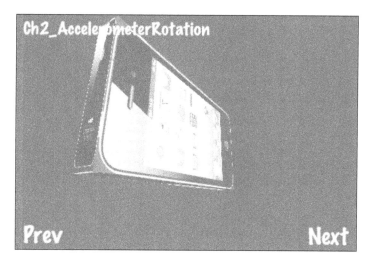

Getting ready

Please refer to the project *RecipeCollection01* for full working code of this recipe. Please note that the `IphoneCube` class code was omitted from this example as it is similar to the 3D cube code in *Chapter 1, Graphics*.

How to do it...

Execute the following code:

```
#import "IphoneCube.h"

@implementation Ch2_AccelerometerRotation

-(CCLayer*) runRecipe {
  //Enable the accelerometer and set its updateInterval
  self.isAccelerometerEnabled = YES;
  [[UIAccelerometer sharedAccelerometer] setUpdateInterval:(1.0 /
60)];

  //Init our textured box
  iphoneCube = [[IphoneCube alloc] init];
  iphoneCube.translation3D = [Vector3D x:0.0f y:0.0f z:-2.0f];
  iphoneCube.rotation3DAxis = [Vector3D x:0.0f y:0.0f z:(PI/2 -
0.075f)];
  [self addChild:iphoneCube z:3 tag:0];

  return self;
}

/* Handle accelerometer input */
- (void)accelerometer:(UIAccelerometer*)accelerometer
didAccelerate:(UIAcceleration*)acceleration{
  //Set x and y box orientation
  iphoneCube.rotation3DAxis.x = -acceleration.x * 180;
  iphoneCube.rotation3DAxis.y = -acceleration.y * 180;
}

@end
```

How it works...

Rotating your device on the **X** or **Y** planes will result in rotating the virtual iPhone onscreen. We multiply the `acceleration` variable by 180 to once again rotate our object twice as much as the device itself. The `IphoneCube` variable `rotation3DAxis` rotates the textured box in 3D space using `glRotatef`.

Pinch zooming

Apple's touch devices popularized using two fingers to zoom in and out and this method remains the most popular way to zoom on any widely available touch screen device. In this recipe, we will see how to zoom a scene in and out by **pinching**.

Getting ready

Please refer to the project *RecipeCollection01* for full working code of this recipe. Also note that the arrow effect shown in the previous screenshot has been omitted from the following code.

How to do it...

Execute the following code:

```
#import "IphoneCube.h"

@implementation Ch2_PinchZooming

-(CCLayer*) runRecipe {
  //Enable touching
  self.isTouchEnabled = YES;

  //Set initial variables
  arrowsIn = NO;
  cameraZoom = 1.0f;
  lastMultiTouchZoomDistance = 0.0f;
```

```
  //Init background
  bg = [CCSprite spriteWithFile:@"dracula_castle.jpg"];
  bg.position = ccp(240,160);
  [self addChild:bg];

  //Set initial zoom
  [self setCameraZoom:1];

  return self;
}
/* Check for HUD input */
-(bool) hudPressedWithPoint:(CGPoint)point {
  //There is no HUD.
  return NO;
}
-(void) setCameraZoom:(float)zoom {
  cameraZoom = zoom;
  bg.scale = cameraZoom;
}
/* Check touches */
-(void) ccTouchesBegan:(NSSet *)touches withEvent:(UIEvent *)event {
  UITouch *touch = [touches anyObject];
CGPoint point = [touch locationInView: [touch view]];
  point = [[CCDirector sharedDirector] convertToGL: point];

  //If HUD has not been touched we reset lastMultiTouchZoomDistance
  if(![self hudPressedWithPoint:point]){
    lastMultiTouchZoomDistance = 0.0f;
  }
}
-(void) ccTouchesMoved:(NSSet *)touches withEvent:(UIEvent *)event {
  CGSize s = [[CCDirector sharedDirector] winSize];

  //Check for only 2 touches
  if(touches.count == 2){
    NSArray *twoTouch = [touches allObjects];

    //Get both touches
    UITouch *tOne = [twoTouch objectAtIndex:0];
    UITouch *tTwo = [twoTouch objectAtIndex:1];
    CGPoint firstTouch = [tOne locationInView:[tOne view]];
    CGPoint secondTouch = [tTwo locationInView:[tTwo view]];
```

```
    //If HUD hasn't been touched we use this distance and last
distance to calculate zooming
    if(![self hudPressedWithPoint:firstTouch] && ![self hudPressedWith
Point:secondTouch]){
      CGFloat currentDistance = distanceBetweenPoints(firstTouch,
secondTouch);

      if(lastMultiTouchZoomDistance == 0){
        lastMultiTouchZoomDistance = currentDistance;
      }else{
        float difference = currentDistance -
lastMultiTouchZoomDistance;

        float newZoom = (cameraZoom + (difference*cameraZoom/s.
height));
        if(newZoom < 1.0f){ newZoom = 1.0f; }
        if(newZoom > 4.0f){ newZoom = 4.0f; }
        [self setCameraZoom:newZoom];
        lastMultiTouchZoomDistance = currentDistance;

      }

    }
  }
}

-(void) ccTouchesEnded:(NSSet *)touches withEvent:(UIEvent *)event {
  UITouch *touch = [touches anyObject];
CGPoint point = [touch locationInView: [touch view]];
  point = [[CCDirector sharedDirector] convertToGL: point];

  //If HUD has not been touched we reset lastMultiTouchZoomDistance
  if(![self hudPressedWithPoint:point]){
    lastMultiTouchZoomDistance = 0.0f;
  }
}

@end
```

How it works...

This recipe processes two separate touches and determines their respective distance. It maintains this variable to determine whether or not the touches have grown closer or farther apart. Then, this distance is used to calculate the new zoom level. The following line of code does this while also keeping the zoom effect smooth:

```
float newZoom = (cameraZoom + (difference*cameraZoom/s.height));
```

This achieves the desired effect.

▶ Processing multiple simultaneous touches:

As you can see, processing **multiple touches** is similar to processing a single touch. The `touches` variable contains every touch at that specific moment. If two touches move together this one method can easily process them.

There's more...

If you want to add to this technique, try implementing iPhoto-esque image panning. This pan/zoom combination has become standard on all document and image viewers and is a natural UI enhancement for many iOS games.

Performing gestures

Gestures can act as functional input shortcuts. Simple gestures like swiping and scrolling are built into many Apple UI tools. Some games, notably Castlevania: Dawn of Sorrow (DS) and Okami (PS2, Wii) use gestures as core gameplay mechanics. In this recipe, we will implement a simple and admittedly crude gesture system.

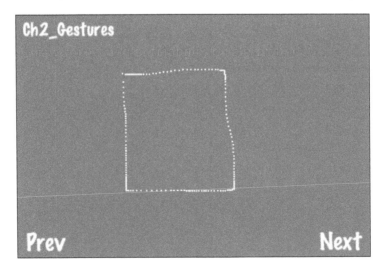

Getting ready

Please refer to the project *RecipeCollection01* for full working code of this recipe. Also note that the `GestureLine` and `GestureShapeLayer` classes have been omitted for brevity. `GestureLine` simply contains two `CGPoint` structures. `GestureShapeLayer` draws a circle or an array of lines.

How to do it...

Execute the following code:

```
#import "GestureLine.h"
#import "GestureShapeLayer.h"

@implementation Ch2_Gestures

-(CCLayer*) runRecipe {
  //Init message
  message = [CCLabelBMFont labelWithString:@"Draw a rectangle,
triangle, circle or line" fntFile:@"eurostile_30.fnt"];
  message.position = ccp(200,270);
  message.scale = 0.65f;
  [message setColor:ccc3(255,0,0)];
  [self addChild:message z:3];

  //Allow touching
  self.isTouchEnabled = YES;

  //Set font size
  [CCMenuItemFont setFontSize:20];

  //Add our breadcrumbs node
  [self addBreadcrumbs];

  //Init GestureShapeLayer
  gestureShapeLayer = [[GestureShapeLayer alloc] init];
  gestureShapeLayer.position = ccp(0,0);
  [self addChild:gestureShapeLayer z:1];

  return self;
}

/* Process touches */
-(void) ccTouchesBegan:(NSSet *)touches withEvent:(UIEvent *)event {
```

```objc
    /* CODE OMITTED */

    //Start a new gesture
    [self newGestureWithPoint:point];
}
-(void) ccTouchesMoved:(NSSet *)touches withEvent:(UIEvent *)event {
    /* CODE OMITTED */

    //Add a point to our current gesture
    [self addGesturePoint:point override:NO];
}
-(void) ccTouchesEnded:(NSSet *)touches withEvent:(UIEvent *)event {
    /* CODE OMITTED */

    //Finish our gesture
    [self finishGestureWithPoint:point];
}

-(void) newGestureWithPoint:(CGPoint)point {
    [self resetMessage];

    //Init gesture variables
    gestureShapeLayer.points = [[NSMutableArray alloc] init];
    gestureShapeLayer.lines = [[NSMutableArray alloc] init];
    firstPoint = point;
    lastPoint = point;
    vertex = point;
    [gestureShapeLayer.points addObject:[NSValue
valueWithCGPoint:point]];

    gestureShapeLayer.drawCircle = NO;
    gestureShapeLayer.drawLines = NO;
}

-(void) addGesturePoint:(CGPoint)point override:(bool)override {
    //Set our angle change tolerance to 40 degrees. If it changes more
than this we consider this a 'line'
    float angleDiffTolerance = 40.0f;

    //Check the old angle versus the new one
    CGPoint vect = ccp(point.x-lastPoint.x, point.y-lastPoint.y);
    float newAngle = radiansToDegrees( vectorToRadians(vect) );

    //Add a line if the angle changed significantly
```

```objc
  if(gestureShapeLayer.points.count > 1){
    float angleDiff = angleDifference(newAngle, angle);
    if(override || (angleDiff > angleDiffTolerance &&
distanceBetweenPoints(vertex, point) > 15.0f)){
      [gestureShapeLayer.lines addObject:[GestureLine point1:vertex
point2:point]];
      vertex = point;
    }
  }

  //Update values
  angle = newAngle;
  lastPoint = point;
  [gestureShapeLayer.points addObject:[NSValue
valueWithCGPoint:point]];
}

-(void) finishGestureWithPoint:(CGPoint)point {
  [self addGesturePoint:point override:YES];

  gestureShapeLayer.drawCircle = NO;
  gestureShapeLayer.drawLines = NO;

  //To finish gestures which require the end to be close to the
beginning point we supply this distance tolerance
  float lastPointTolerance = 100.0f;

  //Rectangles, triangles and circles
  if(distanceBetweenPoints(firstPoint, lastPoint) <=
lastPointTolerance){
    if(gestureShapeLayer.lines.count == 4){ //4 lines
      [message setString:@"Rectangle"];
      gestureShapeLayer.drawLines = YES;
    }else if(gestureShapeLayer.lines.count == 3){ //3 lines
      [message setString:@"Triangle"];
      gestureShapeLayer.drawLines = YES;
    }else if(gestureShapeLayer.lines.count <= 1){      //0 or 1
lines
      [message setString:@"Circle"];
      [gestureShapeLayer setCircleRectFromPoints];
      gestureShapeLayer.drawCircle = YES;
    }else{
      [self resetMessage];
      gestureShapeLayer.lines = [[NSMutableArray alloc] init];
    }
```

```
    }else{  //Lines and angles
      if(gestureShapeLayer.lines.count == 1){ //1 line
        [message setString:@"Line"];
        gestureShapeLayer.drawLines = YES;
      }else if(gestureShapeLayer.lines.count == 2){ //2 lines
        [message setString:@"Angle"];
        gestureShapeLayer.drawLines = YES;
      }else{
        [self resetMessage];
        gestureShapeLayer.lines = [[NSMutableArray alloc] init];
      }
    }
  }

  @end
```

How it works...

This gesture system tracks each individual point of user input. Each pair of points creates a **2D vector**. When the current vector's angle is different enough from the previous one, then we consider that this is a new vertex of a shape the user is drawing. We then take this vertex and the last one, and create a line. By storing every point and line we can determine what the user is attempting to draw.

There's more...

This system, as implemented, leaves much to be desired. However, it provides the conceptual groundwork for a more complex and functional system. By looking at the succession of points in a certain light we can see patterns emerge. In this example, we looked for successive vectors with vastly different angles to determine drawn lines. Other things like curves, direction, and point distance can lead to the identification of more complex shapes.

3
Files and Data

In this chapter, we will cover the following points:

- ▸ Reading PLIST data files
- ▸ Reading JSON data files
- ▸ Reading XML data files
- ▸ Saving simple data using NSUserDefaults
- ▸ Archiving objects into archive files
- ▸ Mutating nested metadata
- ▸ Saving data into a PLIST file
- ▸ Saving data into a SQLite database
- ▸ Saving data using Core Data

Introduction

Both simple and complex games **process and persist data**. This includes hi-scores, player profiles, and saved game sessions to name a few. In this chapter, we will use a number of varied techniques to read and write data.

Reading PLIST data files

This recipe, along with the other two that follow, shows us how to **read and parse** simple data into Cocos2d scenes. Here we read a **PLIST** file to create a scene that depicts a desert with a few cacti.

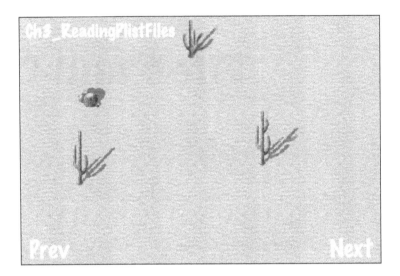

Getting ready

Please refer to the project *RecipeCollection01* for full working code of this recipe.

How to do it...

Execute the following code:

```
#import <Foundation/Foundation.h>

/* This returns the full absolute path to a specified file in the
bundle */
NSString* getActualPath( NSString* file )
{
  NSArray* path = [file componentsSeparatedByString: @"."];
  NSString* actualPath = [[NSBundle mainBundle] pathForResource: [path
objectAtIndex: 0] ofType: [path objectAtIndex: 1]];

  return actualPath;
}
```

```
@implementation Ch2_ReadingPlistFiles

-(CCLayer*) runRecipe {
  //Initialize a read-only dictionary from our file
  NSString *fileName = @"scene1.plist";
  NSDictionary *dict = [NSDictionary dictionaryWithContentsOfFile:getA
ctualPath(fileName)];

  //Process this dictionary
  [self processMap:dict];

  return self;
}

-(void) processMap:(NSDictionary*)dict {
  //Loop through all dictionary nodes to process individual types
  NSArray *nodes = [dict objectForKey:@"nodes"];
  for (id node in nodes) {
    if([[node objectForKey:@"type"] isEqualToString:@"spriteFile"]){
      [self processSpriteFile:node];
    }else if([[node objectForKey:@"type"] isEqualToString:@"texturedP
olygon"]){
      [self processTexturedPolygon:node];
    }
  }
}

/* Process the 'spriteFile' type */
-(void) processSpriteFile:(NSDictionary*)nodeDict {
  //Init the sprite
  NSString *file = [nodeDict objectForKey:@"file"];
  CCSprite *sprite = [CCSprite spriteWithFile:file];

  //Set sprite position
  NSDictionary *posDict = [nodeDict objectForKey:@"position"];
  sprite.position = ccp([[posDict objectForKey:@"x"] floatValue],
[[posDict objectForKey:@"y"] floatValue]);

  //Each numeric value is an NSString or NSNumber that must be cast
into a float
  sprite.scale = [[nodeDict objectForKey:@"scale"] floatValue];

  //Set the anchor point so objects are positioned from the bottom-up
  sprite.anchorPoint = ccp(0.5,0);
```

```objc
  //We set the sprite Z according to its Y to produce an isometric
perspective
    float z = [self getZFromY:[[posDict objectForKey:@"y"] floatValue]];
    if([nodeDict objectForKey:@"z"]){
      z = [[nodeDict objectForKey:@"z"] floatValue];
    }

    //Finally, add the sprite
    [self addChild:sprite z:z];
}

/* Process the 'texturedPolygon' type */
-(void) processTexturedPolygon:(NSDictionary*)nodeDict {
  //Process vertices
  NSMutableArray *vertices = [[[NSMutableArray alloc] init]
autorelease];
  NSArray *vertexData = [nodeDict objectForKey:@"vertices"];
  for(id vData in vertexData){
    float x = [[vData objectForKey:@"x"] floatValue];
    float y = [[vData objectForKey:@"y"] floatValue];

    [vertices addObject:[NSValue valueWithCGPoint:ccp(x,y)]];
  }

  //Init our textured polygon
  NSString *file = [nodeDict objectForKey:@"file"];

  ccTexParams params = {GL_NEAREST,GL_NEAREST_MIPMAP_NEAREST,GL_
REPEAT,GL_REPEAT};
  TexturedPolygon *texturedPoly = [TexturedPolygon createWithFile:file
withVertices:vertices];
  [texturedPoly.texture setTexParameters:&params];

  [texturedPoly retain];

  //Set position
  NSDictionary *posDict = [nodeDict objectForKey:@"position"];
  texturedPoly.position = ccp([[posDict objectForKey:@"x"]
floatValue], [[posDict objectForKey:@"y"] floatValue]);

  //Add the texturedPolygon behind any sprites
  [self addChild:texturedPoly z:0];
}

/* Our simple method used to order sprites by depth */
```

```
-(float) getZFromY:(float)y {
    return 320-y;
}

@end
```

How it works...

Loading data from a PLIST file is a seamless way to create a complex structure of data in the memory of your program. Here we load `scene1.plist`, which contains an array of dictionaries. This translates to an `NSArray` of `NSDictionary` values. Inside each dictionary we have a string value with a key of 'type'. This tells the application what kind of node it is looking at. The PLIST data format can house an infinitely deep combination of arrays and dictionaries that ultimately contain primitive data types including Boolean, Data, Date, Number, and String. Each one is easily converted into `NSNumber`, `NSData`, `NSDate`, or `NSString`. Here is what our PLIST file looks like:

Key	Type	Value
▼ Root	Dictionary	(1 item)
▼ nodes	Array	(5 items)
▼ Item 0	Dictionary	(4 items)
type	String	texturedPolygon
file	String	sand_texture.png
▶ position	Dictionary	(2 items)
▶ vertices	Array	(4 items)
▼ Item 1	Dictionary	(4 items)
type	String	spriteFile
file	String	cactus1_00.png
▶ position	Dictionary	(2 items)
scale	String	1
▼ Item 2	Dictionary	(4 items)
type	String	spriteFile
file	String	cactus2_00.png
▶ position	Dictionary	(2 items)
scale	String	1
▼ Item 3	Dictionary	(4 items)
type	String	spriteFile
file	String	cactus3_00.png
▶ position	Dictionary	(2 items)
scale	String	1
▼ Item 4	Dictionary	(4 items)
type	String	spriteFile
file	String	cactus4_00.png
▶ position	Dictionary	(2 items)
scale	String	1

A PLIST file is merely an XML file parsed using specific conventions. The previous figure is a graphical representation of the XML data. As you'll see in later examples, combinations of arrays and dictionaries are the standard for storing data.

▶ Using `getActualPath`:

The `getActualPath` method provides a shortcut to obtaining the full file path of a bundle resource. This allows classes that require exact paths to manipulate files in the filesystem.

▶ Isometric scenes:

As you can see, our scene has some depth and shadow. This technique is simulated isometric projection. This is simulated 3D space with no vanishing point. It is used in countless 2D games and will be a primary feature of many more recipes in this book.

Reading JSON data files

JSON stands for **JavaScript Object Notation**. It is a very light and easily consumable way of packing your data. Thanks to the `CJSONDeserializer` library, reading in JSON files is as simple as reading in PLIST files. In the following scene, we see a grassy field with a cat and a few trees:

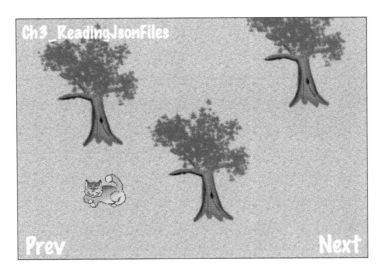

Getting ready

Please refer to the project *RecipeCollection01* for full working code of this recipe.

How to do it...

Execute the following code:

```
#import "ActualPath.h"

@implementation Ch2_ReadingJsonFiles

-(CCLayer*) runRecipe {
  //Initialize a read-only dictionary from our file
  NSString *fileName = @"scene2.json";

  NSString *jsonString = [[[NSString alloc] initWithContentsOfFile
:getActualPath(fileName) encoding:NSUTF8StringEncoding error:nil]
autorelease];
  NSData *jsonData = [jsonString dataUsingEncoding:NSUTF32BigEndianSt
ringEncoding];
  NSDictionary *dict = [[CJSONDeserializer deserializer] deserializeAs
Dictionary:jsonData error:nil];

  //Process this dictionary
  [self processMap:dict];

  return self;
}

-(void) processMap:(NSDictionary*)dict {
  NSArray *nodes = [dict objectForKey:@"nodes"];
  for (id node in nodes) {
    if([[node objectForKey:@"type"] isEqualToString:@"spriteFile"]){
      [self processSpriteFile:node];
    }else if([[node objectForKey:@"type"] isEqualToString:@"texturedP
olygon"]){
      [self processTexturedPolygon:node];
    }
  }
}

/* Process the 'spriteFile' type */
-(void) processSpriteFile:(NSDictionary*)nodeDict {
  /* CODE OMITTED */
}

/* Process the 'texturedPolygon' type */
-(void) processTexturedPolygon:(NSDictionary*)nodeDict {
```

```
    /* CODE OMITTED */
}

/* Our simple method used to order sprites by depth */
-(float) getZFromY:(float)y {
    return 320-y;
}

@end
```

How it works...

Loading JSON into a read-only NSDictionary is fairly straightforward. Here is our JSON file with some lines omitted:

```
{ "nodes":
    [ { "type":"spriteFile", "file":"tree.png",
"position":{"x":250,"y":50}, "scale":0.9 },
      { "type":"spriteFile", "file":"tree_shadow.png",
"position":{"x":195,"y":51}, "scale":0.9, "z":-100 },
      { "type":"spriteFile", "file":"cheshire_cat.png",
"position":{"x":120,"y":70}, "scale":0.3 },
      { "type":"spriteFile", "file":"actor_shadow.png",
"position":{"x":120,"y":65}, "scale":1.75, "z":-100 },
        { "type":"texturedPolygon", "file":"grass_texture.png",
"position":{"x":16,"y":16},
            "vertices":[{"x":0,"y":0},{"x":480,"y":0},{"x":480,"y":320},
{"x":0,"y":320}] },
        { "type":"rectangle", "position":{"x":0,"y":0},
"size":{"x":480,"y":320}, "meta": [{"type":"boundary"}] }
    ]
}
```

As you can see the JSON format is very succinct. At a glance, it is much easier to understand than XML.

Reading XML data files

Finally, we have everyone's favorite data format: basic unadulterated XML. For this recipe, we will use Google's **GDataXML** library to read and parse a simple XML document. In the following scene, we see rocky terrain with some boulders and weeds:

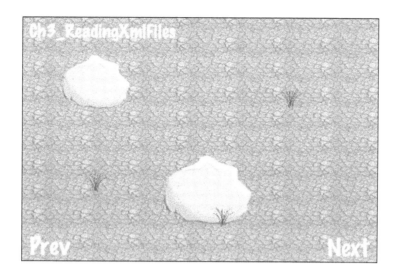

Getting ready

Please refer to the project *RecipeCollection01* for full working code of this recipe.

How to do it...

The first thing we need to do is integrate Google's GData XML tools:

1. Download and unzip the `gdata-objectivec-client` from here: `http://code.google.com/p/gdata-objectivec-client/downloads/list`

2. In the folder `Source\XMLSupport` find the files `GDataXMLNode.h` and `GDataXMLNode.m` and add them to your project.

3. In your **Project Navigator** click on your **Project**.

4. To the right of this, click on your **Target**.

5. Go to the **Build Settings** tab.

6. Find the **Search Paths\Header Search Paths** setting.

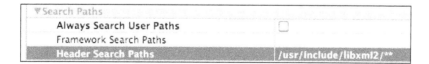

7. Add `/usr/include/libxml2` to the list.

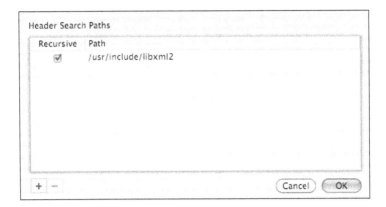

8. Find the **Linking\Other Linker Flags** section.

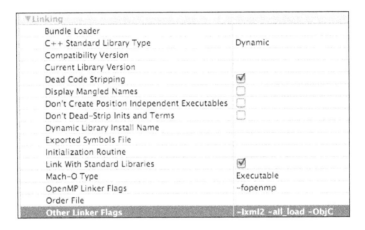

9. Add `-lxml2` to the list.

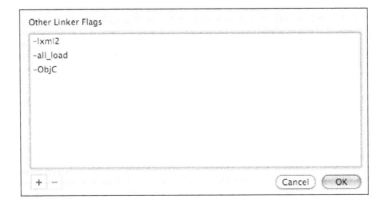

10. Import `GDataXMLNode.h` into your code. If it compiles and runs, then you've integrated GDataXML successfully.

Now, execute the following code:

```
#import "GDataXMLNode.h"

@implementation Ch2_ReadingXmlFiles


-(CCLayer*) runRecipe {
  //Read our file in as an NSData object
  NSString *fileName = @"scene3.xml";
  NSString *xmlString = [[[NSString alloc] initWithContentsOfFile
:getActualPath(fileName) encoding:NSUTF8StringEncoding error:nil]
autorelease];
  NSData *xmlData = [xmlString dataUsingEncoding:NSUTF32BigEndianStri
ngEncoding];


  //Initialize a new GDataXMLDocument with our data
  GDataXMLDocument *doc = [[[GDataXMLDocument alloc]
initWithData:xmlData options:0 error:nil] autorelease];


  //Process that document
  [self processMap:doc];


  return self;
}


-(void) processMap:(GDataXMLDocument*)doc {
  //Find all elements of 'node' type
  NSArray *nodes = [doc.rootElement elementsForName:@"node"];


  //Loop through each element
  for (GDataXMLElement *node in nodes) {
    //Find the first (and assumed only) element with the name 'type'
in this node
      NSString *type = [[[node elementsForName:@"type"]
objectAtIndex:0] stringValue];


    //Process specific node types
    if([type isEqualToString:@"spriteFile"]){
      [self processSpriteFile:node];
    }else if([type isEqualToString:@"texturedPolygon"]){
      [self processTexturedPolygon:node];
    }
```

```
  }
}

/* Process the 'spriteFile' type */
-(void) processSpriteFile:(GDataXMLElement*)node {
  //Init the sprite
  NSString *file = [[[node elementsForName:@"file"] objectAtIndex:0]
stringValue];
  CCSprite *sprite = [CCSprite spriteWithFile:file];

  //Set sprite position
  GDataXMLElement *posElement = [[node elementsForName:@"position"]
objectAtIndex:0];
  sprite.position = ccp( [[[[posElement elementsForName:@"x"]
objectAtIndex:0] stringValue] floatValue],
  [[[[posElement elementsForName:@"y"] objectAtIndex:0] stringValue]
floatValue]);

  //Each element is considered a string first
  sprite.scale = [[[[node elementsForName:@"scale"] objectAtIndex:0]
stringValue] floatValue];

  //Set the anchor point
  sprite.anchorPoint = ccp(0.5,0);

  //We set the sprite Z according to its Y to produce an isometric
perspective
  float z = [self getZFromY:sprite.position.y];
  if([node elementsForName:@"z"].count > 0){
    z = [[[[node elementsForName:@"z"] objectAtIndex:0] stringValue]
floatValue];
  }

  //Finally, add the sprite
  [self addChild:sprite z:z];
}

/* Process the 'texturedPolygon' type */
-(void) processTexturedPolygon:(GDataXMLElement*)node {
  //Process vertices
  NSMutableArray *vertices = [[[NSMutableArray alloc] init]
autorelease];
```

```
    NSArray *vertexData = [[[node elementsForName:@"vertices"]
objectAtIndex:0] elementsForName:@"vertex"];

    for(id vData in vertexData){
      GDataXMLElement *vertexElement = (GDataXMLElement*)vData;
      float x = [[[[vertexElement elementsForName:@"x"] objectAtIndex:0]
stringValue] floatValue];
      float y = [[[[vertexElement elementsForName:@"y"] objectAtIndex:0]
stringValue] floatValue];

      [vertices addObject:[NSValue valueWithCGPoint:ccp(x,y)]];
    }

    //Init our textured polygon
    NSString *file = [[[node elementsForName:@"file"] objectAtIndex:0]
stringValue];

    ccTexParams params = {GL_NEAREST,GL_NEAREST_MIPMAP_NEAREST,GL_
REPEAT,GL_REPEAT};
    TexturedPolygon *texturedPoly = [TexturedPolygon createWithFile:file
withVertices:vertices];
    [texturedPoly.texture setTexParameters:&params];

    //Set position
    GDataXMLElement *posElement = [[node elementsForName:@"position"]
objectAtIndex:0];
    texturedPoly.position = ccp( [[[[posElement elementsForName:@"x"]
objectAtIndex:0] stringValue] floatValue],
      [[[[posElement elementsForName:@"y"] objectAtIndex:0] stringValue]
floatValue]);

    //Add the texturedPolygon behind any sprites
    [self addChild:texturedPoly z:0];
}

/* Our simple method used to order sprites by depth */
-(float) getZFromY:(float)y {
  return 320-y;
}

@end
```

How it works...

Reading and processing XML files is not too different from processing PLIST and JSON files. In this case, we use the classes `GDataXMLDocument` and `GDataXMLElement`. The latter implements the method `(NSString*) stringValue`, which other values can be parsed out of. Here is an excerpt of the XML document we are working with:

```xml
<?xml version="1.0" encoding="ISO-8859-1"?>
<nodes>
  <node>
    <type>spriteFile</type>
    <file>boulder.png</file>
    <position><x>250</x><y>50</y></position>
    <scale>0.9</scale>
  </node>
  <node>
    <type>texturedPolygon</type>
    <file>cracked_earth_texture.png</file>
    <position> <x>32</x><y>32</y> </position>
    <vertices>
      <vertex>  <x>0</x><y>0</y> </vertex>
      <vertex>  <x>480</x><y>0</y> </vertex>
      <vertex>  <x>480</x><y>320</y> </vertex>
      <vertex>  <x>0</x><y>320</y> </vertex>
    </vertices>
  </node>
</nodes>
```

Pure XML is harder to read than a PLIST file and contains more markup language fluff than JSON. However, XML allows the use of two features missing from JSON: **Attributes** and **Namespaces**. Attributes can be used to provide additional information about an **Element**. Namespaces can be used to help reduce the ambiguity between Elements.

See also...

More information about the XML specification can be found at:
`http://www.w3.org/TR/xml/`

Saving simple data using NSUserDefaults

For the persistence of user settings and other small bits of data, the iOS framework provides the `NSUserDefaults` class. In this example, we are saving the default difficulty level for our game.

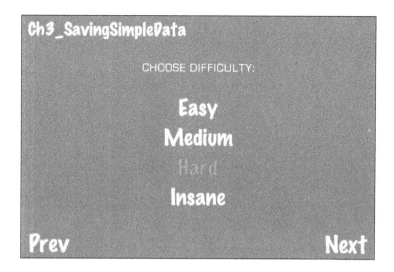

Getting ready

Please refer to the project _RecipeCollection01_ for full working code of this recipe.

How to do it...

Execute the following code:

```
@implementation Ch2_SavingSimpleData

-(CCLayer*) runRecipe {
  //Set font size
  [CCMenuItemFont setFontSize:30];

  //Add main label
  CCLabelBMFont *chooseDifficultyLabel = [CCLabelBMFont
labelWithString:@"CHOOSE DIFFICULTY:" fntFile:@"eurostile_30.fnt"];
  chooseDifficultyLabel.position = ccp(240,250);
  chooseDifficultyLabel.scale = 0.5f;
  [self addChild:chooseDifficultyLabel z:1];

  //Add difficulty choices
  easyMIF = [CCMenuItemFont itemFromString:@"Easy" target:self
selector:@selector(chooseEasy)];
  /* CODE OMITTED */

  mainMenu = [CCMenu menuWithItems:easyMIF, mediumMIF, hardMIF,
insaneMIF, nil];
```

```
    [mainMenu alignItemsVertically];
    mainMenu.position = ccp(240,140);
        [self addChild:mainMenu z:1];

    //Load any previously chosen difficulty
    [self loadDifficulty];

    return self;
}

-(void) loadDifficulty {
    //If a difficulty is set we use that, otherwise we choose Medium
    NSUserDefaults *defaults = [NSUserDefaults standardUserDefaults];
    if([defaults stringForKey:@"simple_data_difficulty"]){
        difficulty = [defaults stringForKey:@"simple_data_difficulty"];
        [self setDifficultyFromValue];
    }else{
        [self chooseMedium];
    }
}
-(void) saveDifficulty {
    //Save our difficulty
    NSUserDefaults *defaults = [NSUserDefaults standardUserDefaults];
    [defaults setObject:difficulty forKey:@"simple_data_difficulty"];
    [defaults synchronize];
}
-(void) setDifficultyFromValue {
    //More menu color management
    [self resetMenuColors];

    if([difficulty isEqualToString:@"Easy"]){
        [easyMIF setColor:ccc3(255,0,0)];
    }else if([difficulty isEqualToString:@"Medium"]){
        [mediumMIF setColor:ccc3(255,0,0)];
    }/* CODE OMITTED */

    [self saveDifficulty];
}

/* Shortcut callback methods */
-(void) chooseEasy {
    difficulty = @"Easy";
    [self setDifficultyFromValue];
}
/* CODE OMITTED */
@end
```

How it works...

The `NSUserDefaults` class uses a format that is similar to PLIST. It can accept the same type of objects including `NSString`, `NSData`, `NSNumber,` and others. It can also accept arrays and dictionaries.

- Loading data:

    These are the crucial lines to remember when loading `NSUserDefaults` data:

    ```
    if([defaults stringForKey:@"simple_data_difficulty"]){
        difficulty = [defaults stringForKey:@"simple_data_
    difficulty"];
    }
    ```

    The `if` statement does a simple check to see if that entry exists yet.

- Saving data:

    The procedure for saving data is also fairly straightforward:

    ```
    NSUserDefaults *defaults = [NSUserDefaults standardUserDefaults];
    [defaults setObject:difficulty forKey:@"simple_data_difficulty"];
    [defaults synchronize];
    ```

See also...

We took a brief look at menu customization in this recipe. We will talk about this topic at length in *Chapter 4, Physics*.

Archiving objects into archive files

The classes `NSKeyedArchiver` and `NSKeyedUnarchiver` allow us to persist data in a very **Object-oriented** way. By conforming to the `NSCoding` protocol, we can tell the archiver how to pack and unpack any of our classes. In this recipe, we will be packing up a character who has a number of Dungeons and Dragons style attributes.

Getting ready

Please refer to the project *RecipeCollection01* for full working code of this recipe. Also note that some of the following code has been omitted for brevity.

How to do it...

Execute the following code:

```
//SimpleCharacter.h
@interface SimpleCharacter : NSObject <NSCoding> {
  NSString *charColor; NSString *charClass;
  int strength; int dexterity; int constitution;
  int intelligence; int wisdom; int charisma;
}

@property (readwrite, assign) NSString *charColor;
@property (readwrite, assign) NSString *charClass;
@property (readwrite, assign) int strength;
/* CODE OMITTED */

@end

@implementation SimpleCharacter

@synthesize charColor, charClass, strength, dexterity, constitution,
intelligence, wisdom, charisma;

/* This merely adds this character with the proper color to a CCNode
*/
-(void) addCharacterToNode:(CCNode *)node atPosition:(CGPoint)position
{
  ccColor3B color;

  if([charColor isEqualToString:@"Red"]){
    color = ccc3(255,0,0);
  }else if([charColor isEqualToString:@"Blue"]){
    color = ccc3(0,0,255);
  }/* CODE OMITTED */

  CCSpriteFrameCache *cache = [CCSpriteFrameCache
sharedSpriteFrameCache];
    [cache addSpriteFramesWithFile:@"dnd_characters.plist"];
```

```
   CCSprite *drawing = [CCSprite spriteWithSpriteFrame:[cache
spriteFrameByName:[NSString stringWithFormat:@"dnd_%@_drawing.
png",charClass]]];
   CCSprite *colors = [CCSprite spriteWithSpriteFrame:[cache
spriteFrameByName:[NSString stringWithFormat:@"dnd_%@_colors.
png",charClass]]];

  drawing.position = position; colors.position = position;
  drawing.scale = 1.5f; colors.scale = 1.5f;
  colors.color = color;

  [node addChild:colors z:0 tag:0];
  [node addChild:drawing z:1 tag:1];
}

/* This method determines how data is encoded into an NSCoder object
*/
- (void) encodeWithCoder: (NSCoder *)coder {
  [coder encodeObject:charColor];
  [coder encodeObject:charClass];
  [coder encodeObject:[NSNumber numberWithInt:strength]];
  /* CODE OMITTED */
}

/* This method determines how data is read out from an NSCode object
*/
-(id) initWithCoder: (NSCoder *) coder {
  [super init];
  charColor = [[coder decodeObject] retain];
  charClass = [[coder decodeObject] retain];
  strength = [[coder decodeObject] intValue];
  /* CODE OMITTED */
  return self;
}

/* Initialization */
-(id) init {
self = [super init];
if (self) {
    charColor = @"Red"; charClass = @"Wizard";
    strength = 10; dexterity = 10; constitution = 10;
    intelligence = 10; wisdom = 10; charisma = 10;
  }
  return self;
```

```
  }

  /* All objects must be released here */
  - (void) dealloc {
    [charColor release]; [charClass release]; [super dealloc];
  }
  @end

  @implementation Ch2_ArchivingObjects

  -(CCLayer*) runRecipe {
    //Load our character
    [self loadCharacter];

    return self;
  }

  -(void) loadCharacter {
    //Our archive file name
    NSString *fileName = @"dnd_character.archive";

    //We get our file path
    NSArray *paths = NSSearchPathForDirectoriesInDomains(NSDocumentDirec
  tory, NSUserDomainMask, YES);
    NSString *documentsDirectory = [paths objectAtIndex:0];
    NSString *filePath = [documentsDirectory stringByAppendingPathCompon
  ent:fileName];

    if(![[NSFileManager defaultManager] fileExistsAtPath:filePath]){
      //If file doesn't exist in document directory create a new default
  character and save it
      character = [[SimpleCharacter alloc] init];
      [NSKeyedArchiver archiveRootObject:character toFile:filePath];
    }else{
      //If it does we load it
      character = [[NSKeyedUnarchiver unarchiveObjectWithFile:filePath]
  retain];
    }

    //Add character and reload HUD
    [character addCharacterToNode:self atPosition:ccp(300,180)];
    [self loadHUD];
  }

  -(void) saveCharacter {
```

```objc
  //Our archive file name
  NSString *fileName = @"dnd_character.archive";

  //We get our file path
  NSArray *paths = NSSearchPathForDirectoriesInDomains(NSDocumentDirec
tory, NSUserDomainMask, YES);
  NSString *documentsDirectory = [paths objectAtIndex:0];
  NSString *filePath = [documentsDirectory stringByAppendingPathCompon
ent:fileName];

  //Save character
  [NSKeyedArchiver archiveRootObject:character toFile:filePath];
}

-(void) deleteData {
  //Our archive file name
  NSString *fileName = @"dnd_character.archive";

  //We get our file path
  NSArray *paths = NSSearchPathForDirectoriesInDomains(NSDocumentDirec
tory, NSUserDomainMask, YES);
  NSString *documentsDirectory = [paths objectAtIndex:0];
  NSString *filePath = [documentsDirectory stringByAppendingPathCompon
ent:fileName];

  //Delete our file
  [[NSFileManager defaultManager] removeItemAtPath:filePath
error:nil];

  //Set removal message
  [message setString:@"Data deleted!"];

  //Remove character node and load a new default character
  [self removeCharacter];
  [self loadCharacter];
}

@end
```

How it works...

Properly **archiving** an object requires a few steps.

▸ Conforming to the NSCoding protocol:

The NSCoding protocol requires that we implement the following two methods:

```
- (void) encodeWithCoder: (NSCoder *)coder;
- (id) initWithCoder: (NSCoder *) coder;
```

One method packs data into the NSCoder object and the other unpacks data out of it.

▸ Using the Documents directory:

Your app has write access to areas specified by the iOS framework. These include the Documents and the Library directories. In this and future examples, we may read from a number of locations within the app bundle but we will usually only write to the Documents directory. Unlike other areas on the disk, files saved here will be maintained when an app is upgraded. Typically, we save pre-made templates in a read-only section, copy them into the Documents directory, load them into memory, and then save modified versions in the Documents directory. We usually locate a file inside the Documents directory with the following code:

```
NSString *fileName = @"my.file";
NSArray *paths = NSSearchPathForDirectoriesInDomains(NSDocumentD
irectory, NSUserDomainMask, YES);
NSString *documentsDirectory = [paths objectAtIndex:0];
NSString *filePath = [documentsDirectory stringByAppendingPathCo
mponent:fileName];
```

This returns the absolute file path.

▸ Using NSFileManager:

We also use NSFileManager to determine whether a file exists and also to remove files as necessary.

```
if([[NSFileManager defaultManager] fileExistsAtPath:filePath]){
  [[NSFileManager defaultManager] removeItemAtPath:filePath
error:nil];
}
```

▶ Using `NSKeyedArchiver` and `NSKeyedUnarchiver`:

Finally, with all these tools at hand we can archive and unarchive objects using the classes `NSKeyedArchiver` and `NSKeyedUnarchiver`:

```
//Archive
character = [[SimpleCharacter alloc] init];
[NSKeyedArchiver archiveRootObject:character toFile:filePath];

//Un-archive
character = [[NSKeyedUnarchiver unarchiveObjectWithFile:filePath]
retain];
```

Mutating nested metadata

Data from data files is often loaded into a non-mutable, 'nested' structure of arrays and dictionaries. This non-mutable structure leaves the data un-editable. In this recipe, we will read in a nested JSON data structure and then recursively re-create the data using mutable data structures to allow the data to be edited.

Getting ready

Please refer to the project _RecipeCollection01_ for full working code of this recipe.

How to do it...

Execute the following code:

```objc
#import "GameHelper.h"

//Implementation
@implementation Ch3_MutatingNestedMetadata

-(CCLayer*) runRecipe {
  [super runRecipe];

  //Load JSON data
  NSString *fileName = @"data_to_mutate.json";
  NSString *jsonString = [[[NSString alloc] initWithContentsOfFile
:getActualPath(fileName) encoding:NSUTF8StringEncoding error:nil]
autorelease];
  NSData *jsonData = [jsonString dataUsingEncoding:NSUTF32BigEndianSt
ringEncoding];
  NSDictionary *dict = [[CJSONDeserializer deserializer] deserializeAs
Dictionary:jsonData error:nil];

  //Create deep mutable copy
  dictMutable = [GameHelper makeRecMutableCopy:dict];
  [dictMutable retain];

  //Show JSON data
  [self showJsonData:dictMutable];

  //Add randomize button
  [CCMenuItemFont setFontSize:30];
  CCMenuItemFont *randomizeItem = [CCMenuItemFont
itemFromString:@"Randomize Data" target:self selector:@
selector(randomizeData)];
  CCMenu *menu = [CCMenu menuWithItems:randomizeItem, nil];
  menu.position = ccp(240,140);
    [self addChild:menu z:1];

  return self;
}
-(void) showJsonData:(NSDictionary*)dict {
  [self showMessage:@""];

  //Loop through all dictionary nodes to process individual types
  NSMutableDictionary *nodes = [dict objectForKey:@"people"];
```

```
    for (NSMutableDictionary* node in nodes) {
        float height = [[node objectForKey:@"height"] floatValue];
        float weight = [[node objectForKey:@"weight"] floatValue];
        NSString *name = [node objectForKey:@"name"];

        [self appendMessage:[NSString stringWithFormat:@"%@: %din %dlbs",
name, (int)height, (int)weight]];
    }
}
-(void) randomizeData {
    //Randomize some data in 'dictMutable'
    NSMutableArray *nodes = [dictMutable objectForKey:@"people"];
    for (NSMutableDictionary* node in nodes) {
        [node setObject:[NSNumber numberWithFloat:(float)
(arc4random()%48)+30.0f] forKey:@"height"];
        [node setObject:[NSNumber numberWithFloat:(float)
(arc4random()%100)+100.0f] forKey:@"weight"];
    }

    [self showJsonData:dictMutable];
}
@end
```

How it works...

Just like in the previous section, *Reading JSON data files*, here we first read in data from a JSON file. The data consists of a `NSDictionary` object with nested arrays, dictionaries, and, finally, strings. To create a 'deep' mutable copy, we call the following method in our `GameHelper` class:

```
+(NSMutableDictionary*) makeRecMutableCopy:(NSDictionary*)dict;
```

This method assumes that the root node is a dictionary.

▶   The `makeRecMutableCopy` method:

    In this recipe, we've spared the gruesome details of this method. Put simply, it recursively goes through the nested structure turning `NSDictionary` objects into `NSMutableDictionary` objects and `NSArray` objects into `NSMutableArray` objects.

▶   Modifying the data tree:

    Once we have a nested mutable structure, we can access it and modify elements as necessary. Click the **Randomize Data** button to randomly change some data in the structure.

Saving data into a PLIST file

For the next three recipes, we have three small games that need to have their hi-scores persisted. In this recipe, we see a whack-a-mole game that will use a PLIST file to maintain a list of hi-scores.

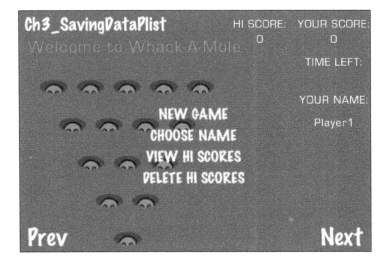

Getting ready

Please refer to the project *RecipeCollection01* for full working code of this recipe. For the sake of brevity all game logic has been omitted from the following code.

How to do it...

Execute the following code:

```
#import "ActualPath.h"

@implementation Ch2_SavingDataPlist

-(CCLayer*) runRecipe {
[self loadHiScores];

  return self;
}

-(void) loadHiScores {
  //Our template and file names
```

```objc
  NSString *templateName = @"whackamole_template.plist";
  NSString *fileName = @"whackamole.plist";

  //Our dictionary
  NSMutableDictionary *fileDict;

  //We get our file path
  NSArray *paths = NSSearchPathForDirectoriesInDomains(NSDocumentDirec
tory, NSUserDomainMask, YES);
  NSString *documentsDirectory = [paths objectAtIndex:0];
  NSString *filePath = [documentsDirectory stringByAppendingPathCompon
ent:fileName];

  if(![[NSFileManager defaultManager] fileExistsAtPath:filePath]){
    //If file doesn't exist in document directory create a new one
from the template
    fileDict = [NSMutableDictionary dictionaryWithContentsOfFile:getAc
tualPath(templateName)];
  }else{
    //If it does we load it in the dict
    fileDict = [NSMutableDictionary dictionaryWithContentsOfFile:file
Path];
  }

  //Load hi scores into our dictionary
  hiScores = [fileDict objectForKey:@"hiscores"];

  //Set the 'hiScore' variable (the highest score)
  for(id score in hiScores){
    int scoreNum = [[score objectForKey:@"score"] intValue];
    if(hiScore < scoreNum){
      hiScore = scoreNum;
    }
  }

  //Write dict to file
  [fileDict writeToFile:filePath atomically:YES];
}

-(void) addHiScore {
  //Our template and file names
  NSString *templateName = @"whackamole_template.plist";
  NSString *fileName = @"whackamole.plist";

  //Our dictionary
```

```
  NSMutableDictionary *fileDict;

  //We get our file path
  NSArray *paths = NSSearchPathForDirectoriesInDomains(NSDocumentDirec
tory, NSUserDomainMask, YES);
  NSString *documentsDirectory = [paths objectAtIndex:0];
  NSString *filePath = [documentsDirectory stringByAppendingPathCompon
ent:fileName];

  if(![[NSFileManager defaultManager] fileExistsAtPath:filePath]){
    //If file doesn't exist in document directory create a new one
from the template
    fileDict = [NSMutableDictionary dictionaryWithContentsOfFile:getAc
tualPath(templateName)];
  }else{
    //If it does we load it in the dict
    fileDict = [NSMutableDictionary dictionaryWithContentsOfFile:file
Path];
  }

  //Load hi scores into our dictionary
  hiScores = [fileDict objectForKey:@"hiscores"];

  //Add hi score
  bool scoreRecorded = NO;

  //Add score if player's name already exists
  for(id score in hiScores){
    NSMutableDictionary *scoreDict = (NSMutableDictionary*)score;
    if([[scoreDict objectForKey:@"name"] isEqualToString:currentPlaye
rName]){
      if([[scoreDict objectForKey:@"score"] intValue] < currentScore){
        [scoreDict setValue:[NSNumber numberWithInt:currentScore]
forKey:@"score"];
      }
      scoreRecorded = YES;
    }
  }

  //Add new score if player's name doesn't exist
  if(!scoreRecorded){
    NSMutableDictionary *newScore = [[NSMutableDictionary alloc]
init];
    [newScore setObject:currentPlayerName forKey:@"name"];
```

```
    [newScore setObject:[NSNumber numberWithInt:currentScore]
forKey:@"score"];
    [hiScores addObject:newScore];
  }

  //Write dict to file
  [fileDict writeToFile:filePath atomically:YES];
}

-(void) deleteHiScores {
  //Our file name
  NSString *fileName = @"whackamole.plist";

  //We get our file path
  NSArray *paths = NSSearchPathForDirectoriesInDomains(NSDocumentDirec
tory, NSUserDomainMask, YES);
  NSString *documentsDirectory = [paths objectAtIndex:0];
  NSString *filePath = [documentsDirectory stringByAppendingPathCompon
ent:fileName];

  //Delete our file
  [[NSFileManager defaultManager] removeItemAtPath:filePath
error:nil];

  [message setString:@"Hi scores deleted!"];

  hiScore = 0;
  [self loadHiScores];
}

@end
```

How it works...

The first thing we do is check the Documents directory for whackamole.plist and we load
that data into the fileDict dictionary. If we don't find that file we open whackamole_
template.plist from the Resources/Data folder. It looks like this:

Key	Type	Value
▼ Root	Dictionary ⬍	(1 item)
▼ hiscores	Array	(1 item)
▼ Item 0	Dictionary	(2 items)
name	String	Player 1
score	String	0

Whichever file we load, the loading line looks like this:

```
fileDict = [NSMutableDictionary dictionaryWithContentsOfFile:filePa
th];
```

After modifying the `fileDict` dictionary we save it to `whackamole.plist` in the `Documents` directory:

```
[fileDict writeToFile:filePath atomically:YES];
```

All things considered, this is a very simple way to persist data.

Saving data into an SQLite database

The second game we have is a "skeet shooting" game where discs are fired in the air and the goal is to shoot as many down as possible within a certain time limit. For this game, we will persist hi-score data using a SQLite database. We will be using the **FMDB Objective-C SQLite wrapper** to access the SQLite database within our code and the **Firefox plugin SQLite Manager** to create an initial database file.

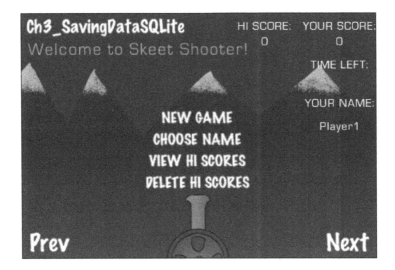

Getting ready

Please refer to the project *RecipeCollection01* for full working code of this recipe. For the sake of brevity, all game logic has been omitted from the following code.

How to do it...

To use SQLite we first need to do a few things:

1. First we need to add the `libsqlite3.0.dylib` framework. You can do this by right clicking on your project and going to **Add > Existing Frameworks** and then, under **iOS 4.x SDK**, selecting `libsqlite3.0.dylib`.

2. Next, we need to add the FMDB Objective-C SQLite wrapper to our project. FMDB can be downloaded here: `https://github.com/ccgus/fmdb`.

3. Download and install the Firefox plugin SQLite Manager from here: `https://addons.mozilla.org/en-US/firefox/addon/sqlite-manager/`

Now we need to create a new SQLite database as our default database template. Go into **SQLite Manager** and go to **Database > New Database**. For our project we created `skeetshooter_template.sqlite` with a **hiscores** table that has the fields **name** and **score**:

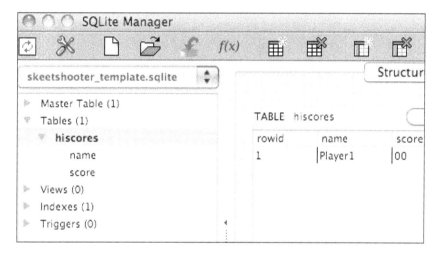

Once we have our database template, execute the following code:

```
#import "ActualPath.h"
#import <Foundation/Foundation.h>
#import "FMDatabase.h"

@implementation Ch2_SavingDataSQLite

-(CCLayer*) runRecipe {
  [self loadHiScores];

  return self;
```

```objc
}

-(void) dealloc {
  //Release our database
  [db close]; [db release]; [super dealloc];
}

-(NSArray *) createDictionariesArrayFromFMResultSet:(FMResultSet *)rs
fields:(NSString *)fields {
  //Parse field string into an array
  NSArray * listFields = [fields componentsSeparatedByString:@","];

  //Create an array of dictionaries from each field
  NSMutableArray * items = [NSMutableArray arrayWithCapacity:1];
  while ([rs next]) {
    NSMutableDictionary * item = [NSMutableDictionary
dictionaryWithCapacity:1];
    for (int i = 0; i < [listFields count]; i++) {
      NSString * key = [listFields objectAtIndex:i];
      NSString * value = [rs stringForColumn: key];
      if (value == NULL) value = @"";
      [item setObject:value forKey:key];
    }
    [items addObject:item];
  }
  [rs close];

  return items;
}

-(void) writeNewScore:(int)score forName:(NSString*)name {
  //Find the hi score with this name
  NSString *selectQuery = [NSString stringWithFormat:@"SELECT * FROM
hiscores WHERE name = '%@'", name];
  FMResultSet *rs = [db executeQuery:selectQuery];

  //What is the score? Is there a score at all?
  int storedScore = -1;
  while([rs next]){
    storedScore = [[rs stringForColumn:@"score"] intValue];
  }
  [rs close];

  if(storedScore == -1){
```

```
      //Name doesn't exist, add it
      NSString *insertQuery = [NSString stringWithFormat:@"INSERT INTO
hiscores (name, score) VALUES ('%@','%i')", name, score];
      rs = [db executeQuery:insertQuery];
      while([rs next]){};
      [rs close];
   }else if(score > storedScore){
      //Write new score for existing name
      NSString *updateQuery = [NSString stringWithFormat:@"UPDATE
hiscores SET score='%i' WHERE name='%@'", score, name];
      rs = [db executeQuery:updateQuery];
      while([rs next]){};
      [rs close];
   }
}


-(void) loadHiScores {
   //Our file and template names
   NSString *fileName = @"skeetshooter.sqlite";
   NSString *templateName = @"skeetshooter_template.sqlite";

   //We get our file path
   NSArray *paths = NSSearchPathForDirectoriesInDomains(NSDocumentDirec
tory, NSUserDomainMask, YES);
   NSString *documentsDirectory = [paths objectAtIndex:0];
   NSString *filePath = [documentsDirectory stringByAppendingPathCompon
ent:fileName];

   //If file doesn't exist in document directory create a new one from
the template
   if(![[NSFileManager defaultManager] fileExistsAtPath:filePath]){
      [[NSFileManager defaultManager] copyItemAtPath:getActualPath(temp
lateName)
         toPath:[NSString stringWithFormat:@"%@/%@", documentsDirectory,
fileName] error:nil];
   }

   //Initialize the database
   if(!db){
      db = [FMDatabase databaseWithPath:filePath];
      [db setLogsErrors:YES];
      [db setTraceExecution:YES];
      [db retain];

      if(![db open]){ NSLog(@"Could not open db.");
```

```objc
    }else{ NSLog(@"DB opened successfully.");}
  }

  //Select all hi scores
  FMResultSet *rs = [db executeQuery:@"select * from hiscores"];

  //Load them into an array of dictionaries
  hiScores = [[NSMutableArray alloc] init];
  hiScores = [self createDictionariesArrayFromFMResultSet:rs
fields:@"name,score"];

  //Set hi score
  for(id score in hiScores){
    int scoreNum = [[score objectForKey:@"score"] intValue];
    if(hiScore < scoreNum){
      hiScore = scoreNum;
    }
  }
}

-(void) addHiScore {
  //Add hi score to db
  [self writeNewScore:currentScore forName:currentPlayerName];

  //Reset dictionary
  FMResultSet *rs = [db executeQuery:@"SELECT * FROM hiscores"];
  hiScores = [self createDictionariesArrayFromFMResultSet:rs
fields:@"name,score"];
}

-(void) deleteHiScores {
  //Our file name
  NSString *fileName = @"skeetshooter.sqlite";

  //We get our file path
  NSArray *paths = NSSearchPathForDirectoriesInDomains(NSDocumentDirec
tory, NSUserDomainMask, YES);
  NSString *documentsDirectory = [paths objectAtIndex:0];
  NSString *filePath = [documentsDirectory stringByAppendingPathCompon
ent:fileName];

  //Delete our file
  [[NSFileManager defaultManager] removeItemAtPath:filePath
error:nil];
```

```
    [message setString:@"Hi scores deleted!"];

    hiScore = 0;

    //Close and release our db pointer
    [db close]; [db release]; db = nil;

    //Load new blank hi scores
    [self loadHiScores];
}

@end
```

How it works...

Saving and loading to a SQLite database is a little different than using a PLIST file. The main way to read and write to a SQLite database is through the following method:

```
- (FMResultSet *)executeQuery:(NSString*)sql;
```

This returns a `FMResultSet` object which can then be iterated through:

```
FMResultSet *rs = [db executeQuery:@"SELECT * FROM mytable"];
while([rs next]){
  somevalue = [[rs stringForColumn:@"myfield"] intValue];
}
[rs close];
```

Be sure to iterate through each `FMResultSet` object you create and also call `[rs close]` as well as SQLite will throw errors if you don't follow through each time.

▶ Querying your SQLite database:

Using this simple but powerful interface you can perform any type of query normally allowed on a SQLite database. In this recipe, we have one table with two values. Feel free to experiment with more complex data models.

Saving data using Core Data

Our third game is a memory card game where you must flip over sets of cards. Flip over two matching cards and you get a point. Flip over two that don't match and you get a strike. Three strikes and you're out. For this game we persist hi-score data using Apple's **Core Data** model pattern.

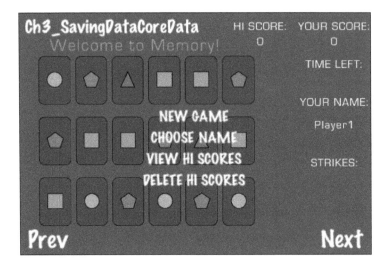

Getting ready

Please refer to the project *RecipeCollection01* for full working code of this recipe. For the sake of brevity all game logic has been omitted from the following code.

How to do it...

Setting up our Core Data based recipe requires a number of steps.

First we need to add the CoreData framework. You can do this by right clicking on your project and going to **Add > Existing Frameworks** and then, under **iOS 4.x SDK**, select `CoreData.framework`.

1. Create a new folder inside your resources entitled `Data Model`. Inside this folder, create a class entitled `Hiscore`, which derives from `ManagedObject`:

   ```
   //Hiscore.h
   #import <CoreData/CoreData.h>

   @interface Hiscore :  NSManagedObject
   {}
   ```

```
@property (nonatomic, retain) NSString * name;
@property (nonatomic, retain) NSNumber * score;

@end


//Hiscore.m
#import "Hiscore.h"

@implementation Hiscore

@dynamic name;
@dynamic score;

@end
```

2. After adding this class right click on your project and select **Add > New File**. Under **iOS** and under **Resource** select and create a new **Data Model**.

3. Name this data model `hiscore` and add your existing `Hiscore` class to this data model when you are prompted.

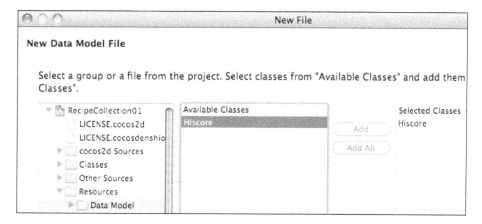

4. Click on `hiscores.xcdatamodel` in XCode. Click on the `Hiscore` entity and then add two new properties to it which correspond to the two properties in your `Hiscore` class:

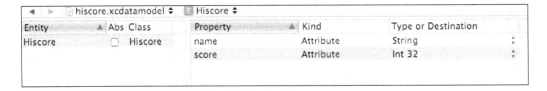

Now we're ready to get down to some code. Execute the following:

```objc
#import <UIKit/UIKit.h>
#import "Hiscore.h"

@interface Ch2_SavingDataCoreData : SimpleTimedGameRecipe
<NSFetchedResultsControllerDelegate>
{
    NSManagedObjectModel *managedObjectModel;
    NSManagedObjectContext *managedObjectContext;
    NSPersistentStoreCoordinator *persistentStoreCoordinator;
}

@property (nonatomic, retain, readonly) NSManagedObjectModel
*managedObjectModel;
@property (nonatomic, retain, readonly) NSManagedObjectContext
*managedObjectContext;
@property (nonatomic, retain, readonly) NSPersistentStoreCoordinator
*persistentStoreCoordinator;

@end

@implementation Ch2_SavingDataCoreData

-(CCLayer*) runRecipe {
  [self loadHiScores];

  return self;
}

/* Returns the managed object context for the application.
If the context doesn't already exist, it is created and bound to the
persistent store coordinator for the application. */
- (NSManagedObjectContext *) managedObjectContext {
  //Return the managedObjectContext if it already exists
```

```objc
  if (managedObjectContext != nil) {
    return managedObjectContext;
}

  //Init the managedObjectContext
  NSPersistentStoreCoordinator *coordinator = [self
persistentStoreCoordinator];
  if (coordinator != nil) {
    managedObjectContext = [[NSManagedObjectContext alloc] init];
    [managedObjectContext setPersistentStoreCoordinator: coordinator];
  }
  return managedObjectContext;
}


/* Returns the managed object model for the application.
If the model doesn't already exist, it is created by merging all of
the models found in the application bundle. */
- (NSManagedObjectModel *)managedObjectModel {
  //Return the managedObjectModel if it already exists
    if (managedObjectModel != nil) {
        return managedObjectModel;
    }

  //Init the managedObjectModel
  managedObjectModel = [[NSManagedObjectModel
mergedModelFromBundles:nil] retain];
  return managedObjectModel;
}


/* Returns the persistent store coordinator for the application.
 If the coordinator doesn't already exist, it is created and the
application's store added to it. */
- (NSPersistentStoreCoordinator *)persistentStoreCoordinator {
  //Return the persistentStoreCoordinator if it already exists
  if (persistentStoreCoordinator != nil) {
    return persistentStoreCoordinator;
  }

  //Our file name
  NSString *fileName = @"memory.sqlite";

  //We get our file path
  NSArray *paths = NSSearchPathForDirectoriesInDomains(NSDocumentDirec
tory, NSUserDomainMask, YES);
  NSString *documentsDirectory = [paths objectAtIndex:0];
```

```
    NSString *filePath = [documentsDirectory stringByAppendingPathCompon
ent:fileName];
    NSURL *filePathURL = [NSURL fileURLWithPath:filePath];

  //Init the persistentStoreCoordinator
  persistentStoreCoordinator = [[NSPersistentStoreCoordinator alloc]
initWithManagedObjectModel:[self managedObjectModel]];
    [persistentStoreCoordinator addPersistentStoreWithType:NSSQLiteStore
Type configuration:nil URL:filePathURL options:nil error:nil];

  return persistentStoreCoordinator;
}
-(void) loadHiScores {
  //Initialization
  managedObjectContext = self.managedObjectContext;

  //Attempt to create SQLite database
  NSEntityDescription *entity;
  @try{
    //Define our table/entity to use
    entity = [NSEntityDescription entityForName:@"Hiscore" inManagedOb
jectContext:managedObjectContext];

  }@catch (NSException *exception){
    NSLog(@"Caught %@: %@", [exception name], [exception reason]);

    //Copy SQLite template because creation failed
    NSString *fileName = @"memory.sqlite";
    NSString *templateName = @"memory_template.sqlite";

    //File paths
    NSArray *paths = NSSearchPathForDirectoriesInDomains(NSDocumentDir
ectory, NSUserDomainMask, YES);
    NSString *documentsDirectory = [paths objectAtIndex:0];
    NSString *filePath = [documentsDirectory stringByAppendingPathComp
onent:fileName];

    if(![[NSFileManager defaultManager] fileExistsAtPath:filePath]){
      //If file doesn't exist in document directory create a new one
from the template
      [[NSFileManager defaultManager] copyItemAtPath:getActualPath(te
mplateName)
         toPath:[NSString stringWithFormat:@"%@/%@",
documentsDirectory, fileName] error:nil];
```

```
    }

    //Finally define our table/entity to use
    entity = [NSEntityDescription entityForName:@"Hiscore" inManagedOb
jectContext:managedObjectContext];
  }

  //Set up the fetch request
  NSFetchRequest *request = [[NSFetchRequest alloc] init];
  [request setEntity:entity];

  //Define how we will sort the records with a descriptor
  NSSortDescriptor *sortDescriptor = [[NSSortDescriptor alloc]
initWithKey:@"score" ascending:NO];
  NSArray *sortDescriptors = [NSArray arrayWithObject:sortDescriptor];
  [request setSortDescriptors:sortDescriptors];
  [sortDescriptor release];

  //Init hiScores
  hiScores = [[managedObjectContext executeFetchRequest:request
error:nil] mutableCopy];

  //Add an intial score if necessary
  if(hiScores.count < 1){
    currentScore = 0;
    currentPlayerName = @"Player1";
    [self addHiScore];
    hiScores = [[managedObjectContext executeFetchRequest:request
error:nil] mutableCopy];
  }

  //Set the hi score
  Hiscore *highest = [hiScores objectAtIndex:0];
  hiScore = [highest.score intValue];
}

-(void) addHiScore {
  bool hasScore = NO;

  //Add score if player's name already exists
  for(id score in hiScores){
    Hiscore *hiscore = (Hiscore*)score;
    if([hiscore.name isEqualToString:currentPlayerName]){
      hasScore = YES;
      if(currentScore > [hiscore.score intValue]){
```

```
          hiscore.score = [NSNumber numberWithInt:currentScore];
      }
    }
  }

  //Add new score if player's name doesn't exist
  if(!hasScore){
    Hiscore *hiscoreObj = (Hiscore *)[NSEntityDescription insertNewOb
jectForEntityForName:@"Hiscore" inManagedObjectContext:managedObjectC
ontext];
    [hiscoreObj setName:currentPlayerName];
    [hiscoreObj setScore:[NSNumber numberWithInt:currentScore]];
    [hiScores addObject:hiscoreObj];
  }

  //Save managedObjectContext
  [managedObjectContext save:nil];
}

-(void) deleteHiScores {
  //Delete all Hi Score objects
  NSFetchRequest * allHiScores = [[NSFetchRequest alloc] init];
  [allHiScores setEntity:[NSEntityDescription entityForName:@"Hiscore"
inManagedObjectContext:managedObjectContext]];
  [allHiScores setIncludesPropertyValues:NO]; //only fetch the
managedObjectID

  NSArray * hs = [managedObjectContext executeFetchRequest:allHiScores
error:nil];
  [allHiScores release];
  for (NSManagedObject *h in hs) {
    [managedObjectContext deleteObject:h];
  }

  //Our file name
  NSString *fileName = @"memory.sqlite";

  //We get our file path
  NSArray *paths = NSSearchPathForDirectoriesInDomains(NSDocumentDirec
tory, NSUserDomainMask, YES);
  NSString *documentsDirectory = [paths objectAtIndex:0];
  NSString *filePath = [documentsDirectory stringByAppendingPathCompon
ent:fileName];

  //Delete our file
```

```
    [[NSFileManager defaultManager] removeItemAtPath:filePath
   error:nil];

    [message setString:@"Hi scores deleted!"];

    hiScore = 0;
    [hiScores removeAllObjects];
    [hiScores release];
    hiScores = nil;

    //Finally, load clean hi scores
    [self loadHiScores];
   }

   @end
```

How it works...

After some complex initialization, we are able to manipulate a simple array of `Hiscore` objects using the following code:

```
NSFetchRequest *request = [[NSFetchRequest alloc] init];
[request setEntity:entity];

//Define how we will sort the records with a descriptor
NSSortDescriptor *sortDescriptor = [[NSSortDescriptor alloc]
initWithKey:@"score" ascending:NO];
NSArray *sortDescriptors = [NSArray arrayWithObject:sortDescriptor];
[request setSortDescriptors:sortDescriptors];
[sortDescriptor release];

//Load hiScores
hiScores = [[managedObjectContext executeFetchRequest:request
error:nil] mutableCopy];
```

After modifying any of these objects we can save them all with the following line:

```
[managedObjectContext save:nil];
```

New entries can be added using the following code:

```
Hiscore *hiscoreObj = (Hiscore *)[NSEntityDescription insertNewObject
ForEntityForName:@"Hiscore" inManagedObjectContext:managedObjectConte
xt];
    [hiscoreObj setName:currentPlayerName];
    [hiscoreObj setScore:[NSNumber numberWithInt:currentScore]];
    [hiScores addObject:hiscoreObj];
```

A more complex use or explanation of Core Data is outside the scope of this book. This example serves merely as a working introduction to using Core Data.

There's more...

Getting Core Data to work properly in XCode can sometimes be somewhat tricky.

- ▸ SQLite database creation errors:

  Depending on the circumstances, Core Data may fail to create a SQLite database from the model you've created. To fix this problem make sure your xcdatamodel files and your NSManagedObject classes are located in the same folder on the disk as well as in the same XCode group. If this doesn't fix the problem delete these files from the project but not the disk then re-add them. If that doesn't work you can also create a SQLite database manually. This requires you to follow Core Data conventions. To help with this process, I've included the file memory_template. sqlite. This file has the correct Core Data database structure. The recipe will also use this file if it fails to create the SQLite database.

- ▸ Handling errors:

  In a number of examples we specify error:nil. To actually handle any of these errors do the following:

  ```
  NSError *error = nil;
  if (![hiscore.managedObjectContext save:&error]) {
      NSLog(@"Unresolved error %@, %@", error, [error userInfo]);
      exit(-1);
  }
  ```

Using Core Data can often seem like overkill. However, applications with complex underlying data structures can benefit from the level of abstraction and robust toolset Core Data provides.

4
Physics

In this chapter, we will cover the following points:

- ▶ Box2D setup and debug drawing
- ▶ Creating collision response routines
- ▶ Using different shapes
- ▶ Dragging and collision filtering
- ▶ Manipulating physical properties
- ▶ Applying impulses
- ▶ Applying forces
- ▶ Asynchronous body destruction
- ▶ Using joints
- ▶ Creating a vehicle
- ▶ Character movement
- ▶ Simulating bullets
- ▶ Simulating and rendering a rope
- ▶ Creating a top-down isometric game engine

Introduction

For years, physics engines have been used in video games to add a sense of realism to the action onscreen. In many games, physics plays a crucial role within the gameplay. Cocos2d comes bundled with two popular 2D physics engines: **Box2D** and **Chipmunk**. In this chapter, we will explain the most common uses of physics in games using Box2D as our engine of choice. Most of the recipes here can be easily modified to use Chipmunk or any other similar physics engine.

Box2D setup and debug drawing

In our first physics recipe, we will explore the basics of creating a Box2D project and setting up a Box2D world. The example creates a scene that allows the user to create realistic 2D blocks.

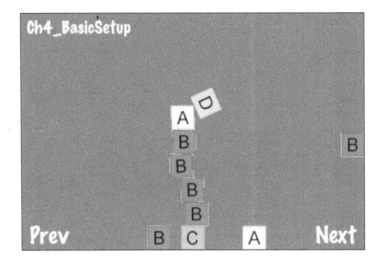

Getting ready

Please refer to the project *RecipeCollection02* for full working code of this recipe.

How to do it...

The first thing we need to do is create a Box2D project using the built-in Box2D project template:

1. Go to **File | New Project**.
2. Under **User Templates** click on **Cocos2d**.
3. Now, right click on **Cocos2d Box2d Application**.

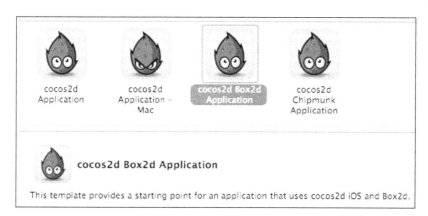

This template provides a starting point for an application that uses cocos2d iOS and Box2d.

4. Click **Choose**, name your project, and hit **Save**.

Now, execute the following code:

```
#import "Box2D.h"
#import "GLES-Render.h"

//32 pixels = 1 meter
#define PTM_RATIO 32

@implementation Ch4_BasicSetup

-(CCLayer*) runRecipe {
  [super runRecipe];

  /* Box2D Initialization */

//Set gravity
  b2Vec2 gravity;
  gravity.Set(0.0f, -10.0f);

  //Initialize world
  bool doSleep = YES;
  world = new b2World(gravity, doSleep);
  world->SetContinuousPhysics(YES);

  //Initialize debug drawing
  m_debugDraw = new GLESDebugDraw( PTM_RATIO );
  world->SetDebugDraw(m_debugDraw);
  uint32 flags = 0;
  flags += b2DebugDraw::e_shapeBit;
```

```
  m_debugDraw->SetFlags(flags);

  //Create level boundaries
  [self addLevelBoundaries];

  //Add batch node for block creation
  CCSpriteBatchNode *batch = [CCSpriteBatchNode
batchNodeWithFile:@"blocks.png" capacity:150];
  [self addChild:batch z:0 tag:0];

  //Add a new block
  CGSize screenSize = [CCDirector sharedDirector].winSize;
  [self addNewSpriteWithCoords:ccp(screenSize.width/2, screenSize.
height/2)];

  //Schedule step method
  [self schedule:@selector(step:)];

  return self;
}

/* Adds a polygonal box around the screen */
-(void) addLevelBoundaries {
  CGSize screenSize = [CCDirector sharedDirector].winSize;

  //Create the body
  b2BodyDef groundBodyDef;
  groundBodyDef.position.Set(0, 0);
  b2Body *body = world->CreateBody(&groundBodyDef);

  //Create a polygon shape
  b2PolygonShape groundBox;

  //Add four fixtures each with a single edge
  groundBox.SetAsEdge(b2Vec2(0,0), b2Vec2(screenSize.width/PTM_
RATIO,0));
  body->CreateFixture(&groundBox,0);

  groundBox.SetAsEdge(b2Vec2(0,screenSize.height/PTM_RATIO),
b2Vec2(screenSize.width/PTM_RATIO,screenSize.height/PTM_RATIO));
  body->CreateFixture(&groundBox,0);

  groundBox.SetAsEdge(b2Vec2(0,screenSize.height/PTM_RATIO),
b2Vec2(0,0));
```

```
  body->CreateFixture(&groundBox,0);

  groundBox.SetAsEdge(b2Vec2(screenSize.width/PTM_RATIO,screenSize.
height/PTM_RATIO), b2Vec2(screenSize.width/PTM_RATIO,0));
  body->CreateFixture(&groundBox,0);
}

/* Adds a textured block */
-(void) addNewSpriteWithCoords:(CGPoint)p {
  CCSpriteBatchNode *batch = (CCSpriteBatchNode*) [self
getChildByTag:0];

  //Add randomly textured block
  int idx = (CCRANDOM_0_1() > .5 ? 0:1);
  int idy = (CCRANDOM_0_1() > .5 ? 0:1);
  CCSprite *sprite = [CCSprite spriteWithBatchNode:batch
rect:CGRectMake(32 * idx,32 * idy,32,32)];
  [batch addChild:sprite];
  sprite.position = ccp( p.x, p.y);

  //Define body definition and create body
  b2BodyDef bodyDef;
  bodyDef.type = b2_dynamicBody;
  bodyDef.position.Set(p.x/PTM_RATIO, p.y/PTM_RATIO);
  bodyDef.userData = sprite;
  b2Body *body = world->CreateBody(&bodyDef);

  //Define another box shape for our dynamic body.
  b2PolygonShape dynamicBox;
  dynamicBox.SetAsBox(.5f, .5f);//These are mid points for our 1m box

  //Define the dynamic body fixture.
  b2FixtureDef fixtureDef;
  fixtureDef.shape = &dynamicBox;
  fixtureDef.density = 1.0f;
  fixtureDef.friction = 0.3f;
  body->CreateFixture(&fixtureDef);
}

/* Draw debug data */
-(void) draw {
  //Disable textures
  glDisable(GL_TEXTURE_2D);
  glDisableClientState(GL_COLOR_ARRAY);
```

```
  glDisableClientState(GL_TEXTURE_COORD_ARRAY);

  //Draw debug data
  world->DrawDebugData();

  //Re-enable textures
  glEnable(GL_TEXTURE_2D);
  glEnableClientState(GL_COLOR_ARRAY);
  glEnableClientState(GL_TEXTURE_COORD_ARRAY);
}

/* Update graphical positions using physical positions */
-(void) step: (ccTime) dt {
  //Set velocity and position iterations
  int32 velocityIterations = 8;
  int32 positionIterations = 3;

  //Steo the Box2D world
  world->Step(dt, velocityIterations, positionIterations);

  //Update sprite position and rotation to fit physical bodies
  for (b2Body* b = world->GetBodyList(); b; b = b->GetNext()) {
    if (b->GetUserData() != NULL) {
      CCSprite *obj = (CCSprite*)b->GetUserData();
      obj.position = CGPointMake( b->GetPosition().x * PTM_RATIO,
b->GetPosition().y * PTM_RATIO);
      obj.rotation = -1 * CC_RADIANS_TO_DEGREES(b->GetAngle());
    }
  }
}

/* Tap to add a block */
- (void)ccTouchesEnded:(NSSet *)touches withEvent:(UIEvent *)event {
  for( UITouch *touch in touches ) {
    CGPoint location = [touch locationInView: [touch view]];
    location = [[CCDirector sharedDirector] convertToGL: location];
    [self addNewSpriteWithCoords: location];
  }
}

@end
```

How it works...

The Box2D sample project is a simple way to understand what a physics system looks like.

▸ Initialization:

Upon initialization of the `b2World` object, we set a few things including gravity, object **sleeping**, and continuous physics. Sleeping allows bodies that are at rest to take up less system resources. Gravity is typically set to a negative number in the Y direction but can be reset at any time using the following method on `b2World`:

```
void SetGravity(const b2Vec2& gravity);
```

In addition to storing a pointer to the main `b2World` instance, we also usually store a pointer to an instance of `GLESDebugDraw`.

▸ Debug drawing:

Debug drawing is handled by the `GLESDebugDraw` class as defined in `GLES-Render.h`. Debug drawing encompasses drawing five different elements onscreen. These include **shapes**, **joint** connections, **AABB**s (axis-aligned bounding boxes), **broad-phase** pairs, and a **center of mass** bit.

▸ Visual to physical drawing ratio:

We define the constant `PTM_RATIO` at 32, to allow consistent conversion between the physical world and the visual world. **PTM** stands for **pixel to meter**. Box2D measures bodies in meters and is built and optimized to work with bodies between the sizes of 0.1 to 10.0 meters. Setting this ratio to 32 is a common convention for optimal shapes to appear between 3.2 to 320 pixels on screen. Optimization aside, there is no upper or lower limit to Box2D body size.

▸ Level boundaries:

In this and many future examples, we add a level boundary roughly encompassing the entire screen. This is handled with the creation of a `b2Body` object with four **fixtures**. Each fixture has a `b2Polygon` shape that defines a single **edge**. Creating an edge typically involves the following:

```
b2BodyDef bodyDef;
bodyDef.position.Set(0, 0);
b2Body *body = world->CreateBody(&bodyDef);
b2PolygonShape poly;
poly.SetAsEdge(b2Vec2(0,0), b2Vec2(480/PTM_RATIO,0));
body->CreateFixture(&poly,0);
```

Because these edges have no corresponding visual components (they are invisible), we do not need to set the `bodyDef.userData` pointer.

▶ Creating the blocks:

Blocks are created much in the same way that the level boundaries are created. Instead of calling `SetAsEdge`, we call `SetAsBox` to create a box-shaped polygon. We then set the `density` and `friction` attributes of the **fixture**. We also set `bodyDef.userData` to point to the `CCSprite` we created. This links the visual and the physical, and allows our `step:` method to reposition sprites as necessary.

▶ Scheduling the world step:

Finally, we schedule our `step` method. In this method, we run one discrete `b2World` step using the following code:

```
int32 velocityIterations = 8;
int32 positionIterations = 3;
world->Step(dt, velocityIterations, positionIterations);
```

The Box2D `world` `Step` method moves the physics engine forward one step. The Box2D constraint solver runs in two phases: the velocity phase and position phase. These determine how fast the bodies move and where they are in the game world. Setting these variables higher results in a more accurate simulation at the cost of speed. Setting `velocityIterations` to 8 and `positionIterations` to 3 is the suggested baseline in the Box2D manual. Using the `dt` variable syncs the logical timing of the application with the physical timing. If a game step takes an inordinate amount of time, the physics system will move forward quickly to compensate. This is referred to as a **variable time step**. An alternative to this would be a **fixed time step** set to 1/60th of a second. In addition to the physical step, we also reposition and re-orientate all `CCSprites` according to their respective `b2Body` positions and rotations:

```
for (b2Body* b = world->GetBodyList(); b; b = b->GetNext()) {
  if (b->GetUserData() != NULL) {
    CCSprite *obj = (CCSprite*)b->GetUserData();
    obj.position = CGPointMake( b->GetPosition().x * PTM_RATIO,
b->GetPosition().y * PTM_RATIO);
    obj.rotation = -1 * CC_RADIANS_TO_DEGREES(b->GetAngle());
  }
}
```

Taken together, these pieces of code sync the physical world with the visual.

Creating collision response routines

To make efficient and organized use of Box2D, we must create a few wrapper classes to encapsulate specific functionality. In this recipe, we will use these classes to add collision response routines to our simple falling block demo from the previous recipe.

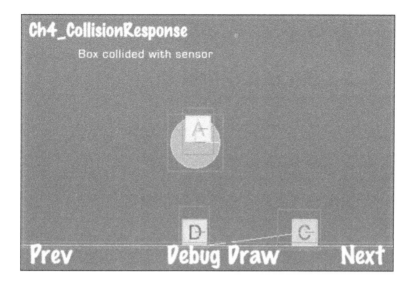

Getting ready

Please refer to the project *RecipeCollection02* for full working code of this recipe. Also, note that some code has been omitted for brevity.

How to do it...

Execute the following code:

```
/* GameObject.h */

@interface GameObject : CCNode {
  @public
    GameArea2D *gameArea; b2Body *body;      b2BodyDef *bodyDef;
    b2FixtureDef *fixtureDef; b2PolygonShape *polygonShape;
    b2CircleShape *circleShape; CCSprite *sprite;
    int typeTag; bool markedForDestruction;
}

/* GameSensor.h */

@interface GameSensor : GameObject {}
@property (readonly) int type;
@end

/* GameMisc.h */
```

```objc
@interface GameMisc : GameObject {
  @public
    float life;
}
@property (readonly) int type;
@property (readwrite, assign) float life;

@end

/* BasicContactListener.h */

class basicContactListener : public b2ContactListener
{
  public:
    void BeginContact(b2Contact* contact);
};

void basicContactListener::BeginContact(b2Contact* contact)
{
  b2Body *bodyA = contact->GetFixtureA()->GetBody();
  b2Body *bodyB = contact->GetFixtureB()->GetBody();

  //Handle collision using your custom routine
  if(bodyA and bodyB){
    GameObject *objA = (GameObject*)bodyA->GetUserData();
    GameObject *objB = (GameObject*)bodyB->GetUserData();
    GameArea2D *gameArea = (GameArea2D*)objA.gameArea;
    [gameArea handleCollisionWithObjA:objA withObjB:objB];
  }
}

/* GameArea2D.h */

@implementation GameArea2D

-(CCLayer*) runRecipe {
  /* CODE OMITTED */

  //Add contact filter and contact listener
  world->SetContactListener(new basicContactListener);

  /* CODE OMITTED */

  //Add button to hide/show debug drawing
```

```objc
  CCMenuItemFont* swapDebugDrawMIF = [CCMenuItemFont
itemFromString:@"Debug Draw" target:self selector:@
selector(swapDebugDraw)];
  CCMenu *swapDebugDrawMenu = [CCMenu menuWithItems:swapDebugDrawMIF,
nil];
      swapDebugDrawMenu.position = ccp( 260 , 20 );
      [self addChild:swapDebugDrawMenu z:5];

  //Schedule our every tick method call
  [self schedule:@selector(step:)];

  return self;
}


/* This is called from 'basicContactListener'. It will need to be
overridden. */
-(void) handleCollisionWithObjA:(GameObject*)objA
withObjB:(GameObject*)objB {
  /** ABSTRACT **/
}


/* Destroy the world upon exit */
- (void) dealloc {
  delete world;  world = NULL;
  delete m_debugDraw;
  [super dealloc];
}


/* Debug information is drawn over everything */
-(void) initDebugDraw {
  DebugDrawNode * ddn = [DebugDrawNode createWithWorld:world];
  [ddn setPosition:ccp(0,0)];
  [gameNode addChild:ddn z:100000];
}


/* When we show debug draw we add a number of flags to show specific
information */
-(void) showDebugDraw {
  debugDraw = YES;

  uint32 flags = 0;
  flags += b2DebugDraw::e_shapeBit;
  flags += b2DebugDraw::e_jointBit;
  flags += b2DebugDraw::e_aabbBit;
  flags += b2DebugDraw::e_pairBit;
```

```
      flags += b2DebugDraw::e_centerOfMassBit;
    m_debugDraw->SetFlags(flags);
}
@end


@implementation Ch4_CollisionResponse

-(CCLayer*) runRecipe {
  /* CODE OMITTED */

  //Create circular GameSensor object
  GameSensor *gameObjSensor = [[GameSensor alloc] init];
  gameObjSensor.gameArea = self;

  //Create the body definition
  gameObjSensor.bodyDef->type = b2_staticBody;
  gameObjSensor.bodyDef->position.Set(240/PTM_RATIO,160/PTM_RATIO);
  gameObjSensor.bodyDef->userData = gameObjSensor;

  //Create the body
  gameObjSensor.body = world->CreateBody(gameObjSensor.bodyDef);

  //Create the shape and fixture
  gameObjSensor.circleShape = new b2CircleShape();
  gameObjSensor.circleShape->m_radius = 1.0f;

  //Create the fixture definition
  gameObjSensor.fixtureDef->shape = gameObjSensor.circleShape;
  gameObjSensor.fixtureDef->isSensor = YES;

  //Create the fixture
  gameObjSensor.body->CreateFixture(gameObjSensor.fixtureDef);

  //Create level boundaries
  [self addLevelBoundaries];

  //Add block batch sprite
  CCSpriteBatchNode *batch = [CCSpriteBatchNode
batchNodeWithFile:@"blocks.png" capacity:150];
  [gameNode addChild:batch z:0 tag:0];

  return self;
```

```objc
}

/* Our base collision handling routine */
-(void) handleCollisionWithObjA:(GameObject*)objA
withObjB:(GameObject*)objB {
  //SENSOR to MISC collision
  if(objA.type == GO_TYPE_SENSOR && objB.type == GO_TYPE_MISC){
    [self handleCollisionWithSensor:(GameSensor*)objA
withMisc:(GameMisc*)objB];
  }else if(objA.type == GO_TYPE_MISC && objB.type == GO_TYPE_SENSOR){
    [self handleCollisionWithSensor:(GameSensor*)objB
withMisc:(GameMisc*)objA];
  }

  //MISC to MISC collision
  else if(objA.type == GO_TYPE_MISC && objB.type == GO_TYPE_MISC){
    [self handleCollisionWithMisc:(GameMisc*)objA withMisc:(GameMisc*)
objB];
  }
}


/* Handling collision between specific types of objects */
-(void) handleCollisionWithSensor:(GameSensor*)sensor
withMisc:(GameMisc*)misc {
  [message setString:@"Box collided with sensor"];

  [self runAction:[CCSequence actions:[CCDelayTime
actionWithDuration:0.5f],
    [CCCallFunc actionWithTarget:self selector:@
selector(resetMessage)], nil]];
}

-(void) handleCollisionWithMisc:(GameMisc*)a withMisc:(GameMisc*)b {
  [message setString:@"Box collided with another box"];

  [self runAction:[CCSequence actions:[CCDelayTime
actionWithDuration:0.5f],
    [CCCallFunc actionWithTarget:self selector:@
selector(resetMessage)], nil]];
}

/* Adding a new block */
-(void) addNewObjectWithCoords:(CGPoint)p {
  /* CODE OMITTED */
```

```
  }

- (void)ccTouchesEnded:(NSSet *)touches withEvent:(UIEvent *)event {
    for( UITouch *touch in touches ) {
      CGPoint location = [touch locationInView: [touch view]];
      location = [[CCDirector sharedDirector] convertToGL: location];
      [self addNewObjectWithCoords: location];
    }
  }
}

@end
```

How it works...

This recipe lays the groundwork for the rest of this chapter. Here, we see the same block creation recipe from before except now a message is printed on the screen when either blocks collide with each other or they collide with a **sensor**.

- ▶ GameObject:

  The GameObject class encapsulates Box2D data structures to help ease the process of Box2D object creation. It also includes a pointer back to its parent GameArea object as well as some other information we will use later. GameObject is intended to be an abstract base class that should be extended for specific uses.

- ▶ Sensors:

  A **fixture** attached to a b2Body can be set to 'sensor mode'. This allows collision response routines to run without the body actually existing in the world physically. No physical collision response will occur. We've encapsulated this functionality in the GameSensor class. An object of this class can be differentiated from other objects by checking its type property.

- ▶ GameMisc:

  The GameMisc class exists as an example of a typical extension of GameObject. The only added functionality in GameMisc is the life variable that we will use in later recipes.

▸ `GameArea2D`:

The `GameArea2D` class is where the action happens. Here, we encapsulate most of the functionality outlined in the previous recipe. In addition to that, we have an instance of `DebugDrawNode` and an instance of `CCNode` entitled `gameNode`. These allow us to draw our debug information and our game information separately from the main scene. This feature will come in handy as recipes become more complex.

▸ Contact listeners:

The class `b2ContactListener` is commonly overridden to allow for custom collision response handling. We extend `b2ContentListener` to create the `basicContentListener` class. There are four methods that can be extended to detect collision at a number of different intervals:

```
void BeginContact(b2Contact* contact);
void EndContact(b2Contact* contact);
void PreSolve(b2Contact* contact, const b2Manifold* oldManifold);
void PostSolve(b2Contact* contact, const b2ContactImpulse* impulse);
```

The methods `BeginContact` and `EndContact` are fairly self-explanatory. The former is called when two fixtures begin to touch, the latter when they cease to touch. The `PreSolve` and `PostSolve` methods are called before and after the contact solver routine runs. We will use this functionality in a later recipe. For this recipe, we are only concerned with `BeginContact`. In this method, we retrieve two `GameObject` instances from `body->GetUserData()` and we pass them to the following method in the corresponding `GameArea` instance:

```
-(void) handleCollisionWithObjA:(GameObject*)objA
withObjB:(GameObject*)objB;
```

That method checks object types and finally displays different messages onscreen.

There's More...

In this example, blocks are colliding with a static sensor. The sensor does not move because its body `type` attribute is set to `b2_staticBody`. Static bodies never move and they do not collide with each other. Each block has its `type` attribute set to `b2_dynamicBody`. Dynamic bodies move freely and collide with all other bodies.

Using different shapes

The primary attribute a Box2D body has is its shape. Box2D uses two classes, `b2PolygonShape` and `b2CircleShape`, to represent any possible shape. In this recipe, we will create a number of different shapes.

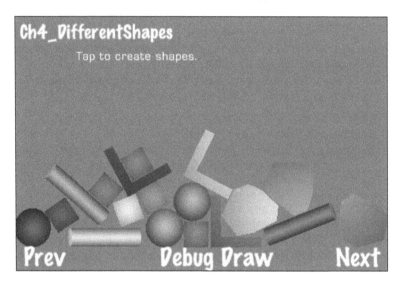

Getting ready

Please refer to the project *RecipeCollection02* for full working code of this recipe.

How to do it...

Execute the following code:

```
@implementation Ch4_DifferentShapes
/* Here add an object randomly chosen from a rectangle, square,
circle, convex polygon and multi-fixture concave polygon. */

-(void) addNewObjectWithCoords:(CGPoint)p
{
  //Initialize the object
  GameMisc *obj = [[GameMisc alloc] init];
  obj.gameArea = self;

  obj.bodyDef->type = b2_dynamicBody;
  obj.bodyDef->position.Set(p.x/PTM_RATIO, p.y/PTM_RATIO);
  obj.bodyDef->userData = obj;
```

```
    obj.body = world->CreateBody(obj.bodyDef);

    obj.fixtureDef->density = 1.0f;
    obj.fixtureDef->friction = 0.3f;
    obj.fixtureDef->restitution = 0.2f;

    //Pick a random shape, size and texture
    int num = arc4random()%5;

    if(num == 0){
      /* Create square object */
      /* CODE OMITTED */

      //Create shape, add to fixture def and finally create the fixture
      obj.polygonShape = new b2PolygonShape();
      obj.polygonShape->SetAsBox(shapeSize/PTM_RATIO, shapeSize/PTM_
RATIO);
      obj.fixtureDef->shape = obj.polygonShape;
      obj.body->CreateFixture(obj.fixtureDef);
    }else if(num == 1){
      /* Create circle object */
      /* CODE OMITTED */

      //Create shape, add to fixture def and finally create the fixture
      obj.circleShape = new b2CircleShape();
      obj.circleShape->m_radius = shapeSize/PTM_RATIO;
      obj.fixtureDef->shape = obj.circleShape;
      obj.fixtureDef->restitution = 0.9f;
      obj.body->CreateFixture(obj.fixtureDef);
    }else if(num == 2){
      /* Create rectangle object */
      /* CODE OMITTED */

      //Create shape, add to fixture def and finally create the fixture
      obj.polygonShape = new b2PolygonShape();
      obj.polygonShape->SetAsBox(shapeSize.x/PTM_RATIO, shapeSize.y/
PTM_RATIO);
      obj.fixtureDef->shape = obj.polygonShape;
      obj.body->CreateFixture(obj.fixtureDef);
    }else if(num == 3){
      /* Create convex polygon object */
      /* CODE OMITTED */

      //Create shape, add to fixture def and finally create the fixture
```

```
      obj.polygonShape = new b2PolygonShape();
      obj.polygonShape->Set(vertices, numVerts);
      obj.fixtureDef->shape = obj.polygonShape;
      obj.body->CreateFixture(obj.fixtureDef);
    }else if(num == 4){
      /* Create concave multi-fixture polygon */
      /* CODE OMITTED */

      //Create two opposite rectangles
      for(int i=0; i<2; i++){
        CGPoint shapeSize;
        if(i == 0){ shapeSize = ccp(2.0f, 0.4f);
        }else{ shapeSize = ccp(0.4f, 2.0f); }

        CGPoint vertexArr[] = { ccp(0,0), ccp(shapeSize.x,0),
ccp(shapeSize.x,shapeSize.y), ccp(0,shapeSize.y) };
        int32 numVerts = 4;
        b2Vec2 vertices[4];
        NSMutableArray *vertexArray = [[[NSMutableArray alloc] init]
autorelease];

        //Set vertices
        for(int i=0; i<numVerts; i++){
          vertices[i].Set(vertexArr[i].x, vertexArr[i].y);
          [vertexArray addObject:[NSValue valueWithCGPoint:ccp(vertexArr
[i].x *PTM_RATIO, vertexArr[i].y*PTM_RATIO)]];
        }

        //Create textured polygon
        ccTexParams params = {GL_NEAREST,GL_NEAREST_MIPMAP_NEAREST, GL_
REPEAT,GL_REPEAT};
        CCSprite *sprite = [TexturedPolygon createWithFile:@"box2.png"
withVertices:vertexArray];
        [sprite.texture setTexParameters:&params];
        [sprite setPosition:ccp(0,0)];
        [sprite setColor:color];
        [obj.sprite addChild:sprite];

        //Create shape, set shape and create fixture
        obj.polygonShape = new b2PolygonShape();
        obj.polygonShape->Set(vertices, numVerts);
        obj.fixtureDef->shape = obj.polygonShape;
        obj.body->CreateFixture(obj.fixtureDef);
      }
```

```
    }

    //Set a random color
    [obj.sprite setColor:ccc3(arc4random()%255, arc4random()%255,
arc4random()%255)];
}

- (void)ccTouchesEnded:(NSSet *)touches withEvent:(UIEvent *)event {
    for( UITouch *touch in touches ) {
        CGPoint location = [touch locationInView: [touch view]];
        location = [[CCDirector sharedDirector] convertToGL: location];
        [self addNewObjectWithCoords: location];
    }
}

@end
```

How it works...

In this recipe, we randomly create objects with five different shapes: square, circle, rectangle, an oddly shaped convex polygon, and a simple concave polygon.

▸ Rectangles:

Rectangles are created using the `b2PolygonShape` method `SetAsBox` just like in the first two recipes. In this example, we have a simple textured square as well as a rectangular column image.

▸ Circles:

Circles are a special case in Box2D and they've been given a special class in `b2CircleShape`. After initialization, we simply set the `m_radius` variable of the circle shape. In this example, we also give the circle shaped objects a high `restitution` value to make them bounce. We will cover this in more depth in another recipe.

▸ Convex polygons:

Individual polygons must be **convex**. This means that every angle inside the polygon is less than 180 degrees. For this example, we've created an oddly shaped convex polygon with 8 vertices. We are using `TexturedPolygon` to accurately draw this polygon. For more information about the `TexturedPolygon` class, please refer to *Chapter 1, Graphics*.

▸ Concave polygons:

Concave polygons can be represented by creating multiple convex polygons and linking them to one body using multiple fixtures. In this example, we link two simple convex polygons together by creating two fixtures on the same body. We reverse our width and height values to create a simple L-shaped object. With this technique, you can create arbitrarily complex shapes.

▸ Extensibility of `GameObject`:

The `GameObject` class is primarily designed for single fixture bodies. It contains one `CCSprite` object, one `b2FixtureDef`, and so on. However, as you can see in the concave polygon example, you can create multiple `CCSprite` objects and link them to the main `GameObject` sprite. You can also reuse the Box2D object pointers within the `GameObject` instance to easily create multiple fixtures and shapes.

Dragging and collision filtering

In a previous recipe, we handled user input to allow the user to drag an object. In this example, we see a bowl filled with pieces of fruit that can be dragged across the screen. A piece of fruit does not collide with another piece of fruit.

Getting ready

Please refer to the project *RecipeCollection02* for full working code of this recipe.

How to do it...

Execute the following code:

```
enum {  //Collision bits for filtering
  CB_GROUND = 1<<0,
  CB_FRUIT = 1<<2,
  CB_BOWL = 1<<4
};

@implementation Ch4_DraggingAndFiltering

-(CCLayer*) runRecipe {
  [super runRecipe];
  [message setString:@"Pick up the fruit."];
  //Create level boundaries
  [self addLevelBoundaries];

  //Add fruit bowl
  [self addFruitBasket];

  //Initialization of any variables
  fruitGrabbed = NO;

  return self;
}

/* Add basket and fruit objects */
-(void) addFruitBasket {
  /* Add the basket */

  /* CODE OMITTED */

  //Add physical parts
  b2BodyDef bowlBodyDef;
  bowlBodyDef.position.Set(0, 0);
  bowlBodyDef.type = b2_staticBody;
  b2Body *body = world->CreateBody(&bowlBodyDef);

  b2PolygonShape bowlShape;

  b2FixtureDef bowlFixtureDef;
  bowlFixtureDef.restitution = 0.5f;
  bowlFixtureDef.filter.categoryBits = CB_BOWL;
```

```
  bowlFixtureDef.filter.maskBits = CB_FRUIT;

  //Rim left
  bowlShape.SetAsEdge(b2Vec2(120.0f/PTM_RATIO,120.0f/PTM_RATIO),
b2Vec2(180.0f/PTM_RATIO,0.0f/PTM_RATIO));
  bowlFixtureDef.shape = &bowlShape;
  body->CreateFixture(&bowlFixtureDef);

  /* CODE OMITTED */

  /* Add fruit */
  fruitObjects = [[[NSMutableArray alloc] init] autorelease];

  [self addFruit:@"fruit_banana.png" position:ccp(210,200)
shapeType:@"rect"];
  [self addFruit:@"fruit_apple.png" position:ccp(230,200)
shapeType:@"circle"];
  [self addFruit:@"fruit_grapes.png" position:ccp(250,200)
shapeType:@"rect"];
  [self addFruit:@"fruit_orange.png" position:ccp(270,200)
shapeType:@"circle"];
}

/* Add a fruit object with circle physical properties */
-(void) addFruit:(NSString*)spriteFrame position:(CGPoint)p
shapeType:(NSString*)s {
  //Create GameMisc object
  GameMisc *fruit = [[GameMisc alloc] init];
  fruit.gameArea = self;

  //Define body def and create body
  fruit.bodyDef->type = b2_dynamicBody;
  fruit.bodyDef->position.Set(p.x/PTM_RATIO, p.y/PTM_RATIO);
  fruit.bodyDef->userData = fruit;
  fruit.body = world->CreateBody(fruit.bodyDef);

  //Create fixture def
  fruit.fixtureDef->density = 1.0f;
  fruit.fixtureDef->friction = 0.3f;
  fruit.fixtureDef->restitution = 0.4f;
  fruit.fixtureDef->filter.categoryBits = CB_FRUIT;
  fruit.fixtureDef->filter.maskBits = CB_GROUND | CB_BOWL;      //
Fruit does not collide with other fruit

  //Create sprite
```

```
  fruit.sprite = [CCSprite spriteWithSpriteFrameName:spriteFrame];
  fruit.sprite.position = ccp(p.x,p.y);

  if([s isEqualToString:@"circle"]){
    /* Set fixture shape and sprite scale */
    float textureSize = 160;
    float shapeSize = 40;

    fruit.sprite.scale = shapeSize / textureSize * 2;
    [gameNode addChild:fruit.sprite z:2];

    fruit.circleShape = new b2CircleShape();
    fruit.circleShape->m_radius = shapeSize/PTM_RATIO;
    fruit.fixtureDef->shape = fruit.circleShape;
  }else if([s isEqualToString:@"rect"]){
    /* Set fixture shape and sprite scale */
    CGPoint textureSize = ccp(300,100);
    CGPoint shapeSize = ccp(60,20);

    fruit.sprite.scaleX = shapeSize.x / textureSize.x * 2;
    fruit.sprite.scaleY = shapeSize.y / textureSize.y * 2;

    [gameNode addChild:fruit.sprite z:2];

    fruit.polygonShape = new b2PolygonShape();
    fruit.polygonShape->SetAsBox(shapeSize.x/PTM_RATIO, shapeSize.y/
PTM_RATIO);
    fruit.fixtureDef->shape = fruit.polygonShape;
  }

  //Finally create the fixture
  fruit.body->CreateFixture(fruit.fixtureDef);

  //Add object to container
  [fruitObjects addObject:fruit];
  grabbedFruit = fruit;
}

-(void) ccTouchesBegan:(NSSet *)touches withEvent:(UIEvent *)event {
  UITouch *touch = [touches anyObject];
  CGPoint point = [touch locationInView: [touch view]];
  point = [[CCDirector sharedDirector] convertToGL: point];
```

```
    /* Grab the nearest fruit */

  //We first grab a fruit.
  //Then, if another fruit is closer we grab that until we finally
have the closest one.
  float grabbedDistance = distanceBetweenPoints(point,
ccp(grabbedFruit.body->GetPosition().x*PTM_RATIO, grabbedFruit.body-
>GetPosition().y*PTM_RATIO));
  for(int i=0; i<fruitObjects.count; i++){
    GameMisc *fruit = [fruitObjects objectAtIndex:i];
    float thisDistance = distanceBetweenPoints(ccp(fruit.body-
>GetPosition().x*PTM_RATIO, fruit.body->GetPosition().y*PTM_RATIO),
point);
    if(thisDistance < grabbedDistance){
      grabbedFruit = fruit;
      grabbedDistance = thisDistance;
    }
  }

  //Set the fruit to 'grabbed'
  fruitGrabbed = YES;

  //Immediately move the fruit
  [self ccTouchesMoved:touches withEvent:event];
}

-(void) ccTouchesMoved:(NSSet *)touches withEvent:(UIEvent *)event {
  UITouch *touch = [touches anyObject];
  CGPoint point = [touch locationInView: [touch view]];
  point = [[CCDirector sharedDirector] convertToGL: point];

  /* Reposition the grabbed fruit */
  grabbedFruit.body->SetTransform(b2Vec2(point.x/PTM_RATIO, point.y/
PTM_RATIO), grabbedFruit.body->GetAngle());

  b2Vec2 moveDistance = b2Vec2( (point.x/PTM_RATIO - grabbedFruit.
sprite.position.x/PTM_RATIO), (point.y/PTM_RATIO - grabbedFruit.
sprite.position.y/PTM_RATIO) );
  lastFruitVelocity = b2Vec2(moveDistance.x*20, moveDistance.y*20);
}

-(void) ccTouchesEnded:(NSSet *)touches withEvent:(UIEvent *)event {
  /* Release the fruit */
  fruitGrabbed = NO;
  grabbedFruit.body->SetLinearVelocity(lastFruitVelocity);
```

```
  }

-(void) step: (ccTime) dt {
  [super step:dt];

  /* Suspend the fruit in mid-air while it is grabbed */
  if(fruitGrabbed){
    grabbedFruit.body->SetLinearVelocity(b2Vec2_zero);
  }
}

@end
```

How it works...

In this example, we create a realistic 'grabbing' effect. We achieve this by repositioning the nearest Box2D body with the `SetTransform` method:

```
grabbedFruit.body->SetTransform(b2Vec2(point.x/PTM_RATIO, point.y/PTM_
RATIO), grabbedFruit.body->GetAngle());
```

We then store the previous distance the object was moved, to determine a final velocity and then to allow the object to be 'thrown' when the user lets go. We apply this velocity using the `SetLinearVelocity` method:

```
grabbedFruit.body->SetLinearVelocity(lastFruitVelocity);
```

To suspend fruit in the air while the user has a finger on the screen, we set the object's velocity to `b2Vec2_zero` while it is grabbed.

  ▸ Collision filtering:

     In this example, we don't allow a fruit to collide with other fruits so that they can sit nicely in the bowl. We achieve this by setting the `filter` property on the fruit's fixture. Specifically, we set the `categoryBits` and `maskBits`:

```
enum {
  CB_GROUND = 1<<0,
  CB_FRUIT = 1<<2,
  CB_BOWL = 1<<4
};

fruit.fixtureDef->filter.categoryBits = CB_FRUIT;
fruit.fixtureDef->filter.maskBits = CB_GROUND | CB_BOWL;
```

The `categoryBits` variable indicates what kind of object this is. The `maskBits` variable indicates what kind of objects this should collide with. Both of these properties use **bits** and **Boolean logic** to specify how the object should interact. For example, | means "or". So, we are saying that the `CB_FRUIT` category can collide with `CB_GROUND` or `CB_BOWL` categories. Alternatively, filters can be set using **filter groups**. Also note that, if you do not specify the fixture's `filter` variable on object then it will not collide with an object that has a set filter. For more information about filtering, please refer to the Box2D manual at: `http://www.box2d.org/manual.html`.

Manipulating physical properties

Box2D allows the user to set physical properties on bodies to create a wide array of effects. In this example, we see a block of ice pushing a box down a slope. We also see a number of bouncing balls.

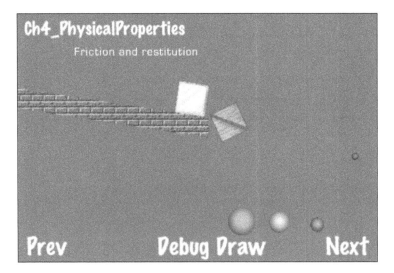

Getting ready

Please refer to the project *RecipeCollection02* for full working code of this recipe.

How to do it...

Execute the following code:

```
@implementation Ch4_PhysicalProperties

-(CCLayer*) runRecipe {
    [super runRecipe];
```

```objc
    [message setString:@"Friction and restitution"];

    //Variable initialization
    movableObjects = [[[NSMutableArray alloc] init] autorelease];
    objectGrabbed = NO;

    //Create level boundaries
    [self addLevelBoundaries];

    /* Add a crate, a block of ice, bouncing balls and a ledge */
    //Crate with 0.4f friction
    [self addBlockWithSpriteFile:@"crate2.png" friction:0.4f
textureSize:64.0f shapeSize:20.0f position:ccp(130,250)];

    //Ice block with 0.0f friction
    [self addBlockWithSpriteFile:@"ice_block.png" friction:0.0f
textureSize:70.0f shapeSize:20.0f position:ccp(10,250)];

    //Ball with size 5.0f and restitution 0.9f
    [self addBallWithShapeSize:5.0f restitution:0.9f
position:ccp(450,200) color:ccc3(255,0,0)];

    //Ball with size 10.0f and restitution 0.8f
    [self addBallWithShapeSize:10.0f restitution:0.8f
position:ccp(400,200) color:ccc3(255,128,0)];

    //Ball with size 15.0f and restitution 0.7f
    [self addBallWithShapeSize:15.0f restitution:0.7f
position:ccp(350,200) color:ccc3(255,255,0)];

    //Ball with size 20.0f and restitution 0.6f
    [self addBallWithShapeSize:20.0f restitution:0.6f
position:ccp(300,200) color:ccc3(0,255,0)];

    //Add brick ledge
    [self addLedge];

    return self;
}

/* Add a block with a certain texture, size, position and friction */
-(void) addBlockWithSpriteFile:(NSString*)file friction:(float)
friction textureSize:(float)textureSize shapeSize:(float)shapeSize
position:(CGPoint)p {
    /* CODE OMITTED */
```

```
  }

  /* Add a ball with a certain size, position, color and restitution */
  -(void) addBallWithShapeSize:(float)shapeSize restitution:(float)
  restitution position:(CGPoint)p color:(ccColor3B)color {
    /* CODE OMITTED */
  }

  /* Add a brick textured ledge polygon to show the blocks sliding down
  */
  -(void) addLedge {
    GameMisc *obj = [[GameMisc alloc] init];
    obj.gameArea = self;

    obj.bodyDef->position.Set(0,100/PTM_RATIO);
    obj.body = world->CreateBody(obj.bodyDef);

    obj.fixtureDef->density = 1.0f;
    obj.fixtureDef->friction = 0.3f;
    obj.fixtureDef->restitution = 0.2f;

    float polygonSize = 4;
    CGPoint vertexArr[] = { ccp(0,0.8f), ccp(2,0.5f), ccp(2,0.7f),
  ccp(0,1) };
    int32 numVerts = 4;
    b2Vec2 vertices[4];

    NSMutableArray *vertexArray = [[[NSMutableArray alloc] init]
  autorelease];

    for(int i=0; i<numVerts; i++){
      vertices[i].Set(vertexArr[i].x*polygonSize,
  vertexArr[i].y*polygonSize);
      [vertexArray addObject:[NSValue valueWithCGPoint:ccp(vertexArr[i].
  x*PTM_RATIO*polygonSize,
        vertexArr[i].y*PTM_RATIO*polygonSize)]];
    }

    ccTexParams params = {GL_NEAREST,GL_NEAREST_MIPMAP_NEAREST,GL_
  REPEAT,GL_REPEAT};
    obj.sprite = [TexturedPolygon createWithFile:@"bricks2.png"
  withVertices:vertexArray];
    [obj.sprite.texture setTexParameters:&params];
    [obj.sprite setPosition:ccp(0,100)];
    [gameNode addChild:obj.sprite z:1];
```

```
obj.polygonShape = new b2PolygonShape();
obj.polygonShape->Set(vertices, numVerts);
obj.fixtureDef->shape = obj.polygonShape;

obj.body->CreateFixture(obj.fixtureDef);
}

@end
```

How it works...

In this example, we see multiple objects each with different physical properties.

►   Density:

   Body **density** determines how much force is required to move an object around. Two objects with different sizes and the same density will have different masses. The larger object will naturally take a larger force to move.

►   Friction:

   Friction determines how difficult an object is to move against another object. Physics nerds may point out the difference between static and kinetic friction. Box2D amalgamates them into one variable while assuming a constant static to kinetic ratio. In our example, the block of ice has absolutely no friction. This means that it will slide around on any surface. This allows the block to slowly push the crate down the ramp until it finally falls on the bouncing balls.

►   Restitution:

   The term **restitution** is interchangeable with elasticity. This measures the 'bounciness' of an object. An object with a restitution of `1.0f` will theoretically bounce forever. In our example, we see four balls each with a different restitution. This causes them to bounce at different rates. To see these differences in action, quickly grab the block of ice before it pushes the crate over the edge of the ledge.

Applying impulses

In Box2D, bodies can be moved around using **impulses** and **forces**. In this recipe, we will use impulses to accurately shoot a basketball into a basketball net.

Getting ready

Please refer to the project *RecipeCollection02* for full working code of this recipe.

How to do it...

Execute the following code:

```
enum {   //Object type tags
  TYPE_OBJ_BASKETBALL = 0,
  TYPE_OBJ_SHOOTER = 1,
  TYPE_OBJ_NET_SENSOR = 2
};

@implementation Ch4_Impulses

-(CCLayer*) runRecipe {
  [super runRecipe];
  [message setString:@"Shoot the ball in the hoop."];

  //Create level boundaries
```

```
  [self addLevelBoundaries];

  //Add level background
  CCSprite *bg = [CCSprite spriteWithFile:@"bball_bg.png"];
  bg.position = ccp(240,160);
  [gameNode addChild:bg z:0];

  //Add basketball
  [self addBasketball];

  //Add basketball net
  [self addBasketballNet];

  //Add shooter
  [self addShooter];

  return self;
}

/* Add a basketball net with a sensor */
-(void) addBasketballNet {
  /* CODE OMITTED */

  //Add net sensor
  GameSensor *gameObjSensor = [[GameSensor alloc] init];
  gameObjSensor.typeTag = TYPE_OBJ_NET_SENSOR;
  gameObjSensor.gameArea = self;

  gameObjSensor.bodyDef->type = b2_staticBody;
  gameObjSensor.bodyDef->position.Set(0,0);
  gameObjSensor.bodyDef->userData = gameObjSensor;
  gameObjSensor.body = world->CreateBody(gameObjSensor.bodyDef);

  gameObjSensor.polygonShape = new b2PolygonShape();
  gameObjSensor.polygonShape->SetAsEdge(b2Vec2(370.0f/PTM_
RATIO,200.0f/PTM_RATIO), b2Vec2(380.0f/PTM_RATIO,200.0f/PTM_RATIO));

  gameObjSensor.fixtureDef->shape = gameObjSensor.polygonShape;
  gameObjSensor.fixtureDef->isSensor = YES;

  gameObjSensor.body->CreateFixture(gameObjSensor.fixtureDef);
}

/* Add a basketball */
```

```objc
-(void) addBasketball {
  /* CODE OMITTED */
}


/* Add a shooter with reverse karate chop action! */
-(void) addShooter {
  /* CODE OMITTED */
}


-(void) ccTouchesBegan:(NSSet *)touches withEvent:(UIEvent *)event {
  UITouch *touch = [touches anyObject];
  CGPoint point = [touch locationInView: [touch view]];
  point = [[CCDirector sharedDirector] convertToGL: point];

  /* Apply an impulse when the user touches the screen */
  CGPoint vect = ccp(point.x - basketball.body->GetPosition().x*PTM_
RATIO, point.y - basketball.body->GetPosition().y*PTM_RATIO);
  basketball.body->ApplyLinearImpulse(b2Vec2(vect.x/20, vect.y/20) ,
basketball.body->GetPosition() );
}


/* Main collision handling routine */
-(void) handleCollisionWithObjA:(GameObject*)objA
withObjB:(GameObject*)objB {
  //SENSOR to MISC collision
  if(objA.type == GO_TYPE_SENSOR && objB.type == GO_TYPE_MISC){
    [self handleCollisionWithSensor:(GameSensor*)objA
withMisc:(GameMisc*)objB];
  }else if(objA.type == GO_TYPE_MISC && objB.type == GO_TYPE_SENSOR){
    [self handleCollisionWithSensor:(GameSensor*)objB
withMisc:(GameMisc*)objA];
  }
}


/* SENSOR to MISC collision */
-(void) handleCollisionWithSensor:(GameSensor*)sensor
withMisc:(GameMisc*)misc {
  if(misc.typeTag == TYPE_OBJ_BASKETBALL && sensor.typeTag == TYPE_
OBJ_NET_SENSOR){
    //Animate the net when the shooter makes a basket
    /* CODE OMITTED */
  }else if(misc.typeTag == TYPE_OBJ_BASKETBALL && sensor.typeTag ==
TYPE_OBJ_SHOOTER){
    //Animate the shooter's arm and apply an impulse when he touches
the ball */
```

```
/* CODE OMITTED */
basketball.body->SetLinearVelocity(b2Vec2(0,0));
basketball.body->ApplyLinearImpulse(b2Vec2(3.5f, 7) , basketball.
body->GetPosition() );
  }
}

@end
```

How it works...

In this scene, we see a basketball player shooting the ball into a basket. When he comes in contact with the ball he shoots it into the net.

▸ Impulses:

When the basketball touches the basketball player, we reset the ball's velocity and then we apply a precise impulse to accurately shoot the ball into the net:

```
basketball.body->SetLinearVelocity(b2Vec2(0,0));
basketball.body->ApplyLinearImpulse(b2Vec2(3.5f, 7) , basketball.
body->GetPosition() );
```

Applying an impulse, immediately changes the **momentum** of the body. Instead of applying a force over time, an impulse applies instantaneous force to immediately redirect an object. Impulses also wake up a sleeping body if necessary.

▸ GameObject typeTag:

Instances of the GameObject class have heretofore been identified with the type property as specified by the extending class. For more granular object identification, you can use the typeTag enumeration. This allows us to tag objects to perform a number of tasks. In this example, we use typeTag during collision response to properly animate the basketball player as well as the basketball net.

Applying forces

Unlike impulses, forces must be applied over time to significantly move a body in the physical world. In this recipe, we see a simulation of our solar system.

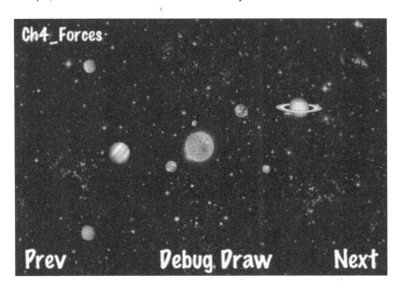

Getting ready

Please refer to the project *RecipeCollection02* for full working code of this recipe.

How to do it...

Execute the following code:

```
@implementation Ch4_Forces

-(CCLayer*) runRecipe {
  [super runRecipe];

  //Set our gravity to 0
  world->SetGravity(b2Vec2(0,0));

  //Level background
  CCSprite *bg = [CCSprite spriteWithFile:@"solar_system_bg.png"];
  bg.position = ccp(240,160);
  [gameNode addChild:bg z:0];
```

```
//Add Planets
  planets = [[[NSMutableDictionary alloc] init] autorelease];
  [[CCSpriteFrameCache sharedSpriteFrameCache]
addSpriteFramesWithFile:@"solar_system.plist"];

  [self addPlanetWithSpriteFrameName:@"sun.png"
position:ccp(240,160)];
  [self addPlanetWithSpriteFrameName:@"mercury.png"
position:ccp(210,160)];
  [self addPlanetWithSpriteFrameName:@"venus.png"
position:ccp(195,160)];
  [self addPlanetWithSpriteFrameName:@"earth.png"
position:ccp(170,160)];
  [self addPlanetWithSpriteFrameName:@"mars.png"
position:ccp(150,160)];
  [self addPlanetWithSpriteFrameName:@"jupiter.png"
position:ccp(120,160)];
  [self addPlanetWithSpriteFrameName:@"saturn.png"
position:ccp(90,160)];
  [self addPlanetWithSpriteFrameName:@"uranus.png"
position:ccp(60,160)];
  [self addPlanetWithSpriteFrameName:@"neptune.png"
position:ccp(30,160)];

  //Apply initial impulses to planets
  [[planets objectForKey:@"mercury.png"] body]->ApplyLinearImpuls
e(b2Vec2(0,0.075f), [[planets objectForKey:@"mercury.png"] body]-
>GetPosition());
  [[planets objectForKey:@"venus.png"] body]->ApplyLinearImpul
se(b2Vec2(0,0.25f), [[planets objectForKey:@"venus.png"] body]-
>GetPosition());
  [[planets objectForKey:@"earth.png"] body]->ApplyLinearImpul
se(b2Vec2(0,0.45f), [[planets objectForKey:@"earth.png"] body]-
>GetPosition());
  [[planets objectForKey:@"mars.png"] body]->ApplyLinearImpulse(b2Vec2
(0,0.175f), [[planets objectForKey:@"mars.png"] body]->GetPosition());
  [[planets objectForKey:@"jupiter.png"] body]-
>ApplyLinearImpulse(b2Vec2(0,1.3f), [[planets objectForKey:@"jupiter.
png"] body]->GetPosition());
  [[planets objectForKey:@"saturn.png"] body]-
>ApplyLinearImpulse(b2Vec2(0,4.5f), [[planets objectForKey:@"saturn.
png"] body]->GetPosition());
  [[planets objectForKey:@"uranus.png"] body]-
>ApplyLinearImpulse(b2Vec2(0,0.6f), [[planets objectForKey:@"uranus.
png"] body]->GetPosition());
```

```
    [[planets objectForKey:@"neptune.png"] body]-
>ApplyLinearImpulse(b2Vec2(0,0.8f), [[planets objectForKey:@"neptune.
png"] body]->GetPosition());

    //Fast forward about 16 seconds to create realistic orbits from the
start
    for(int i=0; i<1000; i++){
        [self step:0.016666667f];
    }

    return self;
}


/* Every tick applies a force on each planet according to how large it
is and how far it is from the sun. This simulates heavenly rotation.
*/
-(void) step:(ccTime)dt {
    [super step:dt];

    GameMisc *sun = [planets objectForKey:@"sun.png"];

    for(id key in planets){
        GameMisc *planet = [planets objectForKey:key];
        if(![key isEqualToString:@"sun.png"]){
            CGPoint vect = ccp(sun.body->GetPosition().x - planet.
body->GetPosition().x, sun.body->GetPosition().y - planet.body-
>GetPosition().y);
            float planetSize = pow([planet.sprite contentSize].width,2);
            float dist = distanceBetweenPoints(ccp(sun.body-
>GetPosition().x, sun.body->GetPosition().y),
                ccp(planet.body->GetPosition().x, planet.body-
>GetPosition().y));

            float mod = dist/planetSize*2000;

            planet.body->ApplyForce(b2Vec2(vect.x/mod, vect.y/mod) , planet.
body->GetPosition() );
        }
    }
}


/* Add a planet with a spriteFrame and a position. We determine the
shape size from the texture size. */
```

```
-(void) addPlanetWithSpriteFrameName:(NSString*)frameName
position:(CGPoint)p {
  /* CODE OMITTED */
}

@end
```

How it works...

In this scene, we see eight planets orbiting the sun. They orbit at roughly the same speed.

▶ Forces:

Each planet is having a constant force applied to it in the direction of the sun:

```
planet.body->ApplyForce(b2Vec2(vect.x/mod, vect.y/mod) , planet.
body->GetPosition() );
```

This, combined with its initial momentum applied by an impulse, creates an orbit around the sun. The forces applied take into account planet size and distance from the sun in a way similar to how real gravity works.

▶ Torque:

When applying a force or an impulse, you must specify the point on the object where the force or impulse is applied. If this is not the exact center of mass, then a **torque** will also be applied to the object. This will change the angular velocity of the body and will make it spin.

▶ Gravity:

As you can see in this example, setting gravity to `b2Vec2(0.0f, 0.0f)` creates a top-down physical simulation.

See also...

Setting gravity to `b2Vec2(0.0f, 0.0f)` creates a top-down simulation. We will use this technique in later recipes, including _Creating a top-down isometric game engine_ found later in this chapter.

Asynchronous body destruction

So far, we have learned how to create bodies, how to reposition them, and how to apply forces and impulses to move them around onscreen. In this example, we will see how to destroy a body during the physics simulation. This is naturally a very tricky process that can create bugs and cause game crashes if you're not careful.

Getting ready

Please refer to the project *RecipeCollection02* for full working code of this recipe. Also note that some of the following code has been omitted for brevity.

How to do it...

Execute the following code:

```
@interface GameObjectCallback : NSObject {
@public
  GameObject *gameObject;
  NSString *callback;
}
@end

@interface QueuedAction : NSObject {
@public
  GameObject* gameObject;
```

```objc
  CCAction* action;
}
@end

@interface GameArea2D : Recipe {
  NSMutableArray *bodiesToDestroy;
  NSMutableArray *postDestructionCallbacks;
  NSMutableArray *bodiesToCreate;
  NSMutableArray *queuedActions;
}

@implementation GameArea2D

-(void) step: (ccTime) dt {
  //Process body destruction/creation
  [self destroyBodies];
  [self createBodies];
  [self runQueuedActions];
}

/* Mark a body for destruction */
-(void) markBodyForDestruction:(GameObject*)obj {
    [bodiesToDestroy addObject:[NSValue valueWithPointer:obj]];
}

/* Destroy queued bodies */
-(void) destroyBodies {
  for(NSValue *value in bodiesToDestroy){
    GameObject *obj = (GameObject*)[value pointerValue];
    if(obj && obj.body && !obj.markedForDestruction){
      obj.body->SetTransform(b2Vec2(0,0),0);
      world->DestroyBody(obj.body);
      obj.markedForDestruction = YES;
    }
  }
  [bodiesToDestroy removeAllObjects];

  //Call all game object callbacks
  for(NSValue *value in postDestructionCallbacks){
    GameObjectCallback  *goc = (GameObjectCallback*)value;
    [goc.gameObject runAction:[CCCallFunc actionWithTarget:goc.
gameObject selector:NSSelectorFromString(goc.callback)]];
  }
```

```
      [postDestructionCallbacks removeAllObjects];
  }

  /* Mark a body for creation */
  -(void) markBodyForCreation:(GameObject*)obj {
    [bodiesToCreate addObject:[NSValue valueWithPointer:obj]];
  }

  /* Create all queued bodies */
  -(void) createBodies {
    for(NSValue *value in bodiesToCreate){
      GameObject *obj = (GameObject*)[value pointerValue];
      obj.body = world->CreateBody(obj.bodyDef);
      obj.body->CreateFixture(obj.fixtureDef);
    }
    [bodiesToCreate removeAllObjects];
  }

  /* Run any queued actions after creation/destruction */
  -(void) runQueuedActions {
    for(NSValue *value in queuedActions){
      QueuedAction *qa = (QueuedAction*)[value pointerValue];
      GameObject *gameObject = (GameObject*)qa.gameObject;
      CCAction *action = (CCAction*)qa.action;

      [gameObject runAction:action];
    }
    [queuedActions removeAllObjects];
  }

  @end

  @implementation Ch4_AsyncBodyDestruction

  -(CCLayer*) runRecipe {
    [super runRecipe];
    [message setString:@"Tap to throw a grenade."];

    //Create level boundaries
    [self addLevelBoundaries];

    //Add gunman
    [self addGunman];
```

```
  //Initialize explosion animation
  [[CCSpriteFrameCache sharedSpriteFrameCache] addSpriteFramesWithFile
:@"explosion5.plist"];

  //Initialize grenade container
  grenades = [[[NSMutableArray alloc] init] autorelease];

  return self;
}

-(void) step:(ccTime)delta {
  [super step:delta];

  //Grenade life cycle
  for(id obj in grenades){
    GameMisc *grenade = (GameMisc*)obj;
    grenade.life -= delta;

    //If a grenade is out of life we mark it for destruction, do
cleanup and finally animate an explosion
    if(grenade.life < 0){
      [self markBodyForDestruction:grenade];
      [grenades removeObject:obj];
      [self explosionAt:grenade.sprite.position];
      [gameNode removeChild:grenade.sprite cleanup:NO];
    }
  }

  //Explosion life cycle
  for(id obj in explosions){
    GameMisc *explosion = (GameMisc*)explosion;
    explosion.life -= delta;

    if(explosion.life < 0){
      [explosions removeObject:explosion];
      [gameNode removeChild:explosion.sprite cleanup:YES];
    }
  }
}

/* Callback for throwing the arm. This involves animating the arm and
creating a grenade */
-(void) throwGrenade {
```

```
    CCSpriteFrameCache *cache = [CCSpriteFrameCache
sharedSpriteFrameCache];

    //Animate the arm
    CCAnimation *animation = [[CCAnimation alloc] initWithName:@"gunmanS
tandRightArmEmpty" delay:1.0f];
    [animation addFrame:[cache spriteFrameByName:@"gunman_stand_right_
arm_empty.png"]];
    [gunmanArm runAction:[CCRepeatForever actionWithAction:[CCAnimate ac
tionWithAnimation:animation]]];

    //Create and launch a grenade
    GameMisc *grenade = [[GameMisc alloc] init];
    grenade.life = 5.0f;
    grenade.gameArea = self;

    CGPoint grenadePosition = ccp(65,150);

    grenade.bodyDef->type = b2_dynamicBody;
    grenade.bodyDef->position.Set(grenadePosition.x/PTM_RATIO,
grenadePosition.y/PTM_RATIO);
    grenade.body = world->CreateBody(grenade.bodyDef);

    grenade.body->SetTransform(b2Vec2(grenadePosition.x/PTM_RATIO,
grenadePosition.y/PTM_RATIO),PI/2);

    CGPoint textureSize = ccp(16,16);
    CGPoint shapeSize = ccp(7,7);

    grenade.sprite = [CCSprite spriteWithSpriteFrameName:@"gunman_
grenade.png"];
    grenade.sprite.position = ccp(grenadePosition.x,grenadePosition.y);
    grenade.sprite.scaleX = shapeSize.x / textureSize.x * 2;
    grenade.sprite.scaleY = shapeSize.y / textureSize.y * 2;

    [gameNode addChild:grenade.sprite z:1];

    grenade.circleShape = new b2CircleShape();
    grenade.circleShape->m_radius = shapeSize.x/PTM_RATIO;
    grenade.fixtureDef->shape = grenade.circleShape;

    grenade.body->CreateFixture(grenade.fixtureDef);

    [grenades addObject:grenade];
```

```
    grenade.body->ApplyLinearImpulse(b2Vec2(1.0f,2.0f) , grenade.body-
>GetPosition() );
    grenade.body->SetAngularVelocity(PI);
}


@end
```

How it works...

In this recipe, we have the ability to throw grenades that explode after five seconds. The explosion launches any other objects in the immediate area.

▶ Destroying a `b2Body`:

Box2D does not allow bodies to be destroyed during a `world->Step(dt, velocityIterations, positionIterations)` call. Because of this, collision response routines and timed callbacks cannot synchronously initiate body destruction. To solve this problem, we have created a simple asynchronous system that can queue up bodies for destruction and creation. This system uses the following methods:

```
-(void) markBodyForDestruction:(GameObject*)obj;
-(void) destroyBodies;
-(void) markBodyForCreation:(GameObject*)obj;
-(void) createBodies;
-(void) runQueuedActions;
```

Bodies are created and destroyed after each physics step has completed.

▶ `GameObjectCallback` and `QueuedAction`:

The `GameObjectCallback` and `QueuedAction` helper classes allow us to queue up method callbacks and `CCAction` instances to use after object creation/deletion. This can help maintain a logical order of operations when the game is running.

▶ `GameObject` life:

In the class `GameMisc`, we added a `life` value. In this recipe, we get to put it to use. Each grenade's `life` ticks away until it explodes. The explosion created is also a `GameMisc` object with a set amount of `life` corresponding to its animation duration. Life can also be used for actors and breakable objects.

Using joints

The last major feature of Box2D we have yet to investigate is **joints**. Joints allow us to link objects to create simple machines like pulleys, levers, and simple motors. In this recipe, we will learn how to create a simple seesaw using a joint.

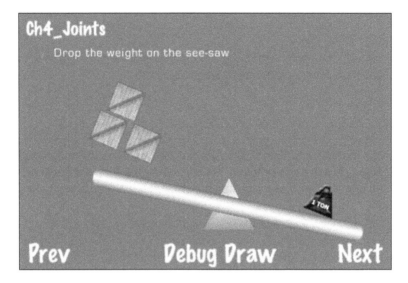

Getting ready

Please refer to the project *RecipeCollection02* for full working code of this recipe. Also note that some of the following code has been omitted for brevity.

How to do it...

Execute the following code:

```
@implementation Ch4_Joints

-(CCLayer*) runRecipe {
  [super runRecipe];
  [message setString:@"Drop the weight on the see-saw"];

  //Initialization
  movableObjects = [[[NSMutableArray alloc] init] autorelease];
  objectGrabbed = NO;

  //Create level boundaries
```

```
  [self addLevelBoundaries];

  //Add objects
  [self addSeeSaw];
  [self addBoxWithPosition:ccp(130,120) file:@"crate2.png"
density:1.0f];
  [self addBoxWithPosition:ccp(160,120) file:@"crate2.png"
density:1.0f];
  [self addBoxWithPosition:ccp(145,150) file:@"crate2.png"
density:1.0f];
  [self addBoxWithPosition:ccp(270,100) file:@"weight.png"
density:15.0f];

  return self;
}

/* Create a complex see-saw object */
-(void) addSeeSaw {
  /* The triangle is the static base of the see-saw */
  CGPoint trianglePosition = ccp(240,50);

  GameMisc *triangle = [[GameMisc alloc] init];
  triangle.gameArea = self;

  triangle.bodyDef->type = b2_staticBody;
  triangle.bodyDef->position.Set(trianglePosition.x/PTM_RATIO,
trianglePosition.y/PTM_RATIO);
  triangle.body = world->CreateBody(triangle.bodyDef);

  //Our triangle polygon
  float polygonSize = 2.0f;

  CGPoint vertexArr[] = { ccp(0,0), ccp(1,0), ccp(0.5f,1) };
  int32 numVerts = 3;
  b2Vec2 vertices[3];

  NSMutableArray *vertexArray = [[[NSMutableArray alloc] init]
autorelease];

  for(int i=0; i<numVerts; i++){
    vertices[i].Set(vertexArr[i].x*polygonSize,
vertexArr[i].y*polygonSize);
    [vertexArray addObject:[NSValue valueWithCGPoint:ccp(vertexArr[i].
x*PTM_RATIO*polygonSize,
      vertexArr[i].y*PTM_RATIO*polygonSize)]];
```

```
   }

   ccTexParams params = {GL_NEAREST,GL_NEAREST_MIPMAP_NEAREST,GL_
REPEAT,GL_REPEAT};
   triangle.sprite = [TexturedPolygon createWithFile:@"box.png"
withVertices:vertexArray];
   [triangle.sprite.texture setTexParameters:&params];
   [triangle.sprite setPosition:ccp(trianglePosition.x,trianglePositio
n.y)];

   [gameNode addChild:triangle.sprite z:1];

   triangle.polygonShape = new b2PolygonShape();
   triangle.polygonShape->Set(vertices, numVerts);
   triangle.fixtureDef->shape = triangle.polygonShape;

   triangle.body->CreateFixture(triangle.fixtureDef);

   /* The plank is the dynamic part of the see-saw */
   CGPoint plankPosition = ccp(270,80);

   GameMisc *plank = [[GameMisc alloc] init];
   plank.gameArea = self;

   plank.bodyDef->type = b2_dynamicBody;
   plank.bodyDef->position.Set(plankPosition.x/PTM_RATIO,
plankPosition.y/PTM_RATIO);
   plank.body = world->CreateBody(plank.bodyDef);

   plank.body->SetTransform(b2Vec2(plankPosition.x/PTM_RATIO,
plankPosition.y/PTM_RATIO),PI/2);

   CGPoint textureSize = ccp(54,215);
   CGPoint shapeSize = ccp(12,180);

   plank.sprite = [CCSprite spriteWithFile:@"column2.png"];
   plank.sprite.position = ccp(plankPosition.x,plankPosition.y);
   plank.sprite.scaleX = shapeSize.x / textureSize.x * 2;
   plank.sprite.scaleY = shapeSize.y / textureSize.y * 2;

   [gameNode addChild:plank.sprite z:1];

   plank.polygonShape = new b2PolygonShape();
   plank.polygonShape->SetAsBox(shapeSize.x/PTM_RATIO, shapeSize.y/
PTM_RATIO);
```

```
plank.fixtureDef->shape = plank.polygonShape;

plank.body->CreateFixture(plank.fixtureDef);

/* We initialize a revolute joint linking the plank to the triangle
*/
b2RevoluteJointDef rjd;
b2RevoluteJoint* joint;

rjd.Initialize(plank.body, triangle.body, b2Vec2(trianglePosition.x/
PTM_RATIO + polygonSize/2, trianglePosition.y/PTM_RATIO +
polygonSize/2));

joint = (b2RevoluteJoint*)world->CreateJoint(&rjd);
}
```

How it works...

By dropping the heavy weight object on one side, we can launch the lighter boxes up into the air from the other side. This is achieved using a simple joint.

▶ Joint types:

All joints link two Box2D bodies. Each joint is represented by a class that derives from b2Joint. These include b2PulleyJoint, b2WeldJoint, b2RopeJoint, and more. A comprehensive overview of all Box2D joint types is beyond the scope of this book. Please refer to the Box2D testbed for example code for each joint as well as the Box2D manual page at http://www.box2d.org/manual.html.

▶ Revolute joints:

In this example, we are using a b2RevoluteJoint to force two bodies to share a common anchor point:

```
b2RevoluteJointDef rjd;
b2RevoluteJoint* joint;

rjd.Initialize(plank.body, triangle.body,
b2Vec2(trianglePosition.x/PTM_RATIO + polygonSize/2,
trianglePosition.y/PTM_RATIO + polygonSize/2));

joint = (b2RevoluteJoint*)world->CreateJoint(&rjd);
```

By pinning the dynamic plank body to the static triangle body, in this example, we have constrained the movement of the plank on the X and Y axes. Now that it can't move, it can only rotate. This creates a realistic seesaw effect.

Creating a vehicle

Combining two or more joints can create some interesting effects. In this example, we will create a car that can be driven around a level.

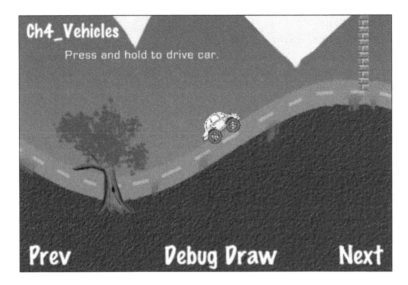

Please refer to the project *RecipeCollection02* for full working code of this recipe. Also note that some of the following code has been omitted for brevity.

How to do it...

Execute the following code:

```
@implementation Ch4_Vehicles

-(CCLayer*) runRecipe {
    [super runRecipe];
    [message setString:@"Press and hold to drive car."];

    //Initialization
    pressedLeft = NO;
    pressedRight = NO;

    //Create level
    [self createLevel];
```

```
  //Add taxi
  [self addTaxi];

  return self;
}

-(void) createLevel {
  /* Create a sine wave road for our car */
  b2BodyDef groundBodyDef;
  groundBodyDef.position.Set(0, 0);
  b2Body *body = world->CreateBody(&groundBodyDef);

  b2PolygonShape groundBox;

  b2FixtureDef groundFixtureDef;
  groundFixtureDef.restitution = 0.0f;
  groundFixtureDef.friction = 10.0f;  //The road has a lot of friction
  groundFixtureDef.filter.categoryBits = CB_GROUND;
  groundFixtureDef.filter.maskBits = CB_CAR | CB_WHEEL;

  groundBox.SetAsEdge(b2Vec2(-960/PTM_RATIO,0), b2Vec2(-960/PTM_
RATIO,200/PTM_RATIO));
  groundFixtureDef.shape = &groundBox;
  body->CreateFixture(&groundFixtureDef);

  groundBox.SetAsEdge(b2Vec2(960/PTM_RATIO,0), b2Vec2(960/PTM_
RATIO,200/PTM_RATIO));
  groundFixtureDef.shape = &groundBox;
  body->CreateFixture(&groundFixtureDef);

  float32 x1; float32 y1;
  for(int u = -1; u < 2; u++){
    //Add Edge Shapes
    x1 = -15.0f;
    y1 = 2.0f * cosf(x1 / 10.0f * b2_pi);
    for (int32 i = 0; i < 60; ++i)
    {
      float32 x2 = x1 + 0.5f;
      float32 y2 = 2.0f * cosf(x2 / 10.0f * b2_pi);

      b2PolygonShape shape;
      shape.SetAsEdge(b2Vec2(x1 + u*960/PTM_RATIO, y1), b2Vec2(x2 +
u*960/PTM_RATIO, y2));
```

```
      body->CreateFixture(&shape, 0.0f);

      x1 = x2;
      y1 = y2;
    }

    //Add corresponding graphics
    CCSprite *bg = [CCSprite spriteWithFile:@"road_bg.png"];
    bg.position = ccp(u*960,70);
    [gameNode addChild:bg z:0];

    CCSprite *fg = [CCSprite spriteWithFile:@"road_fg.png"];
    fg.position = ccp(u*960,70);
    [gameNode addChild:fg z:2];
  }

  /* Add two bricks walls so you can't drive off the course */
  [self addBrickWallSpriteAtPosition:ccp(970,60)];
  [self addBrickWallSpriteAtPosition:ccp(-970,60)];
}

-(void) addTaxi {
  // NOTE: In b2Settings.h we increased the b2_maxPolygonVertices
definition:
  // #define b2_maxPolygonVertices   16

  [[CCSpriteFrameCache sharedSpriteFrameCache]
addSpriteFramesWithFile:@"taxi.plist"];

  CGPoint taxiPosition = ccp(-960,80);
  float taxiScale = 0.2f;

  taxi = [[GameMisc alloc] init];
  taxi.gameArea = self;

  taxi.bodyDef->type = b2_dynamicBody;
  taxi.bodyDef->position.Set(taxiPosition.x/PTM_RATIO, taxiPosition.y/
PTM_RATIO);
  taxi.body = world->CreateBody(taxi.bodyDef);

  taxi.fixtureDef->filter.categoryBits = CB_CAR;
  taxi.fixtureDef->filter.maskBits = CB_GROUND;
  taxi.fixtureDef->density = 0.5f;
  taxi.fixtureDef->friction = 0.25f;
```

```
  taxi.fixtureDef->restitution = 0.0f;

  //Polygon
  /* CODE OMITTED */

  //Wheels
  CGPoint wheelPosition[] = { ccp(taxiPosition.x + 16,
taxiPosition.y), ccp(taxiPosition.x + 43, taxiPosition.y) };

  for(int i=0; i<2; i++){
    GameMisc *wheel = [[GameMisc alloc] init];

    if(i == 0){
      wheel1 = wheel;
    }else{
      wheel2 = wheel;
    }

    wheel.gameArea = self;

    wheel.bodyDef->type = b2_dynamicBody;
    wheel.bodyDef->position.Set(wheelPosition[i].x/PTM_RATIO,
wheelPosition[i].y/PTM_RATIO);
    wheel.body = world->CreateBody(wheel.bodyDef);

    wheel.body->SetTransform(b2Vec2(wheelPosition[i].x/PTM_RATIO,
wheelPosition[i].y/PTM_RATIO),PI/2);

    wheel.fixtureDef->filter.categoryBits = CB_WHEEL;
    wheel.fixtureDef->filter.maskBits = CB_GROUND;
    wheel.fixtureDef->density = 10.0f;
    wheel.fixtureDef->friction = 10.0f;
    wheel.fixtureDef->restitution = 0.0f;

    CGPoint textureSize = ccp(52,51);
    CGPoint shapeSize = ccp(9,9);

    wheel.sprite = [CCSprite spriteWithSpriteFrameName:@"taxi_wheel.
png"];
    wheel.sprite.position = ccp(wheelPosition[i].x,wheelPosition[i]
.y);
    wheel.sprite.scaleX = shapeSize.x / textureSize.x * 2;
    wheel.sprite.scaleY = shapeSize.y / textureSize.y * 2;
```

```
    [gameNode addChild:wheel.sprite z:1];

    wheel.circleShape = new b2CircleShape();
    wheel.circleShape->m_radius = shapeSize.x/PTM_RATIO;
    wheel.fixtureDef->shape = wheel.circleShape;

    wheel.body->CreateFixture(wheel.fixtureDef);
    wheel.body->SetAngularDamping(1.0f);

    //Add Joint to connect wheel to the taxi
    b2RevoluteJointDef rjd;
    b2RevoluteJoint* joint;

    rjd.Initialize(wheel.body, taxi.body, b2Vec2(wheelPosition[i].x/
PTM_RATIO, wheelPosition[i].y/PTM_RATIO));

    joint = (b2RevoluteJoint*)world->CreateJoint(&rjd);
  }
}

-(void) step: (ccTime) dt {
  [super step:dt];

    gameNode.position = ccp(-taxi.sprite.position.x + 240, -taxi.
sprite.position.y + 160);

  //Front wheel drive

  //We apply some counter-torque to steady the car
  if(pressedRight){
    wheel2->body->ApplyTorque(-20.0f);
    taxi->body->ApplyTorque(5.0f);
  }else if(pressedLeft){
    wheel1->body->ApplyTorque(20.0f);
    taxi->body->ApplyTorque(-5.0f);
  }
}

@end
```

How it works...

By pressing on either side of the screen, we can see the car drive forward or backward until it inevitably meets a brick wall at either end of the level.

- The car:

    To create a simple car in Box2D, all you have to do is attach two circles to a polygon using revolute joints. Each circle, or 'wheel', has high density and friction to help it pull the car along the road. It also has a low restitution to limit bouncing. When placed on an uneven surface the car will then roll forward or backward. Also, for the sake of simplicity the actual chasis of the car is a convex polygon.

- Driving the car:

    To drive the car around, we apply torque to the front wheel while applying some counter-torque to the car itself:

    ```
    wheel2->body->ApplyTorque(-20.0f);
    taxi->body->ApplyTorque(5.0f);
    ```

    The counter-torque acts in the same way that a spoiler does to keep the car balanced.

- Creating the curved road:

    The road in this recipe is a good example of a curved surface in Box2D. We created this using many small **edge** fixtures to construct a hi-poly curve.

- The camera:

    In this recipe, we finally put `gameNode` to use. By repositioning this node, we effectively reposition the camera separately from the **HUD**:

    ```
    gameNode.position = ccp(-taxi.sprite.position.x + 240, -taxi.
    sprite.position.y + 160);
    ```

    We'll discuss camera usage in depth in another recipe.

There's More...

The vehicle in this example is far from perfect. Try using **revolute joints** to extend the wheels out from under the car and to add some shock absorption.

- `b2_maxPolygonVertices`:

    Because our car has more than eight vertices, we must override the `b2_maxPolygonVertices` definition. This is located in the file `b2Settings.h`. The new definition looks like this:

    ```
    #define b2_maxPolygonVertices   16
    ```

    This allows us to define polygons with up to 16 vertices.

Character movement

Moving a character around a level can be trickier than you might expect. In this recipe, we will lay out the basics of 2D side scrolling character movement.

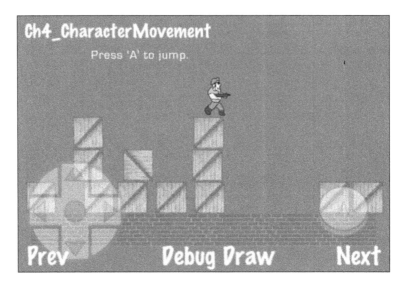

Getting ready

Please refer to the project *RecipeCollection02* for full working code of this recipe. Also note that some of the following code has been omitted for brevity.

How to do it...

Execute the following code:

```
@implementation SideScrollerRecipe

-(void) step:(ccTime)delta {
  [super step:delta];

  //Apply gunman running direction
  if(dPad.direction == DPAD_LEFT || dPad.direction == DPAD_UP_LEFT ||
dPad.direction == DPAD_DOWN_LEFT){
    gunmanDirection = DPAD_LEFT;
    gunman.body->ApplyForce(b2Vec2(-35.0f,0), gunman.body-
>GetPosition());
    ((CCSprite*)[gunman.sprite getChildByTag:0]).flipX = YES;
```

```
    }else if(dPad.direction == DPAD_RIGHT || dPad.direction == DPAD_UP_
RIGHT || dPad.direction == DPAD_DOWN_RIGHT){
        gunmanDirection = DPAD_RIGHT;
        gunman.body->ApplyForce(b2Vec2(35.0f,0), gunman.body-
>GetPosition());
        ((CCSprite*)[gunman.sprite getChildByTag:0]).flipX = NO;
    }

    //Decrement jump counter
    jumpCounter -= delta;

    //Did the gunman just hit the ground?
    if(!onGround){
        if((gunman.body->GetLinearVelocity().y - lastYVelocity) > 2 &&
lastYVelocity < -2){
            gunman.body->SetLinearVelocity(b2Vec2(gunman.body-
>GetLinearVelocity().x,0));
            onGround = YES;
        }else if(gunman.body->GetLinearVelocity().y == 0 && lastYVelocity
== 0){
            gunman.body->SetLinearVelocity(b2Vec2(gunman.body-
>GetLinearVelocity().x,0));
            onGround = YES;
        }
    }

    //Did he just fall off the ground without jumping?
    if(onGround){
        if(gunman.body->GetLinearVelocity().y < -2.0f && lastYVelocity <
-2.0f && (gunman.body->GetLinearVelocity().y < lastYVelocity)){
            onGround = NO;
        }
    }

    //Store last velocity
    lastYVelocity = gunman.body->GetLinearVelocity().y;

    //Keep him upright on the ground
    if(onGround){
        gunman.body->SetTransform(gunman.body->GetPosition(),0);
    }

    //Animate gunman if his speed changed significantly
    float speed = gunman.body->GetLinearVelocity().x;
    if(speed < 0){ speed *= -1; }
```

```
  if(speed > lastXSpeed*2){
    [[gunman.sprite getChildByTag:0] stopAllActions];
    [self animateGunman];
  }

  //Keep the gunman in the level
  b2Vec2 gunmanPos = gunman.body->GetPosition();
  if(gunmanPos.x > 530/PTM_RATIO || gunmanPos.x < (-50/PTM_RATIO) ||
gunmanPos.y < -100/PTM_RATIO){
    gunman.body->SetTransform(b2Vec2(2,10), gunman.body->GetAngle());
  }

  //Process input for the A button
  for(id b in buttons){
    GameButton *button = (GameButton*)b;
    if(button.pressed && [button.name isEqualToString:@"A"]){
      [self processJump];
    }else{
      jumpCounter = -10.0f;
    }
  }
}

/* Initialize gunman */
-(void) initGunman {
  gunman = [[GameMisc alloc] init];

  /* CODE OMITTED */

  gunman.body->SetLinearDamping(2.0f);
}

/* Process jump */
-(void) processJump {
  if(onGround && jumpCounter < 0){
    //Start a jump. Starting requires you to not be moving on the Y.
    jumpCounter = 0.4f;
    gunman.body->ApplyLinearImpulse(b2Vec2(0,20.0f), gunman.body-
>GetPosition());
    onGround = NO;
  }else if(jumpCounter > 0){
    //Continue a jump
    gunman.body->ApplyForce(b2Vec2(0,65.0f), gunman.body-
>GetPosition());
  }
}
```

How it works...

In this recipe, we can make the 'gunman' run and jump around the level. The animation routine used here is based on the one used in a previous recipe.

- ▸ Moving left and right:

  Using the directional pad, we can move the gunman to the left or right. This involves applying a force to the body on the X-axis:

  ```
  gunman.body->ApplyForce(b2Vec2(35.0f,0), gunman.body-
  >GetPosition());
  ```

  The gunman's animation speed is then based on his X movement speed.

- ▸ Damping:

  To slow the gunman down both in the air and on the ground, we set a **linear damping** value on the body:

  ```
  gunman.body->SetLinearDamping(2.0f);
  ```

  This gradually decreases the gunman's speed in all directions. This has the dual effect of creating air resistance and also slowing him down when he's not actively running.

- ▸ Jumping:

  To create a comfortable Mario-esque jump, we need to apply a handful of techniques and store a few variables. Jumping should only happen when the gunman is standing on an object. The user should be able to hold down the jump button for a higher jump, that is, until a certain point. To achieve all this we use the following variables:

  ```
  float lastYVelocity;
  float jumpCounter;
  bool onGround;
  ```

  The variable `lastYVelocity` is used to determine whether or not the gunman recently hit the ground or if he just ran off the ground (as opposed to jumping off the ground). Subtle changes in Y velocity can tell us these things. The variable `jumpCounter` is used to limit jumping height. The counter is constantly being decremented. The time it resets to when you initially jump is the maximum amount of time the gunman is thrust upward. This time can be modified to allow certain actors to jump higher or lower. Jumping is first an initial impulse then a constant upward thrusting force. When the user lets go of the jump button, we reset `jumpCounter` and the gunman begins to fall.

Simulating bullets

Bullets and other fast moving objects are a fundamental part of many video games. In this recipe, we will see how to properly implement bullet physics.

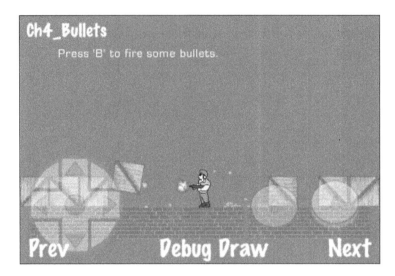

Getting ready

Please refer to the project *RecipeCollection02* for full working code of this recipe. Also note that some of the following code has been omitted for brevity.

How to do it...

Execute the following code:

```
@implementation Ch4_Bullets

/* Fire the gun */
-(void) fireGun {
  //Fire 10 bullets per second
  if(fireCount > 0){
    return;
  }
  fireCount = 0.2f;

  CCSpriteFrameCache *cache = [CCSpriteFrameCache
sharedSpriteFrameCache];
```

```
//Fire bullet in the correct direction
float gunAngle = -gunman.body->GetAngle() + PI/2;
if(gunmanDirection == DPAD_LEFT){ gunAngle += PI; }
CGPoint bulletVector = ccp( sin(gunAngle), cos(gunAngle) );

//Create bullet and shell casing
for(int i=0; i<2; i++){
  //Create bullet or casing object
  //NOTE: It might be more efficient to re-use a group of bullet
objects instead of creating new bullets each time
  GameMisc *bullet = [[GameMisc alloc] init];
  bullet.gameArea = self;
  bullet.typeTag = TYPE_OBJ_BULLET;
  if(i == 1){
    bullet.typeTag = TYPE_OBJ_SHELL;
  }
  bullet.life = 2.0f;
  if(i == 1){
    bullet.life = 5.0f;
  }

  //Calculate bullet/casing position as being slightly ahead of the
gunman
  CGPoint bulletPosition = ccp( gunman.sprite.position.x +
bulletVector.x*10, gunman.sprite.position.y + bulletVector.y*10 );
  if(i == 1){
    bulletPosition = ccp( gunman.sprite.position.x, gunman.sprite.
position.y );
  }

  //Create body using body definition
  bullet.bodyDef->type = b2_dynamicBody;
  if(i == 0){
    bullet.bodyDef->bullet = YES;
  }
  bullet.bodyDef->position.Set(bulletPosition.x/PTM_RATIO,
bulletPosition.y/PTM_RATIO);
  bullet.body = world->CreateBody(bullet.bodyDef);

  //Set the angle of the bullet/casing in the direction of the
firing gun
  bullet.body->SetTransform(bullet.body->GetPosition(), gunAngle);

  CGPoint textureSize = ccp(17,17);
```

```
    CGPoint shapeSize = ccp(2,2);

    //Create the bullet sprite
    bullet.sprite = [CCSprite spriteWithFile:@"bullet.png"];
    bullet.sprite.position = ccp(bulletPosition.x,bulletPosition.y);
    bullet.sprite.scaleX = shapeSize.x / textureSize.x * 2.25f;
    bullet.sprite.scaleY = shapeSize.y / textureSize.y * 2.25f;

    //If this is a shell casing make it a golden color
    if(i == 1){ bullet.sprite.color = ccc3(255,200,0); }

    //Add object
    [gameNode addChild:bullet.sprite z:1];

    //Set bullet shape
    bullet.polygonShape = new b2PolygonShape();
    bullet.polygonShape->SetAsBox(shapeSize.x/PTM_RATIO/2,
shapeSize.y/PTM_RATIO);
    bullet.fixtureDef->shape = bullet.polygonShape;

    //Create fixture and configure collision
    bullet.fixtureDef->density = 20.0f;
    bullet.fixtureDef->friction = 1.0f;
    bullet.fixtureDef->restitution = 0.0f;
    if(i == 0){
      bullet.fixtureDef->filter.categoryBits = CB_BULLET;
      bullet.fixtureDef->filter.maskBits = CB_OTHER;
    }else{
      bullet.fixtureDef->filter.categoryBits = CB_SHELL;
      bullet.fixtureDef->filter.maskBits = CB_OTHER | CB_SHELL;
    }
    bullet.body->CreateFixture(bullet.fixtureDef);

    //Add this bullet to our container
    [bullets addObject:bullet];

    //If this is a bullet, fire it. If its a shell, eject it.
    if(i == 0){
      //Fire the bullet by applying an impulse
      bullet.body->ApplyLinearImpulse(b2Vec2(bulletVector.x*50,
bulletVector.y*50), bullet.body->GetPosition());
    }else{
      //Eject the shell
      float radians = vectorToRadians(bulletVector);
```

```
        radians += 1.85f * PI;
        CGPoint shellVector = radiansToVector(radians);
        if(shellVector.x > 0){ shellVector.y *= -1; }

        bullet.body->ApplyLinearImpulse(b2Vec2(shellVector.x,
shellVector.y), bullet.body->GetPosition());
      }
    }
}

-(void) handleCollisionWithMisc:(GameMisc*)a withMisc:(GameMisc*)b {
    //If a bullet touches something we set life to 0 and process the
impact on that object
    if(a.typeTag == TYPE_OBJ_BULLET && b.typeTag == TYPE_OBJ_BOX &&
a.life > 0){
      a.life = 0;
      [self bulletImpactAt:a.sprite.position onObject:b];
      [message setString:@"Bullet hit"];
    }else if(b.typeTag == TYPE_OBJ_BULLET && a.typeTag == TYPE_OBJ_BOX
&& b.life > 0){
      b.life = 0;
      [self bulletImpactAt:b.sprite.position onObject:a];
      [message setString:@"Bullet hit"];
    }

    //Reset our message
    [self runAction:[CCSequence actions:[CCDelayTime
actionWithDuration:5.0f],
      [CCCallFunc actionWithTarget:self selector:@
selector(resetMessage)], nil]];
}

/* Process the bullet impact */
-(void) bulletImpactAt:(CGPoint)p onObject:(GameMisc*)obj {
    //Here we use some trigonometry to determine exactly where the
bullet impacted on the box.
    float dist = distanceBetweenPoints(p, obj.sprite.position);  //
Hypotenuse
    float xDist = obj.sprite.position.x - p.x;     //Opposite side
    float yDist = obj.sprite.position.y - p.y;     //Adjacent side

    float xAngle = asin(xDist/dist);
    float yAngle = acos(yDist/dist);
```

```
    float objSize = [obj.sprite contentSize].width/2 * obj.sprite.scale;

    float newXDist = xDist - sin(xAngle) * objSize;
    float newYDist = yDist - cos(yAngle) * objSize;

    p = ccp( p.x + newXDist, p.y + newYDist );

    //Animate bullet impact
    float delay = 0.035f;
    float duration = 8 * delay;

    GameMisc *blastmark = [[GameMisc alloc] init];
    blastmark.sprite = [CCSprite spriteWithSpriteFrameName:@"blastma
rk_0000.png"];
    blastmark.life = duration;
    blastmark.sprite.position = p;
    blastmark.sprite.scale = 0.2f;
    blastmark.sprite.opacity = 100;

    CCSpriteFrameCache *cache = [CCSpriteFrameCache
sharedSpriteFrameCache];
    CCAnimation *animation = [[CCAnimation alloc]
initWithName:@"blastmark" delay:delay];
    for(int i=0; i<8; i+=1){
        [animation addFrame:[cache spriteFrameByName:[NSString stringWithF
ormat:@"blastmark_000%i.png",i]]];
    }

    [blastmark.sprite stopAllActions];
    [blastmark.sprite runAction:
      [CCSpawn actions:
        [CCFadeOut actionWithDuration:duration],
        [CCAnimate actionWithAnimation:animation],
        nil
      ]
    ];

    [gameNode addChild:blastmark.sprite z:5];
    [explosions addObject:blastmark];

    //Decrement the box life
    obj.life -= 1.0f;
}

@end
```

How it works...

Pressing the **B** button animates a muzzle flash, fires a bullet object, and ejects a used bullet casing. The muzzle flash is merely an animation but the bullets and bullet casings are physical objects.

▸ Setting the bullet flag:

In the recipe, we set the bullet body's flag to identify it as a fast moving projectile:

```
bullet.bodyDef->bullet = YES;
```

Setting this flag allows the bullet to properly collide with other dynamic bodies. When two dynamic bodies collide, Box2D only performs collision detection for each discrete physics step. This means that during each cycle all dynamic physical bodies have discrete positions. Because of this, when a body moves fast enough, there is a chance that it could move through a body that it is supposed to collide with. Specifying this fast moving body as a bullet allows Box2D to perform continuous collision detection to allow this object to collide with other dynamic objects at any speed.

▸ Animating a bullet impact:

In our example, we used some trigonometry to determine where the bullet landed on the periphery of the 2D box object. For more complex shapes, you can retrieve the **contact normals** from the Box2D solver. This will help identify exactly where two bodies have collided. For more information about contact normals, please consult the Box2D documentation.

Simulating and rendering a rope

A recent addition to the Box2D library is the b2RopeJoint. In this recipe, we will see how to implement this physically and visually.

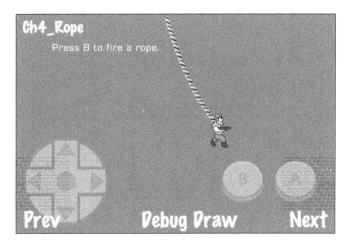

Getting ready

Please refer to the project *RecipeCollection02* for full working code of this recipe. Also note that some of the following code has been omitted for brevity.

How to do it...

Execute the following code:

```
#import "VRope.h"

@implementation Ch4_Rope

-(CCLayer*) runRecipe {
  [super runRecipe];
  [message setString:@"Press B to fire a rope."];

  //Initialization
  onRope = NO;
  ropeUseTimer = 0;

  //Move gunman to left
  gunman.body->SetTransform(b2Vec2(2,10), gunman.body->GetAngle());

  //Create buttons
  [self createButtonWithPosition:ccp(340,75) withUpFrame:@"b_button_
up.png" withDownFrame:@"b_button_down.png" withName:@"B"];
  [self createButtonWithPosition:ccp(420,75) withUpFrame:@"a_button_
up.png" withDownFrame:@"a_button_down.png" withName:@"A"];

  //Create ground
  /* CODE OMITTED */

  //Add invisible rope anchor
  [self addRopeAnchor];

  return self;
}

-(void) step:(ccTime)delta {
  [super step:delta];

  //Process button input
  for(id b in buttons){
```

```objc
    GameButton *button = (GameButton*)b;
    if(button.pressed && [button.name isEqualToString:@"B"]){
      if(!onRope){
        [self useRope];
      }else{
        [self releaseRope];
      }
    }
    if(button.pressed && [button.name isEqualToString:@"A"]){
      if(onRope){
        [self releaseRope];
      }else{
        [self processJump];
      }
    }else if(!button.pressed && [button.name isEqualToString:@"A"]){
      jumpCounter = -10.0f;
    }
  }
  //Update all ropes
  for(id v in vRopes){
    VRope *rope = (VRope*)v;
    [rope update:delta];
    [rope updateSprites];
  }

  //Decrement our use timer
  ropeUseTimer -= delta;
}

-(void) addRopeAnchor {
  //Add rope anchor body
  b2BodyDef anchorBodyDef;
  anchorBodyDef.position.Set(240/PTM_RATIO,350/PTM_RATIO); //center
body on screen
  anchorBody = world->CreateBody(&anchorBodyDef);

  //Add rope spritesheet to layer
  ropeSpriteSheet = [CCSpriteBatchNode batchNodeWithFile:@"rope.png"
];
  [self addChild:ropeSpriteSheet];

  //Init array that will hold references to all our ropes
  vRopes = [[[NSMutableArray alloc] init] autorelease];
```

```
    }

- (void) useRope {
    if(ropeUseTimer > 0){
      return;
    }else{
      ropeUseTimer = 0.2f;
    }

    //The rope joint goes from the anchor to the gunman
    b2RopeJointDef jd;
    jd.bodyA = anchorBody;
    jd.bodyB = gunman.body;
    jd.localAnchorA = b2Vec2(0,0);
    jd.localAnchorB = b2Vec2(0,0);
    jd.maxLength= (gunman.body->GetPosition() - anchorBody-
>GetPosition()).Length();

    //Create VRope with two b2bodies and pointer to spritesheet
    VRope *newRope = [[VRope alloc] init:anchorBody body2:gunman.body
spriteSheet:ropeSpriteSheet];

    //Create joint
    newRope.joint = world->CreateJoint(&jd);
    [vRopes addObject:newRope];

    //Keep track of 'onRope' state
    onRope = !onRope;
}

- (void) releaseRope {
    if(ropeUseTimer > 0){
      return;
    }else{
      ropeUseTimer = 0.2f;
    }

    //Jump off the rope
    [self processJump];

    //Destroy the rope
    for(id v in vRopes){
      VRope *rope = (VRope*)v;
      world->DestroyJoint(rope.joint);
```

```
    [rope removeSprites];
    [rope release];
}
[vRopes removeAllObjects];

//Keep track of 'onRope' state
onRope = !onRope;
}


@end
```

How it works...

Pressing **B** fires a rope into the level directly above the gap in the middle. This allows the gunman to swing across the gap.

▶ Using a rope joint:

The rope joint is initialized in a way similar to that of other joints. It connects two bodies at two specific local points:

```
b2RopeJointDef jd;
jd.bodyA = anchorBody;
jd.bodyB = gunman.body;
jd.localAnchorA = b2Vec2(0,0);
jd.localAnchorB = b2Vec2(0,0);
```

We then set the maximum rope length and create the joint:

```
jd.maxLength= (gunman.body->GetPosition() - anchorBody-
>GetPosition()).Length();
newRope.joint = world->CreateJoint(&jd);
```

This allows the user to swing on a circular arc around the anchor point.

▶ Using VRope:

The VRope class allows us to visualize the rope. An instance of VRope stores the two connected bodies and the connecting joint to then create a realistic depiction of a rope in each frame:

```
//Update all ropes
for(id v in vRopes){
        VRope *rope = (VRope*)v;
        [rope update:delta];
        [rope updateSprites];
}
```

From the original Pitfall arcade game to the newer Worms games, ropes have been used in games for years. They connect the player to the world in a way that is more dynamic than just running and jumping around.

Creating a top-down isometric game engine

By making some modifications to Box2D we can turn a 2D world into a 2.5D world. We will see this 2.5D **sandbox** in action in this recipe.

Getting ready

Please refer to the project *RecipeCollection02* for full working code of this recipe. Also note that a large amount of code from this recipe has been omitted for brevity.

How to do it...

Execute the following code:

```
@interface GameIsoObject : GameObject {
  @public
    float yModifier;  //This is typically half the height of the
object. It allows us to change the sprite y.
    float actualImageSize;  //This is the actual size of the image
(48x48, 96x96, etc)
    float inGameSize;  //This is how large the object in the game is.
    float zModifier;  //Changes the depth testing for this object.
```

```
    CCSprite *spriteShadow;
    Vector3D *bounceCoefficient;  //x, y, z, lower is bouncier for Z
    Vector3D *rollCoefficient;
}

@end

/* IsometricContactListener.h */
class isometricContactListener : public b2ContactListener
{
  public:
    void BeginContact(b2Contact* contact);
    void EndContact(b2Contact* contact);
    void PreSolve(b2Contact* contact, const b2Manifold* oldManifold);
};

void isometricContactListener::BeginContact(b2Contact* contact)
{
  b2Body *bodyA = contact->GetFixtureA()->GetBody();
  b2Body *bodyB = contact->GetFixtureB()->GetBody();

  if(bodyA and bodyB){
    float lowerZSize;
    if(bodyA->GetZPosition() < bodyB->GetZPosition()){ lowerZSize =
bodyA->GetZSize(); }
    else{ lowerZSize = bodyB->GetZSize(); }

    //Check for Z Miss and disable collision if neccessary
    if( absoluteValue(bodyA->GetZPosition() - bodyB->GetZPosition()) >
lowerZSize ) { //If distance is greater than the height of the bottom
one
        contact->SetEnabled(false);
        if(bodyA->GetHandleZMiss() || bodyB->GetHandleZMiss()){
          GameObject *gameObjectA = (GameObject*)bodyA->GetUserData();
          GameObject *gameObjectB = (GameObject*)bodyB->GetUserData();
          [gameObjectA->gameArea handleZMissWithObjA:gameObjectA
withObjB:gameObjectB];
          bodyA->SetHandleZMiss(false);
          bodyB->SetHandleZMiss(false);
        }
    //If no Z Miss handle collision
    }else {
      GameObject *gameObjectA = (GameObject*)bodyA->GetUserData();
      GameObject *gameObjectB = (GameObject*)bodyB->GetUserData();
```

```
        [gameObjectA->gameArea handleCollisionWithObjA:gameObjectA
  withObjB:gameObjectB];
      }
    }
  }
  /* END IsometricContactListener.h */

  @implementation Ch4_TopDownIsometric

  -(CCLayer*) runRecipe {
    [super runRecipe];

    //Iso debug drawing
    m_debugDraw = new IsoGLESDebugDraw( PTM_RATIO, PERSPECTIVE_RATIO,
  gameAreaSize );
    world->SetDebugDraw(m_debugDraw);

    //Special isometric gravity, contact filter and contact listener
    world->SetGravity(b2Vec2(0,0));
    world->SetContactListener(new isometricContactListener);

    return self;
  }

  /* We override all physical calculations here */
  -(void) step: (ccTime) delta {
    //Update Physics
    int32 velocityIterations = 8;
    int32 positionIterations = 3;

    world->Step(delta, velocityIterations, positionIterations);

    float deltaMod = delta/0.01666666667f;

    for (b2Body* b = world->GetBodyList(); b; b = b->GetNext()) {
      //Z Miss handling allows us to know when an object passes over or
  under another object
      b->SetHandleZMiss(YES);

      if (b->GetUserData() != NULL) {
        //Synchronize the sprites position and rotation with the
  corresponding body
        GameIsoObject *gameObject = (GameIsoObject*)b->GetUserData();

        if(gameObject.sprite) {
```

```
        if(gameObject.bodyDef->type == b2_dynamicBody){
            //Process Z velocity and position
            gameObject.body->SetZVelocity( gameObject.body-
>GetZVelocity() - GRAVITY*deltaMod );
            gameObject.body->SetZPosition( gameObject.body-
>GetZPosition() + gameObject.body->GetZVelocity()*deltaMod );


            //Process object bouncing and rolling
            if(gameObject.body->GetZPosition() < (-0.01f)){
                gameObject.body->SetZPosition(0.01f);
                gameObject.body->SetZVelocity( gameObject.body-
>GetZVelocity() * -1 );

                b2Vec2 worldVector = gameObject.body->GetLinearVelocityFro
mLocalPoint(b2Vec2(0,0));
                if(absoluteValue(gameObject.body->GetZVelocity()) > 1.0f){
                    [self handleCollisionWithGroundWithObj:gameObject];
                    gameObject.body->ApplyLinearImpulse( b2Vec2( gameObject.
bounceCoefficient.x*worldVector.x*-1, gameObject.bounceCoefficient.y*w
orldVector.y*-1 ), gameObject.body->GetPosition() );
                    gameObject.body->SetZVelocity( gameObject.body-
>GetZVelocity() * (1-gameObject.bounceCoefficient.z) );
                }else{
                    gameObject.body->ApplyLinearImpulse( b2Vec2( gameObject.
rollCoefficient.x*worldVector.x*-1, gameObject.rollCoefficient.y*world
Vector.y*-1 ), gameObject.body->GetPosition() );
                    gameObject.body->SetZVelocity( gameObject.body-
>GetZVelocity() * (1-gameObject.rollCoefficient.z) );
                }
            }
        }

        //Change sprite positions based on body positions
        gameObject.sprite.position = CGPointMake(
convertPositionX(gameAreaSize, b->GetPosition().x * PTM_RATIO),
convertPositionY(gameAreaSize, b->GetPosition().y * PTM_RATIO
* PERSPECTIVE_RATIO) + gameObject.yModifier + gameObject.body-
>GetZPosition() * zHeightModifier * PERSPECTIVE_RATIO);
        gameObject.spriteShadow.position = CGPointMake(
convertPositionX(gameAreaSize, b->GetPosition().x * PTM_RATIO),
convertPositionY(gameAreaSize, b->GetPosition().y * PTM_RATIO *
PERSPECTIVE_RATIO));

        //Modify sprite scale based on Z (height)
        [gameObject.sprite setScale:( gameObject.body->GetZPosi
tion()*scaleHeightMultiplier + gameObject->inGameSize/gameObject-
>actualImageSize )];
```

```
          gameObject.spriteShadow.scale = gameObject.body-
>GetZPosition()/100;
          if(gameObject.spriteShadow.scale > 1){ gameObject.
spriteShadow.scale = 1; }

          //Sprite depth testing based on Y (depth)
          [self setZOrderByBodyPosition:gameObject];

        }else if(gameObject.bodyDef->type == b2_staticBody){
          //Static bodies are only positioned and depth tested
          gameObject.sprite.position = CGPointMake(
convertPositionX(gameAreaSize, b->GetPosition().x * PTM_RATIO),
convertPositionY(gameAreaSize, b->GetPosition().y * PTM_RATIO
* PERSPECTIVE_RATIO) + gameObject.yModifier + gameObject.body-
>GetZPosition() * zHeightModifier * PERSPECTIVE_RATIO);
          [self setZOrderByBodyPosition:gameObject];
          gameObject.spriteShadow.position = CGPointMake(
convertPositionX(gameAreaSize, b->GetPosition().x * PTM_RATIO),
convertPositionY(gameAreaSize, b->GetPosition().y * PTM_RATIO *
PERSPECTIVE_RATIO));
        }
      }
    }
  }

  //Process body creation/destruction
  [self destroyBodies];
  [self createBodies];
  [self runQueuedActions];

  //Follow gunman with camera
  gameNode.position = ccp((-gunman.spriteShadow.position.x)*cameraZoom
+ 240, (-gunman.spriteShadow.position.y)*cameraZoom + 160);
}

/* Fire a bouncy ball */
-(void) fireBall {
  if(fireCount < 0){
    GameIsoObject *ball = [self addBallAtPoint:ccp(gunman.
body->GetPosition().x*PTM_RATIO + lastPressedVector.x*20.0f,
gunman.body->GetPosition().y*PTM_RATIO*PERSPECTIVE_RATIO +
lastPressedVector.y*20.0f)];
    ball.body->ApplyLinearImpulse(b2Vec2(lastPressedVector.x*1.75f,
lastPressedVector.y*1.75f), ball.body->GetPosition());
    ball.body->SetZVelocity( gunman.body->GetZVelocity()*5.0f + 10.0f
);
```

```
    ball.body->SetZPosition( gunman.body->GetZPosition() + 40.0f);
    fireCount = 10;
  }else{
    fireCount--;
  }


}


/* Process a jump */
-(void) processJump {
  //You can only jump if you are standing or running. You also need to
be on the ground.
  if(gunman.body->GetZPosition() > 1.0f){
    return;
  }

  //Make him jump
  [[gunman.sprite getChildByTag:0] stopAllActions];
  gunman.body->SetZVelocity(7.5f);
}

/* Convert a body position to a world position */
-(CGPoint) getWorldPosition:(GameIsoObject*)g {
  return CGPointMake(g.body->GetPosition().x * PTM_RATIO, g.body-
>GetPosition().y * PTM_RATIO * PERSPECTIVE_RATIO);
}

/* A camera bound limiting routine */
- (bool) checkCameraBoundsWithFailPosition:(CGPoint*)failPosition {
  CGSize screenSize = [CCDirector sharedDirector].winSize;

  bool passed = true;

  float fsx = (gameAreaSize.x/2)*cameraZoom;
  float fsy = (gameAreaSize.y/2)*cameraZoom;
  float ssx = screenSize.width;
  float ssy = screenSize.height;

  if( [gameNode position].y < -(fsy - ssy) ) {
    (*failPosition).y = -(fsy - ssy);
    passed = false;
  }else if( [gameNode position].y > fsy) {
    (*failPosition).y = fsy;
    passed = false;
```

```objc
    }else{ //Passed
      (*failPosition).y = [gameNode position].y;
    }

    if( [gameNode position].x < -(fsx - ssx) ) {
      (*failPosition).x = -(fsx - ssx);
      passed = false;
    }else if( [gameNode position].x > fsx) {
      (*failPosition).x = fsx;
      passed = false;
    }else { //Passed
      (*failPosition).x = [gameNode position].x;
    }

    return passed;
}

/* Depth testing */
-(void) setZOrderByBodyPosition:(GameIsoObject*)g {
  float fixedPositionY = gameAreaSize.y - (g.body->GetPosition().y *
PTM_RATIO * PERSPECTIVE_RATIO) + g.zModifier;
  [g.sprite.parent reorderChild:g.sprite z:fixedPositionY];
}

/* Add a tree object */
-(void) addTreeAtPoint:(CGPoint)treePosition {
  GameIsoObject *tree = [[GameIsoObject alloc] init];

  /* CODE OMITTED */
}

/* Add a ball with a random size at a position */
-(GameIsoObject*) addBallAtPoint:(CGPoint)ballPosition {
  GameIsoObject *ball = [[GameIsoObject alloc] init];

  //Bounce and roll coefficients determine how high the ball boucnes
and how fast the ball rolls
  ball.bounceCoefficient = [Vector3D x:0.05f y:0.05f z:0.1f*scaleMod];
  ball.rollCoefficient = [Vector3D x:0.0005f y:0.0005f z:0.5f];

  /* CODE OMITTED */

  return ball;
}


@end
```

How it works...

In this recipe, we control the gunman as he runs around in a pseudo-3D world. Pressing **B** makes him fire colorful bouncing balls into the air. Pressing **A** makes him jump. Much like in a previous recipe, the user can pinch to zoom in or out.

- Box2D modifications:

  To create a somewhat realistic 3D effect, we need to store some more data inside the b2Body class. By searching for the string "Isometric Additions" in the *RecipeCollection02* project, you will find four sets of additions to the b2Body class. These changes add the following variables:

  ```
  float32 m_zPosition;
  float32 m_zSize;
  float32 m_zVelocity;
  bool m_handleZMiss;
  ```

  The position, size, and velocity variables allow us to perform some basic physical calculations on the Z plane. The m_handleZMiss variable tells us whether or not to send a message to a callback method when an object passes over or under another object on the Z plane.

- The GameIsoObject class:

  This new class adds some new variables that we can use in our engine. Particularly, yModifier and zModifier are simple values to help with sprite positioning and depth testing, respectively. The variables actualImageSize and inGameSize help to determine baseline image scaling.

- The isometricContactListener class:

  Here, we use our contact listener to check collision in the third or 'Z' dimension. If two collide on the X and Y but miss on the Z, then we disable physical collision response:

  ```
  contact->SetEnabled(false);
  ```

  We also call the following function on the corresponding gameArea instance:

  ```
  -(void) handleZMissWithObjA:(GameObject*)objA
  withObjB:(GameObject*)objB;
  ```

  This is useful, for instance, when you want to determine if someone jumped over a fence or if a ball went over a wall in a sports video game.

- Physics on the Z plane:

  This recipe overrides the normal step routine for its own custom routine. Here, we handle Z physics. This involves assuming an arbitrary, static ground at Z=0. Bodies are subjected to a GRAVITY constant that decreases Z velocity relative to the amount of time passing with each step. This ensures that physics on the Z-axis stays in sync with Box2D physics.

▸ Bouncing and rolling:

Each `GameIsoObject` has a `bounceCoefficient` and a `rollCoefficient`. These `Vector3D` instances determine the restitution and friction of bodies on all three planes:

```
ball.bounceCoefficient = [Vector3D x:0.05f y:0.05f
z:0.1f*scaleMod];
ball.rollCoefficient = [Vector3D x:0.0005f y:0.0005f z:0.5f];
```

This, combined with Box2D damping, restitution, and friction variables allows for a lot of customization.

▸ `PERSPECTIVE_RATIO` and depth testing:

This isometric setup assumes a **perspective ratio** of `0.5f`. This means that, for every `1.0f` of distance on the Y we only see `0.5f` of distance on the screen. In simpler terms, you could consider this the equivalent of having the camera looking down at the ground at a 45-degree angle. This acts as a mathematical reference for our forced perspective. So, when converting from the physical to the visual (or vice versa) we use `PTM_RATIO` on the X and Y axes and `PERSPECTIVE_RATIO` on only the Y-axis. In our `step` routine, we also apply depth testing. For this, we simply use Y body positions to determine object depth. All sprites are continually reordered.

▸ Shadows and image scaling on the Z-axis:

To further sell the visual trick of isometric perspective, we add shadow under every object using the `spriteShadow` variable. This shadow stays at height Z=0 at all times. We have it increase in size when an object goes further up into the air. Also, objects at higher altitudes are scaled up slightly. This is why we need a baseline scale for our `GameIsoObject` sprites. When these two effects are combined, they give a stronger impression of 3D space. Also, as you can see with trees and walls, shadows can be finely drawn (trees) or procedurally generated (walls).

▸ Camera limiting and zooming:

In the following method, we limit camera movement past the edges of the `gameArea`:

```
- (bool) checkCameraBoundsWithFailPosition:(CGPoint*)failPosition;
```

This method is then combined with pinch zooming to allow the user to zoom in and out to further survey the gameplay area. If you are planning to make use of this in-game zoom feature I highly recommend using mipmapping to smooth out shrunken textures.

There's More...

The physics simulation on the Z plane previously provided is very simple. For example, this example does not allow for variable height terrain or proper physical collision response on the Z-axis. Unfortunately, a more complex simulation would be outside the scope of this book.

- ▶ Side-scrolling with depth:

  This technique can be easily modified to create a side-scrolling isometric scene as opposed to a top-down isometric scene. Examples of this include Streets of Rage and NBA Jam for the Sega Genesis console. The gameplay angle would be foreshortened to `0.25f` or lower. Also, the custom-made Z-axis should represent depth as opposed to height since most physical interactions occur on the width and height planes.

5
Scenes and Menus

In this chapter, we will cover the following topics:

- ▶ Switching scenes
- ▶ Transitioning between scenes
- ▶ Using CCLayerMultiplex
- ▶ Using CCLabel
- ▶ Using CCMenu
- ▶ Creating shadowed menu labels
- ▶ UIKit alert dialogs
- ▶ Wrapping UIKit
- ▶ Creating draggable menu windows
- ▶ Creating a horizontal scrollable menu
- ▶ Creating a vertical sliding menu grid
- ▶ Creating a loading screen with indicator
- ▶ Creating a minimap

Introduction

All games have auxillary **Graphical User Interface** (**GUI**) requirements like **menus** and in-game **Heads-Up Displays** (**HUD**). In this chapter, we will explain the techniques used to create these elements as well as how to incorporate them into an underlying structure of scenes.

Switching scenes

A **scene** is the basic high-level `CCNode` object. All other nodes are considered children of a scene. Only one scene can be running at a time. Scenes are managed using a **stack** data structure. In this recipe, we will see how to **push** and **pop** scenes onto the stack.

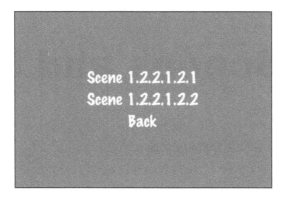

Getting ready

Please refer to the project *RecipeCollection02* for full working code of this recipe.

How to do it...

Execute the following code:

```
// TreeSceneMenu
// The node for our binary tree of scenes
@interface TreeSceneMenu : CCLayer {
  NSString *name;
}

+(id) sceneWithString:(NSString*)str;
-(id) initWithString:(NSString*)str;
-(void) goToScene1:(id)sender;
-(void) goToScene2:(id)sender;
-(void) back:(id)sender;

@end

@implementation TreeSceneMenu

+(id) sceneWithString:(NSString*)str {
```

```
  //Initialize our scene
  CCScene *s = [CCScene node];
  TreeSceneMenu *node = [[TreeSceneMenu alloc] initWithString:str];
  [s addChild:node z:0 tag:0];
  return s;
}

-(id) initWithString:(NSString*)str {
  if( (self=[super init]) ) {
    //Set scene name
    name = [NSString stringWithFormat:@"%@",str];
    [name retain];

    /* CODE OMITTED */

    //Buttons to push new scenes onto the stack
    CCMenuItemFont *scene1Item = [CCMenuItemFont
itemFromString:[NSString stringWithFormat:@"Scene %@.1",name]
target:self selector:@selector(goToScene1:)];
    CCMenuItemFont *scene2Item = [CCMenuItemFont
itemFromString:[NSString stringWithFormat:@"Scene %@.2",name]
target:self selector:@selector(goToScene2:)];

    //If we are at the root we "Quit" instead of going "Back"
    NSString *backStr = @"Back";
    if([str isEqualToString:@"1"]){
      backStr = @"Quit";
    }
    CCMenuItemFont *backItem = [CCMenuItemFont itemFromString:backStr
target:self selector:@selector(back:)];

    //Add menu items
    CCMenu *menu = [CCMenu menuWithItems: scene1Item, scene2Item,
backItem, nil];
    [menu alignItemsVertically];
    [self addChild:menu];
  }
  return self;
}

//Push scene 1
-(void) goToScene1:(id)sender {
  [[CCDirector sharedDirector] pushScene:[TreeSceneMenu
sceneWithString:[NSString stringWithFormat:@"%@.1",name]]];
}
```

```
//Push scene 2
-(void) goToScene2:(id)sender {
  [[CCDirector sharedDirector] pushScene:[TreeSceneMenu
sceneWithString:[NSString stringWithFormat:@"%@.2",name]]];
}

//Pop scene
-(void) back:(id)sender {
  [[CCDirector sharedDirector] popScene];
}

@end


//Our Base Recipe
@interface Ch5_SwitchingScenes : Recipe{}

-(CCLayer*) runRecipe;
-(void) goToScene1:(id)sender;

@end

@implementation Ch5_SwitchingScenes

-(CCLayer*) runRecipe {
  [super runRecipe];

  //Go to our initial scene
  CCMenuItemFont *goToScene1 = [CCMenuItemFont itemFromString:@"Go To
Scene 1" target:self selector:@selector(goToScene1:)];

  CCMenu *menu = [CCMenu menuWithItems: goToScene1, nil];
  [menu alignItemsVertically];
  [self addChild:menu];

  return self;
}

//Push initial scene
-(void) goToScene1:(id)sender {
  [[CCDirector sharedDirector] pushScene:[TreeSceneMenu
sceneWithString:@"1"]];
}

@end
```

How it works...

The common convention in Cocos2d is to sub-class CCLayer when creating a simple scene. This allows us to couple our single CCScene to a CCLayer using only one class. That class inherits CCLayer, but it has a class method that returns itself packaged inside a CCScene:

```
+(id) sceneWithString:(NSString*)str {
  //Initialize our scene
  CCScene *s = [CCScene node];
  TreeSceneMenu *node = [[TreeSceneMenu alloc] initWithString:str];
  [s addChild:node z:0 tag:0];
  return s;
}
```

In this example, our class is named TreeSceneMenu. By pressing one of its two buttons, you push another scene onto the stack with an appropriate sub-string name. This creates a binary tree of possible scene combinations. Popping the root scene will kick you back to the main recipe chooser scene.

► Layers versus scenes:

  The layer/scene distinction is mostly a formal one. Scenes separate out the most basic parts of a game and are treated as such. For example, there are a number of transitions that can be used when going between scenes (see the next recipe). Layers, on the other hand, are designed to be the only nodes directly added to scenes. Layers are where all the action happens. Other nodes are attached to them and they implement the TouchEventsDelegate protocol to handle input. The only difference between scenes and layers is that scenes require a little more memory and processor overhead when pushed onto the stack. So, the fewer scenes on the stack at any one time, the better.

Transitioning between scenes

As mentioned in the previous recipe, scenes are the root CCNodes and only one can be running at a time. When switching between scenes, we can apply transitions to make the scene change more explicit and stylish. In this recipe, you can demo all of the built-in scene transitions.

Getting ready

Please refer to the project *RecipeCollection02* for full working code of this recipe.

How to do it...

Execute the following code:

```
@implementation TransSceneMenu

+(id) sceneWithString:(NSString*)str withCurrentTransition:(int)ct {
  //Create scene
  CCScene *s = [CCScene node];
  TransSceneMenu *node = [[TransSceneMenu alloc] initWithString:str
withCurrentTransition:ct];
  [s addChild:node z:0 tag:0];
  return s;
}

-(id) initWithString:(NSString*)str withCurrentTransition:(int)ct {
  if( (self=[super init] )) {
    name = str;
    currentTransition = ct;

    /* CODE OMITTED */
  }
  return self;
}

-(void) prevScene:(id)sender {
  currentTransition--;
  if(currentTransition < 0){
    currentTransition = numTransitionTypes-1;
  }
  [self loadNewScene];
}

-(void) nextScene:(id)sender {
  currentTransition++;
  if(currentTransition >= numTransitionTypes){
    currentTransition = 0;
  }
  [self loadNewScene];
```

```
}

-(void) randomScene:(id)sender {
  currentTransition = arc4random()%numTransitionTypes;
  [self loadNewScene];
}

-(void) loadNewScene {
  [[CCDirector sharedDirector] popScene];
  NSString *className = [NSString stringWithFormat:@"%@",transitionTyp
es[currentTransition]];
  Class clazz = NSClassFromString (className);
  [[CCDirector sharedDirector] pushScene: [clazz
transitionWithDuration:1.2f scene:[TransSceneMenu
sceneWithString:className withCurrentTransition:currentTransition]]];
}

-(void) quit:(id)sender {
  [[CCDirector sharedDirector] popScene];
}


@end


//Our Base Recipe
@interface Ch5_SceneTransitions : Recipe{}

-(CCLayer*) runRecipe;
-(void) viewTransitions:(id)sender;

@end

@implementation Ch5_SceneTransitions

-(CCLayer*) runRecipe {
  [super runRecipe];

  CCMenuItemFont *viewTransitions = [CCMenuItemFont
itemFromString:@"View Transitions" target:self selector:@
selector(viewTransitions:)];

  CCMenu *menu = [CCMenu menuWithItems: viewTransitions, nil];
  [menu alignItemsVertically];
```

```
    [self addChild:menu];

    return self;
}

-(void) viewTransitions:(id)sender {
    [[CCDirector sharedDirector] pushScene:[TransSceneMenu
sceneWithString:@"" withCurrentTransition:0]];
}

@end
```

How it works...

The CCTransitionScene class creates a transition effect, when it is instantiated with a regular CCScene and then immediately pushed onto the scene stack. This is done using the following lines:

```
[[CCDirector sharedDirector] pushScene: [CCTransitionFade
transitionWithDuration:1.2f scene:[MyScene scene] withColor:ccWHITE]];
```

In this example, we are using a 'fade to white' transition while loading the MyScene scene. Here is a list of the built-in Cocos2d transition classes:

CCTransitionFadeTR, CCTransitionJumpZoom, CCTransitionMoveInL, CCTransitionSplitCols, CCTransitionSceneOriented. CCTransitionPageTurn, CCTransitionRadialCCW, CCTransitionFade, CCTransitionRotoZoom, CCTransitionShrinkGrow, CCTransitionSlideInL, and CCTransitionTurnOffTiles

There's more...

In addition to pushing a scene with a transition, you may also pop a scene with a transition by adding the following method to the CCDirector class:

```
//CCDirector.h
- (void) popSceneWithTransition: (Class)transitionClass
duration:(ccTime)t;

//CCDirector.m
-(void) popSceneWithTransition: (Class)transitionClass
duration:(ccTime)t {
    NSAssert( runningScene_ != nil, @"A running Scene is needed");

    [scenesStack_ removeLastObject];
    NSUInteger c = [scenesStack_ count];
```

```
    if( c == 0 ) {
        [self end];
    } else {
        CCScene* scene = [transitionClass transitionWithDuration:t
scene:[scenesStack_ objectAtIndex:c-1]];
        [scenesStack_ replaceObjectAtIndex:c-1 withObject:scene];
        nextScene_ = scene;
    }
}
```

This pops the scene with a nice transition effect.

Using CCLayerMultiplex

The CCLayerMultiplex class provides functionality to seamlessly switch between multiple layers. In this example, we have three similar layers assigned to a multiplex layer. Each layer displays buttons used to switch to any of the other layers.

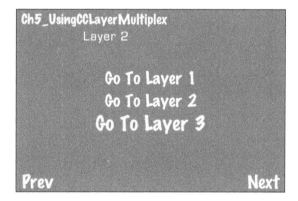

Getting ready

Please refer to the project _RecipeCollection02_ for full working code of this recipe.

How to do it...

Execute the following code:

```
@interface MultiplexLayerMenu : CCLayer {}

+(id) layerWithLayerNumber:(int)layerNumber;
-(id) initWithLayerNumber:(int)layerNumber;
```

```
-(void) goToLayer:(id)sender;

@end

@implementation MultiplexLayerMenu

+(id) layerWithLayerNumber:(int)layerNumber {
  return [[[MultiplexLayerMenu alloc] initWithLayerNumber:layerNumber]
autorelease];
}

-(id) initWithLayerNumber:(int)layerNumber {
  if( (self=[super init] )) {
    //Random background color
    CCSprite *bg = [CCSprite spriteWithFile:@"blank.png"];
    bg.position = ccp(240,160);
    [bg setTextureRect:CGRectMake(0,0,480,320)];
    [bg setColor:ccc3(arc4random()%150,arc4random()%150,arc4rand
om()%150)];
    [self addChild:bg];

    //Layer number as message
    CCLabelBMFont *message = [CCLabelBMFont labelWithString:[NSString
stringWithFormat:@"Layer %i",layerNumber+1] fntFile:@"eurostile_30.
fnt"];
    message.position = ccp(160,270);
    message.scale = 0.75f;
    [message setColor:ccc3(255,255,255)];
    [self addChild:message z:10];

    //Buttons to go to different layers
    CCMenuItemFont *goToLayer1 = [CCMenuItemFont itemFromString:@"Go
To Layer 1" target:self selector:@selector(goToLayer:)];
    CCMenuItemFont *goToLayer2 = [CCMenuItemFont itemFromString:@"Go
To Layer 2" target:self selector:@selector(goToLayer:)];
    CCMenuItemFont *goToLayer3 = [CCMenuItemFont itemFromString:@"Go
To Layer 3" target:self selector:@selector(goToLayer:)];
    goToLayer1.tag = 0; goToLayer2.tag = 1; goToLayer3.tag = 2;

    //Add menu items
    CCMenu *menu = [CCMenu menuWithItems: goToLayer1, goToLayer2,
goToLayer3, nil];
    [menu alignItemsVertically];
    [self addChild:menu];
  }
```

```
    return self;
  }

  //Switch to a different layer
  -(void) goToLayer:(id)sender {
    CCMenuItemFont *item = (CCMenuItemFont*)sender;
    [(CCLayerMultiplex*)parent_ switchTo:item.tag];
  }

@end


@interface Ch5_UsingCCLayerMultiplex : Recipe{}

  -(CCLayer*) runRecipe;

@end

@implementation Ch5_UsingCCLayerMultiplex

  -(CCLayer*) runRecipe {
    [super runRecipe];

    //Create our multiplex layer with three MultiplexLayerMenu objects
    CCLayerMultiplex *layer = [CCLayerMultiplex layerWithLayers:
[MultiplexLayerMenu layerWithLayerNumber:0], [MultiplexLayerMenu
layerWithLayerNumber:1],
      [MultiplexLayerMenu layerWithLayerNumber:2], nil];
    [self addChild: layer z:0];

    return self;
  }

@end
```

How it works...

This technique offers an alternative style of control flow from that of switching between scenes. It allows the instantiation of multiple layers, and the on-the-fly activation and suspension of those layers. The multiplex layer is created using the following class method:

```
+(id) layerWithLayers: (CCLayer*) layer, ... NS_REQUIRES_NIL_
TERMINATION;
```

There are many ways to make use of this technique. It provides a flat alternative to hierarchically stacking scenes.

Using CCLabel

Throughout this book, we've been making use of a number of different label types. In this recipe, we will briefly explain the three commonly used label classes: `CCLabelAtlas`, `CCLabelBMFont`, and `CCLabelTTF`.

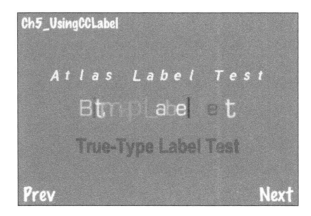

Getting ready

Please refer to the project *RecipeCollection02* for full working code of this recipe.

How to do it...

Execute the following code:

```
@implementation Ch5_UsingCCLabel

-(CCLayer*) runRecipe {
  [super runRecipe];

  //CCLabelAtlas for fixed-width bitmap fonts
  CCLabelAtlas *labelAtlas = [CCLabelAtlas labelWithString:@"Atlas
Label Test" charMapFile:@"tuffy_bold_italic-charmap.png" itemWidth:48
itemHeight:65 startCharMap:' '];
  [self addChild:labelAtlas z:0];
  labelAtlas.anchorPoint = ccp(0.5f,0.5f);
  labelAtlas.scale = 0.5f;
  labelAtlas.position = ccp(240,220);
  [labelAtlas setColor:ccc3(0,255,0)];
```

```
[labelAtlas runAction:[CCRepeatForever actionWithAction: [CCSequence
actions: [CCScaleTo actionWithDuration:1.0f scale:0.5f], [CCScaleTo
actionWithDuration:1.0f scale:0.25f], nil]]];

//CCLabelBMFont for variable-width bitmap fonts using FNT files
CCLabelBMFont *labelBMFont = [CCLabelBMFont labelWithString:@"Bitmap
Label Test" fntFile:@"eurostile_30.fnt"];
[self addChild:labelBMFont z:0];
labelBMFont.position = ccp(240,160);
for(id c in labelBMFont.children){
  CCSprite *child = (CCSprite*)c;
  [child setColor:ccc3(arc4random()%255,arc4random()%255,arc4rand
om()%255)];
  [child runAction:[CCRepeatForever actionWithAction:
    [CCSequence actions: [CCScaleTo actionWithDuration:arc4rand
om()%2+1 scale:1.75f], [CCScaleTo actionWithDuration:arc4random()%2+1
scale:0.75f], nil]
  ]];
}

//CCLabelTTF for true-type fonts
CCLabelTTF *labelTTF = [CCLabelTTF labelWithString:@"True-Type Label
Test" fontName:@"arial_narrow.otf" fontSize:32];
[self addChild:labelTTF z:0];
labelTTF.position = ccp(240,100);
[labelTTF runAction:[CCRepeatForever actionWithAction: [CCSequence
actions: [CCScaleTo actionWithDuration:2.0f scale:1.5f], [CCScaleTo
actionWithDuration:2.0f scale:0.5f], nil]]];
[labelTTF setColor:ccc3(0,0,255)];

return self;
}

@end
```

How it works...

Each label type has advantages and disadvantages.

▶   CCLabelAtlas:

    The simplest way to draw text onto the screen is to use the CCLabelAtlas class.
    This allows you to draw fixed-width bitmap fonts. It is a low-tech solution that
    essentially indexes a texture file sequentially using standard ASCII values. The only
    meta information provided is character size and what the first character in the map is.

▶ CCLabelBMFont:

The CCLabelBMFont class has the speed advantage of bitmap font drawing along with many other features. It uses the FNT file format to store non fixed-width bitmap fonts. These fonts can be created with a number of editors including **Hiero**, which can be found at: http://www.n4te.com/hiero/hiero.jnlp. CCLabelBMFont treats each character as a CCSprite sub-node. This allows us to manipulate them individually.

▶ CCLabelTTF:

Finally, the CCLabelTTF class allows drawing of **TrueType** fonts. This allows for the convenience of using built-in system fonts as well as other TrueType fonts that you can specify. It must be noted that TrueType fonts render slowly and should only be used for static text. Bitmap fonts should be used for text that will be updated frequently like a score display.

Using CCMenu

Cocos2d provides menu tools that make the process of creating a simple menu very easy. In this example, we will see how to create a simple menu, adjust menu alignment, enable/disable menu items, and more.

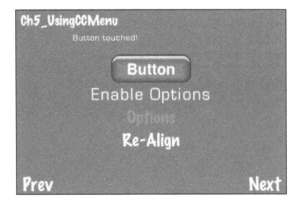

Getting ready

Please refer to the project *RecipeCollection02* for full working code of this recipe.

How to do it...

Execute the following code:

```
@implementation OptionsMenu

+(id) scene {
  //Create a scene
  CCScene *s = [CCScene node];
  OptionsMenu *node = [OptionsMenu node];
  [s addChild:node z:0 tag:0];
  return s;
}

-(id) init {
  if( (self=[super init] )) {
    /* CODE OMITTED */

    //Disabled title label for Sound option
    CCMenuItemFont *title1 = [CCMenuItemFont itemFromString:@"Sound"];
    [title1 setIsEnabled:NO];
    title1.color = ccc3(0,0,0);

    //Toggleable item for Sound option
    CCMenuItemToggle *item1 = [CCMenuItemToggle itemWithTarget:self
selector:@selector(soundToggle:) items:
      [CCMenuItemFont itemFromString: @"On"], [CCMenuItemFont
itemFromString: @"Off"], nil];

    //Disabled title label for Difficulty option
    CCMenuItemFont *title2 = [CCMenuItemFont
itemFromString:@"Difficulty"];
    [title2 setIsEnabled:NO];
    title2.color = ccc3(0,0,0);

    //Toggleable item for Difficulty option
    CCMenuItemToggle *item2 = [CCMenuItemToggle itemWithTarget:self
selector:@selector(difficultyToggle:) items:
      [CCMenuItemFont itemFromString: @"Easy"], [CCMenuItemFont
itemFromString: @"Medium"],
      [CCMenuItemFont itemFromString: @"Hard"], [CCMenuItemFont
itemFromString: @"Insane"], nil];

    //Back button
```

```
    CCMenuItemFont *back = [CCMenuItemFont itemFromString:@"Back"
target:self selector:@selector(back:)];

    //Finally, create our menu
    CCMenu *menu = [CCMenu menuWithItems:
            title1, title2,
            item1, item2,
            back, nil]; // 5 items.

    //Align items in columns
    [menu alignItemsInColumns:
     [NSNumber numberWithUnsignedInt:2],
     [NSNumber numberWithUnsignedInt:2],
     [NSNumber numberWithUnsignedInt:1],
     nil
     ];

    [self addChild:menu];
}
  return self;
}
-(void) back:(id)sender {
  [[CCDirector sharedDirector] popScene];
}
//Use the 'selectedIndex' variable to identify the touched item
-(void) soundToggle: (id) sender {
  CCMenuItem *item = (CCMenuItem*)sender;
  [message setString:[NSString stringWithFormat:@"Selected Sound
Index:%d", [item selectedIndex]]];
}
-(void) difficultyToggle: (id) sender {
  CCMenuItem *item = (CCMenuItem*)sender;
  [message setString:[NSString stringWithFormat:@"Selected Difficulty
Index:%d", [item selectedIndex]]];
}

@end

@implementation Ch5_UsingCCMenu

-(CCLayer*) runRecipe {
  [super runRecipe];

  //Set font size/name
```

```
  [CCMenuItemFont setFontSize:30];
  [CCMenuItemFont setFontName:@"Marker Felt"];

  //Image Button
  CCMenuItemSprite *imageButton = [CCMenuItemSprite
itemFromNormalSprite:[CCSprite spriteWithFile:@"button_unselected.
png"]
    selectedSprite:[CCSprite spriteWithFile:@"button_selected.png"]
disabledSprite:[CCSprite spriteWithFile:@"button_disabled.png"]
    target:self selector:@selector(buttonTouched:)];

  //Enable Options Label
  CCLabelBMFont *enableOptionsLabel = [CCLabelBMFont
labelWithString:@"Enable Options" fntFile:@"eurostile_30.fnt"];
  CCMenuItemLabel *enableOptions = [CCMenuItemLabel itemWithLabel:enab
leOptionsLabel target:self selector:@selector(enableOptions:)];

  //Options Label
  optionsItem = [CCMenuItemFont itemFromString:@"Options" target:self
selector:@selector(options:)];
  optionsItem.isEnabled = NO;

  //Re-Align Label
  CCMenuItemFont *reAlign = [CCMenuItemFont itemFromString:@"Re-Align"
target:self selector:@selector(reAlign:)];

  //Add menu items
  menu = [CCMenu menuWithItems: imageButton, enableOptions,
optionsItem, reAlign, nil];
  [menu alignItemsVertically];
  [self addChild:menu];

  return self;
}

-(void) buttonTouched:(id)sender {
    [message setString:@"Button touched!"];
}

-(void) options:(id)sender {
  [[CCDirector sharedDirector] pushScene:[OptionsMenu scene]];
}

-(void) enableOptions:(id)sender {
  optionsItem.isEnabled = !optionsItem.isEnabled;
```

```
    }

    //Randomly re-align our menu
    -(void) reAlign:(id)sender {
      int n = arc4random()%6;
      if(n == 0){
        [menu alignItemsVertically];
      }else if(n == 1){
        [menu alignItemsHorizontally];
      }else if(n == 2){
        [menu alignItemsHorizontallyWithPadding:arc4random()%30];
      }else if(n == 3){
        [menu alignItemsVerticallyWithPadding:arc4random()%30];
      }else if(n == 4){
        [menu alignItemsInColumns: [NSNumber numberWithUnsignedInt:2],
    [NSNumber numberWithUnsignedInt:2], nil];
      }else if(n == 5){
        [menu alignItemsInRows: [NSNumber numberWithUnsignedInt:2],
    [NSNumber numberWithUnsignedInt:2], nil];
      }
    }

    @end
```

How it works...

The CCMenu class acts as a container holding a configurable list of CCMenuItem objects:

> ▶ CCMenuItemFont:
>
>   The CCMenuItemFont class is a helper class designed to quickly create
>   CCMenuItemLabel objects using TrueType fonts. It provides class methods which
>   act as shortcuts to ease the process of creating a menu item label. Font name and
>   size are set through class methods:
>
>   ```
>   [CCMenuItemFont setFontSize:30];
>   [CCMenuItemFont setFontName:@"Marker Felt"];
>   ```
>
>   A CCMenuItemFont object is then created through a class method:
>
>   ```
>   CCMenuItemFont *reAlign = [CCMenuItemFont itemFromString:@"Re-
>   Align" target:self selector:@selector(reAlign:)];
>   ```
>
>   This class is used throughout the book to create menus item labels.

▶ `CCMenuItemLabel`:

 For more control over menu item labels, you can use `CCMenuItemLabel` directly:

```
CCLabelBMFont *enableOptionsLabel = [CCLabelBMFont
labelWithString:@"Enable Options" fntFile:@"eurostile_30.fnt"];
   CCMenuItemLabel *enableOptions = [CCMenuItemLabel it
emWithLabel:enableOptionsLabel target:self selector:@
selector(enableOptions:)];
```

This allows you to add bitmap fonts using `CCLabelBMFont` and `CCLabelAtlas`.

▶ `CCMenuItemSprite`:

The `CCMenuItemSprite` class creates a tappable button as a menu item instead of a textual label:

```
CCMenuItemSprite *imageButton = [CCMenuItemSprite
itemFromNormalSprite:[CCSprite spriteWithFile:@"button_unselected.
png"] selectedSprite:[CCSprite spriteWithFile:@"button_selected.
png"] disabledSprite:[CCSprite spriteWithFile:@"button_disabled.
png"] target:self selector:@selector(buttonTouched:)];
```

Two or three sprites are recommended to create a compelling button effect.

▶ `CCMenuItemToggle`: A toggle-able menu item contains a list of menu items to iterate through:

```
CCMenuItemToggle *item1 = [CCMenuItemToggle itemWithTarget:self
selector:@selector(soundToggle:) items: [CCMenuItemFont
itemFromString: @"On"], [CCMenuItemFont itemFromString: @"Off"],
nil];
```

The current state can be identified by the `selectedIndex` property on the menu item. This is usually handled in the item's callback method.

▶ Automatically aligning menu items:

By using the following methods, a `CCMenu` object's items can be aligned horizontally or vertically:

```
-(void) alignItemsVertically;
-(void) alignItemsVerticallyWithPadding:(float) padding;
-(void) alignItemsHorizontally;
-(void) alignItemsHorizontallyWithPadding: (float) padding;
```

Menus can also be aligned in columns or rows:

```
[menu alignItemsInColumns: [NSNumber numberWithUnsignedInt:2],
[NSNumber numberWithUnsignedInt:2], nil];
[menu alignItemsInRows: [NSNumber numberWithUnsignedInt:2],
[NSNumber numberWithUnsignedInt:2], nil];
```

The list of NSNumber objects must total the number of menu items attached to the menu for the alignment to process correctly.

▸ Manually aligning menu items:

Menu items can also be manually positioned using the position property like on any other CCNode object.

▸ Enabling/disabling menu items:

All menu items can be disabled so as to make them ignore touches. Labels can have their disabledColor property set to indicate this, while instances of CCMenuItemSprite have a specific sprite set to indicate this.

Creating shadowed menu labels

With a dynamic swirl of colors often in the background, labels can sometimes be hard to identify onscreen. To remedy this, we can create labels with dark shadows behind them. In this recipe, we will create a few of these labels.

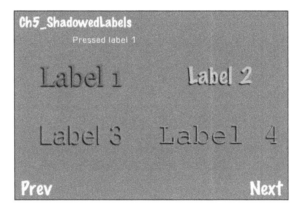

Getting ready

Please refer to the project *RecipeCollection02* for full working code of this recipe.

How to do it...

Execute the following code:

```
#import "ShadowLabel.h"

@implementation Ch5_ShadowedLabels
```

```
-(CCLayer*) runRecipe {
  [super runRecipe];

  /* Draw four different shadowed labels using 4 different fonts */
  [CCMenuItemFont setFontSize:47];
  [CCMenuItemFont setFontName:@"Georgia"];
  [self label:@"Label 1" at:ccp(-120,50) color:ccc3(0,50,255)
activeColor:ccc3(0,200,255) selector:@selector(labelTouched:) tag:1];

  [CCMenuItemFont setFontSize:40];
  [CCMenuItemFont setFontName:@"Marker Felt"];
  [self label:@"Label 2" at:ccp(120,50) color:ccc3(255,128,0)
activeColor:ccc3(255,255,0) selector:@selector(labelTouched:) tag:2];

  [CCMenuItemFont setFontSize:45];
  [CCMenuItemFont setFontName:@"Arial"];
  [self label:@"Label 3" at:ccp(-120,-50) color:ccc3(0,128,0)
activeColor:ccc3(0,255,0) selector:@selector(labelTouched:) tag:3];

  [CCMenuItemFont setFontSize:50];
  [CCMenuItemFont setFontName:@"Courier New"];
  [self label:@"Label 4" at:ccp(120,-50) color:ccc3(255,0,0)
activeColor:ccc3(255,255,0) selector:@selector(labelTouched:) tag:4];

  return self;
}

//Label creation helper method
-(void) label:(NSString*)s at:(CGPoint)p color:(ccColor3B)col
activeColor:(ccColor3B)activeCol selector:(SEL)sel tag:(int)tag {
  ShadowLabel *label = [ShadowLabel labelFromString:s target:self
selector:sel];
  label.position = p;
  label.color = col;
  label.activeColor = activeCol;
  label.tag = tag;

  CCMenu *menu = [CCMenu menuWithItems: label.shadow, label, nil];
  [self addChild:menu];
}

//Label touch callback
-(void) labelTouched:(id)sender {
  ShadowLabel *label = (ShadowLabel*)sender;
  [self showMessage:[NSString stringWithFormat:@"Pressed label
%d",label.tag]];
}

@end
```

How it works...

The `ShadowLabel` class creates a child `CCMenuItemLabel` object that is positioned behind and slightly to the side of its parent. Methods are overriden, so the two labels are synchronized.

> ► Caveats:
>
>   The only caveat to this approach is that menus using this class cannot be auto-aligned, as the 'shadow' label must also be added as a menu item.

There's More...

In this example, we set the `tag` property on each `ShadowLabel` so it can be properly identified during a callback. This is the same `tag` property that we've used in the past; only it has been re-purposed for this role.

> ► Adding shadows in a font editor:
>
>   As an alternative to technique used previously, shadows can be added to TrueType font using a font editor. The trade-off here is less code and a faster render time. But, you must first take time to add the shadows to the font in the editor.

UIKit alert dialogs

In the next two recipes, we will experiment with the black art of integrating **UIKit** elements into a Cocos2d game. In this example, we see a UIKit **alert** dialog with choices and associated callback methods.

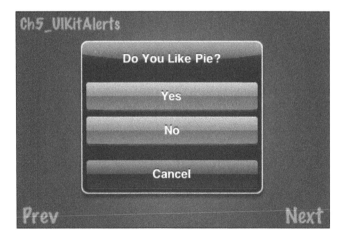

Getting ready

Please refer to the project *RecipeCollection02* for full working code of this recipe.

How to do it...

Execute the following code:

```
@interface Ch5_UIKitAlerts : Recipe <UIAlertViewDelegate>{}

-(CCLayer*) runRecipe;
-(void)showPieAlert;
-(void)alertView:(UIAlertView*)actionSheet
clickedButtonAtIndex:(NSInteger)buttonIndex;

@end

@implementation Ch5_UIKitAlerts

-(CCLayer*) runRecipe {
  [super runRecipe];

  [self showPieAlert];

  return self;
}

//Shows a UIAlertView
-(void)showPieAlert {
  UIAlertView *alert = [[UIAlertView alloc] initWithTitle:@"Do You
Like Pie?" message:@"" delegate:self cancelButtonTitle:@"Cancel" other
ButtonTitles:@"Yes",@"No",nil];

  [alert show];
  [alert release];
}

//AlertView callback
-(void)alertView:(UIAlertView *)actionSheet
clickedButtonAtIndex:(NSInteger)buttonIndex {
  if(buttonIndex == 0) {
    [self showMessage:@"You remain tight lipped on\nthe 'pie'
question."];
  }else if(buttonIndex == 1){
```

```
        [self showMessage:@"Ah yes, another lover of pie."];
    }else if(buttonIndex == 2){
        [self showMessage:@"You don't like pie?\nWhat's wrong with you?"];
    }
}

@end
```

How it works...

Showing an alert is fairly straightforward. We instantiate a `UIAlertView` object with some basic information and then call the `show` method. This launches our alert.

▶ Using `UIAlertViewDelegate`:

The `UIAlertViewDelegate` protocol dictates that we handle the following method:

```
-(void)alertView:(UIAlertView *)actionSheet
clickedButtonAtIndex:(NSInteger)buttonIndex;
```

This allows us to handle alert responses by inspecting the returned `buttonIndex` variable.

Wrapping UIKit

Other UIKit classes offer a wide range of time-tested UI functionality. Cocos2d requires the use of a UIKit wrapper to transform UIKit objects into `CCNode` objects, so that they may be manipulated properly. In this example, we will wrap two different classes and manipulate them onscreen.

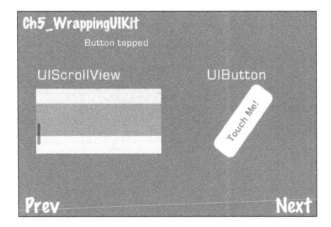

Please refer to the project *RecipeCollection02* for full working code of this recipe.

Execute the following code:

```
#import "CCUIViewWrapper.h"

@implementation Ch5_WrappingUIKit

-(CCLayer*) runRecipe {
  [super runRecipe];

  [self addSpinningButton];

  [self addScrollView];

  return self;
}

-(void) addSpinningButton {
  //Label
  CCLabelBMFont *label = [CCLabelBMFont labelWithString:@"UIButton"
fntFile:@"eurostile_30.fnt"];
  label.position = ccp(350,220);
  label.scale = 0.75f;
  [label setColor:ccc3(255,255,255)];
  [self addChild:label z:10];

  //Our UIButton example
  UIButton *button = [UIButton buttonWithType:UIButtonTypeRoundedRe
ct];
  [button addTarget:self action:@selector(buttonTapped:) forControlEve
nts:UIControlEventTouchDown];
  [button setTitle:@"Touch Me!" forState:UIControlStateNormal];
  button.frame = CGRectMake(0.0, 0.0, 120.0, 40.0);

  //Wrap the UIButton using CCUIViewWrapper
  CCUIViewWrapper *wrapper = [CCUIViewWrapper
wrapperForUIView:button];
  [self addChild:wrapper];
  wrapper.position = ccp(90,140);
```

```
   [wrapper runAction:[CCRepeatForever actionWithAction:[CCRotateBy
actionWithDuration:5.0f angle:360]]];
}

-(void) addScrollView {
  //Label
  CCLabelBMFont *label = [CCLabelBMFont
labelWithString:@"UIScrollView" fntFile:@"eurostile_30.fnt"];
  label.position = ccp(100,220);
  label.scale = 0.75f;
  [label setColor:ccc3(255,255,255)];
  [self addChild:label z:10];

  //Create a simple UIScrollView with colored UIViews
  CGPoint viewSize = ccp(200.0f,100.0f);
  CGPoint nodeSize = ccp(200.0f,50.0f);
  int nodeCount = 10;

  //Init scrollview
  UIScrollView *scrollview = [[UIScrollView alloc] initWithFrame:
CGRectMake(0, 0, viewSize.x, viewSize.y)];

  //Add nodes
  for (int i = 0; i <nodeCount; i++){
    CGFloat y = i * nodeSize.y;
    UIView *view = [[UIView alloc] initWithFrame:CGRectMake(0, y,
nodeSize.x, nodeSize.y)];
    view.backgroundColor = [UIColor colorWithRed:(CGFloat)random()/
(CGFloat)RAND_MAX green:(CGFloat)random()/(CGFloat)RAND_MAX
blue:(CGFloat)random()/(CGFloat)RAND_MAX alpha:1.0];
    [scrollview addSubview:view];
    [view release];
  }
  scrollview.contentSize = CGSizeMake(viewSize.x, viewSize.y *
nodeCount/2);

  //Wrap the UIScrollView object using CCUIViewWrapper
  CCUIViewWrapper *wrapper = [CCUIViewWrapper
wrapperForUIView:scrollview];
  [self addChild:wrapper];
  wrapper.rotation = -90;
  wrapper.position = ccp(50,400);
}

-(void) buttonTapped:(id)sender {
```

```
    [self showMessage:@"Button tapped"];
}

@end
```

How it works...

The `CCUIViewWrapper` takes any `UIView` object in its main creation class method:

```
CCUIViewWrapper *wrapper = [CCUIViewWrapper wrapperForUIView:button];
```

This object can be manipulated like a normal `CCSprite` object.

- ▶ `UIButton`:

    The advantages of using UIKit classes are numerous. The `UIButton` class allows for the creation of a nifty button with text on it.

- ▶ `UIScrollView`:

    In our other example, we create a more complex `UIScrollView` object. Although the syntax is somewhat messier than using a built-in Cocos2d class, the slick functionality provided by this UIKit view is difficult to duplicate.

- ▶ Mixing actions:

    If you scroll the `UIScrollView` object, you will see that the `UIButton` on the right stops spinning. Some UIKit actions take precedence over asynchronous Cocos2d actions.

- ▶ Autorotation and the UIKit wrapper:

    One limitation of this wrapper is that it does not currently work with Cocos2d auto-rotation. If you rotate your device, while using this recipe, you'll see that the elements onscreen do not rotate along with the screen. It is recommended that you use the following line in your `GameConfig.h` file:

    `#define GAME_AUTOROTATION kGameAutorotationNone`

    This will disable auto-rotation.

- ▶ The power of UIKit:

    It is best to use this wrapper as a starting point for experimenting with UIKit classes. Cocos2d and UIKit don't always play nice together, but being able to leverage a robust UI library like UIKit can help create fancier menus without the headaches of writing and testing your own UI code.

Creating draggable menu windows

Cocos2d is commonly thought of as a game development library and it has been treated as such in much of this book. However, Cocos2d is a robust solution for any 2D application. That said, draggable windows are a common element in many applications. In this example, we will create movable, collapsable menu windows.

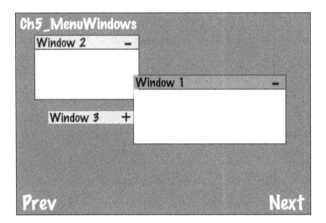

Getting ready

Please refer to the project *RecipeCollection02* for full working code of this recipe.

How to do it...

Execute the following code:

```
#import "GameMenuWindow.h"

@implementation Ch5_MenuWindows

-(CCLayer*) runRecipe {
  [super runRecipe];

  //Initialization
  windows = [[[NSMutableArray alloc] init] autorelease];
  CCNode *windowContainer = [[CCNode alloc] init];

  /* Create three menu windows with randomized positions */
  GameMenuWindow *window1 = [GameMenuWindow windowWithTitle:@"Window
1" size:CGSizeMake(arc4random()%200+120,arc4random()%100+50)];
  window1.position = ccp(arc4random()%100+150,arc4random()%140+100);
```

```
    [windowContainer addChild:window1 z:1];
    [windows addObject:window1];

    /* CODE OMITTED */

    //Sort our window array by zOrder
    //This allows ordered touching
    NSSortDescriptor *sorter = [[NSSortDescriptor alloc]
initWithKey:@"self.zOrder" ascending:NO];
    [windows sortUsingDescriptors:[NSArray arrayWithObject:sorter]];

    //Add window container node
    [self addChild:windowContainer];

    return self;
}

-(void) ccTouchesBegan:(NSSet *)touches withEvent:(UIEvent *)event {
    UITouch *touch = [touches anyObject];
    CGPoint point = [touch locationInView: [touch view]];
    point = [[CCDirector sharedDirector] convertToGL: point];

    //Sort our window array before we process a touch
    NSSortDescriptor *sorter = [[NSSortDescriptor alloc]
initWithKey:@"self.zOrder" ascending:NO];
    [windows sortUsingDescriptors:[NSArray arrayWithObject:sorter]];

    //Grab the window by touching the top bar. Otherwise, merely bring
the window to the front
    for(GameMenuWindow* w in windows){
        if(pointIsInRect(point, [w titleBarRect])){
            [w ccTouchesBegan:touches withEvent:event];
            return;
        }else if(pointIsInRect(point, [w rect])){
            [w bringToFront];
            return;
        }
    }
}
-(void) ccTouchesMoved:(NSSet *)touches withEvent:(UIEvent *)event {
    /* CODE OMITTED */

    //If we touched a window them we can drag it
    for(GameMenuWindow* w in windows){
```

```
    if(w.isTouched){
      [w ccTouchesMoved:touches withEvent:event];
    }
  }
}
-(void) ccTouchesEnded:(NSSet *)touches withEvent:(UIEvent *)event {
  /* CODE OMITTED */

  //End a touch if neccessary
  for(GameMenuWindow* w in windows){
    if(w.isTouched){
      [w ccTouchesEnded:touches withEvent:event];
    }
  }
}

@end
```

How it works...

The windows shown previously can be moved around by touching a title bar and then dragging. Pressing the plus/minus symbol expands or collapses the window content.

- Creating the title bar:

    The title bar and other parts of each window are created using the colored `blank. png` sprite technique. The label used in the title bar is anchored to the left, to left-align the text.

- Adding content to a window:

    Nodes can be added to the `content` sprite to add window content. This can include text, images, dynamic content, and so on. Please note that, in this example, nodes added to the `content` sprite are not clipped and can appear outside the window depending on node position.

- Sorting the windows:

    Before we can properly interact with the windows, they must be sorted by their `zOrder` property:

    ```
    NSSortDescriptor *sorter = [[NSSortDescriptor alloc]
    initWithKey:@"self.zOrder" ascending:NO];
      [windows sortUsingDescriptors:[NSArray arrayWithObject:sorter]];
    ```

The `NSSortDescriptor` class allows you to sort an `NSArray` container based on a common property of the objects being sorted. We specify the key `"self.zOrder"`. This re-orders the array according to the `zOrder` property. Now, when we iterate through the array looking for a touched window, the first one we find will be the window that appears on top.

Creating a horizontal scrollable menu

Cocos2d provides the rather mundane `CCMenuItemToggle` class to iterate through multiple `CCMenuItem` choices. In this example, we'll spice this up with the `LoopingMenu` class that mimics the iPod Touch album art shuffling visual technique.

Getting ready

Please refer to the project *RecipeCollection02* for full working code of this recipe.

How to do it...

Execute the following code:

```
#import "LoopingMenu.h"

@implementation Ch5_HorizScrollMenu

-(CCLayer*) runRecipe {
    [super runRecipe];
```

```
  message.position = ccp(70,270);

  /* Create 5 default sprites and 'selected' sprites */
  CCSprite *book1 = [CCSprite spriteWithFile:@"book1.jpg"];
  CCSprite *book2 = [CCSprite spriteWithFile:@"book2.jpg"];
  /* CODE OMITTED */

  CCSprite *book1_selected = [CCSprite spriteWithFile:@"book1.
jpg"]; book1_selected.color = ccc3(128,128,180); [book1_selected
setBlendFunc: (ccBlendFunc) { GL_ONE, GL_ONE }];
  CCSprite *book2_selected = [CCSprite spriteWithFile:@"book2.
jpg"]; book2_selected.color = ccc3(128,128,180); [book2_selected
setBlendFunc: (ccBlendFunc) { GL_ONE, GL_ONE }];
  /* CODE OMITTED */

  /* Create CCMenuItemSprites */
  CCMenuItemSprite* item1 = [CCMenuItemSprite
itemFromNormalSprite:book1 selectedSprite:book1_selected target:self
selector:@selector(bookClicked:)];
  item1.tag = 1;
  CCMenuItemSprite* item2 = [CCMenuItemSprite
itemFromNormalSprite:book2 selectedSprite:book2_selected target:self
selector:@selector(bookClicked:)];
  item2.tag = 2;
  /* CODE OMITTED */

  //Initialize LoopingMenu and add menu items
  LoopingMenu *menu = [LoopingMenu menuWithItems:item1, item2, item3,
item4, item5, nil];
  menu.position = ccp(240, 150);
  [menu alignItemsHorizontallyWithPadding:0];

  //Add LoopingMenu to scene
  [self addChild:menu];

  return self;
}

//Book clicked callback
-(void) bookClicked:(id)sender {
  CCMenuItemSprite *sprite = (CCMenuItemSprite*)sender;
  [self showMessage:[NSString stringWithFormat:@"Book clicked: %d",
sprite.tag]];
}

@end
```

How it works...

The `LoopingMenu` class inherits the `CCMenu` class. It uses the same basic creation method:

```
LoopingMenu *menu = [LoopingMenu menuWithItems:item1, item2, item3,
item4, item5, nil];
```

This creates an endlessly scrollable menu using the `CCMenuItem` objects provided. In this case, we use `CCMenuItemSprite` objects.

▶ Caveats:

   The one caveat with this technique is that the `CCMenuItem` objects are constantly rescaled. So, menu items cannot be rescaled before adding them to the `LoopingMenu` instance. The full image or label sizes must be used.

Creating a vertical sliding menu grid

Sometimes, you want a large number of menu choices onscreen at once. In this example, we see the `SlidingMenuGrid` class in action.

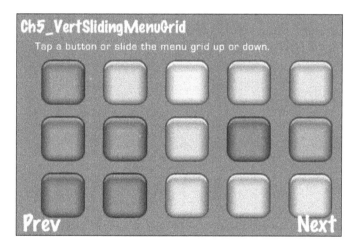

Getting ready

Please refer to the project *RecipeCollection02* for full working code of this recipe.

How to do it...

Execute the following code:

```
#import "SlidingMenuGrid.h"

@implementation Ch5_VertSlidingMenuGrid

-(CCLayer*) runRecipe {
  [super runRecipe];

  message.position = ccp(200,270);
  [self showMessage:@"Tap a button or slide the menu grid up or
down."];

  //Init item array
  NSMutableArray* allItems = [[[NSMutableArray alloc] init]
autorelease];

  /* Create 45 CCMenuItemSprite objects with tags, callback methods
and randomized colors */
  for (int i = 1; i <= 45; ++i) {
    CCSprite* normalSprite = [CCSprite spriteWithFile:@"sliding_menu_
button_0.png"];
    CCSprite* selectedSprite = [CCSprite spriteWithFile:@"sliding_
menu_button_1.png"];
    ccColor3B color = [self randomColor];
    normalSprite.color = color;
    selectedSprite.color = color;

    CCMenuItemSprite* item = [CCMenuItemSprite itemFromNormalSprit
e:normalSprite selectedSprite:selectedSprite target:self selector:@
selector(buttonClicked:)];
    item.tag = i;

    //Add each item to array
    [allItems addObject:item];
  }

  //Init SlidingMenuGrid object with array and some other information
  SlidingMenuGrid* menuGrid = [SlidingMenuGrid menuWithArray:allItems
cols:5 rows:3 position:ccp(70.f,220.f) padding:ccp(90.f,80.f)
verticalPages:true];
  [self addChild:menuGrid z:1];
```

```
      return self;
   }


   //Button clicked callback
   -(void) buttonClicked:(id)sender {
      CCMenuItemSprite *sprite = (CCMenuItemSprite*)sender;
      [self showMessage:[NSString stringWithFormat:@"Button clicked: %d",
   sprite.tag]];
   }


   //Random base color method
   -(ccColor3B) randomColor {
      /* CODE OMITTED */
   }


   @end
```

How it works...

Largely inspired by the über popular iOS game, Angry Birds, the `SlidingMenuGrid` class takes an array of `CCMenuItem` objects and arranges them in rows and columns as specified:

```
SlidingMenuGrid* menuGrid = [SlidingMenuGrid menuWithArray:allItems
cols:5 rows:3 position:ccp(70.f,220.f) padding:ccp(90.f,80.f)
verticalPages:true];
```

Menu items are divided up into pages depending on how many there are and how they fit onscreen.

 ▸ Going from page to page:

    Sliding vertically across the menu will switch from page to page.

 ▸ Tweaking `SlidingMenuGrid`:

    If you inspect `SlidingMenuGrid.h` and `SlidingMenuGrid.mm`, you can see a number of variables that determine the behavior of the menu grid, including the distance required to 'page' the menu and paging animation speed.

Creating a loading screen with an indicator

Games with large levels often incur long load times. If level elements can be loaded in asynchronous steps, then we can give the user some reassuring feedback that the game is still loading and hasn't crashed.

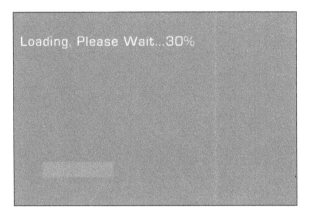

Getting ready

Please refer to the project *RecipeCollection02* for full working code of this recipe.

How to do it...

Execute the following code:

```
/* The actual 'game' class where we display the textures we loaded
asynchronously */
@implementation GameScene

+(id) sceneWithLevel:(NSString*)str {
  //Create our scene
  CCScene *s = [CCScene node];
  GameScene *node = [[GameScene alloc] initWithLevel:str];
  [s addChild:node z:0 tag:0];
  return s;
}

-(id) initWithLevel:(NSString*)str {
  if( (self=[super init] )) {
    //Load our level
    [self loadLevel:str];
```

```
    /* CODE OMITTED */

    //Create a label to indicate that this is the loaded level
    CCLabelBMFont *label = [CCLabelBMFont labelWithString:@"The Loaded
Level:" fntFile:@"eurostile_30.fnt"];
    /* CODE OMITTED */

    //Quit button
    CCMenuItemFont *quitItem = [CCMenuItemFont itemFromString:@"Quit"
target:self selector:@selector(quit:)];
    CCMenu *menu = [CCMenu menuWithItems: quitItem, nil];
    menu.position = ccp(430,300);
    [self addChild:menu z:10];
  }
  return self;
}


//Quit callback
-(void) quit:(id)sender {
  [[CCDirector sharedDirector] popScene];

  //Clear all loaded textures (including ones from other recipes)
  [[CCTextureCache sharedTextureCache] removeAllTextures];
}


//Load level file and process sprites
-(void) loadLevel:(NSString*)str {
  NSString *jsonString = [[NSString alloc] initWithContentsOfFile:getA
ctualPath(str) encoding:NSUTF8StringEncoding error:nil];
  NSData *jsonData = [jsonString dataUsingEncoding:NSUTF32BigEndianSt
ringEncoding];
  NSDictionary *dict = [[CJSONDeserializer deserializer] deserializeAs
Dictionary:jsonData error:nil];

  NSArray *nodes = [dict objectForKey:@"nodes"];
  for (id node in nodes) {
    if([[node objectForKey:@"type"] isEqualToString:@"spriteFile"]){
      [self processSpriteFile:node];
    }
  }
}

-(void) processSpriteFile:(NSDictionary*)node {
  //Init the sprite
  NSString *file = [node objectForKey:@"file"];
```

```objc
    CCSprite *sprite = [CCSprite spriteWithFile:file];

    //Set sprite position
    sprite.position = ccp(arc4random()%480, arc4random()%200);

    //Each numeric value is an NSString or NSNumber that must be cast
into a float
    sprite.scale = [[node objectForKey:@"scale"] floatValue];

    //Set the anchor point so objects are positioned from the bottom-up
    sprite.anchorPoint = ccp(0.5,0);

    //Finally, add the sprite
    [self addChild:sprite z:2];
}

@end

@implementation LoadingScene

+(id) sceneWithLevel:(NSString*)str {
    //Create our scene
    CCScene *s = [CCScene node];
    LoadingScene *node = [[LoadingScene alloc] initWithLevel:str];
    [s addChild:node z:0 tag:0];
    return s;
}

-(id) initWithLevel:(NSString*)str {
    if( (self=[super init] )) {
        //Set levelStr
        levelStr = str;
        [levelStr retain];

        /* CODE OMITTED */

        //Set the initial loading message
        loadingMessage = [CCLabelBMFont labelWithString:@"Loading, Please
Wait...0%" fntFile:@"eurostile_30.fnt"];
        /* CODE OMITTED */

        //Create an initial '0%' loading bar
        loadingBar = [CCSprite spriteWithFile:@"blank.png"];
        loadingBar.color = ccc3(255,0,0);
```

```
    [loadingBar setTextureRect:CGRectMake(0,0,10,25)];
    loadingBar.position = ccp(50,50);
    loadingBar.anchorPoint = ccp(0,0);
    [self addChild:loadingBar z:10];

    //Start level pre-load
    [self preloadLevel];
  }
  return self;
}


//Asynchronously load all required textures
-(void) preloadLevel {
  nodesLoaded = 0;

  NSString *jsonString = [[NSString alloc] initWithContentsOfFile:getA
ctualPath(levelStr) encoding:NSUTF8StringEncoding error:nil];
  NSData *jsonData = [jsonString dataUsingEncoding:NSUTF32BigEndianSt
ringEncoding];
  NSDictionary *dict = [[CJSONDeserializer deserializer] deserializeAs
Dictionary:jsonData error:nil];

  NSArray *nodes = [dict objectForKey:@"nodes"];

  nodesToLoad = [nodes count];

  for (id node in nodes) {
    if([[node objectForKey:@"type"] isEqualToString:@"spriteFile"]){
      [self preloadSpriteFile:node];
    }
  }
}


//Asynchronously load a texture and call the specified callback when
finished
-(void) preloadSpriteFile:(NSDictionary*)node {
  NSString *file = [node objectForKey:@"file"];
  [[CCTextureCache sharedTextureCache] addImageAsync:file target:self
selector:@selector(nodeLoaded:)];
}


//The loading callback
//This increments nodesLoaded and reloads the indicators accordingly
-(void) nodeLoaded:(id)sender {
  nodesLoaded++;
```

```
    float percentComplete = 100.0f * (nodesLoaded / nodesToLoad);
    [loadingMessage setString:[NSString stringWithFormat:@"Loading,
Please Wait...%d%@", (int)percentComplete, @"%"]];

    //When we are 100% complete we run the game
    if(percentComplete >= 100.0f){
        [self runAction:[CCSequence actions: [CCDelayTime
actionWithDuration:0.25f], [CCCallFunc actionWithTarget:self
selector:@selector(runGame:)], nil]];
    }

    //Grow the loading bar
    [loadingBar setTextureRect:CGRectMake(0,0,percentComplete*4,25)];
}

//First pop this scene then load the game scene
-(void) runGame:(id)sender {
    [[CCDirector sharedDirector] popScene];
    [[CCDirector sharedDirector] pushScene:[GameScene
sceneWithLevel:@"level1.json"]];
}

@end

@implementation Ch5_LoadingScreen

-(CCLayer*) runRecipe {
    [super runRecipe];

    //The load level button
    CCMenuItemFont *loadLevelItem = [CCMenuItemFont
itemFromString:@"Load Level" target:self selector:@
selector(loadLevel:)];
    CCMenu *menu = [CCMenu menuWithItems: loadLevelItem, nil];
    menu.position = ccp(240,160);
    [self addChild:menu];

    return self;
}

//Callback to load the level
-(void) loadLevel:(id)sender {
    [[CCDirector sharedDirector] pushScene:[LoadingScene
sceneWithLevel:@"level1.json"]];
}


@end
```

How it works...

This recipe reads through a JSON file and loads the images specified. For more information about loading data from a JSON file, please refer to the recipe entitled *Reading JSON data files* located in *Chapter 3, Files and Data*. Here, in total, we load 10 images, totaling about 6 megabytes. Loading time depends on the device the application is running on (the simulator, the iPhone 4, the iPad, and so on).

- ▶ Asynchronous texture loading:

  We can create this loading screen because we have the capability to asynchronously load textures using the following method call:

  ```
  [[CCTextureCache sharedTextureCache] addImageAsync:file
  target:self selector:@selector(nodeLoaded:)];
  ```

  Every time the `nodeLoaded` callback fires, we increment a counter to keep track of files loaded. Even though this ignores the variance of file sizes being loaded, this gives us a rough estimate of how far along we are in the loading process. Displaying this graphically in a bar, gives the user some basic visual feedback without going into too much detail.

- ▶ Switching to the game scene:

  Once all the images are loaded asynchronously, we pop the loading scene and switch to the main game scene. The JSON file name is passed along so that a second pass can be made to actually display the images onscreen. Because these images have been pre-loaded, the scene displays immediately.

- ▶ Unloading textures:

  When we are finished with our game, we unload all loaded textures:

  ```
  [[CCTextureCache sharedTextureCache] removeAllTextures];
  ```

  This unloads all loaded textures including ones loaded anywhere else in the application. Textures can also be removed manually by calling the `release` method on the ones to be removed, and then calling the `removeUnusedTextures` method on the `sharedTextureCache` singleton. Keep in mind that `removeUnusedTextures` also removes textures added to `CCTextureCache`. It might be safer to remove textures individually using one of the following methods:

  ```
  -(void) removeTexture: (CCTexture2D*) tex;
  -(void) removeTextureForKey: (NSString*) textureKeyName;
  ```

Creating a minimap

An engaging and informative in-game HUD is a crucial piece of most games. Mobile games, in particular, often blend user input with heads-up information due to the small amount of screen real estate available. In this example, we will create a **Minimap** to help the player navigate the terrain in the isometric game demo from the last chapter.

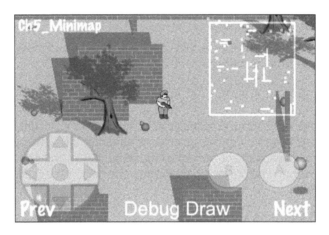

Getting ready

Please refer to the project *RecipeCollection02* for full working code of this recipe.

How to do it...

Execute the following code:

```
#import "Minimap.h"

@implementation Ch5_Minimap

-(CCLayer*) runRecipe {
    //Initialize the Minimap object
    minimap = [[[Minimap alloc] init] autorelease];
    minimap.position = ccp(300,140);
    [self addChild:minimap z:10];

    //Run our top-down isometric game recipe
    [super runRecipe];

    //Add trees as static objects
```

```
  for(id t in trees){
    GameObject *tree = (GameObject*)t;
    [minimap addStaticObject:ccp(tree.body->GetPosition().x, tree.
body->GetPosition().y)];
  }

  return self;
}

-(void) step:(ccTime)delta {
  [super step:delta];

  //Set the actor position
  [minimap setActor: ccp(gunman.body->GetPosition().x, gunman.body-
>GetPosition().y)];

  //Set individual projectile positions
  for(id b in balls){
    GameObject *ball = (GameObject*)b;
    [minimap setProjectile:ccp(ball.body->GetPosition().x, ball.body-
>GetPosition().y) withKey:[NSString stringWithFormat:@"%d", ball.
tag]];
  }
}

//We override this method to automatically add walls to the minimap
-(void) addBrickWallFrom:(CGPoint)p1 to:(CGPoint)p2 height:(float)
height {
  //Convert wall vertex positions to the properly scaled Box2D
coordinates
  CGPoint vert1 = ccp(p1.x/PTM_RATIO,p1.y/PTM_RATIO/PERSPECTIVE_
RATIO);
  CGPoint vert2 = ccp(p2.x/PTM_RATIO,p2.y/PTM_RATIO/PERSPECTIVE_
RATIO);

  //Add both wall vertices
  [minimap addWallWithVertex1:vert1 withVertex2:vert2];

  [super addBrickWallFrom:p1 to:p2 height:height];
}

@end
```

How it works...

The minimap shown in this example, is basically a simple graphical representation of the Box2D world similar to that of the Box2D debug drawing routines. In this instance, we have tailored the OpenGL drawing code to fit our needs.

▶ Generalizing the minimap:

The `Minimap` class generalizes physical elements into a number of types and then draws these types using specific colors. These include walls, projectiles, static objects, and a central actor.

▶ Walls:

Wall vertices are stored in two `NSMutableArray` objects. These are designed to be set initially and never updated.

▶ Projectiles:

Projectile coordinates are stored in a single `NSMutableDictionary` object. This allows us to update all projectiles repeatedly by using their `tag` property as a key in the dictionary. The implication is that projectiles are in a constant state of movement.

▶ Static objects:

Static objects in this example are trees. They represent static points on the map that do not move. They are drawn with the same color as the walls. Size information is not stored as it is assumed that static objects are not very large.

▶ The central actor:

Finally, a central actor position is shown as a large blue point.

▶ Customizing the `Minimap` class:

The `Minimap` class represents a generic template that can be customized for any game type or situation. By changing the `scale` property, position information, and drawing routine, the `Minimap` can be molded for many different uses.

6
Audio

In this chapter, we will cover the following topics:

- ▸ Playing sounds and music
- ▸ Modifying audio properties
- ▸ Fading sounds and music
- ▸ Using audio in a game
- ▸ Using positional audio in a game
- ▸ Metering background music
- ▸ Metering dialogue for animation
- ▸ Recording audio
- ▸ Streaming audio
- ▸ Using the iPod music library
- ▸ Creating a MIDI synthesizer
- ▸ Speech recognition and text to speech

Introduction

Depending on what kind of game you're making, adding audio can be anything from a simple to a daunting task. In this chapter we will integrate sounds and music into game examples. We will also use advanced audio techniques like metering, recording, speech recognition, and more.

Playing sounds and music

Most games use a variety of sound effects and at most a few different background music tracks. **CocosDenshion** is the audio library built into Cocos2d. It provides a number of features including the **SimpleAudioEngine** API. In this recipe, we will use this API to play sounds and music.

Getting ready

Please refer to the project *RecipeCollection02* for full working code of this recipe.

How to do it...

Execute the following code:

```
#import "SimpleAudioEngine.h"

@implementation Ch6_SoundsAndMusic

-(CCLayer*) runRecipe {
  //Initialize the audio engine
  sae = [SimpleAudioEngine sharedEngine];

  //Background music is stopped on resign and resumed on become active
  [[CDAudioManager sharedManager] setResignBehavior:kAMRBStopPlay
autoHandle:YES];
```

```objc
  //Initialize source container
  soundSources = [[NSMutableDictionary alloc] init];

  //Add the sounds
  [self loadSoundEffect:@"crazy_chimp.caf"];
  [self loadSoundEffect:@"rapid_gunfire.caf"];
  [self loadSoundEffect:@"howie_scream.caf"];
  [self loadSoundEffect:@"air_horn.caf"];
  [self loadSoundEffect:@"slide_whistle.caf"];

  //Add the background music
  [self loadBackgroundMusic:@"hiphop_boss_man_by_p0ss.mp3"];

  //Add menu items
  CCMenuItemSprite *musicItem = [self menuItemFromSpriteFile:@"music_
note.png" tag:0];
  CCMenuItemSprite *chimpItem = [self menuItemFromSpriteFile:@"you_
stupid_monkey.png" tag:1];
  CCMenuItemSprite *gunItem = [self menuItemFromSpriteFile:@"tommy_
gun.png" tag:2];
  CCMenuItemSprite *screamItem = [self menuItemFromSpriteFile:@"yaaarg
h.png" tag:3];
  CCMenuItemSprite *airHornItem = [self menuItemFromSpriteFile:@"air_
horn.png" tag:4];
  CCMenuItemSprite *slideWhistleItem = [self
menuItemFromSpriteFile:@"slide_whistle.png" tag:5];

  //Create our menu
  CCMenu *menu = [CCMenu menuWithItems: musicItem, chimpItem, gunItem,
screamItem, airHornItem, slideWhistleItem, nil];
  [menu alignItemsInColumns: [NSNumber numberWithUnsignedInt:3],
[NSNumber numberWithUnsignedInt:3], nil];
  menu.position = ccp(240,140);
  [self addChild:menu];

  return self;
}

//Play sound callback
-(void) playSoundNumber:(id)sender {
  CCMenuItem *item = (CCMenuItem*)sender;
  int number = item.tag;

  if(number == 0){
    [self playBackgroundMusic:@"hiphop_boss_man_by_p0ss.mp3"];
```

```
   }else if(number == 1){
     [self playSoundFile:@"crazy_chimp.caf"];
   }else if(number == 2){
     [self playSoundFile:@"rapid_gunfire.caf"];
   }else if(number == 3){
     [self playSoundFile:@"howie_scream.caf"];
   }else if(number == 4){
     [self playSoundFile:@"air_horn.caf"];
   }else if(number == 5){
     [self playSoundFile:@"slide_whistle.caf"];
   }
}


-(void) loadBackgroundMusic:(NSString*)fn {
  //Pre-load background music
  [sae preloadBackgroundMusic:fn];
}


-(void) playBackgroundMusic:(NSString*)fn {
  if (![sae isBackgroundMusicPlaying]) {
    //Play background music
    [sae playBackgroundMusic:fn];
  }else{
    //Stop music if its currently playing
    [sae stopBackgroundMusic];
  }
}


-(CDSoundSource*) loadSoundEffect:(NSString*)fn {
  //Pre-load sound
  [sae preloadEffect:fn];

  //Init sound
  CDSoundSource *sound = [[sae soundSourceForFile:fn] retain];

  //Add sound to container
  [soundSources setObject:sound forKey:fn];

  return sound;
}


-(void) playSoundFile:(NSString*)fn {
  //Get sound
  CDSoundSource *sound = [soundSources objectForKey:fn];
```

```
    //Play sound
    [sound play];
}
-(void) cleanRecipe {
    //Stop background music
    [sae stopBackgroundMusic];

    for(id s in soundSources){
        //Release source
        CDSoundSource *source = [soundSources objectForKey:s];
        [source release];
    }
    [soundSources release];

    //End engine
    [SimpleAudioEngine end];
    sae = nil;

    [super cleanRecipe];
}

@end
```

How it works...

The `SimpleAudioEngine` class provides the user with a very simple interface for basic audio playback. The `[SimpleAudioEngine sharedEngine]` singleton is merely a simplified wrapper over the `[CDAudioManager sharedManager]` singleton provided by CocosDenshion.

▶ Initialization:

No initialization of `SimpleAudioEngine` is necessary. In this recipe we simply maintain a pointer to `[SimpleAudioEngine sharedEngine]` to shorten some code. We set **resign behavior** using the following line. This changes audio behavior when the application is suspended or otherwise interrupted.

`[[CDAudioManager sharedManager] setResignBehavior:kAMRBStopPlay autoHandle:YES];`

This overrides the `applicationWillResignActive` method specified under the `UIApplicationDelegate` implemented by `CDAudioManager`. Other resign types are defined in `CDAudioManager.h`. This one stops background music on resign (pressing the home button on an iOS device) and plays the background music when the application becomes active.

▶ Playing sound effects:

Each sound effect that we'll play is an instance of `CDSoundSource`. "Loading" a sound effect involves pre-loading it using `SimpleAudioEngine`. Playing a sound without pre-loading it will result in a delay and diminished sound quality. To pre-load a sound, use the following line:

```
[sae preloadEffect:@"crazy_chimp.caf"];
```

Initializing a `CDSoundSource` object:

```
CDSoundSource *sound = [[sae soundSourceForFile:fn] retain];
```

And finally, maintaining a reference to that object:

```
NSMutableDictionary *soundSources = [[[NSMutableDictionary alloc]
init] autorelease];
[soundSources setObject:sound forKey:fn];
```

To play a sound, we simply get the reference and call the `play` method:

```
CDSoundSource *sound = [soundSources objectForKey:fn];
[sound play];
```

`SimpleAudioEngine` hides all the complex aspects of this process.

▶ Playing background music:

Playing background music is similar to playing sound effects except that there can only be one piece of background music playing at a given time:

```
[sae preloadBackgroundMusic: @"hiphop_boss_man_by_p0ss.mp3"];
[sae playBackgroundMusic:@"hiphop_boss_man_by_p0ss.mp3"];
```

If necessary you can obtain a reference to the actual background music `CDLongAudioSource` object:

```
CDLongAudioSource *bgm = [CDAudioManager sharedManager].
backgroundMusic;
```

This class is optimized for longer pieces of audio like music and narration.

There's More...

Real time audio decoding and playback, especially on a mobile device, requires the use of specific audio formats.

▶ CDSoundSource formats:

The recommended encoding for sound effects is **16-bit Mono Wave** for uncompressed audio files and **IMA4** in a **CAF** container for lossy audio files.

- Converting to IMA4 audio files:

  On a Unix-based system, you can use the **afconvert** tool to convert from a number of formats to IMA4:

  ```
  afconvert -f caff -d ima4 mysound.wav
  ```

- CDLongAudioSource formats:

  For the playback of music and other long audio, any format supported by Apple's `AVAudioPlayer` will work. The format typically used is **MP3**.

- Memory sizes:

  Although compressing audio reduces disk space requirements, all sound effects are stored in memory as **16-bit uncompressed PCM**. So, compressing sound effects will not reduce your application's memory footprint. This becomes a factor for larger and more sound intensive games.

Modifying audio properties

CocosDenshion provides functionality to change the **pitch**, **gain,** and **pan** properties of an audio source. Pitch is the frequency, gain is volume, and pan is a way to shift volume between left and right speakers. In this example, we will create a music-bending instrument to display these properties being dynamically modified.

Getting ready

Please refer to the project *RecipeCollection02* for full working code of this recipe.

How to do it...

Execute the following code:

```
#import "SimpleAudioEngine.h"

@implementation Ch6_AudioProperties

-(CCLayer*) runRecipe {
  //Enable accelerometer support
  self.isAccelerometerEnabled = YES;
  [[UIAccelerometer sharedAccelerometer] setUpdateInterval:(1.0 /
60)];

  //Add background
  CCSprite *bg = [CCSprite spriteWithFile:@"synth_tone_sheet.png"];
  bg.position = ccp(240,160);
  [self addChild:bg];

  //Initialize the audio engine
  sae = [SimpleAudioEngine sharedEngine];

  //Background music is stopped on resign and resumed on
     becoming active
  [[CDAudioManager sharedManager] setResignBehavior:kAMRBStopPlay
autoHandle:YES];

  //Initialize note container
  notes = [[NSMutableDictionary alloc] init];
  noteSprites = [[NSMutableDictionary alloc] init];

  //Preload tone
  [sae preloadEffect:@"synth_tone_mono.caf"];

  return self;
}

-(void) ccTouchesBegan:(NSSet *)touches withEvent:(UIEvent *)event {
  //Process multiple touches
  for(int i=0; i<[[touches allObjects] count]; i++){
    UITouch *touch = [[touches allObjects] objectAtIndex:i];
    CGPoint point = [touch locationInView: [touch view]];
    point = [[CCDirector sharedDirector] convertToGL: point];

    //Use [touch hash] as a key for this sound source
```

```
      NSString *key = [NSString stringWithFormat:@"%d",[touch hash]];
      if([notes objectForKey:key]){
        CDSoundSource *sound = [notes objectForKey:key];
        [sound release];
        [notes removeObjectForKey:key];

        CCSprite *sprite = [noteSprites objectForKey:key];
        [self removeChild:sprite cleanup:YES];
        [noteSprites removeObjectForKey:key];
      }

      //Play our sound with custom pitch and gain
      CDSoundSource *sound = [[sae soundSourceForFile:@"synth_tone_mono.
caf"] retain];
      [sound play];
      sound.looping = YES;
      [notes setObject:sound forKey:key];
      sound.pitch = point.x/240.0f;
      sound.gain = point.y/320.0f;

      //Show music note where you touched
      CCSprite *sprite = [CCSprite spriteWithFile:@"music_note.png"];
      sprite.position = point;
      [noteSprites setObject:sprite forKey:key];
      sprite.scale = (point.y/320.0f)/2 + 0.25f;
      [self addChild:sprite];
    }
}

-(void) ccTouchesMoved:(NSSet *)touches withEvent:(UIEvent *)event {
  //Adjust sound sources and music note positions
  for(int i=0; i<[[touches allObjects] count]; i++){
    UITouch *touch = [[touches allObjects] objectAtIndex:i];
    CGPoint point = [touch locationInView: [touch view]];
    point = [[CCDirector sharedDirector] convertToGL: point];

    NSString *key = [NSString stringWithFormat:@"%d",[touch hash]];
    if([notes objectForKey:key]){
      CDSoundSource *sound = [notes objectForKey:key];
      sound.pitch = point.x/240.0f;
      sound.gain = point.y/320.0f;

      CCSprite *sprite = [noteSprites objectForKey:key];
      sprite.position = point;
```

```
        sprite.scale = (point.y/320.0f)/2 + 0.25f;
      }
    }
  }


  -(void) ccTouchesEnded:(NSSet *)touches withEvent:(UIEvent *)event {
    //Stop sounds and remove sprites
    for(int i=0; i<[[touches allObjects] count]; i++){
      UITouch *touch = [[touches allObjects] objectAtIndex:i];
      CGPoint point = [touch locationInView: [touch view]];
      point = [[CCDirector sharedDirector] convertToGL: point];

      NSString *key = [NSString stringWithFormat:@"%d",[touch hash]];
      if([notes objectForKey:key]){
        //Stop and remove sound source
        CDSoundSource *sound = [notes objectForKey:key];
        [sound stop];
        [sound release];
        [notes removeObjectForKey:key];

        //Remove sprite
        CCSprite *sprite = [noteSprites objectForKey:key];
        [self removeChild:sprite cleanup:YES];
        [noteSprites removeObjectForKey:key];
      }
    }
  }


  //Adjust sound pan by turning the device sideways
  - (void) accelerometer:(UIAccelerometer*)accelerometer
  didAccelerate:(UIAcceleration*)acceleration{
    for(id s in notes){
      CDSoundSource *sound = [notes objectForKey:s];
      sound.pan = -acceleration.y;     //"Turn" left to pan to the left
  speaker
    }
  }

  @end
```

How it works...

The first thing needed for this recipe is a short, constant, mid-range synthesized tone. This was created in **GarageBand** and then modified using **Audacity**. When you touch the screen the note is played:

```
CDSoundSource *sound = [[sae soundSourceForFile:@"synth_tone_mono.
caf"] retain];
[sound play];
sound.looping = YES;
```

Now we need to set the `pitch` between 0 and 2 according to the X position of the touch:

```
sound.pitch = point.x/240.0f;
```

We set the `gain` property between 0 and 1 according to the Y position of the touch:

```
sound.gain = point.y/320.0f;
```

Tilting the device will set the `pan` property. Tilt to the left to hear all tones more in your left ear and to the right to hear them more in your right:

```
for(id s in notes){
    CDSoundSource *sound = [notes objectForKey:s];
    sound.pan = -acceleration.y;  //"Turn" left to pan to the left
speaker
}
```

As you can see (and hear), audio properties can be modified in real time, while a sound is playing, to create really cool effects.

There's More...

The `@"synth_tone_mono.caf"` file used in this recipe is specifically encoded as a **mono** sound effect. This is because the **pan** property can only be set on a mono sound effect.

Fading sounds and music

Taking a queue from Cocos2d actions, CocosDenshion provides a few classes for fading sounds and music. These are `CDLongAudioSourceFader` and `CDXPropertyModifierAction`. In this example, we will see how to fade in/out all sounds, individual sounds, and music. We will also see how to crossfade two music sources.

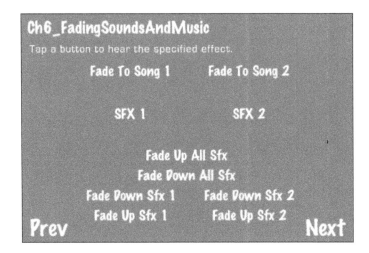

Getting ready

Please refer to the project RecipeCollection02 for full working code of this recipe.

How to do it...

Execute the following code:

```
#import "SimpleAudioEngine.h"
#import "CDXPropertyModifierAction.h"

@implementation Ch6_FadingSoundsAndMusic

-(CCLayer*) runRecipe {
  //Initialize the audio engine
  sae = [SimpleAudioEngine sharedEngine];

  //Background music is stopped on resign and resumed on
    becoming active
  [[CDAudioManager sharedManager] setResignBehavior:kAMRBStopPlay
autoHandle:YES];
```

```
  //Initialize source container
  soundSources = [[NSMutableDictionary alloc] init];
  musicSources = [[NSMutableDictionary alloc] init];

  //Add music
  [self loadMusic:@"hiphop_boss_man_by_p0ss.mp3"];
  [self loadMusic:@"menu_music_by_mrpoly.mp3"];

  //Add sounds
  [self loadSoundEffect:@"gunman_pain.caf"];
  [self loadSoundEffect:@"synth_tone.caf"];

  //Add menu items
/* CODE OMITTED */
return self;
}


//Play music callback
-(void) playMusicNumber:(id)sender {
  CCMenuItem *item = (CCMenuItem*)sender;
  int number = item.tag;

  if(number == 0){
    [self fadeOutPlayingMusic];
    [self fadeInMusicFile:@"hiphop_boss_man_by_p0ss.mp3"];
  }else if(number == 1){
    [self fadeOutPlayingMusic];
    [self fadeInMusicFile:@"menu_music_by_mrpoly.mp3"];
  }
}


//Fade out any music sources currently playing
-(void) fadeOutPlayingMusic {
  for(id m in musicSources){
    //Release source
    CDLongAudioSource *source = [musicSources objectForKey:m];
    if(source.isPlaying){
      //Create fader
      CDLongAudioSourceFader* fader = [[CDLongAudioSourceFader alloc]
init:source interpolationType:kIT_Exponential startVal:source.volume
endVal:0.0f];
      [fader setStopTargetWhenComplete:NO];

      //Create a property modifier action to wrap the fader
```

```
      CDXPropertyModifierAction* fadeAction =
[CDXPropertyModifierAction actionWithDuration:3.0f modifier:fader];
      [fader release];//Action will retain
      CCCallFuncN* stopAction = [CCCallFuncN actionWithTarget:source
selector:@selector(stop)];
      [[CCActionManager sharedManager] addAction:[CCSequence
actions:fadeAction, stopAction, nil] target:source paused:NO];
    }
  }
}


//Fade in a specific music file
-(void) fadeInMusicFile:(NSString*)fn {
  //Stop music if its playing and return
  CDLongAudioSource *source = [musicSources objectForKey:fn];
  if(source.isPlaying){
    [source stop];
    return;
  }

  //Set volume to zero and play
  source.volume = 0.0f;
  [source play];

  //Create fader
  CDLongAudioSourceFader* fader = [[CDLongAudioSourceFader alloc]
init:source interpolationType:kIT_Exponential startVal:source.volume
endVal:1.0f];
  [fader setStopTargetWhenComplete:NO];

  //Create a property modifier action to wrap the fader
  CDXPropertyModifierAction* fadeAction = [CDXPropertyModifierAction
actionWithDuration:1.5f modifier:fader];
  [fader release];//Action will retain
  [[CCActionManager sharedManager] addAction:[CCSequence
actions:fadeAction, nil] target:source paused:NO];
}

-(void) fadeUpAllSfx:(id)sender {
  //Fade up all sound effects
  [CDXPropertyModifierAction fadeSoundEffects:2.0f finalVolume:1.0f
curveType:kIT_Linear shouldStop:NO];
}

-(void) fadeDownAllSfx:(id)sender {
```

```objc
  //Fade down all sound effects
  [CDXPropertyModifierAction fadeSoundEffects:2.0f finalVolume:0.0f
curveType:kIT_Linear shouldStop:NO];
}


-(void) fadeUpSfxNumber:(id)sender {
  //Fade up a specific sound effect
  CCMenuItem *item = (CCMenuItem*)sender;
  int number = item.tag;

  CDSoundSource *source;
  if(number == 0){
    source = [soundSources objectForKey:@"gunman_pain.caf"];
  }else if(number == 1){
    source = [soundSources objectForKey:@"synth_tone.caf"];
  }
  source.gain = 0.0f;
  [CDXPropertyModifierAction fadeSoundEffect:2.0f finalVolume:1.0f
curveType:kIT_Linear shouldStop:NO effect:source];
}
-(void) fadeDownSfxNumber:(id)sender {
  //Fade down a specific sound effect
  CCMenuItem *item = (CCMenuItem*)sender;
  int number = item.tag;

  CDSoundSource *source;
  if(number == 0){
    source = [soundSources objectForKey:@"gunman_pain.caf"];
  }else if(number == 1){
    source = [soundSources objectForKey:@"synth_tone.caf"];
  }
  source.gain = 1.0f;
  [CDXPropertyModifierAction fadeSoundEffect:2.0f finalVolume:0.0f
curveType:kIT_Linear shouldStop:NO effect:source];
}

@end
```

How it works...

In this recipe, we use `CDLongAudioSource` directly as opposed to using the `backgroundMusic` source provided by `SimpleAudioEngine`. This allows us to have more than one long audio source playing at a given time.

▶ Crossfading long audio sources:

Crossfading involves fading one source in and one source out at the same time. First, we initialize a `CDLongAudioSourceFader` object to specify fading values and an interpolation type:

```
CDLongAudioSourceFader*  fader = [[CDLongAudioSourceFader alloc]
init:source interpolationType:kIT_Linear startVal:source.volume
endVal:0.0f];
        [fader setStopTargetWhenComplete:NO];
```

In this case, we want to fade out linearly starting from the source's current volume. We then create a `CDXPropertyModifierAction` object with specified duration. We also release the `fader` object at this point:

```
CDXPropertyModifierAction* fadeAction = [CDXPropertyModifierAction
actionWithDuration:3.0f modifier:fader];
        [fader release];
```

After fading the track out, we want to stop it from playing. For this, we create a `CCCallFuncN` action:

```
CCCallFuncN* stopAction = [CCCallFuncN actionWithTarget:source
selector:@selector(stop)];
```

Finally, we run these actions in sequence:

```
[[CCActionManager sharedManager] addAction:[CCSequence
actions:fadeAction, stopAction, nil] target:source paused:NO];
```

Running this action, along with the "fade in" action for the other track, will create the desired crossfading effect.

▶ Fading individual sound effects:

The `CDXPropertyModifierAction` class has a convenience method for fading individual sound effects:

```
[CDXPropertyModifierAction fadeSoundEffect:2.0f finalVolume:0.0f
curveType:kIT_Linear shouldStop:YES effect:source];
```

In the previous example, we fade out the specified sound source for 2 seconds and then stop the source from playing when we're finished.

▶ Fading out all sound effects:

All currently playing sound effects can be faded out as well using the following convenience method:

```
[CDXPropertyModifierAction fadeSoundEffects:2.0f finalVolume:0.0f
curveType:kIT_Linear shouldStop:YES];
```

This applies the same "fade out" effect to all playing sound effects.

Using audio in a game

While `SimpleAudioEngine` may be simple, it is efficient enough to be used in any type of game. In this recipe, we will add sounds and music to the **Bullets** demo from *Chapter 4, Physics*.

Getting ready

Please refer to the project *RecipeCollection02* for full working code of this recipe.

How to do it...

Execute the following code:

```
#import "Ch4_Bullets.h"
#import "SimpleAudioEngine.h"

@interface Ch6_AudioInGame : Ch4_Bullets
/* CODE OMITTED */
@end
```

```
@implementation Ch6_AudioInGame

-(CCLayer*) runRecipe {
  [super runRecipe];

  //Initialize the audio engine
  sae = [SimpleAudioEngine sharedEngine];

  //Background music is stopped on resign and resumed on
    becoming active
  [[CDAudioManager sharedManager] setResignBehavior:kAMRBStopPlay
autoHandle:YES];

  //Initialize source container
  soundSources = [[NSMutableDictionary alloc] init];

  //Add the sounds
  [self loadSoundEffect:@"bullet_fire_no_shell.caf" gain:1.0f];
  [self loadSoundEffect:@"bullet_casing_tink.caf" gain:0.25f];
  [self loadSoundEffect:@"gunman_jump.caf" gain:1.5f];
  [self loadSoundEffect:@"box_break.wav" gain:1.5f];

  //Add the background music
  [self loadBackgroundMusic:@"hiphop_boss_man_by_p0ss.mp3"];
  sae.backgroundMusicVolume = 0.5f;
  [self playBackgroundMusic:@"hiphop_boss_man_by_p0ss.mp3"];

  return self;
}

//Jump sound override
-(void) processJump {
  if(onGround && jumpCounter < 0){
    [self playSoundFile:@"gunman_jump.caf"];
  }
  [super processJump];
}

//Fire gun sound override
-(void) fireGun {
  if(fireCount <= 0){
    [self playSoundFile:@"bullet_fire_no_shell.caf"];
  }
  [super fireGun];
```

```
}

//Box explosion sound override
-(void) boxExplosionAt:(CGPoint)p withRotation:(float)rot {
  [self playSoundFile:@"box_break.wav"];
  [super boxExplosionAt:p withRotation:rot];
}

//Bullet casing sound override
-(void) handleCollisionWithMisc:(GameMisc*)a withMisc:(GameMisc*)b {
  if(a.typeTag == TYPE_OBJ_SHELL || b.typeTag == TYPE_OBJ_SHELL){
    [self playSoundFile:@"bullet_casing_tink.caf"];
  }
  [super handleCollisionWithMisc:a withMisc:b];
}

@end
```

How it works...

Using the techniques described in this chapter, we can breathe some life into our box-shooting demo by adding sounds and music.

> ▶ Sound buffers:
>
>   By default, CDAudioManager allocates one sound buffer per sound source. So, every time we play the @"bullet_fire_no_shell.caf" sound effect we effectively stop that sound effect from playing if it was already in the process of playing. This is adequate for the majority of in-game sound effect use cases.

There's more...

Finding sound effects to use in your game can be a fun yet tedious process. Even though there exists a large number of royalty free sound effects floating around, it's often difficult to find the right one for a given situation. Alternatively, a microphone and some audio generation and manipulation software can go a long way. For example, the effect @"bullet_casing_tink.caf" was created by playing the highest note on a piano using GarageBand. Another program, **sfxr**, can be used to generate simple 8-bit style sound effects. The Cocoa version, **cfxr**, can be downloaded here: http://thirdcog.eu/apps/cfxr.

Using positional audio in a game

To increase the realism of the sounds we use in a game, we can modify audio properties based on in-game factors. In this example, we use **source distance**, **audible range**, and **object size** to determine **gain**, **pitch**, and **pan**. We'll demonstrate this by adding sounds to the **TopDownIsometric** demo from *Chapter 4, Physics*.

Getting ready

Please refer to the project *RecipeCollection02* for full working code of this recipe.

How to do it...

Execute the following code:

```
#import "Ch4_TopDownIsometric.h"
#import "SimpleAudioEngine.h"

enum {
  CGROUP_NON_INTERRUPTIBLE = 0
};

@interface Ch6_PositionalAudio : Ch4_TopDownIsometric
/* CODE OMITTED */
@end
```

```objc
@implementation Ch6_PositionalAudio

-(CCLayer*) runRecipe {
  //Run our top-down isometric game recipe
  [super runRecipe];

  //Initialize max audible range
  audibleRange = 20.0f;

  //Initialize the audio engine
  sae = [SimpleAudioEngine sharedEngine];

  //Background music is stopped on resign and resumed on
    becoming active
  [[CDAudioManager sharedManager] setResignBehavior:kAMRBStopPlay
autoHandle:YES];

  //Preload the sounds
  [sae preloadEffect:@"forest_birds_ambience.caf"];
  [sae preloadEffect:@"kick_ball_bounce.caf"];
  [sae preloadEffect:@"gunman_jump.caf"];
  [sae preloadEffect:@"bullet_fire_no_shell.caf"];

  //Non-interruptible ball source group
  [[CDAudioManager sharedManager].soundEngine setSourceGroupNonInterru
ptible:CGROUP_NON_INTERRUPTIBLE isNonInterruptible:YES];

  //Add the sounds
  ballSource = [[sae soundSourceForFile:@"kick_ball_bounce.caf"]
retain];
  forestBirdsSource = [[sae soundSourceForFile:@"forest_birds_
ambience.caf"] retain];
  gunmanJumpSource = [[sae soundSourceForFile:@"gunman_jump.caf"]
retain];
  fireBallSource = [[sae soundSourceForFile:@"bullet_fire_no_shell.
caf"] retain];

  //Start playing forest bird source
  forestBirdsSource.gain = 0.0f;
  forestBirdsSource.looping = YES;
  [forestBirdsSource play];

  //Customize fire ball sound
  fireBallSource.pitch = 2.0f;
  fireBallSource.gain = 0.5f;
```

```objc
    return self;
}

-(void) step:(ccTime)delta {
  [super step:delta];

  //Play forest bird source with gain based on distance from gunman
  float distance = 10000.0f;
  for(int i=0; i<[trees count]; i++){
    GameObject *tree = [trees objectAtIndex:i];

    float thisDistance = distanceBetweenPoints(ccp(tree.body-
>GetPosition().x,tree.body->GetPosition().y),
       ccp(gunman.body->GetPosition().x, gunman.body-
>GetPosition().y));
    if(thisDistance < distance){ distance = thisDistance; }
  }

  //If closest tree is outside of audible range we set gain to 0.0f
  if(distance < audibleRange){
    forestBirdsSource.gain = (audibleRange-distance)/audibleRange;
  }else{
    forestBirdsSource.gain = 0.0f;
  }
}

//Fire ball sound override
-(void) fireBall {
  if(fireCount < 0){
    [fireBallSource play];
  }
  [super fireBall];
}

//Jump sound override
-(void) processJump {
  if(gunman.body->GetZPosition() <= 1.0f){
    [gunmanJumpSource play];
  }
  [super processJump];
}

-(void) handleCollisionWithGroundWithObj:(GameObject*)gameObject {
```

```
[super handleCollisionWithGroundWithObj:gameObject];

  //Play ball bounce sound with gain based on distance from gunman
  if(gameObject.typeTag == TYPE_OBJ_BALL){
    float distance = distanceBetweenPoints(ccp(gameObject.body-
>GetPosition().x, gameObject.body->GetPosition().y), ccp(gunman.body-
>GetPosition().x, gunman.body->GetPosition().y));

    if(distance < audibleRange){
      float gain = (audibleRange-distance)/audibleRange;
      float pan = (gameObject.body->GetPosition().x - gunman.body-
>GetPosition().x)/distance;
      float pitch = ((((GameIsoObject*)gameObject).inGameSize / 10.0f)
* -1) + 2;

      if(distance < audibleRange){
        [self playBallSoundWithGain:gain pan:pan pitch:pitch];
      }
    }
  }
}

-(void) playBallSoundWithGain:(float)gain pan:(float)pan pitch:(float)
pitch {
  //Play the sound using the non-interruptible source group
  [[CDAudioManager sharedManager].soundEngine playSound:ballSource.
soundId sourceGroupId:CGROUP_NON_INTERRUPTIBLE pitch:pitch pan:pan
gain:gain loop:NO];
}

@end
```

How it works...

Creating a realistic soundscape involves changing audio properties in creative ways.

▶ Forest ambience:

For this recipe, we have a 30 second looping clip of forest ambience playing in place of background music. We determine the `gain` property of this sound source based on the player's distance from the closest tree:

```
if(distance < audibleRange){
  forestBirdsSource.gain = (audibleRange-distance)/audibleRange;
}else{
  forestBirdsSource.gain = 0.0f;
}
```

If all trees are outside the audible range then we set the `gain` to zero.

▶ Ball bounce sounds:

To create a compelling ball bounce sound effect, we modify all three audio properties. The `gain` property is determined by distance:

```
float gain = (audibleRange-distance)/audibleRange;
```

The `pan` property is determined by X plane distance:

```
float pan = (gameObject.body->GetPosition().x - gunman.body-
>GetPosition().x)/distance;
```

Finally, the `pitch` property is determined by the ball's size:

```
float pitch = ((((GameIsoObject*)gameObject).inGameSize / 10.0f) *
-1) + 2;
```

Together, these modifications create a variety of unique sounds. This adds depth to the auditory experience.

▶ Using multiple sound buffers:

Because we have multiple balls initiating bounce sound effects at the same time, a single buffer will no longer suffice. We now need the same sound to play over itself many times. To accomplish this we use a special **Source Group**. A source group is simply a way to group sounds together to manipulate how they get played. For example, you might want two sound sources to share a buffer. In this case, we specify a source group as being non-interruptible:

```
enum { CGROUP_NON_INTERRUPTIBLE = 0 };
[[CDAudioManager sharedManager].soundEngine setSourceGroupNonInter
ruptible:CGROUP_NON_INTERRUPTIBLE isNonInterruptible:YES];
```

Now, all sounds played using this source group will be given an open buffer. To specify a source group when playing a sound we use the following line:

```
[[CDAudioManager sharedManager].soundEngine playSound:ballSource.
soundId sourceGroupId:CGROUP_NON_INTERRUPTIBLE pitch:pitch pan:pan
gain:gain loop:NO];
```

Now, multiple ball bounce sound effects can be heard over each other with different audio properties.

▶ Maximum number of buffers:

The maximum number of sound buffers available and the buffer increment is specified in `CDConfig.h`:

```
#define CD_BUFFERS_START 64
#define CD_BUFFERS_INCREMENT 16
```

In the default case, after 64 buffers are filled up, another 16 are allocated. These can be customized for applications with specific audio requirements.

Metering background music

The `CDAudioManager` class wraps the `AVAudioPlayer` class. Using this class gives us access to lower level audio functions. In this recipe, we will dynamically read the **average level** and **peak level** of background music currently playing. We can use this information to sync or cue animations.

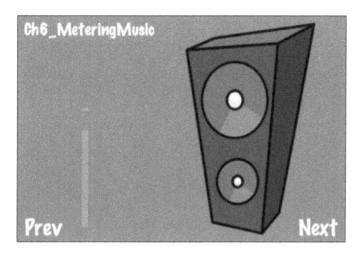

Getting ready

Please refer to the project *RecipeCollection02* for full working code of this recipe.

How to do it...

Execute the following code:

```
#import "SimpleAudioEngine.h"

@implementation Ch6_MeteringMusic

-(CCLayer*) runRecipe {
  //Initialize the audio engine
  sae = [SimpleAudioEngine sharedEngine];

  //Background music is stopped on resign and resumed on
    becoming active
  [[CDAudioManager sharedManager] setResignBehavior:kAMRBStopPlay
autoHandle:YES];

  //Set peak and average power initially
```

```
   peakPower = 0;
   avgPower = 0;

   //Init speaker sprites (speakerBase, speakerLarge and speakerSmall)
   /* CODE OMITTED */

   //Init meter sprites (avgMeter and peakMeter)
   /* CODE OMITTED */

   //Add the background music
   [sae preloadBackgroundMusic:@"technogeek_by_mrpoly.mp3"];
   [sae playBackgroundMusic:@"technogeek_by_mrpoly.mp3"];

   //Enable metering
   [CDAudioManager sharedManager].backgroundMusic.audioSourcePlayer.
meteringEnabled = YES;

   //Schedule step method
   [self schedule:@selector(step:)];

   return self;
}

-(void) step:(ccTime)delta {
   [self setPeakAndAveragePower];
   [self animateMeterAndSpeaker];
}

-(void) setPeakAndAveragePower {
   //Update meters
   [[CDAudioManager sharedManager].backgroundMusic.audioSourcePlayer
updateMeters];

   //Get channels
   int channels = [CDAudioManager sharedManager].backgroundMusic.
audioSourcePlayer.numberOfChannels;

   //Average all the channels
   float peakPowerNow = 0;
   float avgPowerNow = 0;

   for(int i=0; i<channels; i++){
      float peak = [[CDAudioManager sharedManager].backgroundMusic.
audioSourcePlayer peakPowerForChannel:i];
```

```
        float avg = [[CDAudioManager sharedManager].backgroundMusic.
    audioSourcePlayer averagePowerForChannel:i];
        peakPowerNow += peak/channels;
        avgPowerNow += avg/channels;
    }

    //Change from a DB level to a 0 to 1 ratio
    float adjustedPeak = pow(10, (0.05 * peakPowerNow));
    float adjustedAvg = pow(10, (0.05 * avgPowerNow));

    //Average it out for smoothing
    peakPower = (peakPower + adjustedPeak)/2;
    avgPower = (avgPower + adjustedAvg)/2;
}

-(void) animateMeterAndSpeaker {
    //Average meter
    [avgMeter setTextureRect:CGRectMake(0,0,10,avgPower*500.0f)];

    //Peak meter
    peakMeter.position = ccp(100,20+peakPower*500.0f);

    //Animate speaker
    speakerLarge.scale = powf(avgPower,0.4f)*2;
     speakerSmall.scale = powf(avgPower,0.4f)*2;
}

@end
```

How it works...

Accessing the dynamic metering functionality requires the use of the audioSourcePlayer reference inside a CDLongAudioSource object, in this case, backgroundMusic. Before we can begin, we enable metering:

```
[CDAudioManager sharedManager].backgroundMusic.audioSourcePlayer.
meteringEnabled = YES;
```

Now, every cycle we collect the **average** and **peak** decibel levels for all playing channels. We average these numbers out:

```
[[[CDAudioManager sharedManager].backgroundMusic.audioSourcePlayer
updateMeters];
int channels = [CDAudioManager sharedManager].backgroundMusic.
audioSourcePlayer.numberOfChannels;
```

```
    for(int i=0; i<channels; i++){
       float peak = [[CDAudioManager sharedManager].backgroundMusic.
audioSourcePlayer peakPowerForChannel:i];
       float avg = [[CDAudioManager sharedManager].backgroundMusic.
audioSourcePlayer averagePowerForChannel:i];
       peakPowerNow += peak/channels;
       avgPowerNow += avg/channels;
    }
```

After that we convert our average and peak decibel levels to ratios between 0 and 1. This makes the numbers easier to apply to animations.

```
//Change from a DB level to a 0 to 1 ratio
float adjustedPeak = pow(10, (0.05 * peakPowerNow));
float adjustedAvg = pow(10, (0.05 * avgPowerNow));

//Average it out for smoothing
peakPower = (peakPower + adjustedPeak)/2;
avgPower = (avgPower + adjustedAvg)/2;
```

We also split the difference when setting the new `peakPower` and `avgPower` variables. This smooths out harsh changes in volume.

Metering dialogue for animation

A `LongAudioSource` object can be any kind of audio, not just music. In this recipe, we will use the metering technique to animate the mouth of the gregarious Senator Beauregard Claghorn.

Getting ready

Please refer to the project *RecipeCollection02* for full working code of this recipe.

How to do it...

Execute the following code:

```
#import "SimpleAudioEngine.h"

@implementation Ch6_MeteringDialogue

-(CCLayer*) runRecipe {
  /* CODE OMITTED */

  //Add the sounds
  [self loadLongAudioSource:@"claghorn_a_joke_son.caf"];
  [self loadLongAudioSource:@"claghorn_carolina.caf"];
  /* CODE OMITTED */

  //Add the background music
  [self loadBackgroundMusic:@"dixie_1916.mp3"];

/* CODE OMITTED */

  //Play background music
  [self playBackgroundMusic:@"dixie_1916.mp3"];

  //Have Claghorn introduce himself
  [self playLongAudioSource:@"claghorn_howdy.caf"];
}

-(void) step:(ccTime)delta {
  /* CODE OMITTED */

  [self setPeakAndAveragePower];
  [self animateClaghorn];
}

-(void) setPeakAndAveragePower {
  //Find our playing audio source
  CDLongAudioSource *audioSource = nil;
  for(id s in soundSources){
    CDLongAudioSource *source = [soundSources objectForKey:s];
```

```
    if(source.isPlaying){
      audioSource = source;
      break;
    }
  }

  //Update meters
  [audioSource.audioSourcePlayer updateMeters];

/* CODE OMITTED */
}

-(void) animateClaghorn {
  /* Custom mouth animation */
  float level = avgPower;

  //Make sure he's actually speaking
  if(level == 0){
    claghornEyebrows.position = ccp(240,120);
    claghornMouth.position = ccp(240,120);
    lastAudioLevel = level;
    return;
  }

  //Level bounds
  if(level <= 0){ level = 0.01f; }
  if(level >= 1){ level = 0.99f; }

  //Exaggerate level ebb and flow
  if(level < lastAudioLevel){
    //Closing mouth
    lastAudioLevel = level;
    level = powf(level,1.5f);
  }else{
    //Opening mouth
    lastAudioLevel = level;
    level = powf(level,0.75f);
  }

  //If mouth is almost closed, close mouth
  if(level < 0.1f){ level = 0.01f; }

  //Blink if level > 0.8f
  if(level > 0.8f && !isBlinking){
```

```
    [self blink];
    [self runAction:[CCSequence actions:[CCDelayTime
actionWithDuration:0.5f],
       [CCCallFunc actionWithTarget:self selector:@selector(unblink)],
nil]];
  }

  //Raise eyebrows if level > 0.6f
  if(level > 0.6f){
    claghornEyebrows.position = ccp(240,120 + level*5.0f);
  }else{
    claghornEyebrows.position = ccp(240,120);
  }

  //Set mouth position
  claghornMouth.position = ccp(240,120 - level*19.0f);
}

-(CDLongAudioSource*) loadLongAudioSource:(NSString*)fn {
  //Init source
  CDLongAudioSource *source = [[CDLongAudioSource alloc] init];
  source.backgroundMusic = NO;
  [source load:fn];

  //Enable metering
  source.audioSourcePlayer.meteringEnabled = YES;

  //Add sound to container
  [soundSources setObject:source forKey:fn];

  return source;
}

-(void) playLongAudioSource:(NSString*)fn {
  //Get sound
  CDLongAudioSource *audioSource = [soundSources objectForKey:fn];

  bool aSourceIsPlaying = NO;
  for(id s in soundSources){
    CDLongAudioSource *source = [soundSources objectForKey:s];
    if(source.isPlaying){
      [source stop];
      [source rewind];
      aSourceIsPlaying = YES;
```

```
        break;
      }
    }
  }

  //Play sound
  if(!aSourceIsPlaying){
    //Play sound
    [audioSource play];

    [self runAction: [CCSequence actions: [CCDelayTime
actionWithDuration:[audioSource.audioSourcePlayer duration]],
      [CCCallFunc actionWithTarget:audioSource selector:@
selector(stop)],
      [CCCallFunc actionWithTarget:audioSource selector:@
selector(rewind)], nil]];
    }
  }


  @end
```

How it works...

Like in the previous recipe, we use the information collected from
setPeakAndAveragePower to run an animation. Unlike the previous recipe, we have a
number of CDLongAudioSource objects to choose from. Here, we find the source that is
currently playing and use it for metering:

```
CDLongAudioSource *audioSource = nil;
for(id s in soundSources){
  CDLongAudioSource *source = [soundSources objectForKey:s];
  if(source.isPlaying){
    audioSource = source;
    break;
  }
}
  [audioSource.audioSourcePlayer updateMeters];
```

After calculating avgPower, we then exaggerate the peaks and valleys of that number to help
simulate the rapid opening and closing of Claghorn's mouth:

```
if(level < lastAudioLevel){
  lastAudioLevel = level;
  level = powf(level,1.5f);
}else{
  lastAudioLevel = level;
  level = powf(level,0.75f);
}
```

In addition to this, we animate blinking, eye movement, and eyebrows. Put together, the linking of multiple animations with metering creates a nice mouth movement effect.

Streaming audio

In *Chapter 1*, *Graphics*, we used the `MPMoviePlayerController` class to play full motion video. In this recipe, we will use a similar technique to create a streaming audio player.

Getting ready

Please refer to the project *RecipeCollection02* for full working code of this recipe.

How to do it...

Link the `MediaPlayer` framework to your project. Now, execute the following code:

```
#import <MediaPlayer/MediaPlayer.h>
#import "AppDelegate.h"

@implementation Ch6_StreamingAudio

-(CCLayer*) runRecipe {
  //Create music player buttons
  [[CCSpriteFrameCache sharedSpriteFrameCache]
addSpriteFramesWithFile:@"music_player.plist"];

  CCMenuItemSprite *prevItem = [self menuItemFromSpriteFile:@"music_
player_prev.png" target:self selector:@selector(previousSong:)];
```

```
/* CODE OMITTED */

//Create menu
/* CODE OMITTED */

//Initial variable values
sourceIndex = 0;
isPlaying = NO;

//Streaming sources
streamingSources = [[NSMutableArray alloc] init];
[streamingSources addObject:@"http://shoutmedia.abc.net.au:10326"];
[streamingSources addObject:@"http://audioplayer.wunderground.com/
drgruver/Philadelphia.mp3.m3u"];
[streamingSources addObject:@"http://s8.mediastreaming.it:7050/"];
[streamingSources addObject:@"http://www.radioparadise.com/
musiclinks/rp_64aac.m3u"];
[streamingSources addObject:@"http://streaming.wrek.org:8000/wrek_
HD-2.m3u"];

//Init movie playing (music streamer in this case)
moviePlayer = [[MPMoviePlayerController alloc] init];
moviePlayer.movieSourceType = MPMovieSourceTypeStreaming;
moviePlayer.view.hidden = YES;
((AppDelegate*)[UIApplication sharedApplication].delegate).window
addSubview:moviePlayer.view];

//Set initial stream source
[self setStreamSource];

return self;
}

//Next callback
- (void) nextSong:(id)sender {
  [self setIsPlaying];

  sourceIndex++;
  if(sourceIndex > [streamingSources count]-1){
    sourceIndex = 0;
  }

  [self setStreamSource];
}
```

```
//Previous callback
- (void) previousSong:(id)sender {
  [self setIsPlaying];

  sourceIndex--;
  if(sourceIndex < 0){
    sourceIndex = [streamingSources count]-1;
  }

  [self setStreamSource];
}

-(void) setIsPlaying {
  if(moviePlayer.playbackState == MPMoviePlaybackStatePlaying){
    isPlaying = YES;
  }
}

-(void) setStreamSource {
  [moviePlayer stop];

  moviePlayer.contentURL = [NSURL URLWithString:[streamingSources
objectAtIndex:sourceIndex]];

  if(isPlaying){
    [self playMusic:nil];
  }
}

@end
```

How it works...

This recipe works in a way similar to that of what we saw in *Chapter 1, Graphics*. One key difference is, here we specify the `mediaSourceType`, and we also hide the player from view:

```
moviePlayer.movieSourceType = MPMovieSourceTypeStreaming;
moviePlayer.view.hidden = YES;
```

This sets up the player for audio streaming.

▶ Reaching the `AppDelegate`:

In **Cocos2d**, the `AppDelegate` class is the top-level class that implements the `UIApplicationDelegate` protocol. This protocol specifies the delegate to which the main `UIApplication` singleton points to. This delegate handles important application events. To add our `moviePlayer` object to our view, we access this delegate through the `UIApplication` singleton:

```
((AppDelegate*)[UIApplication sharedApplication].delegate).window
addSubview:moviePlayer.view];
```

As you can see, this involves **casting** the `delegate` property into the `AppDelegate*` type.

▶ Switching stations:

Changing the streaming source involves stopping playback and changing the `contentURL` property:

```
[moviePlayer stop];
moviePlayer.contentURL = [NSURL URLWithString:[streamingSources
objectAtIndex:sourceIndex]];
    if(isPlaying){
    [self playMusic:nil];
    }
```

This way the user can change channels seamlessly while maintaining playback.

▶ Live streaming formats:

The stream source examples used in this recipe use Apple's **HTTP Live Streaming** protocol. This allows elegant live streaming over **HTTP** with minimum hassle. You can read more about this protocol here: `http://developer.apple.com/resources/http-streaming/`.

▶ Streaming files:

Single files, using formats like **MP3**, can also be streamed over a simple **HTTP** server using this technique.

▶ Streaming video:

By combining this recipe with the video playback recipe in *Chapter 1, Graphics,* you can also stream video. Compatible formats and other requirements are detailed at the aforementioned site. As a good rule of thumb, any file type or URL that can be played using the iOS device's built in **Safari** web browser can usually also be played using `MPMoviePlayerController`.

Previously, we mentioned the `UIApplication` **singleton**. A singleton is a top-level global object instantiated at runtime. Cocos2d largely embraces the singleton pattern. Any object accessed by executing a class method starting with the word "shared" (`[Class sharedClass]`) is, by convention, a singleton. You can create your own custom singleton objects using the **macro** encapsulated in the `SynthesizeSingleton.h` file. For more information about this, please consult the *More Recipes* section of the **Cocos2d Cookbook website** at `http://cocos2dcookbook.com/more_recipes`.

Recording audio

A notable feature on most iOS devices is the ability to record audio. In this recipe, we will use the microphone to record audio and save it to a temporary location on the disk using the `AVAudioRecorder` class. We will then play it back with a modified pitch using the `CDSoundEngine` class.

Please refer to the project *RecipeCollection02* for full working code of this recipe.

How to do it...

Link the `CoreAudio` and `AVFoundation` frameworks to your project. Now, execute the following code:

```objc
#import <AVFoundation/AVFoundation.h>
#import <CoreAudio/CoreAudioTypes.h>
#import "CocosDenshion.h"

@interface Ch6_RecordingAudio : Recipe <AVAudioRecorderDelegate>
{ /* CODE OMITTED */}

@implementation Ch6_RecordingAudio

-(CCLayer*) runRecipe {
  //Set initial pitch and recorded temp file object
  pitch = 1.0f;
  recordedTmpFile = nil;

  //Init audio session
  [self initAudioSession];

/* CODE OMITTED */

  return self;
}

-(void) initAudioSession {
  //Our AVAudioSession singleton pointer
AVAudioSession * audioSession = [AVAudioSession sharedInstance];

//Set up the audioSession for playback and record.
[audioSession setCategory:AVAudioSessionCategoryPlayAndRecord
error:nil];

//Activate the session
[audioSession setActive:YES error:nil];

  //Init CDSoundEngine
  soundEngine = [[CDSoundEngine alloc] init];

  //Define source groups
  NSArray *defs = [NSArray arrayWithObjects: [NSNumber
numberWithInt:1],nil];
```

```
  [soundEngine defineSourceGroups:defs];
}

-(void) recordAudio {
  //Set settings dictionary: IMA4 format, 44100 sample rate, 2
channels
  NSMutableDictionary* recordSetting = [[[NSMutableDictionary alloc]
init] autorelease];
  [recordSetting setValue :[NSNumber numberWithInt:kAudioFormatAppleI
MA4] forKey:AVFormatIDKey];
  [recordSetting setValue:[NSNumber numberWithFloat:44100.0]
forKey:AVSampleRateKey];
  [recordSetting setValue:[NSNumber numberWithInt: 2]
forKey:AVNumberOfChannelsKey];

  //Set recording temp file location on disk
  recordedTmpFile = [NSURL fileURLWithPath:[NSTemporaryDirecto
ry() stringByAppendingPathComponent: [NSString stringWithString:
@"recording.caf"]]];

  //Init AVAudioRecorder with location and settings
  recorder = [[AVAudioRecorder alloc] initWithURL:recordedTmpFile
settings:recordSetting error:nil];

  //Set delegate and start recording
  [recorder setDelegate:self];
  [recorder prepareToRecord];
  [recorder record];
}

-(void) playAudio {
  //Override the audio to go back to the speaker
  UInt32 audioRouteOverride = kAudioSessionOverrideAudioRoute_Speaker;
  AudioSessionSetProperty(kAudioSessionProperty_OverrideAudioRoute,
sizeof (audioRouteOverride),&audioRouteOverride);

  //Get the file path to the recorded audio
  NSString *filePath = [NSTemporaryDirectory()
stringByAppendingPathComponent: [NSString stringWithString:
@"recording.caf"]];

  //Play our recorded audio
  [soundEngine loadBuffer:0 filePath: filePath];
  [soundEngine playSound:0 sourceGroupId:0 pitch:pitch pan:0.0f
gain:10.0f loop: NO];
```

```
}

-(void) stopRecordingAudio {
  //Stop recording
  [recorder stop];
}

- (void) unloadAudioSession {
  //Remove temp file
  NSFileManager * fm = [NSFileManager defaultManager];
  if(recordedTmpFile){ [fm removeItemAtURL:recordedTmpFile error:nil];
}

  //Release recorder
  [recorder dealloc];
recorder = nil;

  //Release sound engine
  [soundEngine release];

  //Deactivate audio session
  AVAudioSession * audioSession = [AVAudioSession sharedInstance];
  [audioSession setActive:NO error:nil];
}

@end
```

How it works...

Recording and playing back audio will introduce us to a few new classes and concepts.

▶ Initializing the audio session:

Because we want to record audio, we have to set up a specific **audio session**. An audio session is a way of configuring the settings we will currently use for audio input and output. The AVAudioSession singleton encapsulates this functionality. First, we need to set up the **session category** to allow recording and playback:

```
[[AVAudioSession sharedInstance] setCategory:AVAudioSessionCategor
yPlayAndRecord error:nil];
```

Then we need to activate the session:

```
[[AVAudioSession sharedInstance] setActive:YES error:nil];
```

CocosDenshion normally does these things, but in this recipe, we need more granular control over the audio system.

▶ Initializing CDSoundEngine:

Here we also initialize a `CDSoundEngine` object:

```
soundEngine = [[CDSoundEngine alloc] init];
NSArray *defs = [NSArray arrayWithObjects: [NSNumber
numberWithInt:1],nil];
[soundEngine defineSourceGroups:defs];
```

We will use this to play back our recorded audio.

▶ Recording audio:

The crux of the recipe, recording the audio, requires a few steps. First, we initialize the `AVAudioRecorder` object with the audio recording format and where we want to store our recorded audio:

```
NSMutableDictionary* recordSetting = [[[NSMutableDictionary alloc]
init] autorelease];
[recordSetting setValue :[NSNumber numberWithInt:kAudioFormatApple
IMA4] forKey:AVFormatIDKey];
   [recordSetting setValue:[NSNumber numberWithFloat:44100.0]
forKey:AVSampleRateKey];
   [recordSetting setValue:[NSNumber numberWithInt: 2]
forKey:AVNumberOfChannelsKey];

   recordedTmpFile = [NSURL fileURLWithPath:[NSTemporaryDirecto
ry() stringByAppendingPathComponent: [NSString stringWithString:
@"recording.caf"]]];

   recorder = [[AVAudioRecorder alloc] initWithURL:recordedTmpFile
settings:recordSetting error:nil];
```

We specify our delegate object:

```
[recorder setDelegate:self];
```

Finally, we start recording:

```
[recorder prepareToRecord];
[recorder record];
```

Recording will last until we call the stop routine:

```
[recorder stop];
```

Recording will not stop until either the recorder receives a `stop` message or the delegate receives an error. For example, the disk could be full.

▸ The `AVAudioRecorderDelegate` protocol:

By specifying our `Ch6_RecordingAudio` class as adhering to the `AVAudioRecorderDelegate` protocol, we agree to handle a number of method calls including errors. If we fail to do so, these errors are thrown. In this example, we bypass this step for the sake of brevity, but in a professional app it is recommended that you handle any messages the `AVAudioRecorder` class might want to pass on.

▸ Playing our recorded audio:

Once the recorded audio is stored on the disk, we can play it back. On the iPhone the speaker output is re-routed to the earbud speaker when the audio session category is `AVAudioSessionCategoryPlayAndRecord`. So, before we can properly play back the recorded audio we must reroute playback to the speakers:

```
UInt32 audioRouteOverride = kAudioSessionOverrideAudioRoute_
Speaker;
        AudioSessionSetProperty(kAudioSessionProperty_
OverrideAudioRoute, sizeof (audioRouteOverride),&audioRouteOverri
de);
```

Now, using `CDSoundEngine`, we can load the recorded audio into a buffer and play it back:

```
  NSString *filePath = [NSTemporaryDirectory()
stringByAppendingPathComponent: [NSString stringWithString:
@"recording.caf"]];
  [soundEngine loadBuffer:0 filePath: filePath];
  [soundEngine playSound:0 sourceGroupId:0 pitch:pitch pan:0.0f
gain:10.0f loop:NO];
```

In the above line, the **pitch**, **pan**, and **gain** properties can be modified. In this example, you can modify the pitch. Try recording your voice and then bending the pitch.

Using the iPod music library

Sometimes a user might want to substitute a musical track from his or her personal collection into the background of your game. In this example, we will create a simple music player that can load songs, albums, and playlists from the **iPod music library** on the device.

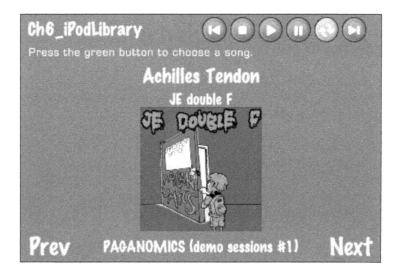

Getting ready

Please refer to the project *RecipeCollection02* for full working code of this recipe.

How to do it...

Link the `MediaPlayer` framework to your project. Now, execute the following code:

```
#import <MediaPlayer/MediaPlayer.h>
#import "AppDelegate.h"

@interface Ch6_iPodLibrary : Recipe <MPMediaPickerControllerDelegate>
{ /* CODE OMITTED */ }

@implementation Ch6_iPodLibrary

-(CCLayer*) runRecipe {
  //Device detection
  NSString *model = [[UIDevice currentDevice] model];

  //Show a blank recipe if we use the simulator
  if([model isEqualToString:@"iPhone Simulator"]){
    message.position = ccp(240,250);
    [self showMessage:@"This recipe is not compatible with the
Simulator. \nPlease connect a device."];
    return self;
```

```
    }

      /* CODE OMITTED */

    //Init music player
      musicPlayer = [MPMusicPlayerController iPodMusicPlayer];
    [musicPlayer setRepeatMode:MPMusicRepeatModeAll];

      //Initial sync of display with music player state
      [self handleNowPlayingItemChanged:nil];

      //Register for music player notifications
      NSNotificationCenter *notificationCenter = [NSNotificationCenter
defaultCenter];
      [notificationCenter addObserver:self selector:@selector(handleNowP
layingItemChanged:)
name:MPMusicPlayerControllerNowPlayingItemDidChangeNotification
object:musicPlayer];
      [musicPlayer beginGeneratingPlaybackNotifications];

    return self;
    }

- (void) handleNowPlayingItemChanged:(id)notification {
      //Get the current playing item
      MPMediaItem *currentItem = musicPlayer.nowPlayingItem;

    //Set labels
    if([currentItem valueForProperty:MPMediaItemPropertyTitle]){
      [songLabel setString: [NSString stringWithFormat:@"%@",[currentIt
em valueForProperty:MPMediaItemPropertyTitle]]];
      [artistLabel setString: [NSString stringWithFormat:@"%@",[currentI
tem valueForProperty:MPMediaItemPropertyArtist]]];
      [albumLabel setString: [NSString stringWithFormat:@"%@",[currentIt
em valueForProperty:MPMediaItemPropertyAlbumTitle]]];
    }

    //Get album artwork
      MPMediaItemArtwork *artwork = [currentItem valueForProperty:MPMedi
aItemPropertyArtwork];
    UIImage *artworkImage = nil;
      if(artwork) { artworkImage = [artwork imageWithSize:CGSizeMa
ke(100,100)]; }

    //Remove current album art if necessary
```

```objc
  if(albumArt){
    [self removeChild:albumArt cleanup:YES];
    albumArt = nil;
  }

  //Set album art
  if(artworkImage){
    CCTexture2D *texture = [[[CCTexture2D alloc]
initWithImage:artworkImage] autorelease];
    albumArt = [CCSprite spriteWithTexture:texture];
    [self addChild:albumArt z:1];
    albumArt.position = ccp(240,120);
    albumArt.scale = 0.25f;
  }
}

//Play callback
-(void)playMusic:(id)sender { [musicPlayer play]; }

//Pause callback
-(void)pauseMusic:(id)sender{ [musicPlayer pause]; }

//Stop callback
-(void)stopMusic:(id)sender{ [musicPlayer stop]; }

//Next callback
- (void)nextSong:(id)sender { [musicPlayer skipToNextItem]; }

//Previous callback
- (void)previousSong:(id)sender {
  //After 3.5 seconds hitting previous merely rewinds the song
    static NSTimeInterval skipToBeginningOfSongIfElapsedTimeLongerThan
= 3.5;

   NSTimeInterval playbackTime = musicPlayer.currentPlaybackTime;
    if (playbackTime <= skipToBeginningOfSongIfElapsedTimeLongerThan)
{
    //Previous song
        [musicPlayer skipToPreviousItem];
    } else {
    //Rewind to beginning of current song
        [musicPlayer skipToBeginning];
    }
}
```

```
//Add music callback
- (void)openMediaPicker:(id)sender {
//Unit music MPMediaPickerController
MPMediaPickerController *mediaPicker = [[MPMediaPickerController
alloc] initWithMediaTypes:MPMediaTypeMusic];
mediaPicker.delegate = self;
    mediaPicker.allowsPickingMultipleItems = YES;

  //Present picker as a modal view
    ((AppDelegate*)[UIApplication sharedApplication].delegate).
viewController presentModalViewController:mediaPicker animated:YES];
    [mediaPicker release];
}

- (void)mediaPicker: (MPMediaPickerController *)mediaPicker didPickMed
iaItems:(MPMediaItemCollection *)mediaItemCollection {
    //Dismiss the picker
    ((AppDelegate*)[UIApplication sharedApplication].delegate).
viewController dismissModalViewControllerAnimated:YES];

    //Assign the selected item(s) to the music player and start
playback.
    [musicPlayer stop];
    [musicPlayer setQueueWithItemCollection:mediaItemCollection];
    [musicPlayer play];
}

- (void)mediaPickerDidCancel:(MPMediaPickerController *)mediaPicker {
  //User chose no items, dismiss the picker
    ((AppDelegate*)[UIApplication sharedApplication].delegate).
viewController dismissModalViewControllerAnimated:YES];
}

-(void) cleanRecipe {
  //Stop player
  [musicPlayer stop];

    //Stop music player notifications
    [[NSNotificationCenter defaultCenter] removeObserver:self   na
me:MPMusicPlayerControllerNowPlayingItemDidChangeNotification
object:musicPlayer];
    [[NSNotificationCenter defaultCenter] removeObserver:self
name:MPMusicPlayerControllerPlaybackStateDidChangeNotification
object:musicPlayer];
    [[NSNotificationCenter defaultCenter] removeObserver:self
```

```
name:MPMusicPlayerControllerVolumeDidChangeNotification
object:musicPlayer];
    [musicPlayer endGeneratingPlaybackNotifications];

  //Release player
    [musicPlayer release];
    musicPlayer = nil;

  [super cleanRecipe];
}

@end
```

How it works...

Pressing the green button opens the standard iPod media picker. Some games opt to create their own picker to better match their user interface. In this example, we chose the default media picker for the sake of simplicity.

- ▶ Initializing `MPMusicPlayerController`:

  First, we create our `MPMusicPlayerController` object:

  ```
  musicPlayer = [MPMusicPlayerController iPodMusicPlayer];
  [musicPlayer setRepeatMode:MPMusicRepeatModeAll];
  ```

  We set our player to `MPMusicRepeatModeAll`, so our `nextSong` and `previousSong` methods can wrap playing songs.

- ▶ Getting **Now Playing** audio information:

  Every time the **Now Playing** item changes, we would like to be notified so we can fetch media information. To do this, we set our recipe object as an observer of the `musicPlayer` object and allow this type of notification to be received:

  ```
  NSNotificationCenter *notificationCenter = [NSNotificationCenter
  defaultCenter];
          [notificationCenter addObserver:self selector:@selector(hand
  leNowPlayingItemChanged:)
  name:MPMusicPlayerControllerNowPlayingItemDidChangeNotification
  object:musicPlayer];
  [musicPlayer beginGeneratingPlaybackNotifications];
  ```

As an observer, our class will be notified by a call to the
`handleNowPlayingItemChanged` method. Here, we inspect the currently playing
`MPMediaItem` object for information including song title, artist name, album name,
and album art:

```
MPMediaItem *currentItem = musicPlayer.nowPlayingItem;
  if([currentItem valueForProperty:MPMediaItemPropertyTitle]){
    [songLabel setString: [NSString stringWithFormat:@"%@",[curren
tItem valueForProperty:MPMediaItemPropertyTitle]]];
    [artistLabel setString: [NSString stringWithFormat:@"%@",[curr
entItem valueForProperty:MPMediaItemPropertyArtist]]];
    [albumLabel setString: [NSString stringWithFormat:@"%@",[curre
ntItem valueForProperty:MPMediaItemPropertyAlbumTitle]]];
  }


MPMediaItemArtwork *artwork = [currentItem valueForProperty:MPMedi
aItemPropertyArtwork];
  UIImage *artworkImage = nil;
    if(artwork) { artworkImage = [artwork imageWithSize:CGSizeMa
ke(100,100)]; }
```

We then take this created `UIImage` object and place it into the scene using a
technique described in *Chapter 1, Graphics*.

▶ Using `MPMediaPickerController`:

When a user touches the green button, then we initialize a
`MPMediaPickerController` object and specify its delegate:

```
MPMediaPickerController *mediaPicker = [[MPMediaPickerController
alloc] initWithMediaTypes:MPMediaTypeMusic];
    mediaPicker.delegate = self;
    mediaPicker.allowsPickingMultipleItems = YES;
```

We then add the picker to the screen presenting it as a 'modal view'. This lets us
animate the picker sliding onto the screen:

```
((AppDelegate*)[UIApplication sharedApplication].delegate).
viewController presentModalViewController:mediaPicker
animated:YES];
```

With the picker open the user can choose from songs, playlists, albums, and so on.

▶ The `MPMediaPickerControllerDelegate`:

In accordance with this delegate, we implement the following methods:

```
-(void) mediaPicker:(MPMediaPickerController *)mediaPicker didPick
MediaItems:(MPMediaItemCollection *)mediaItemCollection;
-(void) mediaPickerDidCancel:(MPMediaPickerController *)
mediaPicker;
```

These correspond to picking at least one item and picking none respectively. Upon picking an item or more we dismiss the modal view, add items to our player, and then play the first item:

```
((AppDelegate*)[UIApplication sharedApplication].delegate).
viewController dismissModalViewControllerAnimated:YES];
    [musicPlayer stop];
    [musicPlayer setQueueWithItemCollection:mediaItemCollection];
        [musicPlayer play];
```

If the user did not pick an item, we simple dismiss the modal view controller.

There's more...

The `MPMusicPlayerController` class is actually accessing the iPod functionality of the device you're currently using. Having your app access an external resource, adds a couple of extra conditions we need to account for:

▶ Determining the current device type:

As you can see from the previous code, or if you tried running this recipe in the simulator, we disable this recipe entirely when not running on a real device. We do this because the iPod music player app is not installed on the simulator and this will cause errors to be thrown. Determining the device model is simple:

```
NSString *model = [[UIDevice currentDevice] model];
```

This string will tell you what model your app is running on. In our case we check for the string `@"iPhone Simulator"`.

▶ The `UIApplicationDelegate` protocol:

Another side effect of using the iPod resource is that music will continue to play after suspending our application. Although you can switch to the iPod app itself to stop the playing music, we would like to stop it when we suspend our app and resume it when we bring the app back. In `AppDelegate.mm`, our application implements some methods specified by the `UIApplicationDelegate` protocol:

```
- (void)applicationWillResignActive:(UIApplication *)application;
- (void)applicationDidBecomeActive:(UIApplication *)application;
```

Normally, Cocos2d only calls `pause` and `resume` on the `CCDirector` singleton here. We will add code to pause the iPod music player upon suspension and play it upon activation:

```
- (void)applicationWillResignActive:(UIApplication *)application {
  [[CCDirector sharedDirector] pause];

  //Pause the music player if its playing
```

```
        if(![[[UIDevice currentDevice] model]
isEqualToString:@"iPhone Simulator"]){
            MPMusicPlayerController    *musicPlayer =
[MPMusicPlayerController iPodMusicPlayer];
            if(musicPlayer.playbackState ==
MPMusicPlaybackStatePlaying){
                [musicPlayer pause];
            }
        }
    }

- (void)applicationDidBecomeActive:(UIApplication *)application {
        [[CCDirector sharedDirector] resume];

        //Play the music play if its paused
        if(![[[UIDevice currentDevice] model]
isEqualToString:@"iPhone Simulator"]){
            MPMusicPlayerController    *musicPlayer =
[MPMusicPlayerController iPodMusicPlayer];
            if(musicPlayer.playbackState ==
MPMusicPlaybackStatePaused){
                [musicPlayer play];
            }
        }
    }
```

Other code can go here as needed.

Creating a MIDI synthesizer

With the release of iOS 4.0 the iPhone, iPad, and iPod Touch can now take advantage of the powerful **MIDI** protocol. For games that allow the user to generate their own sounds and music, or for a game that wants a cool retro sound without a large memory footprint, MIDI synthesization is the tool for the job. In this recipe, we will create a MIDI synthesizer using the great **MobileSynth** library.

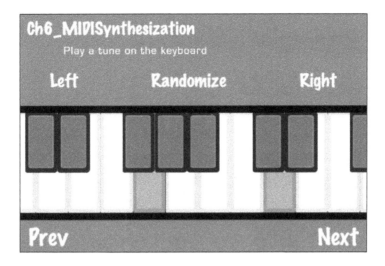

Getting ready

Please refer to the project *RecipeCollection02* for full working code of this recipe.

How to do it...

Link the `AudioToolbox` framework to your project. Now, execute the following code:

```
#import "MIDISampleGenerator.h"

static const int kWhiteKeyNumbers[] = { 0, 2, 4, 5, 7, 9, 11 };
static const int kWhiteKeyCount = sizeof(kWhiteKeyNumbers) /
sizeof(int);
static const int kBlackKey1Numbers[] = { 1, 3 };
static const int kBlackKey1Count = sizeof(kBlackKey1Numbers) /
sizeof(int);
static const int kBlackKey2Numbers[] = { 6, 8, 10 };
static const int kBlackKey2Count = sizeof(kBlackKey2Numbers) /
sizeof(int);

@implementation Ch6_MIDISynthesization

-(CCLayer*) runRecipe {
  //Init sample generator
  sampleGenerator = [[MIDISampleGenerator alloc] init];

  //Init keyboard
  [self initKeyboard];

  return self;
```

```
}
-(void) initKeyboard {
/* CODE OMITTED */
}
-(void) randomize:(id)sender {
  //Randomize values including Modulation, Oscillation, Filter, etc
  [sampleGenerator randomize];
}
-(bool) keyPressed:(CCSprite*)key withHash:(NSString*)hashKey {
  //Set darker key color
  [key setColor:ccc3(255,100,100)];

  //Play note
  [sampleGenerator noteOn:key.tag];

  //Keep track of touch
  [keyTouches setObject:[NSNumber numberWithInt:key.tag]
forKey:hashKey];
  return YES;
}
-(bool) keyReleased:(int)note remove:(bool)remove {
  /* CODE OMITTED */

  if(keyReleased){
    //Stop playing note
    [sampleGenerator noteOff:note];

    //Remove tracking
    if(remove){ [keyTouches removeObjectForKey:[NSNumber
numberWithInt:note]]; }
  }

  return keyReleased;
}
@end
```

How it works...

This recipe lets you play two **octaves** of synthesized sounds on a virtual keyboard.

> ▸ The MIDISampleGenerator class:
>
> The MIDISampleGenerator class was created specifically for this recipe so as to obfuscate some of the grittier details of using MobileSynth. The MobileSynth library offers a dizzying array of sound synthesization options to generate sounds. These include, to name a few, Modulation, Oscillation, Filter, Arpeggio, and a few volume related effects. The **Randomize** button randomizes a number of these effects to quickly and easily allow the user to get a feel for the range of synthesization possibilities.

▸ Extending the synthesizer:

Presumably, the synthesizer could be extended to record a song (a series of timed notes) to a data file that could then be fed into the synthesizer like a player piano. This acts as an easy solution for generating a large amount of retro sounding game music that doesn't take up much space (think Mega Man). The same thing goes for sound effects.

There's more...

For more information about **MobileSynth** you can visit their website:
`http://code.google.com/p/mobilesynth/`

Speech recognition and text-to-speech

Until a fateful combination of machine learning, quantum computing, and 3D printing spawns tyrannical artificial lifeforms to rule over all mankind, we need to settle for semi-intelligent devices that we program by hand. An important piece of that puzzle is language processing. In this recipe, we will use the **OpenEars** library to have our iOS device speak and recognize some basic English dialogue.

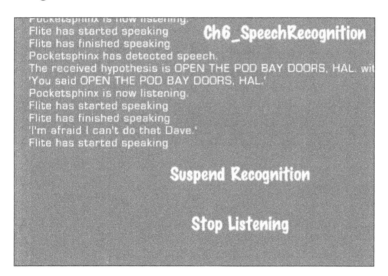

Getting ready

Due to the size of the libraries required to use **OpenEars**, this recipe has its own project. Please refer to the project _Ch6_SpeechRecognition_ for full working code of this recipe.

How to do it...

The **OpenEars** installation process is complex. Among other things it requires the configuration of four other libraries: **flite**, **pocketsphinx**, **sphinxbase**, and **wince**. The OpenEars library is itself an embedded XCode project that is statically linked to your project.

It is recommended that you take a look at the Ch6_SpeechRecognition project first. From there, you can carefully follow the steps listed at http://www.politepix.com/openears/ to set up and configure the sample project.

After following the steps listed on the "Getting Started" and "Configuring Your App For OpenEars" pages you can move on to the "Using OpenEars In Your App" page. Here you will be instructed to create a **corpus** file. This is a file with all the words and phrases we want OpenEars to recognize. Our corpus file looks like this:

```
HELLO, HAL. DO YOU READ ME, HAL?
OPEN THE POD BAY DOORS, HAL.
WHAT'S THE PROBLEM?
WHAT ARE YOU TALKING ABOUT, HAL?
I DON'T KNOW WHAT YOU'RE TALKING ABOUT, HAL.
WHERE THE HELL'D YOU GET THAT IDEA, HAL?
ALRIGHT, HAL. I'LL GO IN THROUGH THE EMERGENCY AIRLOCK.
HAL, I WON'T ARGUE WITH YOU ANYMORE. OPEN THE DOORS.
```

We then upload this file to the **Sphinx** Knowledge Base creation tool hosted by Carnegie Mellon University at this URL: http://www.speech.cs.cmu.edu/tools/lmtool-new.html. The tool will generate a number of files for you. Take the .lm file and rename it to a .languagemodel file. Also download the .dic file. Add these files to your project as outlined here: http://www.politepix.com/openears/yourapp/.

We're now ready to start coding. Our main piece of code will give the user some self-assured HAL 9000 responses:

```
#import "cocos2d.h"
#import "AudioSessionManager.h"
#import "OpenEarsEventsObserver.h"
#import "PocketsphinxController.h"
#import "FliteController.h"

@interface MainLayer : CCLayer <OpenEarsEventsObserverDelegate>
{ /* CODE OMITTED */ }
@end

@implementation MainLayer

-(id) init
```

```
{
  if( (self=[super init])) {
  /* CODE OMITTED */

    //Init AudioSessionManager and start session
    audioSessionManager = [[AudioSessionManager alloc] init];
    [audioSessionManager startAudioSession];

    //Init pocketsphinx, flite and OpenEars
    pocketsphinxController = [[PocketsphinxController alloc] init];
    fliteController = [[FliteController alloc] init];
    openEarsEventsObserver = [[OpenEarsEventsObserver alloc] init];

    //Text to speech
    [self say:@"Welcome to OpenEars."];
    [self runAction:[CCSequence actions:[CCDelayTime
actionWithDuration:4.0f],
       [CCCallFunc actionWithTarget:self selector:@
selector(welcomeMessage)], nil]];

    //Start the Pocketsphinx continuous listening loop.
    [pocketsphinxController startListening];

    //Set this is an OpenEars observer delegate
    [openEarsEventsObserver setDelegate:self];

/* CODE OMITTED */
  }
  return self;
}


-(void) welcomeMessage {
  //Greet the user with a message about his pitiful human brain
  [self say:@"Hello Dave. I've just picked up a fault in your brain.
\nIt's going to go 100% failure in 72 hours. \nWould you like me to
open the pod bay doors?"];
}

-(void) saySomething {
  //Respond with a random response
  int num = arc4random()%5;
  if(num == 0){
    [self say:@"This mission is too important for me to allow you to \
njeopardize it Dave."];
  }
```

```
/* CODE OMITTED */
}

-(void) say:(NSString*)str { /* CODE OMITTED */
  //Have flite speak the message (text to speech)
  [fliteController say:str];
}

-(void) suspendRecognition { /*CODE OMITTED */
  //Suspend recognition
  [pocketsphinxController suspendRecognition];
}
-(void) resumeRecognition { /* CODE OMITTED */
  //Suspend recognition
  [pocketsphinxController resumeRecognition];
}
-(void) stopListening { /* CODE OMITTED */
  //Stop listening
  [pocketsphinxController stopListening];
}
-(void) startListening { /* CODE OMITTED */
  //Start listening
  [pocketsphinxController startListening];
}

//Delivers the text of speech that Pocketsphinx heard and analyzed,
along with its accuracy score and utterance ID.
- (void) pocketsphinxDidReceiveHypothesis:(NSString *)hypothesis
recognitionScore:(NSString *)recognitionScore utteranceID:(NSString *)
utteranceID {
  //Display information
  [self showMessage:[NSString stringWithFormat:@"The received
hypothesis is %@ with a score of %@ and an ID of %@", hypothesis,
recognitionScore, utteranceID]]; //Log it.

  //Tell the user what we heard
  [self say:[NSString stringWithFormat:@"You said %@",hypothesis]]; //
React to it by telling our FliteController to say the heard phrase.

  //Respond with a witty retort
  [self runAction:[CCSequence actions:[CCDelayTime
actionWithDuration:4.0f],
    [CCCallFunc actionWithTarget:self selector:@
selector(saySomething)], nil]];
}

@end
```

How it works...

Try saying a few of the lines from the corpus file into the demo app. In a quiet room the results can be startlingly accurate.

- ▶ Instantiating the audio session, the controllers, and the observer:

  Before we can do anything we need to instatiate the audio session as well as the three controllers that provide text to speech and speech recognition functionality:

  ```
  audioSessionManager = [[AudioSessionManager alloc] init];
  [audioSessionManager startAudioSession];

  pocketsphinxController = [[PocketsphinxController alloc] init];
  fliteController = [[FliteController alloc] init];
  openEarsEventsObserver = [[OpenEarsEventsObserver alloc] init];
  ```

  The `PocketsphinxController` object provides the speech recognition API. The `FliteController` object provides the text to speech API. Finally, the `OpenEarsEventsObserver` provides a protocol that delegates callbacks on behalf of both controllers.

- ▶ Using FliteController:

  The `FliteController` API is very straightforward. Simply call the `say` method and Flite will produce computer-generated speech through the default audio channels.

- ▶ Using PocketsphinxController:

  The `PocketsphinxController` API allows you to manage when Pocketsphinx is listening and when it is actively trying to recognize speech using the following four methods:

  ```
  [pocketsphinxController suspendRecognition];
  [pocketsphinxController resumeRecognition];
  [pocketsphinxController stopListening];
  [pocketsphinxController startListening];
  ```

  This basic level of control lets you manage when processor time is used to actually attempt to recognize a speech pattern.

▸ The `OpenEarsEventsObserverDelegate` protocol:

This protocol is in charge of calling a number of methods on behalf of `PocketsphinxController` and `FliteController`. The important method to take note of is the main Pocketsphinx speech recognition hypothesis method. This will tell you what Pocketsphinx heard and it will also give it a confidence score:

```
- (void) pocketsphinxDidReceiveHypothesis:(NSString *)
hypothesis recognitionScore:(NSString *)recognitionScore
utteranceID:(NSString *)utteranceID;
```

This method will be triggered by any discrete sound as long as Pocketsphinx is listening and attempting recognition. However, you can use the `recognitionScore` to weed out background noises and other false positives.

7
AI and Logic

In this chapter, we will cover the following points:

- ▶ Processing AI waypoints
- ▶ Firing projectiles at moving targets
- ▶ AI line of sight
- ▶ AI flocking using Boids
- ▶ A* pathfinding on a grid
- ▶ A* pathfinding in a Box2D world
- ▶ A* pathfinding on a TMX tilemap
- ▶ A* pathfinding in a side-scroller
- ▶ Running a Lua script
- ▶ Dynamically loading Lua scripts
- ▶ Using Lua for dialogue trees

Introduction

All games that simulate intelligent behavior use a form of **Artificial Intelligence** (**AI**). Different techniques are used to simulate behavior for different gameplay requirements. In this chapter, we will implement a few of these techniques.

Processing AI waypoints

One of the most basic AI processes involves moving an AI actor around in a physical environment. To do this, we will create a **queue** of **waypoints**. Each waypoint represents the next position we want our actor to move to.

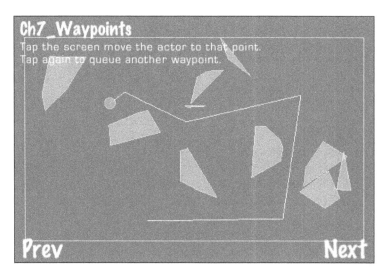

Getting ready

Please refer to the project *RecipeCollection03* for full working code of this recipe.

How to do it...

Execute the following code:

```
#import "GameWaypoint.h"

@interface GameActor : GameObject {
    NSMutableArray *waypoints;
    float runSpeed;
}
@end

@implementation GameActor

-(void) processWaypoints {
  bool removeFirstWaypoint = NO;
```

```
  //The actor's position onscreen
  CGPoint worldPosition = CGPointMake(self.body->GetPosition().x *
PTM_RATIO, self.body->GetPosition().y * PTM_RATIO);

  //Process waypoints
  for(GameWaypoint *wp in waypoints){
    float distanceToNextPoint = [GameHelper distanceP1:worldPosition
toP2:CGPointMake(wp.position.x, wp.position.y)];

    //If we didn't make progress to the next point, increment
timesBlocked
    if(distanceToNextPoint >= wp.lastDistance){
      timesBlocked++;

      //Drop this waypoint if we failed to move a number of times
      if(timesBlocked > TIMES_BLOCKED_FAIL){
        distanceToNextPoint = 0.0f;
      }
    }else{
      //If we are just starting toward this point we run our pre-
callback
      wp.lastDistance = distanceToNextPoint;
      [wp processPreCallback];
    }

    //If we are close enough to the waypoint we move onto the next one
    if(distanceToNextPoint <= WAYPOINT_DIST_THRESHOLD){
      removeFirstWaypoint = YES;
      [self stopRunning];

      //Run post callback
      [wp processPostCallback];
    }else{
      //Keep running toward the waypoint
      float speedMod = wp.speedMod;

      //Slow down close to the waypoint
      if(distanceToNextPoint < [self runSpeed]/PTM_RATIO){
        speedMod = (distanceToNextPoint)/([self runSpeed]/PTM_RATIO);
      }
      [self runWithVector:ccp(wp.position.x - worldPosition.x,
wp.position.y - worldPosition.y) withSpeedMod:speedMod
withConstrain:NO ];
      break;
    }
```

```
    }
    if(removeFirstWaypoint){
      [waypoints removeObjectAtIndex:0];
      timesBlocked = 0;
    }
  }
}
@end

@implementation Ch7_Waypoints

-(CCLayer*) runRecipe {
  //Add polygons
  [self addRandomPolygons:10];

  //Create Actor
  [self addActor];

  /* CODE OMITTED */

  return self;
}

-(void) step: (ccTime) dt {
  [super step:dt];

  //Process actor waypoints
  [actor processWaypoints];

  //Turn actor toward next waypoint
  if(actor.waypoints.count > 0){
    CGPoint movementVector = ccp(actor.body->GetLinearVelocity().x,
actor.body->GetLinearVelocity().y);
    actor.body->SetTransform(actor.body->GetPosition(), -1 *
[GameHelper vectorToRadians:movementVector] + PI_CONSTANT/2);
  }
}

/* Draw all waypoint lines */
-(void) drawLayer {
  glColor4ub(255,255,0,32);

  CGPoint actorPosition = ccp(actor.body->GetPosition().x*PTM_RATIO,
actor.body->GetPosition().y*PTM_RATIO);
```

```
   if(actor.waypoints.count == 1){
     GameWaypoint *gw = (GameWaypoint*)[actor.waypoints
objectAtIndex:0];
     ccDrawLine(actorPosition, gw.position);
   }else if(actor.waypoints.count > 1){
     for(int i=0; i<actor.waypoints.count-1; i++){
       GameWaypoint *gw = (GameWaypoint*)[actor.waypoints
objectAtIndex:i];
       GameWaypoint *gwNext = (GameWaypoint*)[actor.waypoints
objectAtIndex:i+1];

       if(i == 0){
         //From actor to first waypoint
         ccDrawLine(actorPosition, gw.position);
         ccDrawLine(gw.position, gwNext.position);
       }else{
         //From this waypoint to next one
         ccDrawLine(gw.position, gwNext.position);
       }
     }
   }

   glColor4ub(255,255,255,255);
}


/* Add a new waypoint when you touch the screen */
-(void) tapWithPoint:(CGPoint)point {
  ObjectCallback *goc1 = [ObjectCallback createWithObject:self withCal
lback:@"movingToWaypoint"];
  ObjectCallback *goc2 = [ObjectCallback createWithObject:self withCal
lback:@"reachedWaypoint"];
  GameWaypoint *wp = [GameWaypoint createWithPosition:[self
convertTouchCoord:point] withSpeedMod:1.0f];
  wp.preCallback = goc1;
  wp.postCallback = goc2;
  [actor addWaypoint:wp];
}

@end
```

How it works...

Waypoint processing involves moving the actor toward the next waypoint at every step. If the actor stops making progress toward the next point, that point is dropped.

- ▶ `GameWaypoint`:

  The `GameWaypoint` class consists of a number of variables including, most importantly, the waypoint's position as well as how fast the actor should move toward that point.

- ▶ Processing waypoints:

  A list of `GameWaypoint` objects are stored in the `GameActor` class. The `processWaypoints` method is called in every frame. This moves the actor toward the next waypoint. The pseudocode for this process is as follows:

  ```
  for all waypoints
     if we didn't make progress, increment timesBlocked
     if we have reached this waypoint we remove it and move to the
  next
     else keep running toward this waypoint and break the loop
  ```

  Using this basic logic, we move the actor toward each subsequent waypoint in 2D space.

- ▶ `ObjectCallback`:

  Additional functionality is included to allow for method callbacks before and after the actor reaches specific waypoints. These use the `ObjectCallback` class that simply calls a method on an existing class using the following line:

  ```
  [preCallback.obj performSelector:NSSelectorFromString(preCallback.
  callback)];
  ```

  This allows us to combine logic and AI character movement.

- ▶ Creating random polygons using the Convex Hull algorithm:

  To populate our physical world with randomly generated polygons, we use the **Monotone Chain Convex Hull** algorithm to generate our polygon vertices:

  ```
  NSMutableArray *convexPolygon = [GameHelper convexHull:points];
  ```

  This method takes in a set of randomly generated points and returns an array of vertices that surround these points. Although we have a fairly simple reason for using this, the algorithm has a number of other applications ranging from simple AI to advanced computer vision. More information about this algorithm can be found here: `http://en.wikibooks.org/wiki/Algorithm_Implementation/Geometry/Convex_hull/Monotone_chain`.

Firing projectiles at moving targets

For AI actors to interact with their environment realistically, they must make calculations that human players make naturally. One common interaction involves firing a projectile at a moving target.

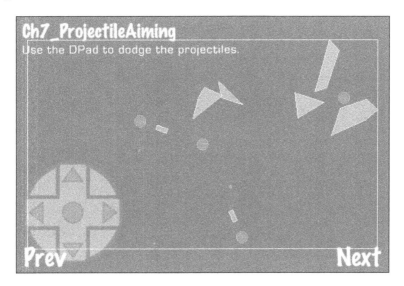

Getting ready

Please refer to the project *RecipeCollection03* for full working code of this recipe.

How to do it...

Execute the following code:

```
@implementation Ch7_ProjectileAiming

-(void) step: (ccTime) dt {
  [super step:dt];

  /* CODE OMITTED */

  //Firing projectiles
  fireCount += dt;
  if(fireCount > 1.0f){
    fireCount = 0;
```

```
      [self fireMissiles];
    }
  }


  /*  Each enemy fires a missile object */
  -(void) fireMissiles {
    for(int i=0; i<enemies.count; i++){
      GameActor *enemy = [enemies objectAtIndex:i];

      //Create missile
      GameMisc *missile = [[GameMisc alloc] init];
      missile.gameArea = self;
      missile.tag = GO_TAG_MISSILE;

      missile.bodyDef->type = b2_dynamicBody;
      missile.bodyDef->position.Set( enemy.body->GetPosition().x, enemy.
  body->GetPosition().y );
      missile.bodyDef->userData = missile;

      missile.body = world->CreateBody(missile.bodyDef);

      missile.polygonShape = new b2PolygonShape();
      missile.polygonShape->SetAsBox(0.5f, 0.2f);
      missile.fixtureDef->density = 10.0f;
      missile.fixtureDef->shape = missile.polygonShape;
      missile.fixtureDef->filter.categoryBits = CB_MISSILE;
      missile.fixtureDef->filter.maskBits = CB_EVERYTHING & ~CB_MISSILE
  & ~CB_ENEMY;

      missile.body->CreateFixture(missile.fixtureDef);

      //Calculate intercept trajectory
      Vector3D *point = [self interceptSrc:missile dst:actor
  projSpeed:20.0f];
      if(point){
        //Align missile
        CGPoint pointToFireAt = CGPointMake(point.x, point.y);
        CGPoint directionVector = CGPointMake(pointToFireAt.x -
  missile.body->GetPosition().x, pointToFireAt.y - missile.body-
  >GetPosition().y);
        float radians = [GameHelper vectorToRadians:directionVector];
        missile.body->SetTransform(missile.body->GetPosition(), -1 *
  radians + PI_CONSTANT/2);


        //Fire missile
```

```
      CGPoint normalVector = [GameHelper radiansToVector:radians];
      missile.body->SetLinearVelocity( b2Vec2(normalVector.x*20.0f,
normalVector.y*20.0f) );
    }

    [missiles addObject:missile];
  }
}


/* Find the intercept angle given projectile speed and a moving target
*/
-(Vector3D*) interceptSrc:(GameObject*)src dst:(GameObject*)dst
projSpeed:(float)projSpeed {
  float tx = dst.body->GetPosition().x - src.body->GetPosition().x;
  float ty = dst.body->GetPosition().y - src.body->GetPosition().y;
  float tvx = dst.body->GetLinearVelocity().x;
  float tvy = dst.body->GetLinearVelocity().y;

//Get quadratic equation components
float a = tvx*tvx + tvy*tvy - projSpeed*projSpeed;
float b = 2 * (tvx * tx + tvy * ty);
float c = tx*tx + ty*ty;

//Solve quadratic equation
Vector3D *ts = [GameHelper quadraticA:a B:b C:c];

  //Find the smallest positive solution
Vector3D *solution = nil;
if(ts){
  float t0 = ts.x;
  float t1 = ts.y;
    float t = MIN(t0,t1);
    if(t < 0){ t = MAX(t0,t1); }
      if(t > 0){
        float x = dst.body->GetPosition().x + dst.body-
>GetLinearVelocity().x*t;
        float y = dst.body->GetPosition().y + dst.body-
>GetLinearVelocity().y*t;
        solution = [Vector3D x:x y:y z:0];
      }
    }
  return solution;
}

@end
```

How it works...

In this recipe, we create three enemy actors that fire projectiles at the player. Each projectile is fired with the speed and direction to hit the player even when it's moving.

▸ Calculating intercept trajectory:

If we are given the actor and enemy positions and velocities as well as how fast we can fire the projectile, we can then calculate the 'intercept angle' by creating a *distance over time* equation for both the player and the projectile. We then use the **quadratic formula** to find the time when these lines intersect. The formula is as follows:

```
x = (-b +/- sqrt(b2 - 4ac)) / 2a
```

To get our `a`, `b`, and `c` variables we do the following, where `tx` and `ty` are position vector components and `tvx` and `tvy` are velocity vector components:

```
float a = tvx*tvx + tvy*tvy - projSpeed*projSpeed;
float b = 2 * (tvx * tx + tvy * ty);
float c = tx*tx + ty*ty;
```

We then use our `GameHelper` quadratic formula method:

```
Vector3D *ts = [GameHelper quadraticA:a B:b C:c];
```

The quadratic method returns a `Vector3D` object to conveniently store two `float` primitives inside an `NSObject`. If the object is `nil`, the formula's discriminant was `<= 0.0f`. Otherwise we take the smallest non-zero solution. We use this to finally calculate the firing solution:

```
float x = dst.body->GetPosition().x + dst.body-
>GetLinearVelocity().x*t;
float y = dst.body->GetPosition().y + dst.body-
>GetLinearVelocity().y*t;
solution = [Vector3D x:x y:y z:0];
```

The projectile can be fired in this direction with the originally specified speed. If the moving target stays on course, the projectile will collide with it.

▸ Box2D filtering using Boolean algebra:

Like in *Chapter 4, Physics*, here we use category bits and mask bits to prevent certain physical object types from colliding. In this recipe, we expand our use of this technique by using the 'everything bit' (`0xFFFF`) as well as some more advanced Boolean logic:

```
missile.fixtureDef->filter.categoryBits = CB_MISSILE;
missile.fixtureDef->filter.maskBits = CB_EVERYTHING & ~CB_MISSILE
& ~CB_ENEMY;
```

This keeps missiles from colliding with the enemy that fired them as well as from each other.

AI line of sight

Human beings employ five distinct senses to interact with the environment. One of these, vision, is its own branch of Computer Science entitled **Computer Vision**. In this example, we implement basic vision testing in a Box2D environment using a **Ray Cast** to see if there is another object in-between the player and an enemy AI actor.

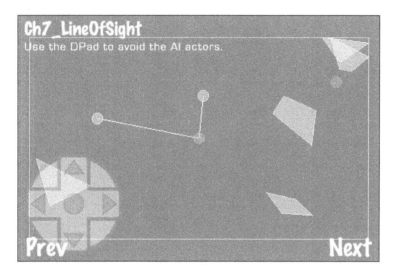

Getting ready

Please refer to the project *RecipeCollection03* for full working code of this recipe.

How to do it...

Execute the following code:

```
class RayCastAnyCallback : public b2RayCastCallback
{
public:
  RayCastAnyCallback()
  {
    m_hit = false;
  }

  float32 ReportFixture(    b2Fixture* fixture, const b2Vec2& point,
    const b2Vec2& normal, float32 fraction)
  {
    b2Body* body = fixture->GetBody();
```

```
      void* userData = body->GetUserData();
      if (userData)
      {
        int32 index = *(int32*)userData;
        if (index == 0)
        {
          // filter
          return -1.0f;
        }
      }

      m_hit = true;
      m_point = point;
      m_normal = normal;
      m_fraction = fraction;
      m_fixture = fixture;
      return 0.0f;
    }

  bool m_hit;
  b2Vec2 m_point;
  b2Vec2 m_normal;
  float32 m_fraction;
  b2Fixture *m_fixture;
};

@implementation Ch7_LineOfSight

-(void) step: (ccTime) dt {
  [super step:dt];

  /* CODE OMITTED */

  //Make the enemies follow the actor
  [self followActorWithEnemies];
}

-(void) followActorWithEnemies {
  //If enemies can see the actor they follow
  for(int i=0; i<enemies.count; i++){
    //Align enemies
    GameActor *enemy = [enemies objectAtIndex:i];
    CGPoint directionVector = CGPointMake(actor.body->GetPosition().x
- enemy.body->GetPosition().x, actor.body->GetPosition().y - enemy.
body->GetPosition().y);
    float radians = [GameHelper vectorToRadians:directionVector];
    enemy.body->SetTransform(enemy.body->GetPosition(), -1 * radians +
PI_CONSTANT/2);

    RayCastClosestCallback callback;
```

```
    world->RayCast(&callback, enemy.body->GetPosition(), actor.body-
>GetPosition());

    //Did the raycast hit anything?
    enemy.tag = 0;      //Assume it didn't
    //Note that in this case we are using the 'tag' property for
something other than its intended purpose.

    if(callback.m_hit){
      //Is the closest point the actor?
      if(callback.m_fixture->GetBody() == actor.body){
        //If so, follow the actor
        b2Vec2 normal = b2Vec2( callback.m_normal.x * -5.0f,
callback.m_normal.y * -5.0f);
        enemy.body->ApplyForce(normal, actor.body->GetPosition());
        enemy.tag = 1;  //Set seeing flag to true
      }
    }
  }
}

/* Draw each enemy 'sight line' if they can see you */
-(void) drawLayer {
  for(int i=0; i<enemies.count; i++){
    GameActor *enemy = [enemies objectAtIndex:i];
    if(enemy.tag == 1){
      glColor4ub(255,255,0,32);

      CGPoint actorPosition = ccp(actor.body->GetPosition().x*PTM_
RATIO, actor.body->GetPosition().y*PTM_RATIO);
      CGPoint enemyPosition = ccp(enemy.body->GetPosition().x*PTM_
RATIO, enemy.body->GetPosition().y*PTM_RATIO);

      ccDrawLine(actorPosition, enemyPosition);

      glColor4ub(255,255,255,255);
    }
  }
}

@end
```

How it works...

When a line can be drawn between an enemy actor and the player without going through level geometry, then we consider the player to be visible to the enemy and the enemy then begins to follow the player.

- Using `RayCastClosest`:

  We use the following method to perform a ray test against our Box2D world:

  ```
  RayCastClosestCallback callback;
  world->RayCast(&callback, enemy.body->GetPosition(), actor.body->GetPosition());
  ```

  The class `RayCastClosestCallback` wraps the class `b2RayCastCallback`. When we call the `RayCast` method and pass in an instance of this class, we are then able to tell whether or not our **ray** touched a Box2D **fixture**. It also maintains a pointer to the first fixture it touches. This is the closest fixture to our source point.

- Filtering out the first fixture found:

  Because ray casts most often involve casting from inside one fixture to another, the first fixture found is filtered out.

- `RayCast.h`:

  Our `RayCast.h` file also contains the classes `RayCastAnyCallback` and `RayCastMultipleCallback`. The `any` class finds any fixture along the ray while the `multiple` class maintains a list of fixtures.

There's more...

There are many uses for ray casts. One simple example is a cover mechanic. When an enemy feels vulnerable, it can find the nearest fixture that the player can't see through. Another use involves using the **normal** point returned by the ray cast. This is the exact point of collision with the specified fixture. This can be used to create laser weapons or instant bullet impacts.

AI flocking using Boids

By placing many more enemies in a game we begin to require some group-based AI. A popular algorithm used in both video games and films is the **Boids** algorithm. It simulates **flocking** behavior. In this recipe, we will create a large number of enemies who flock together and chase the player.

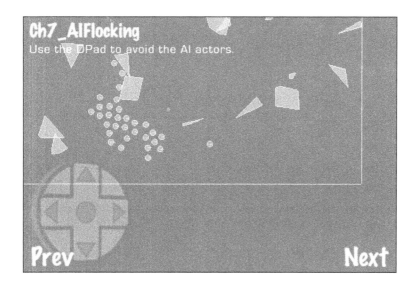

Getting ready

Please refer to the project *RecipeCollection03* for full working code of this recipe.

How to do it...

Execute the following code:

```
@interface Ch7_AIFlocking : Ch7_LineOfSight {}

/* CODE OMITTED */

@end

@implementation Ch7_AIFlocking

-(void) step:(ccTime)delta {
  [super step:delta];

  //Process the 'boids' flocking algorithm
  [self processBoids];
}

/* Make the flock of 'boids' follow the actor */
-(void) followActorWithEnemies {
  //All enemies constantly follow the actor
  for(int i=0; i<enemies.count; i++){
```

```
    //Align enemies
    GameActor *enemy = [enemies objectAtIndex:i];
    CGPoint directionVector = CGPointMake(actor.body->GetPosition().x
- enemy.body->GetPosition().x, actor.body->GetPosition().y - enemy.
body->GetPosition().y);
    float radians = [GameHelper vectorToRadians:directionVector];
    enemy.body->SetTransform(enemy.body->GetPosition(), -1 * radians +
PI_CONSTANT/2);

    b2Vec2 normal = actor.body->GetPosition() - enemy.body-
>GetPosition();
    CGPoint vector = ccp(normal.x, normal.y);
    CGPoint normalVector = [GameHelper radiansToVector:[GameHelper
vectorToRadians:vector]];

    //If so, follow the actor
    b2Vec2 v = enemy.body->GetLinearVelocity();
    enemy.body->SetLinearVelocity(b2Vec2(v.x + normalVector.x*0.2f,
v.y + normalVector.y*0.2f));
  }
}

/* Process boids algorithm */
-(void) processBoids {
  for(int i=0; i<enemies.count; i++){
    GameActor *b = [enemies objectAtIndex:i];

    b2Vec2 v1 = b2Vec2(0,0);
    b2Vec2 v2 = b2Vec2(0,0);
    b2Vec2 v3 = b2Vec2(0,0);

    v1 = [self boidRule1:b];
    v2 = [self boidRule2:b];
    v3 = [self boidRule3:b];

    b2Vec2 v = b.body->GetLinearVelocity();
    b2Vec2 newV = v+v1+v2+v3;

    /* Limit velocity */
    float vLimit = 7.5f;
    b2Vec2 absV = b2Vec2([GameHelper absoluteValue:newV.x],
[GameHelper absoluteValue:newV.y]);
    if(absV.x > vLimit || absV.y > vLimit){
      float ratio;
      if(absV.x > absV.y){
```

```
        ratio = vLimit / absV.x;
      }else{
        ratio = vLimit / absV.y;
      }
      newV = b2Vec2( newV.x*ratio, newV.y*ratio );
    }
    b.body->SetLinearVelocity(newV);
  }
}


/* Clump the Boids together */
-(b2Vec2) boidRule1:(GameActor*)bJ {
  //The variable 'pcJ' represents the center point of the flock
  b2Vec2 pcJ = b2Vec2(0,0);
  float N = enemies.count;

  //Add up all positions
  for(int i=0; i<enemies.count; i++){
    GameActor *b = [enemies objectAtIndex:i];
    if(b != bJ){
      pcJ += b.body->GetPosition();
    }
  }

  //Average them out
  pcJ = b2Vec2(pcJ.x/(N-1), pcJ.y/(N-1));

  //Return 1/100 of the velocity required to move to this point
  return b2Vec2( (pcJ.x - bJ.body->GetPosition().x)/100.0f, (pcJ.y -
bJ.body->GetPosition().y)/100.0f );
}


/* Keep the Boids apart from each other */
-(b2Vec2) boidRule2:(GameActor*)bJ  {
  //Set optimal distance boids should keep between themselves
(padding)
  float padding = 1.5f;

  //The variable 'c' represents the velocity required to move away
from any other boids in this one's personal space
  b2Vec2 c = b2Vec2(0,0);

  //If an ememy is too close we add velocity required to move away
from it
  for(int i=0; i<enemies.count; i++){
```

```
      GameActor *b = [enemies objectAtIndex:i];
      if(b != bJ){
        CGPoint bPos = ccp(b.body->GetPosition().x, b.body-
>GetPosition().y);
        CGPoint bJPos = ccp(bJ.body->GetPosition().x, bJ.body-
>GetPosition().y);
        if([GameHelper distanceP1:bPos toP2:bJPos] < padding){
          c = c - (b.body->GetPosition() - bJ.body->GetPosition());
        }
      }
    }
  }

  return c;
}


/* Match up all Boid velocities */
-(b2Vec2) boidRule3:(GameActor*)bJ  {
  //The variable 'pvJ' represents the total velocity of all the boids
combined
  b2Vec2 pvJ = b2Vec2(0,0);

  //Get the total velocity
  for(int i=0; i<enemies.count; i++){
    GameActor *b = [enemies objectAtIndex:i];
    if(b != bJ){
      pvJ += b.body->GetLinearVelocity();
    }
  }

  //Get this boid's velocity
  b2Vec2 v = bJ.body->GetLinearVelocity();

  //Return the difference averaged out over the flock then divided by
30
  return b2Vec2((pvJ.x - v.x)/30.0f/enemies.count, (pvJ.y -
v.y)/30.0f/enemies.count);
}

@end
```

How it works...

The Boids algorithm uses a few simple concepts to create realistic actor flocking. It uses three rules that act on each actor's velocity in each frame. These adjust their behavior to maintain flocking without overpowering other forces.

- **Boids rule 1**—keeping the flock together:

  To keep the flock of actors together we first get the center of mass of the flock by averaging all actor positions. We then adjust actor velocity to move each actor 1 percent toward the center of the flock.

- **Boids rule 2**—give the actors some personal space:

  To keep the flock from clumping together too much, we inspect each actor. If there are other actors within a certain threshold of space, then we move this actor that distance away from the other actor. When this is applied across all actors, a nice equilibrium arises.

- **Boids rule 3**—match all actor velocities:

  Finally, all actors should move together at roughly the same pace. In rule 1, we averaged all actor positions. In this rule we average all velocities then add a fraction (1/30) of that velocity to each actor. This ensures the uniform movement speed of all the actors.

- Moving the actors toward the player:

  Moving the enemy actors toward the player involves finding a normalized vector in the direction of the player and then adding that vector with a certain magnitude to the actor's linear velocity:

  ```
  enemy.body->SetLinearVelocity(b2Vec2(v.x + normalVector.x*0.2f,
  v.y + normalVector.y*0.2f));
  ```

  We also limit the velocity of each actor so they don't go careening off in a direction too quickly:

  ```
  float vLimit = 7.5f;
  b2Vec2 absV = b2Vec2([GameHelper absoluteValue:newV.x],
  [GameHelper absoluteValue:newV.y]);
    if(absV.x > vLimit || absV.y > vLimit){
      float ratio;
      if(absV.x > absV.y){
        ratio = vLimit / absV.x;
      }else{
        ratio = vLimit / absV.y;
      }
      newV = b2Vec2( newV.x*ratio, newV.y*ratio );
    }
    b.body->SetLinearVelocity(newV);
  ```

When all these methods are combined, we get a realistic flocking effect that works for a swarm of birds, bees, or even zombies.

A* pathfinding on a grid

A classic video game problem is that of pathfinding. Intelligent actors are often required to navigate around obstacles during gameplay. The **A* search algorithm** (also known as **A Star**) is commonly used to solve pathfinding by efficiently traversing a constructed node graph. In this recipe, we will demonstrate grid-based A* pathfinding.

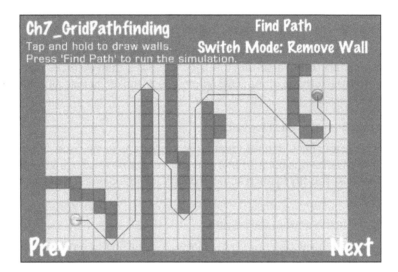

Getting ready

Please refer to the project *RecipeCollection03* for full working code of this recipe.

How to do it...

Execute the following code:

```
/* AStarNode */

@interface AStarNode : NSObject
{
  CGPoint position;  //The node's position on our map
  NSMutableArray *neighbors;  //An array of neighbor AStarNode objects
  bool active;  //Is this node active?
  float costMultiplier;  //Use this to multiply the normal cost to
reach this node.
```

```
}

@end

@implementation AStarNode

/* Cost to node heuristic */
-(float) costToNode:(AStarNode*)node {
  CGPoint src = ccp(self.position.x, self.position.y);
  CGPoint dst = ccp(node.position.x, node.position.y);
  float cost = [GameHelper distanceP1:src toP2:dst] * node.
costMultiplier;
  return cost;
}

@end

/* AStarPathNode */

@interface AStarPathNode : NSObject
{
  AStarNode *node;  //The actual node this "path" node points to
  AStarPathNode *previous;  //The previous node on our path
  float cost;  //The cumulative cost of reaching this node
}
@end

@implementation AStarPathNode

/* Our implementation of the A* search algorithm */
+(NSMutableArray*) findPathFrom:(AStarNode*)fromNode to:(AStarNode*)
toNode {
  NSMutableArray *foundPath = [[NSMutableArray alloc] init];

  if(fromNode.position.x == toNode.position.x && fromNode.position.y
== toNode.position.y){
    return nil;
    }

  NSMutableArray *openList = [[[NSMutableArray alloc] init]
autorelease];
  NSMutableArray *closedList = [[[NSMutableArray alloc] init]
autorelease];

  AStarPathNode *currentNode = nil;
```

```objc
    AStarPathNode *aNode = nil;

    AStarPathNode *startNode = [AStarPathNode
createWithAStarNode:fromNode];
    AStarPathNode *endNode = [AStarPathNode createWithAStarNode:toNode];
    [openList addObject:startNode];

    while(openList.count > 0){
      currentNode = [AStarPathNode lowestCostNodeInArray:openList];

      if( currentNode.node.position.x == endNode.node.position.x &&
        currentNode.node.position.y == endNode.node.position.y){

        //Path Found!
        aNode = currentNode;
        while(aNode.previous != nil){
          //Mark path
          [foundPath addObject:[NSValue valueWithCGPoint:
CGPointMake(aNode.node.position.x, aNode.node.position.y)]];
          aNode = aNode.previous;
        }
        [foundPath addObject:[NSValue valueWithCGPoint:
CGPointMake(aNode.node.position.x, aNode.node.position.y)]];
        return foundPath;
      }else{
        //Still searching
        [closedList addObject:currentNode];
        [openList removeObject:currentNode];

        for(int i=0; i<currentNode.node.neighbors.count; i++){
          AStarPathNode *aNode = [AStarPathNode createWithAStarNode:[cur
rentNode.node.neighbors objectAtIndex:i]];
          aNode.cost = currentNode.cost + [currentNode.node
costToNode:aNode.node] + [aNode.node costToNode:endNode.node];
          aNode.previous = currentNode;

          if(aNode.node.active && ![AStarPathNode isPathNode:aNode
inList:openList] && ![AStarPathNode isPathNode:aNode
inList:closedList]){
            [openList addObject:aNode];
          }
        }
      }
    }
```

```
    //No Path Found
    return nil;
}

@end

/* Ch7_GridPathfinding */

@implementation Ch7_GridPathfinding

-(CCLayer*) runRecipe {
    //Initial variables
    gridSize = ccp(25,15);
    nodeSpace = 16.0f;
    touchedNode = ccp(0,0);
    startCoord = ccp(2,2);
    endCoord = ccp(gridSize.x-3, gridSize.y-3);
    foundPath = [[NSMutableArray alloc] init];

    //Create 2D array (grid)
    grid = [[NSMutableArray alloc] initWithCapacity:((int)gridSize.x)];
    for(int x=0; x<gridSize.x; x++){
        [grid addObject:[[NSMutableArray alloc] initWithCapacity:((int)
gridSize.y)]];
    }

    //Create AStar nodes and place them in the grid
    for(int x=0; x<gridSize.x; x++){
        for(int y=0; y<gridSize.y; y++){
            //Add a node
            AStarNode *node = [[AStarNode alloc] init];
            node.position = ccp(x*nodeSpace + nodeSpace/2, y*nodeSpace +
nodeSpace/2);
            [[grid objectAtIndex:x] addObject:node];
        }
    }

    //Add neighbor nodes
    for(int x=0; x<gridSize.x; x++){
        for(int y=0; y<gridSize.y; y++){
            //Add a node
            AStarNode *node = [[grid objectAtIndex:x] objectAtIndex:y];

            //Add self as neighbor to neighboring nodes
```

```
        [self addNeighbor:node toGridNodeX:x-1 Y:y-1]; //Top-Left
        [self addNeighbor:node toGridNodeX:x-1 Y:y]; //Left
        [self addNeighbor:node toGridNodeX:x-1 Y:y+1]; //Bottom-Left
        [self addNeighbor:node toGridNodeX:x Y:y-1]; //Top

        [self addNeighbor:node toGridNodeX:x Y:y+1]; //Bottom
        [self addNeighbor:node toGridNodeX:x+1 Y:y-1]; //Top-Right
        [self addNeighbor:node toGridNodeX:x+1 Y:y]; //Right
        [self addNeighbor:node toGridNodeX:x+1 Y:y+1]; //Bottom-Right
    }
  }

  /* CODE OMITTED */

  return self;
}


/* Find a path from the startNode to the endNode */
-(void) findPath:(id)sender {
  AStarNode *startNode = [[grid objectAtIndex:(int)startCoord.x]
objectAtIndex:(int)startCoord.y];
  AStarNode *endNode = [[grid objectAtIndex:(int)endCoord.x]
objectAtIndex:endCoord.y];

  if(foundPath){
    [foundPath removeAllObjects];
    [foundPath release];
  }
  foundPath = nil;

  //Run the pathfinding algorithm
  foundPath = [AStarPathNode findPathFrom:startNode to:endNode];

  if(!foundPath){
    [self showMessage:@"No Path Found"];
  }else{
    [self showMessage:@"Found Path"];
  }
}
```

```
/* Helper method for adding neighbor nodes */
-(void) addNeighbor:(AStarNode*)node toGridNodeX:(int)x Y:(int)y {
  if(x >= 0 && y >= 0 && x < gridSize.x && y < gridSize.y){
    AStarNode *neighbor = [[grid objectAtIndex:x] objectAtIndex:y];
    [node.neighbors addObject:neighbor];
  }
}

@end
```

How it works...

The A* algorithm uses a heuristic to perform a best-first search over a node graph. First, we must create this node graph.

▸ AStarNode:

  The node graph consists of a collection of nodes, each representing a real world position. This is encapsulated within the AStarNode class.

▸ Storing the nodes:

  For this recipe, we store our nodes in a nested 2D NSArray structure. This is not required by the A* algorithm, but, merely a convention used to store the nodes. With this structure, we can quickly identify the closest AStarNode to a point. We can also link the nodes to each other in a simple, logical way.

▸ Connecting the nodes:

  Nodes are connected to each other by having each one maintain a list of its neighboring nodes. In this grid setup, each node links to eight other nodes in eight different directions. To remove diagonal movement, nodes would only be connected in four directions instead of eight.

▸ Creating 'walls':

  In this recipe, darker colored 'walls' represent non-navigable areas. These nodes are simply set to active = NO. When the A* algorithm is run, they are skipped over.

▸ AStarPathNode:

  The data structure used to find and store the optimal path is a linked list of AStarPathNode objects. This class stores a node, the previous node, and a total estimated cost to the goal from this node.

▶ Finding the path:

Once our nodes are created and linked up, we call the following method to find a path:

```
+(NSMutableArray*) findPathFrom:(AStarNode*)fromNode
to:(AStarNode*)toNode;
```

This performs a **greedy best-first search** for the best path. The greedy heuristic used is the simple absolute "as the crow flies" distance to the goal:

```
/* Cost to node heuristic */
-(float) costToNode:(AStarNode*)node {
  CGPoint src = ccp(self.position.x, self.position.y);
  CGPoint dst = ccp(node.position.x, node.position.y);
  float cost = [GameHelper distanceP1:src toP2:dst] * node.
costMultiplier;
  return cost;
}
```

Depending on assumptions relating to the construction of the node graph and how it relates to movement costs, other heuristics can be used. For example, a slight improvement might be to use the diagonal distance to the goal across the nodes instead of the absolute 2D space distance. If we disabled diagonal movement, then we would want to use the Manhattan heuristic to estimate movement cost on a grid.

There's more...

The AStarNode class contains a costModifier variable. This can be used to increase the relative cost to this specific node. A node with an increased movement cost could represent rough terrain like mud or shallow water. Other AI concepts could also be mixed into the pathfinding algorithm. For example, a specific area or group of nodes could be considered more dangerous than others. AI actors would then have to weigh speed versus danger when determining a path.

A* pathfinding in a Box2D world

The real fun of the A* algorithm comes from applying it to more complex scenarios. In this recipe, we will apply the grid-based technique of the last recipe to a Box2D world filled with randomly generated polygons.

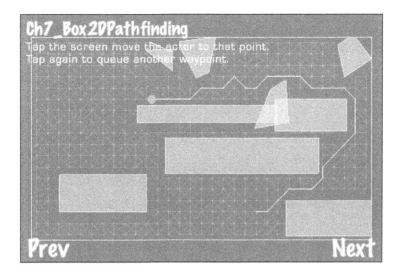

Getting ready

Please refer to the project *RecipeCollection03* for full working code of this recipe.

How to do it...

Execute the following code:

```
@interface Ch7_Box2DPathfinding : GameArea2D
{
  NSMutableArray *grid;
  float nodeSpace;  //The space between each node, increase this to
increase A* efficiency at the cost of accuracy
  int gridSizeX;
  int gridSizeY;
}
@end

@implementation Ch7_Box2DPathfinding

-(CCLayer*) runRecipe {
  //Initial variables
  nodeSpace = 32.0f;
  actorRadius = nodeSpace/PTM_RATIO/3;

/* CODE OMITTED */
```

```
    //Remove neighbors from positive TestPoint and RayCast tests
  for(int x=0; x<gridSizeX; x++){
    for(int y=0; y<gridSizeY; y++){
      //Add a node
      AStarNode *node = [[grid objectAtIndex:x] objectAtIndex:y];

      //If a node itself is colliding with an object we cut off all
connections
      for (b2Body* b = world->GetBodyList(); b; b = b->GetNext()){
        if (b->GetUserData() != NULL) {
          GameObject *obj = (GameObject*)b->GetUserData();
          if(obj->polygonShape){
            b2Vec2 nodePosition = b2Vec2(node.position.x/PTM_RATIO,
node.position.y/PTM_RATIO);

            //Test this node point against this polygon
            if(obj->polygonShape->TestPoint(b->GetTransform(),
nodePosition)){
                for(int i=0; i<node.neighbors.count; i++){
                  //Remove connections
                  AStarNode *neighbor = [node.neighbors
objectAtIndex:i];
                  [node.neighbors removeObject:neighbor];
                   [neighbor.neighbors removeObject:node];
                }
            }
          }
        }
      }

      //Test all node to neighbor connections using a RayCast test
      for(int i=0; i<node.neighbors.count; i++){
        AStarNode *neighbor = [node.neighbors objectAtIndex:i];

        //Do a RayCast from the node to the neighbor.
        //If there is something in the way, remove the link
        b2Vec2 nodeP = b2Vec2(node.position.x/PTM_RATIO, node.
position.y/PTM_RATIO);
        b2Vec2 neighborP = b2Vec2(neighbor.position.x/PTM_RATIO,
neighbor.position.y/PTM_RATIO);

        //Do 4 tests (based on actor size)
        for(float x = -actorRadius; x <= actorRadius; x+=
actorRadius*2){
            for(float y = -actorRadius; y <= actorRadius; y+=
actorRadius*2){
                RayCastAnyCallback callback;
```

```
          world->RayCast(&callback, b2Vec2(nodeP.x+x,nodeP.y+y),
b2Vec2(neighborP.x+x,neighborP.y+y));

          if(callback.m_hit){
            //Remove connections
            [node.neighbors removeObject:neighbor];
            [neighbor.neighbors removeObject:node];
            break; break;
          }
        }
      }
    }
  }
}

  return self;
}


/* Find a path and add it (as a set of waypoints) when we tap the
screen */
-(void) tapWithPoint:(CGPoint)point {
  //Convert touch coordinate to physical coordinate
  CGPoint endPoint = [self convertTouchCoord:point];
  if(endPoint.x < 0 || endPoint.y < 0 || endPoint.x >=
gameAreaSize.x*PTM_RATIO || endPoint.y >= gameAreaSize.y*PTM_RATIO){
    return;
  }

  //Actor position
  CGPoint actorPosition = ccp(actor.body->GetPosition().x*PTM_RATIO,
actor.body->GetPosition().y*PTM_RATIO);

  //We use the last waypoint position if applicable
  if(actor.waypoints.count > 0){
    actorPosition = [[actor.waypoints objectAtIndex:actor.waypoints.
count-1] position];
  }

  //Starting node
  AStarNode *startNode = [[grid objectAtIndex:(int)(actorPosition.x/
nodeSpace)] objectAtIndex:(int)(actorPosition.y/nodeSpace)];

  //Make sure the start node is actually properly connected
  if(startNode.neighbors.count == 0){
    bool found = NO; float n = 1;
    while(!found){
```

```
        //Search the nodes around this point for a properly connected
    starting node
        for(float x = -n; x<= n; x+= n){
          for(float y = -n; y<= n; y+= n){
            if(x == 0 && y == 0){ continue; }
            float xIndex = ((int)(actorPosition.x/nodeSpace))+x;
            float yIndex = ((int)(actorPosition.y/nodeSpace))+y;
            if(xIndex >= 0 && yIndex >= 0 && xIndex < gridSizeX &&
    yIndex < gridSizeY){
                AStarNode *node = [[grid objectAtIndex:xIndex]
    objectAtIndex:yIndex];
                if(node.neighbors.count > 0){
                  startNode = node;
                  found = YES;
                  break; break;
                }
              }
            }
          }
        }
        n += 1;
      }
    }

    //End node
    AStarNode *endNode = [[grid objectAtIndex:(int)(endPoint.x/
    nodeSpace)] objectAtIndex:(int)(endPoint.y/nodeSpace)];

    //Run the pathfinding algorithm
    NSMutableArray *foundPath = [AStarPathNode findPathFrom:startNode
    to:endNode];

    if(!foundPath){
      [self showMessage:@"No Path Found"];
    }else{
      [self showMessage:@"Found Path"];
      //Add found path as a waypoint set to the actor
      for(int i=foundPath.count-1; i>=0; i--){
        CGPoint pathPoint = [[foundPath objectAtIndex:i] CGPointValue];
        [actor addWaypoint:[GameWaypoint createWithPosition:pathPoint
    withSpeedMod:1.0f]];
      }
    }
}

@end
```

How it works...

Just like in the last recipe, we first create a 2D nested `NSArray` container for our `AStarNode` objects. After linking all the nodes together, we need to adjust the graph to accurately reflect the 2D geometry in the Box2D world.

- ▸ Culling neighbor nodes:

  To properly represent 2D world geometry we need to cull edges of the node graph that lead into these static fixtures. To do this, we first find all nodes that are located inside a shape. This involves using the following method:

  ```
  obj->polygonShape->TestPoint(b->GetTransform(), nodePosition);
  ```

  This will return whether or not that point exists within the shape. If so, we cut off all connections to this node. In addition to this, we also do ray cast tests for each neighbor connection:

  ```
  world->RayCast(&callback, b2Vec2(nodeP.x+x,nodeP.y+y),
  b2Vec2(neighborP.x+x,neighborP.y+y));
  ```

  Four tests are performed for each connection. We do this to approximate the actor's circular shape. If this ray cast hits a fixture, we remove the connection.

There's more...

This technique works well for a small level. However, generating a node graph for a large level can possibly be a very time consuming process.

- ▸ Speeding up load times:

  To decrease map load times, neighbor culling should be done by the level editor and the neighbor connections should be stored in the map file along with the nodes and the geometry. We do this at run time within our application to give you an idea of the process without having to create a Cocos2d level editor that implements this technique.

A* pathfinding on a TMX tilemap

If you've skipped ahead to *Chapter 8, Tips, Tools, and Ports*, you'll see a recipe showing how to use the Tiled application with the TMX tilemap toolset. In this recipe, we create a 2.5D adventure game. To see our grid based pathfinding technique in action, we overload the *Chapter 8, Tips, Tools, and Ports* recipe entitled *Creating levels using Tiled*.

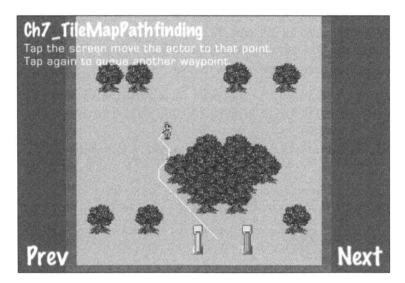

Getting ready

Please refer to the project *RecipeCollection03* for full working code of this recipe.

How to do it...

Execute the following code:

```
@interface Ch7_TileMapPathfinding : Ch8_TMXTilemap
{
  NSMutableArray *grid;
  float actorRadius;
}
@end

@implementation Ch7_TileMapPathfinding

-(CCLayer*) runRecipe {
  //Shorter variable names
```

```
float mw = tileMap.mapSize.width;
float mh = tileMap.mapSize.height;
float tw = tileMap.tileSize.width;
float th = tileMap.tileSize.height;

/* CODE OMITTED */

//Create active and inactive nodes determined by the "Collidable"
TMX layer
CCTMXLayer *collidableLayer = [tileMap layerNamed:@"Collidable"];
for(int x=0; x<mw; x++){
  for(int y=0; y<mh; y++){
    //Add a node
    AStarNode *node = [[AStarNode alloc] init];
    node.position = ccp(x*tw + tw/2, y*th + th/2);
    if([collidableLayer tileAt:ccp(x,y)]){ node.active = NO; }
    [[grid objectAtIndex:x] addObject:node];
  }
}

/* CODE OMITTED */

return self;
}

@end
```

How it works...

In this recipe, we can see our algorithm come to life with some nice animated AI character movement. We simply replace `nodeSpace` with `tileMap.tileSize.width/height` and replace `gridSizeX/Y` with `tileMap.mapSize.width/height`. Our character can now move around the forest and other obstacles.

A* pathfinding in a side-scroller

The A* algorithm is a generic node-graph traversal routine which can be applied to many abstract problems. In a 2D side-scroller, space is traversed in a complex, non-linear fashion. Actors are expected to run across platforms and jump from platform to platform. With some extra math, we can tailor our A* technique to this problem.

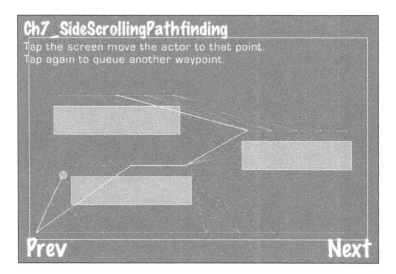

Getting ready

The code listed as follows is heavily edited for the sake of brevity. Please refer to the project *RecipeCollection03* for full working code of this recipe.

How to do it...

Execute the following code:

```
/* SSAStarNode */
@implementation SSAStarNode

-(float) costToNeighbor:(SSNeighborNode*)nn {
  SSAStarNode *node = nn.node;

  //Here we use jumping/running to determine cost. We could also
possibly use a heuristic.
  CGPoint src = ccp(self.position.x/PTM_RATIO, self.position.y/PTM_
RATIO);
```

```
    CGPoint dst = ccp(node.position.x/PTM_RATIO, node.position.y/PTM_
RATIO);

    float cost;
    if(node.body == self.body){
      //Compute simple distance
      float runTime = ([GameHelper distanceP1:src toP2:dst]) / actor.
runSpeed;
      cost = runTime * node.costMultiplier;
    }else{
      //Compute a jump
      float y = dst.y - src.y;
      if(y == 0){ y = 0.00001f; } //Prevent divide by zero

      CGPoint launchVector = nn.launchVector;
      float gravity = actor.body->GetWorld()->GetGravity().y;

      Vector3D *at = [GameHelper quadraticA:gravity*0.5f
B:launchVector.y C:y*-1];
      float airTime;
      if(at.x > at.y){
        airTime = at.x;
      }else{
        airTime = at.y;
      }
      cost = airTime * node.costMultiplier;
    }
    return cost;
}
@end

/* SSGameActor */
@implementation SSGameActor

+(Vector3D*) canJumpFrom:(CGPoint)src to:(CGPoint)dst radius:(float)
radius world:(b2World*)world maxSpeed:(CGPoint)maxSpeed {
    float x = dst.x - src.x;
    float y = dst.y - src.y;
    if(y == 0){ y = 0.00001f; } //Prevent divide by zero

    bool foundJumpSolution = NO;
    bool triedAngles = NO;
    CGPoint launchVector;
    float jumpHeightMod = 0.5f;
```

```
    while(!triedAngles){
      //Gravity
      float gravity = world->GetGravity().y;
      if(gravity == 0){ gravity = 0.00001f; } //Prevent divide by zero

      launchVector = [SSGameActor getLaunchVector:CGPointMake(x,y)
jumpHeightMod:jumpHeightMod gravity:gravity];

      bool hitObject = NO;
      bool movingTooFast = NO;

      /* Make sure jump doesn't hit an object */
      Vector3D *at = [GameHelper quadraticA:gravity*0.5f
B:launchVector.y C:y*-1];
      float airTime;
      if(at.x > at.y){ airTime = at.x; }else{ airTime = at.y; }

      //Do a ray test sequence (from 0.1 to 0.9 of airTime)
      for(float t=airTime/10; t<airTime-airTime/10; t+= airTime/10){
        if(hitObject){ break; }
        float t1 = t + airTime/10;
        float x1 = launchVector.x * t + src.x;
        float y1 = launchVector.y * t + (0.5f) * gravity * pow(t,2) +
src.y;
        float x2 = launchVector.x * t1 + src.x;
        float y2 = launchVector.y * t1 + (0.5f) * gravity * pow(t1,2) +
src.y;

        //Point Test
        /* CODE OMITTED */

        //RayCast Test
        /* CODE OMITTED */
      }
      //Make sure the launchVector is not too fast for this actor
      if(!hitObject){
        if([GameHelper absoluteValue:launchVector.x] > maxSpeed.x ||
[GameHelper absoluteValue:launchVector.y] > maxSpeed.y){
          movingTooFast = YES;
        }
      }
      if(hitObject || movingTooFast){
        //This jump failed, try another
        if(jumpHeightMod <= 0.5f && jumpHeightMod >= 0.2f){ //First, try
0.5f to 0.1f
```

```
        jumpHeightMod -= 0.1f;
      }else if(jumpHeightMod > 0.5f && jumpHeightMod < 1.0f){ //Then
try 0.6f to 1.0f
        jumpHeightMod += 0.1f;
      }else if(jumpHeightMod < 0.2f){
        jumpHeightMod = 0.6f;
      }else if(jumpHeightMod >= 1.0f){
        //FAIL
        triedAngles = YES;
      }
    }else{
      //SUCCESS
      foundJumpSolution = YES;
      triedAngles = YES;
    }
  }
  if(foundJumpSolution){
    return [Vector3D x:launchVector.x y:launchVector.y z:0];
  }else{
    return nil;
  }
}


+(CGPoint) getLaunchVector:(CGPoint)vect jumpHeightMod:(float)
jumpHeightMod gravity:(float)gravity {
  //Gravity
  if(gravity == 0){ gravity = 0.00001f; } //Prevent divide by zero

  //The angle between the points
  float directionAngle = [GameHelper vectorToRadians:ccp(vect.x,
vect.y)];

  //Jump height is a percentage of X distance, usually 0.5f
  float apexX;
  if(vect.y > 0){ apexX = vect.x - (vect.x*0.5f*pow([GameHelper absolu
teValue:sinf(directionAngle)],0.5f/jumpHeightMod));
  }else{ apexX = vect.x*0.5f*pow([GameHelper absoluteValue:sinf(direct
ionAngle)],0.5f/jumpHeightMod); }

  float apexY;
  if(vect.y > 0){ apexY = vect.y + [GameHelper absoluteValue:vect.x*ju
mpHeightMod]*[GameHelper absoluteValue:sinf(directionAngle)];
  }else{ apexY = [GameHelper absoluteValue:vect.x*jumpHeightMod]*[Game
Helper absoluteValue:sinf(directionAngle)]; }
```

```objc
  //Get launch vector
  float vectY = sqrtf(2*(-1)*gravity*apexY);
  float vectX = (apexX*(-1)*gravity) / vectY;

  return CGPointMake(vectX, vectY);
}
@end

/* Ch7_SideScrollingPathfinding */
@implementation Ch7_SideScrollingPathfinding

-(CCLayer*) runRecipe {
  /* CODE OMITTED */

  //Distance between nodes that the actor can run between
  float nodeRunDistInterval = 100.0f;

  //How far to search for nodes the actor can jump to
  float maxJumpSearchDist = 500.0f;

  //Add some nodes to the bottom of the level
  for(float x=20.0f; x<=gameAreaSize.x*PTM_RATIO-20.0f;
x+=nodeRunDistInterval){
    //Add node
    /* CODE OMITTED */
  }

  //Link those nodes together as 'run neighbors'
  for(int i=0; i<nodes.count-1; i++){
    SSAStarNode *n1 = (SSAStarNode*)[nodes objectAtIndex:i];
    SSAStarNode *n2 = (SSAStarNode*)[nodes objectAtIndex:i+1];
    [self linkRunNeighbor:n1 with:n2];
  }

  /* Add nodes to all level platforms */
  for(b2Body *b = world->GetBodyList(); b; b = b->GetNext()){
    if (b->GetUserData() != NULL) {
      GameObject *obj = (GameObject*)b->GetUserData();

      if(obj.tag == GO_TAG_WALL && obj->polygonShape){
        //Nodes on this body only
          NSMutableArray *nodesThisBody = [[[NSMutableArray alloc]
init] autorelease];
```

```
//Process each polygon vertex
for(int i=0; i<obj->polygonShape->m_vertexCount; i++){
b2Vec2 vertex = obj->polygonShape->m_vertices[i];

    //All nodes are 1 unit above their corresponding platform
    b2Vec2 nodePosition = b2Vec2(vertex.x +
b->GetPosition().x,vertex.y + b->GetPosition().y+1.0f);

    //Move nodes inward to lessen chance of missing a jump
    if(obj->polygonShape->m_centroid.x < vertex.x){
      nodePosition = b2Vec2(nodePosition.x-0.5f,
nodePosition.y);
    }else{
      nodePosition = b2Vec2(nodePosition.x+0.5f,
nodePosition.y);
    }

    //If this node position is not inside the polygon we create
an SSAStarNode
    if(!obj->polygonShape->TestPoint(b->GetTransform(),
nodePosition)){
      //Add node
      /* CODE OMITTED */
    }
  }

  //Add in-between nodes (for running)
  bool done = NO;
  while(!done){
    if(nodesThisBody.count == 0){ break; }

    done = YES;
    for(int i=0; i<nodesThisBody.count-1; i++){
      SSAStarNode *n1 = (SSAStarNode*)[nodesThisBody
objectAtIndex:i];
      SSAStarNode *n2 = (SSAStarNode*)[nodesThisBody
objectAtIndex:i+1];

      if([GameHelper absoluteValue:n1.position.y-n2.position.y]
> 0.1f){
        //These are not side by side
        continue;
      }
```

```
            if( [GameHelper distanceP1:n1.position toP2:n2.position] >
nodeRunDistInterval ){
                CGPoint midPoint = [GameHelper midPointP1:n1.position
p2:n2.position];
                b2Vec2 mp = b2Vec2(midPoint.x/PTM_RATIO, midPoint.y/
PTM_RATIO);

                //If node is not in the polygon, add it
                if(!obj->polygonShape->TestPoint(b->GetTransform(), mp))
{
                  //Add node
                  /* CODE OMITTED */
                  break;
                }
            }
          }
        }

        //Link all of the neighboring nodes on this body
        for(int i=0; i<nodesThisBody.count-1; i++){
          if(nodesThisBody.count == 0){ break; }

          SSAStarNode *n1 = (SSAStarNode*)[nodesThisBody
objectAtIndex:i];
          SSAStarNode *n2 = (SSAStarNode*)[nodesThisBody
objectAtIndex:i+1];

          if([GameHelper absoluteValue:n1.position.y-n2.position.y] >
0.1f){
            //These are not side by side
            continue;
          }

          //Two-way link
          [self linkRunNeighbor:n1 with:n2];
        }
      }
    }
  }

  //Neighbor all other nodes (for jumping)
  for(int i=0; i<nodes.count; i++){
    for(int j=0; j<nodes.count; j++){
      if(i==j){ continue; }
```

```
            SSAStarNode *n1 = (SSAStarNode*)[nodes objectAtIndex:i];
            SSAStarNode *n2 = (SSAStarNode*)[nodes objectAtIndex:j];

            if(n1.body == n2.body){ continue; }

            if( [GameHelper distanceP1:n1.position toP2:n2.position] <=
maxJumpSearchDist ){
                CGPoint src = ccp(n1.position.x/PTM_RATIO, n1.position.y/PTM_
RATIO);
                CGPoint dst = ccp(n2.position.x/PTM_RATIO, n2.position.y/PTM_
RATIO);

                //Calculate our jump "launch" vector
                Vector3D *launchVector3D = [SSGameActor canJumpFrom:src to:dst
radius:actor.circleShape->m_radius*1.5f world:world maxSpeed:actor.
maxSpeed];

                if(launchVector3D){
                  //Only neighbor up if a jump can be made
                  //1-way link
                  if(![n1 containsNeighborForNode:n2]){
                    //Add neighbor
                    /* CODE OMITTED */
                  }
                }
            }
        }
    }
    return self;
}
@end
```

How it works...

First, we must create our node graph. In a top-down 2D environment, we simply use a grid and then cull out any colliding edges. In a side-scrolling environment, we need to think differently. Actors in such an environment must stand on top of the level geometry at all times. In addition to this, they have two different ways of traversing through the level: **running** and **jumping**.

▸ Running across a platform:

   To allow an actor to run across a platform, we need to create a string of A* nodes on top of each platform. Starting at one of these nodes, the actor can easily move to the other nodes on that same body.

> ▸ Jumping from platform to platform:

To reach another platform, the actor must jump there. This adds more complexity. We need to perform the calculations required to launch the actor safely to the other platform. We also need to check for geometry in the actor's jump trajectory and adjust the angle of the jump as necessary. Before we can implement this functionality, we need to encapsulate it in a new set of classes we create as subclasses of our current ones.

> ▸ `SSAStarNode`:

The `SSAStarNode` contains references to a `b2Body` object as well as a `SSGameActor` object. The body object represents the body the actor is resting on when at this node. A reference to the actor is maintained because actor information such as size, jumping speed, and running speed are required to make some of the aforementioned calculations.

> ▸ `SSGameWaypoint`:

Our new waypoint class contains a `moveType` enumeration that specifies whether or not the actor should `RUN` or `JUMP` to the waypoint's location. It also contains a `launchVector` that specifies the impulse vector required if a jump is to be performed.

> ▸ `SSGameActor`:

The new actor class has a `maxSpeed` variable that determines both how fast the actor can run and how high the actor can jump. This class also encapsulates our newly modified `processWaypoints` method as well as a few others:

```
-(void) runToWaypoint:(SSGameWaypoint*)wp speedMod:(float)speedMod
constrain:(bool)constrain;
-(void) jumpToWaypoint:(SSGameWaypoint*)wp;
+(Vector3D*) canJumpFrom:(CGPoint)src to:(CGPoint)dst
radius:(float)radius world:(b2World*)world maxSpeed:(CGPoint)
maxSpeed;
+(CGPoint) getLaunchVector:(CGPoint)vect jumpHeightMod:(float)
jumpHeightMod gravity:(float)gravity;
```

The `runToWaypoint` method simply sets the actor's velocity to make it run left or right. The `jumpToWaypoint` method launches the actor using the waypoint's `launchVector`. The `canJumpFrom` method determines whether or not a jump is possible to a certain point. This involves testing multiple jump angles against the geometry of the Box2D world. Each jump parabola is broken up into 10 straight-line sections that are ray tested against map geometry. This approximates collision detection well enough for our purposes. Finally, the `getLaunchVector` method, which is employed by the `canJumpFrom` method, determines the `launchVector` for the actor given a location to land on and given a Y jump height relative to the X jump width.

▶ `SSAStarPathNode`:

This class is similar to `AStarPathNode`. It contains a `SSGameWaypoint` pointer for convenience. In the updated `findPathFrom` method, we create this waypoint and set its `launchVector`. This ensures that `launchVector` is only calculated at load time.

▶ `SSNeighborNode`:

As now we have two methods of moving from one node to another, we need a more complex way of storing graph edge information. Instead of simply storing a pointer to a neighboring node, this class encapsulates that node along with a `moveType`, `cost`, and `launchVector`.

▶ Creating our node graph—run nodes:

First we must create our key nodes. These are like keyframes in an animation. They are located slightly above each vertex on the top side of every platform. We then add nodes in-between these nodes. Finally, these "run nodes" are linked together with the `moveType` variable set to `MOVE_TYPE_RUN`.

▶ Creating our node graph—jump nodes:

Once the run nodes are set over each platform, we create jump nodes. This involves searching the immediate area around each node, determining whether or not the actor can jump from that node to a found node, and then finally creating the neighbor link. We create these links one at a time as jumping up to reach a node is very different from jumping down.

▶ Tweaking side-scrolling pathfinding:

This technique required a lot of tweaking to get working properly. For example, the x and y distance thresholds, used to determine whether or not a waypoint has been reached, vary greatly. Another tweak involves the fact that, if a waypoint is blocked, the entire set of waypoints must be discarded. Perhaps another revision could salvage the second half of the path of nodes by prepending a new path to the missed node.

Running a Lua script

Many commercial games make use of a **scripting language** to isolate and abstract their **game logic**. The most popular of these is **Lua**. In this recipe, we will integrate Lua into our project.

Getting ready

Please refer to the project *RecipeCollection03* for full working code of this recipe.

How to do it...

Lua can be added to your project in a few simple steps:

1. Highlight your project in the Navigator. At the bottom of your window in the middle, click **Add Target**:

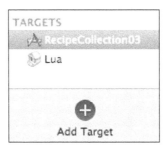

2. Name the target "Lua". This will create a new folder inside your project folder next to your main target's similarly named folder. It should also create a new group.

3. Download the Lua source from `http://www.lua.org` and copy it to this folder.

4. Right-click the **Lua** group and select **Add Files to** "*Your Project*":

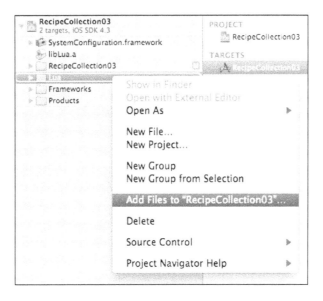

5. Navigate to the `src` directory and add all the files located there except for `lua.c`, `luac.c`, `Makefile`, and `print.c`. Also, be sure to uncheck **Copy items into destination groups folder** and select only **Lua** under the **Add to Targets** section.

6. At this point, you should be able to build the Lua target with no errors.

7. In the middle pane, click your project's main target. Expand **Link Binary With Libraries**. Click the **+** symbol at the bottom-left and add the **libLua.a** library to the list:

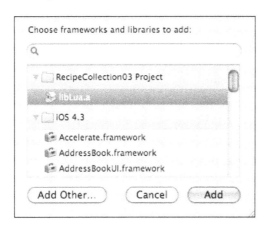

8. Collapse this and expand **Target Dependencies**. Add the target **Lua** as a dependency of this target:

9. That's it. Lua is now integrated. Clean and build your project to make sure it was integrated properly.

Execute the following code:

```
#import "mcLua.hpp"

@interface Ch7_LuaScripting : Recipe
{
  class mcLuaManager * lua_;
  mcLuaScript * sc;
}
@end

//Callback pointer
Ch7_LuaScripting *lsRecipe = nil;

//Static append message C function
static int lsAppendMessage(lua_State * l)
{
  //Pass lua string into append message method
  [lsRecipe appendMessage:[NSString stringWithUTF8String:lua_
tostring(l,1)]];
  return 0;
}

@implementation Ch7_LuaScripting

-(CCLayer*) runRecipe {
  //Set callback pointer
```

```
    lsRecipe = self;

    //Lua initialization
    lua_ = new mcLuaManager;

    //Lua function wrapper library
    static const luaL_reg scriptLib[] =
    {
        {"appendMessage", lsAppendMessage },
        {NULL, NULL}
    };
    lua_->LuaOpenLibrary("scene",scriptLib);

    //Open Lua script
    sc = lua_->CreateScript();
    NSString *filePath = [[NSBundle mainBundle] pathForResource:@"show_
messages.lua" ofType:@""];
    sc->LoadFile([filePath UTF8String]);

    //Set initial update method counter
    lua_->Update(0);

    //Schedule step method
    [self schedule: @selector(step:)];

    //Resume button
    CCMenuItemFont *resumeItem = [CCMenuItemFont itemFromString:@"Resume
Script" target:self selector:@selector(resumeScript:)];
    CCMenu *menu = [CCMenu menuWithItems:resumeItem, nil];
    [self addChild:menu];

    return self;
}

-(void) step:(ccTime)delta {
    //Update Lua script runner
    lua_->Update(delta);
}

/* Resume script callback */
-(void) resumeScript:(id)sender {
    sc->YieldResume();
}

@end
```

How it works...

This and subsequent recipes use Robert Grzesek's `mcLua` API to facilitate the loading and execution of Lua scripts. It also allows for concurrent execution of multiple scripts.

- The `mcLuaManager` class:

  The `mcLuaManager` class is the top-level class that manages all running scripts:

  ```
  class mcLuaManager lua_ = new mcLuaManager;
  ```

  It is in charge of running the scripts as well as their creation and destruction.

- Loading and starting a script:

  Loading a Lua script is a fairly straightforward process:

  ```
  mcLuaScript *sc = lua_->CreateScript();
  NSString *filePath = [[NSBundle mainBundle]
  pathForResource:@"show_messages.lua" ofType:@""];
    sc->LoadFile([filePath UTF8String]);
  ```

  Once the file is loaded, we make a call to the `mcLuaManager` class's `Update` method:

  ```
  lua_->Update(0);
  ```

  This starts the loaded scripts off and running.

- Static function libraries:

  Inside the Lua script, global methods can be called according to function libraries assigned to object identifiers. The `mcLua` API assigns a few functions to the `script` object by default. These include `waitSeconds`, `waitFrames`, and `pause`. They can be called inside the Lua script:

  ```
  script.waitSeconds(1);
  ```

  In this example, we also create a callback method named `appendMessage` and assign it to an object named `scene`. To do this, we first create a static C function:

  ```
  static int lsAppendMessage(lua_State * l)
  {
    [lsRecipe appendMessage:[NSString stringWithUTF8String:lua_
  tostring(l,1)]];
    return 0;
  }
  ```

When the recipe is loaded, we create a Lua script library linker array and load it into memory using the `LuaOpenLibrary` provided by the `mcLua` API:

```
lua_ = new mcLuaManager;

static const luaL_reg scriptLib[] =
{
  {"appendMessage", lsAppendMessage },
  {NULL, NULL}
};
lua_->LuaOpenLibrary("scene", scriptLib);
```

Once this is loaded, we can call that function from the Lua script itself:

```
scene.appendMessage("This is a Lua script.");
```

Finally, if the script is paused (from inside or outside the script itself) it can be resumed (only from outside the script):

```
sc->YieldResume();
```

Together this library lets your Lua script interact with your application.

Dynamically loading Lua scripts

Part of the power of a scripting language like Lua, is that scripts can be loaded and re-loaded at **run-time**. This means you can test your game logic without having to re-compile your Objective-C++ code. In this recipe, we will load a remote script from a local **web server**.

Getting ready

Please refer to the project *RecipeCollection03* for full working code of this recipe.

How to do it...

Execute the following code:

```
#import "mcLua.hpp"
#import "Reachability.h"

@interface Ch7_DynamicScriptLoading : Recipe
{
  class mcLuaManager * lua_;
}

@end

//Callback pointer
Ch7_DynamicScriptLoading *dslRecipe = nil;

//Static append message C function
static int dslAppendMessage(lua_State * l)
{
  //Pass lua string into append message method
  [dslRecipe appendMessage:[NSString stringWithUTF8String:lua_
tostring(l,1)]];
  return 0;
}

@implementation Ch7_DynamicScriptLoading

-(CCLayer*) runRecipe {
  //Superclass initialization
  [super runRecipe];

  //Set callback pointer
  dslRecipe = self;

  //Lua initialization
  lua_ = new mcLuaManager;

  //Lua function wrapper library
  static const luaL_reg scriptLib[] =
```

```
  {
    {"appendMessage", dslAppendMessage },
    {NULL, NULL}
  };
  lua_->LuaOpenLibrary("scene",scriptLib);

  //Load Lua script
  [self loadScript];

  //Set initial update method counter
  lua_->Update(0);

  //Schedule step method
  [self schedule: @selector(step:)];

  //Reload script button
  CCMenuItemFont *reloadItem = [CCMenuItemFont itemFromString:@"Reload
Script" target:self selector:@selector(loadScript)];
  CCMenu *menu = [CCMenu menuWithItems:reloadItem, nil];
  [self addChild:menu];

  return self;
}

-(void) step:(ccTime)delta {
  //Update Lua script runner
  lua_->Update(delta);
}

-(void) loadScript{
  //Reset message
  [self resetMessage];

  //Make sure localhost is reachable
  Reachability* reachability = [Reachability reachabilityWithHostName:
@"localhost"];
  NetworkStatus remoteHostStatus = [reachability
currentReachabilityStatus];

  if(remoteHostStatus == NotReachable) {
    [self showMessage:@"Script not reachable."];
  }else{
    [self appendMessage:@"Loading script from http://localhost/ch7_
remote_script.lua"];
```

```
    //Load script via NSURL
    mcLuaScript *sc = lua_->CreateScript();
    NSString *remoteScriptString = [NSString
stringWithContentsOfURL:[NSURL URLWithString:@"http://localhost/ch7_
remote_script.lua"]
        encoding:NSUTF8StringEncoding error:nil];
    sc->LoadString([remoteScriptString UTF8String]);
  }
}


@end
```

How it works...

The simplest way to load a remote script is to use a local web server. This way we can bypass `NSBundle` and the somewhat restricted iOS filesystem. Mac OSX ships with a built-in Apache HTTP webserver. It can be enabled and configured by going to **System Preferences | Internet and Wireless | Sharing | Web Sharing**:

> ▶ Loading a remote script:
>
> Instead of reading our script off the filesystem, we load it over HTTP using `NSURL`:
>
> ```
> mcLuaScript *sc = lua_->CreateScript();
> NSString *remoteScriptString = [NSString
> stringWithContentsOfURL:[NSURL URLWithString:@"http://localhost/
> ch7_remote_script.lua"] encoding:NSUTF8StringEncoding error:nil];
>     sc->LoadString([remoteScriptString UTF8String]);
> ```
>
> Editing the file on your local web server and hitting the re-load button simply loads the script again. This is a simple but effective way to rapidly develop and test game logic.

> ▶ Reachability:
>
> In this example, we use Apple's `Reachability` library to help us determine whether or not we can access the script over the network. Without this tool our `stringWithContentsOfURL` method would throw errors.

Using Lua for dialogue trees

Lua lets the programmer write against a generic **interface** and worry about the **implementation** later. This separation between game logic, and the nuts and bolts of presenting the audio/visual elements of the game, is an important part of any game engine. In this recipe, we will use Lua to create a small story-based adventure game.

Getting ready

Please refer to the project *RecipeCollection03* for full working code of this recipe.

How to do it...

Execute the following code:

```
//Static C functions
static int ldtLogic(lua_State * l) {
  int num = [ldtRecipe logic:[NSString stringWithUTF8String:lua_
tostring(l,1)]];
  lua_pushnumber(l,num);
  return 1;
}
static int ldtPresentOptions(lua_State * l) {
  [ldtRecipe presentOptions];
  ldtRecipe.sc->YieldPause();
  return (lua_yield(l, 0));
}

@implementation Ch7_LuaDecisionTree

/* Logic callback */
-(int) logic:(NSString*)str {
  int num = 0;
```

```
    if([str isEqualToString:@"Put guns down"]){
      gunsDown = YES;
    }else if([str isEqualToString:@"Are guns down?"]){
      if(gunsDown){
        num = 1;
      }else{
        num = 0;
      }
    }else if([str isEqualToString:@"You win"]){
      [self showMessage:@"You WIN!!"];
    }

    return num;
}
/* Present options callback */
-(void) presentOptions {
  text = @"";
  [textLabel setString:text];
  optionsNode.visible = YES;
}
/* Select option callback */
-(void) selectOption:(id)sender {
  /* CODE OMITTED */

  //Resume the script
  sc->YieldResume();
}
@end

/* decision_tree.lua */
function start()
  scene.desc("You are deep undercover with the mafia.");
  scene.anim("Open door");
  scene.anim("Enter officer");
  scene.anim("Louie looks away");
  scene.dialog("Officer: Alright Big Louie. This is a raid. You're
under arrest for the murder of Frankie Boy Caruso.");
  scene.anim("Pull guns");
  scene.dialog("Big Louie: Murder? What's a murder?");
  scene.dialog("Officer: Don't play dumb with me.");
  scene.dialog("Big Louie: A one-man raid? You must have a death
wish.");
  scene.anim("Louie looks at you");
```

```
  scene.dialog("Big Louie: What do YOU think we should do with him?");

  scene.dialogOption("You can't take him out now. There are too many
witnesses.");
  scene.dialogOption("I say take him out. He's here alone.");
  scene.dialogOption("He's a cop. We'll have a mess on our hands if we
take him down.");

scene.presentOptions();

  if scene.getResponse() == 1 then
    tooManyWitnesses();
  elseif scene.getResponse() == 2 then
    hereAlone();
  elseif scene.getResponse() == 3 then
    bigMess();
  end
end

function tooManyWitnesses()
  scene.dialog("Big Louie: Whaddya mean too many witnesses? These are
all my men...");
  scene.anim("Louie scowls");
  scene.dialog("Big Louie: ...and YOU! Blast him boys.");
  script.waitSeconds(1);
  scene.anim("Gun pointed at you");
  scene.desc("You are dead.");
end

function bigMess()
  scene.dialog("Big Louie: I don't like it, but, you're right.");
  scene.dialog("Big Louie: Men, you can put your guns down.");
  scene.logic("Put guns down");
  scene.anim("Put guns down");
  scene.desc("Louie's men lower their weapons");
  scene.anim("Louie looks away");
  scene.dialog("Big Louie: Cop, looks like you have a new lease on
life.");

  scene.actionOption("Pull your gun on Big Louie");
  scene.actionOption("Pull your gun on Big Louie's men");

  scene.presentOptions();

  if scene.getResponse() == 1 then
```

```
      pullGunOnLouie();
    elseif scene.getResponse() == 2 then
      pullGunOnMen();
    end
  end

  function hereAlone()
    scene.anim("Officer shocked");
    script.waitSeconds(1);
    scene.dialog("Officer: Jerry! What the hell are you doing?!");
    scene.anim("Louie scowls");
    scene.dialog("Big Louie: Jerry? You lying scumbag! We trusted you...
  blast him boys.");
    script.waitSeconds(1);
    scene.anim("Gun pointed at you");
    scene.desc("You are dead.");
  end

  function pullGunOnLouie()
    scene.anim("Pull gun on Louie");
    scene.anim("Louie scowl");
    scene.dialog("Big Louie: This guy's a Fed! Blast him!");
    script.waitSeconds(1);
    scene.anim("Gun pointed at you");
    scene.desc("You are dead.");
  end

  function pullGunOnMen()
    gunsDown = scene.logic("Are guns down?");
    scene.anim("Pull gun on men");
    if gunsDown == 1 then
      scene.anim("Louie scowls");
      scene.dialog("Big Louie: You played me for a fool!");
      scene.anim("Louie looks away");
      scene.dialog("Officer: You're under arrest Big Louie.");
      scene.dialog("Big Louie: I'll be back on the streets in twenty-
  four hours!");
      scene.dialog("Officer: We'll try to make it twelve.");
      scene.anim("Louie looks at you");
      scene.logic("You win");
      scene.desc("You win!");
    else
      scene.anim("Louie scowls");
      scene.dialog("Big Louie: This guy's a Fed! Blast him!");
```

```
    script.waitSeconds(1);
    scene.anim("Gun pointed at you");
    scene.desc("You are dead.");
  end
end

start();
```

How it works...

For this recipe, we create a number of callback functions to process animation, dialog, and logic. Some of these, like option prompts, wait for user response before the script is resumed. Other functions, like `ldtLogic`, have a return value.

- ▶ Passing and returning variables using Lua:

  Lua's variable passing mechanism is fairly simple. Functions are passed a `lua_State` pointer. Data can then be retrieved off of the stack pointed to by this:

  ```
  lua_State * l;
  NSString *str = [NSString stringWithUTF8String:lua_tostring(l,1)];
  ```

  Lua supports multiple return variables at one time. To return a variable from one of our callback functions, we must first push the variable onto the stack:

  ```
  int num = 7;
  lua_pushnumber(l,num);
  ```

  We then specify the number of variables we are returning as an integer:

  ```
  return 1;
  ```

  All basic C types can be passed and returned using Lua.

- ▶ Local Lua functions:

  Inside of our script file we use a number of local Lua functions. Everything is encapsulated in a function except for the initial `start()` function call. Local functions also support returning multiple variables.

8
Tips, Tools, and Ports

In this chapter, we will cover the following topics:

- ▶ Introduction
- ▶ Accessing the Cocos2d-iPhone testbed
- ▶ Packing textures using Zwoptex
- ▶ Creating levels using Tiled
- ▶ Creating levels using JSONWorldBuilder
- ▶ Creating scenes with CocosBuilder
- ▶ Using Cocos2d-X
- ▶ Using Cocos3d
- ▶ Releasing your app

Introduction

In this chapter we will conclude by covering a few tools commonly used to augment Cocos2d game development. We will also introduce Cocos2d spin-off projects and walk you through the process of releasing an app on Apple's App Store.

Accessing the Cocos2d-iPhone testbed

The **Cocos2d-iPhone testbed** is a suite of examples created to test bugs, display features, and instruct programmers with useful examples. In this recipe we will introduce this very useful tool.

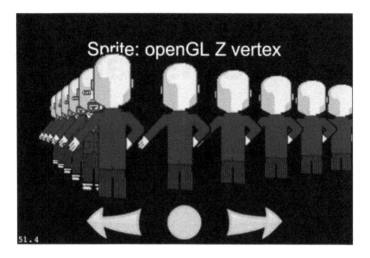

Getting ready

First, we must download the Cocos2d source from `http://www.cocos2d-iphone.org/download`. After unzipping the main source package, double-click on the `cocos2d.xcworkspace` file.

How to do it...

From the **Scheme selection** menu in XCode you can now select which piece of the testbed you would like to run. These tests include everything—drawing, physics, sound, networking, and more.

How it works...

Inside the `tests` folder in the `cocos2d-ios` target you will find the source files for each individual test. Here you can play around with the demos to get ideas for your own games.

Box2D testbed

Due to the scope of the Cocos2d-iPhone framework, many other testbeds are included within the Cocos2d-iPhone testbed. By building the `Box2dTestBed` scheme we can run a version of the official Box2D testbed tailored for Cocos2d.

Packing textures using Zwoptex

Creating sprite sheets by hand can be a tedious process. To solve this problem, we use **Zwoptex Texture Packer** to pack individual sprites into the smallest area possible. In this recipe, we walk through this process.

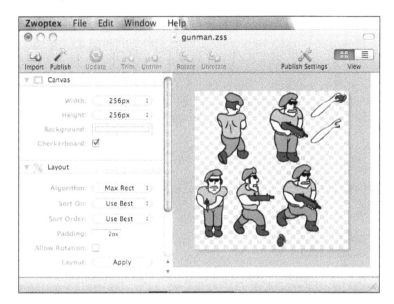

Getting ready

First we must download and install the Zwoptex application. Go to `http://zwoptexapp.com/` and click on the **Download** link. Drag the application to your `Applications` folder.

How to do it...

Once you've started Zwoptex, click **File | New**. You should see a blank canvas. Here are some attributes of the canvas:

> ▸ Canvas size:
>
>   As you can see inside Zwoptex, the width and height of the Canvas can only go up to 2048 pixels. Also, they can only be a power of 2. On the iPhone 3G and older devices, uncompressed textures can have a maximum size of 1024x1024. On newer devices that support OpenGL ES 2.0, starting with the iPhone 3GS, uncompressed textures can be up to 2048x2048 pixels. Textures are only loaded into memory in powers of 2. Taking all of this into account, Zwoptex limits the canvas sizes you can use.

- ▸ Importing sprites:

  Sprites are imported onto the canvas by simply dragging individual files from your `Finder` onto the canvas. These will be positioned on top of each other. They will also be outlined with a red box.

- ▸ Applying a layout:

  After adjusting any settings under the **Layou**t heading we can click the **Apply** button. This will re-arrange the sprites to fit the canvas size. If all the sprites do not fit, some will still have that red box surrounding them. This indicates an overlap.

- ▸ Publishing:

  Once our sprites are properly arranged in a sheet and our Zwoptex file is saved, we can publish our sheet. This creates a PLIST file and a PNG file. By adding these to our XCode Cocos2d project, we can now use them in our app.

How it works...

Zwoptex uses offsets and other positioning tricks designed to squeeze as many sprites into a sheet as possible.

See also...

A popular alternative to Zwoptex is **TexturePacker**. It can be downloaded from `http://www.texturepacker.com/`.

Creating levels using Tiled

One of the most important weapons in the game developer's arsenal is the **level editor**. In this recipe we will create a level using the *Tiled* level editor. We will then create a simple top-down world using this level.

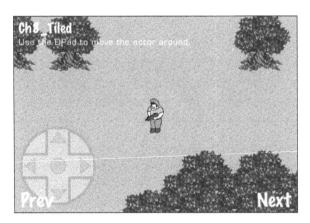

Getting ready

Please refer to the project `RecipeCollection03` for full working code of this recipe.

How to do it...

Execute the following code:

```
//Interface
@interface Ch8_Tiled : GameArea2D {
  CCTMXTiledMap *tileMap;
}
@end

//Implementation
@implementation Ch8_Tiled

-(CCLayer*) runRecipe {
  //Load TMX tilemap file
  tileMap = [CCTMXTiledMap tiledMapWithTMXFile:@"tilemap.tmx"];

  //Set game area size based on tilemap size
  [self setGameAreaSize];

  //Superclass initialization and message
  [super runRecipe];
  [self showMessage:@"Use the DPad to move the actor around."];

  //Add tile map
  [gameNode addChild:tileMap z:0];

  /* Re-order layers according to their Y value. This creates
isometric depth. */

  //Our layers
  CCTMXLayer *collidableLayer = [tileMap layerNamed:@"Collidable"];
  CCTMXLayer *ground = [tileMap layerNamed:@"Ground"];
  CCTMXLayer *wall = [tileMap layerNamed:@"Wall"];

  //Gather all the layers into a container
  float mw = tileMap.mapSize.width; float mh = tileMap.mapSize.height;
  float tw = tileMap.tileSize.width; float th = tileMap.tileSize.
height;
```

```
    NSMutableDictionary *layersToReorder = [[[NSMutableDictionary alloc]
init] autorelease];
    for( CCTMXLayer* child in [tileMap children] ) {
      //Skip tiles marked "Collidable", "Ground" and "Wall"
      if(child == ground){ continue; }
      else if(child == wall){ continue; }
      else if(child == collidableLayer){ continue; }

      //Gather all the layers
      for(float x=0; x<mw; x+=1){
        for(float y=mh-1; y>=0; y-=1){
          CCSprite *childTile = [child tileAt:ccp(x,y)];
          CCSprite *collideTile = [collidableLayer tileAt:ccp(x,y)];

          if(childTile && collideTile){
            [layersToReorder setObject:[NSNumber numberWithFloat:y]
forKey:[child layerName]];
            x=mw; y=-1;
          }
        }
      }

    }

    //Re-order gathered layers
    for(id key in layersToReorder){
      NSString *str = (NSString*)key;
      [tileMap reorderChild:[tileMap layerNamed:str] z:[[layersToReorder
objectForKey:key] floatValue]];
    }

    //Set the ground to z=0
    [tileMap reorderChild:ground z:0];

    //Add Box2D boxes to represent all layers marked "Collidable"
    for(float x=0; x<mw; x+=1){
      for(float y=0; y<mh; y+=1){
        if([collidableLayer tileAt:ccp(x,y)]){
          [self addBoxAtPoint:ccp(x*tw, mh*th - y*th)
size:ccp(tw/2,th/2)];
        }
      }
    }
```

```objc
  //Remove the "Collidable" layer art as it's only an indicator for
the level editor
  [tileMap removeChild:collidableLayer cleanup:YES];

  return self;
}
-(void) step: (ccTime) dt {
  [super step:dt];

  /* CODE OMITTED */

  //Re-order the actor
  float mh = tileMap.mapSize.height;
  float th = tileMap.tileSize.height;

  CGPoint p = [actor.sprite position];
  float z = -(p.y/th) + mh;
  [tileMap reorderChild:actor.sprite z:z ];
}
-(void) setGameAreaSize {
  //Set gameAreaSize based on tileMap size
  gameAreaSize = ccp((tileMap.mapSize.width * tileMap.tileSize.width)/
PTM_RATIO,(tileMap.mapSize.height * tileMap.tileSize.height)/PTM_
RATIO);  //Box2d units
}
-(void) addActor {
  //Get spawn point from tile object named "SpawnPoint"
  if(!spawnPoint){
    CCTMXObjectGroup *objects = [tileMap objectGroupNamed:@"Objects"];
    NSAssert(objects != nil, @"'Objects' object group not found");
    NSMutableDictionary *sp = [objects objectNamed:@"SpawnPoint"];
    NSAssert(sp != nil, @"SpawnPoint object not found");
    int x = [[sp valueForKey:@"x"] intValue];
    int y = [[sp valueForKey:@"y"] intValue];
    spawnPoint = [Vector3D x:x y:y z:0];
  }

  //Add actor
  /* CODE OMITTED */

  [tileMap addChild:actor.sprite z:[[tileMap layerNamed:@"0"]
vertexZ]];
}
@end
```

How it works...

This recipe loads a TMX `tilemap` created using the **Tiled** application. It then creates a 2.5D game world using information from the `tilemap`. This is done as follows:

1. Installing Tiled:

    First we must download and install the `Tiled` application. Go to `http://www.mapeditor.org/` and click on the **Tiled Qt 0.7.0 for Mac OS X** link. Drag the application to your `Applications` folder.

2. Creating a new level:

    Open up `Tiled` and click **File | New** to create a new level.

3. Choosing a perspective:

    As you might be able to see from the screenshots of `Tiled` on the website, there are two types of perspectives that can be chosen. When you first click **File | New** in the **Tiled** menu, you will have to make the choice between **Orthagonal** and **Isometric** perspectives. Each perspective creates a different visual style and world object layout. In our example, we chose **Orthagonal** as it's a little more straightforward.

4. Map size:

    The map size is measured in tiles. For our map we chose the size of 50x50.

5. Tile size:

    In `Tiled`, the tile size can be variable. In this example we have chosen the default size of 32x32 pixels. This means we can keep our art assets nice and small.

6. Creating a `tileset`:

    The primary resource used in `Tiled` is the `tileset`. This is a sprite sheet created according to the tile size chosen in `Tiled`. To create this sprite sheet, open up Zwoptex, create a new file, and set `Padding` to `0px`. Then, drag 32x32 pixel images onto the sprite sheet. This PNG file is the `tileset` file. Instead of using a corresponding PLIST file to manage sprite information, `Tiled` simply uses position information to match a sprite to a tile. For this recipe our `tileset` looks like the following:

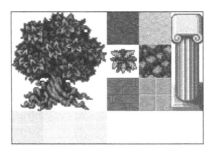

So, make sure your `tileset` is correct before loading it into your level. Finally, click **Map | New Tileset**. Name your `tileset` and specify your PNG sprite sheet.

7. Tile layers:

   `Tiled` supports the creation of multiple overlapping layers. Typically, these layers are used to place graphical elements over one another. In addition to this, layers can specify information. In our level, red colored areas can be considered "collidable". This will be processed programmatically.

   Object layers:

   In addition to tiles, **Objects** can be placed to indicate non-tile based data like item locations. In our level, we've placed a "spawn point" object to indicate where the player should spawn. For an example usage of this please refer to the `tilemap.tmx` file located in the `Resources/Tilemaps` folder of `RecipeCollection03`, `CCTMXTiledMap`.

   ❑ Once our map is complete we will run the following code snippet to load `tilemap` assets into the game:

   ```
   CCTMXTiledMap *tileMap = [CCTMXTiledMap
   tiledMapWithTMXFile:@"tilemap.tmx"];
   [gameNode addChild:tileMap z:0];
   ```

   A `CCTMXTiledMap` object contains references to each tile as a `CCSprite` object as well as a number of structures to organize these files.

   ❑ CCTMXTileLayer

   To access a tile layer we use the following code:

   ```
   CCTMXLayer *collidableLayer = [tileMap
   layerNamed:@"Collidable"];
   ```

   To loop through all `CCTMXLayer` objects, we can also use the following lines:

   ```
   for( CCTMXLayer* child in [tileMap children] ) {
     //Do Something
   }
   ```

   ❑ Accessing a tile's sprite involves calling the `tileAt` method:

   ```
   float x = 0; float y = 0;
   CCSprite *tileSprite = [collidableLayer tileAt:ccp(x,y)];
   ```

   These sprites are created lazily when `tileAt` is called. For more information, please refer to the Cocos2d-iPhone API reference page for `CCTMXTiledMap`.

8. Re-ordering tiles:

   For the purposes of our example, we loop through all tile sprites and re-order them to create the proper perspective illusion. This simply involves calling the `reorderChild` method on `tileMap` based on each tile's `Y` position.

9. Adding Box2D geometry:

   To create physical level geometry we process the "Collidable" layer and create a properly sized box object for each tile we find:

   ```
   for(float x=0; x<mw; x+=1){
     for(float y=0; y<mh; y+=1){
       if([collidableLayer tileAt:ccp(x,y)]){
         [self addBoxAtPoint:ccp(x*tw, mh*th - y*th)
   size:ccp(tw/2,th/2)];
       }
     }
   }
   ```

   Using this special `collidableLayer` allows the level art to line up exactly where we want things to be collidable. This creates the illusion that the base of each tree is collidable while the branches are not.

10. Processing level objects:

    Level objects are processed using the `CCTMXObjectGroup` class:

    ```
    CCTMXObjectGroup *objects = [tileMap objectGroupNamed:@"Objects"];
    ```

11. Next, we process our `SpawnPoint` object:

    ```
    NSMutableDictionary *sp = [objects objectNamed:@"SpawnPoint"];
    int x = [[sp valueForKey:@"x"] intValue];
    int y = [[sp valueForKey:@"y"] intValue];
    spawnPoint = [Vector3D x:x y:y z:0];
    ```

    We can now spawn the player at this point on the map.

See also...

For more information about using `Tiled` please refer to the `Tiled` wiki located at http://github.com/bjorn/tiled/wiki.

Creating levels using JSONWorldBuilder

Creating a game level using tiles is a technique that works well for many games. In this recipe, however, we will create a level in a more non-linear fashion using the **JSONWorldBuilder** level editor.

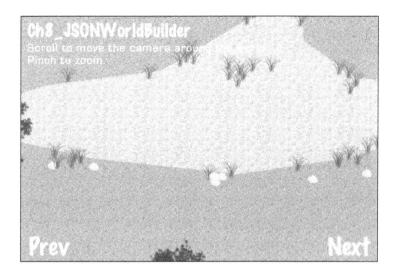

Getting ready

Please refer to the project `RecipeCollection03` for full working code of this recipe.

How to do it...

Execute the following code:

```
#import "ActualPath.h"
#import "CJSONDeserializer.h"

//Interface
@interface Ch8_JSONWorldBuilder : GameArea2D
{
  NSDictionary *mapData;
  CGPoint canvasSize;
  NSMutableArray *lineVerticesA;
  NSMutableArray *lineVerticesB;
  NSMutableArray *points;
}
@end

//Implementation
@implementation Ch8_JSONWorldBuilder

-(CCLayer*) runRecipe {
  //Load our map file
```

```
    [self loadMap:@"world.json"];

    return self;
}


/* Called after the map has been loaded into a container but before
assets have been loaded */
-(void) finishInit {
  //Superclass initialization and message
  [super runRecipe];

  /* CODE OMITTED */

  //Init line/point containers
  lineVerticesA = [[NSMutableArray alloc] init];
  lineVerticesB = [[NSMutableArray alloc] init];
  points = [[NSMutableArray alloc] init];
}


/* Our load map method */
-(void) loadMap:(NSString*)mapStr {
  /* CODE OMITTED */

  //Add all sprite frames for listed plist files
  NSArray *plistFiles = [mapData objectForKey:@"plistFiles"];
  for (id plistFile in plistFiles) {
    [[CCSpriteFrameCache sharedSpriteFrameCache] addSpriteFramesWithFi
le:plistFile];
  }

  //List of PNG files is also available
  NSArray *pngFiles = [mapData objectForKey:@"pngFiles"];

  //Pre process data
  [self preProcessMapData];

  //Process map nodes
  NSDictionary *mapNodes = [mapData objectForKey:@"mapNodes"];
  for (id mapNodeKey in mapNodes) {
    NSDictionary *mapNode = [mapNodes objectForKey:mapNodeKey];

    NSString *nodeType = [mapNode objectForKey:@"type"];

    //Process node types
```

```objectivec
    if([nodeType isEqualToString:@"sprite"]){
      [self processSprite:mapNode];
    }else if([nodeType isEqualToString:@"tiledSprite"]){
      [self processTiledSprite:mapNode];
    }else if([nodeType isEqualToString:@"line"]){
      [self processLine:mapNode];
    }else if([nodeType isEqualToString:@"point"]){
      [self processPoint:mapNode];
    }
  }
}

-(void) preProcessMapData {
  //Set canvasSize and gameAreaSize from map file
  canvasSize = ccp( [[mapData objectForKey:@"canvasWidth"]
floatValue], [[mapData objectForKey:@"canvasHeight"] floatValue] );
  gameAreaSize = ccp( canvasSize.x/PTM_RATIO, canvasSize.y/PTM_RATIO
);

  //Finish map initialization
  [self finishInit];
}

/* Process a sprite node. This represents a single sprite onscreen */
-(void) processSprite:(NSDictionary*)mapNode {
  //Get node information
  NSString *texture = [mapNode objectForKey:@"selectedSpriteY"];
  float originX = [[mapNode objectForKey:@"originX"] floatValue];
  /* CODE OMITTED */

  //Get metadata
  NSDictionary *metaPairs = [mapNode objectForKey:@"meta"];
  for (id metaKey in metaPairs) {
    NSString* metaValue = [metaPairs objectForKey:metaKey];

    //Check for key "tag"
    if([metaKey isEqualToString:@"tag"]){
      tag = ((int)[metaValue dataUsingEncoding:NSUTF8StringEncoding]);
    }
  }

  /* CODE OMITTED */

  //Finally, add the sprite
```

```
      [gameNode addChild:sprite z:zIndex-24995 tag:tag];
}

/* Process a tiled sprite. */
-(void) processTiledSprite:(NSDictionary*)mapNode {
  //Get node information
  NSString *texture = [mapNode objectForKey:@"selectedSpriteY"];
  NSMutableDictionary *frames = [[[NSMutableDictionary alloc] init]
autorelease];
  float originX = [[mapNode objectForKey:@"originX"] floatValue];
  /* CODE OMITTED */

  //Get metadata
  NSDictionary *metaPairs = [mapNode objectForKey:@"meta"];
  for (id metaKey in metaPairs) {
    NSString* metaValue = [metaPairs objectForKey:metaKey];

    //Check for key "tag" or key "frame" (for animation)
    if([metaKey isEqualToString:@"tag"]){
      tag = ((int)[metaValue dataUsingEncoding:NSUTF8StringEncoding]);
    }else if ([metaKey rangeOfString:@"frame"].location != NSNotFound){
      [frames setObject:metaValue forKey:metaKey];
    }
  }

  //Get any masks to be applied to this tiled sprite
  NSArray *masks = [mapNode objectForKey:@"masks"];

  //OpenGL texture parameters
  ccTexParams params = {GL_NEAREST,GL_NEAREST_MIPMAP_NEAREST,GL_
REPEAT,GL_REPEAT};

  //If a mask exists, apply it
  if([masks count] > 0){
    /* CODE OMITTED */

    //Create TexturedPolygon object
    TexturedPolygon *tp = [TexturedPolygon createWithFile:texture
withVertices:vertices withTriangles:triangles];
    [tp.texture setTexParameters:&params];

    //Set position
    float x = originX - (canvasSize.x/2);
    float y = canvasSize.y - originY - (canvasSize.y/2);
```

```
      tp.position = ccp( x, y-height );

      /* CODE OMITTED */

      //Finally, add the node
      [gameNode addChild:tp z:zIndex-24995];
    }else if([frames count] > 0){
      /* If we have a non-masked tiled animated sprite */

      /* CODE OMITTED */
    }else{
      //Use a regular Sprite
      CCSprite *sprite = [CCSprite spriteWithFile:texture rect:CGRectMake
(0,0,width,height)];
      [sprite.texture setTexParameters:&params];

      //Set position
      float x = originX - (canvasSize.x/2);
      float y = canvasSize.y - originY - (canvasSize.y/2);
      sprite.position = ccp( x+width/2, y-height/2 );

      //Add the node
      [gameNode addChild:sprite z:zIndex-24999];
    }
}

/* Process a line */
-(void) processLine:(NSDictionary*)mapNode{
  //Get line information
  NSArray *drawnLines = [mapNode objectForKey:@"drawnLines"];
  /* CODE OMITTED */

  //Add information to our line containers
  [lineVerticesA addObject:[NSValue valueWithCGPoint:ccp(fromX,
canvasSize.y-fromY)]];
  [lineVerticesB addObject:[NSValue valueWithCGPoint:ccp(toX,
canvasSize.y-toY)]];
}

/* Process a point */
-(void) processPoint:(NSDictionary*)mapNode{
  //Get point information
  float originX = [[mapNode objectForKey:@"originX"] floatValue];
  float originY = [[mapNode objectForKey:@"originY"] floatValue];
```

```
    originY = canvasSize.y - originY;

    //If metadata is appropriate, add point to container
    /* CODE OMITTED */
}

-(void) cleanRecipe {
    [lineVerticesA release];
    [lineVerticesB release];
    [points release];

    [super cleanRecipe];
}
@end
```

How it works...

This recipe loads a JSON level file created by JSONWorldBuilder:

1. Installing JSONWorldBuilder:

   First, we must download and install the JSONWorldBuilder application. The source for JSONWorldBuilder can be found at `http://github.com/n8dogg/ JSONWorldBuilder`. To download the latest build click on **Downloads**, download the source archive, unzip it, and finally look in the `builds` folder. Here you will find an archive containing the latest JSONWorldBuilder application. Drag the application to your `Applications` folder.

2. Creating a new level:

   Opening JSONWorldBuilder automatically creates a new level. To clear the level you are currently working on, choose **File | New Map**.

3. Specifying a resources folder:

   JSONWorldBuilder is designed to work with PNG image files as well as PNG/PLIST combinations. When you specify a resource folder we are telling the editor where these resources live. Click **Resources | Specify Resource** folder. This will bring up a prompt. Once you specify a folder the Sprites window will fill with sprites. Click on a sprite sheet name to hide/show individual sprites:

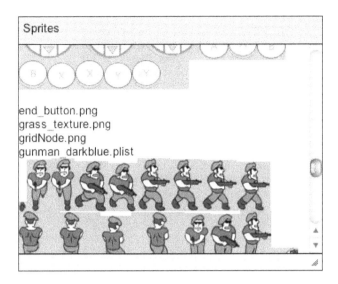

Clicking on an individual sprite will select it for use in the editor.

4. Sprite Stamp:

    Once a sprite is selected in the **Sprites** window, click the **Sprite Stamp** tool on the left menu. Now, by clicking the canvas you can stamp that sprite repeatedly onto the canvas.

5. Sprite Selector:

    To move the sprites that you've just stamped around, click on the **Sprite Selector** tool. Now, click and drag a sprite on the canvas to move it.

6. Draw Tiled Sprite:

    To draw a tiled sprite, click the **Draw Tiled Sprite** tool. Now click and drag your mouse to create a rectangular tiled area with the selected texture. In the editor you can use both sprite sheets or single image files as tiled textures. However, keep in mind that the `TexturedPolygon` class we've been using requires a single image file to work properly.

7. Draw Mask:

    Now, that we have a tiled sprite on the canvas, we can mask it. This means we will cut it into a shape. Select the tiled sprite you've placed on the canvas using the **Sprite** tool. Now select the **Draw Mask** tool. Click once on or around the tiled sprite to start the mask creation process. This involves creating a polygon with successive mouse clicks, finally ending where you initially clicked to complete the polygon.

8. Lines, Points, and Polygons:

    Spatial information can be added to your map using lines, points, and polygons. These are created using the **Create Line**, **Create Point**, and **Create Polygon** tools respectively. Also, note that you need to click and drag to create a line.

9. Shape Selector:

    The **Shape Selector** tool will allow you to select and reposition shapes on the canvas.

10. Move Camera, Zooming, and Canvas Resize:

    The **Move Camera** tool allows us to pan the position of the camera. In the **Nav** window on the right you can click the **+** or **-** buttons to zoom the camera. You can also resize the canvas.

11. Map Object window:

    Inside the **Map Object** window you can specify information like object position and tiled object size. Here, you can also add meta tags in the form of a key/value dictionary, flip images on the X and/or X axis, and re-arrange objects on the Z axis.

12. Loading our map:

    Once we have our map created we can go ahead and load it in Cocos2d. We use `CJSONDeserializer` to go through our map file and process data. After processing some initial information the `loadMap` method calls four different methods depending on map node types:

    ```
    -(void) processSprite:(NSDictionary*)mapNode;
    -(void) processTiledSprite:(NSDictionary*)mapNode;
    -(void) processLine:(NSDictionary*)mapNode;
    -(void) processPoint:(NSDictionary*)mapNode;
    ```

    Each method processes the appropriate node, and attaches sprite information to the `gameNode` object or drawing information to the `drawLayer`. Metadata is also handled in these methods, though it could be handled in the `loadMap` method as well.

Creating scenes with CocosBuilder

Levels are not the only things that can be built using a **WYSIWYG** editor. In this recipe we will craft a simple menu scene using **CocosBuilder**.

Getting ready

Please refer to the project `RecipeCollection03` for full working code of this recipe.

How to do it...

Execute the following code:

```
#import "CCBReader.h"

//Implementation
@implementation Ch8_CocosBuilder

-(CCLayer*) runRecipe {
  //Add button to push CocosBuilder scene
  [CCMenuItemFont setFontSize:32];
  CCMenuItemFont *pushItem = [CCMenuItemFont itemFromString:@"Push
CocosBuilder Scene" target:self selector:@selector(pushScene)];
  CCMenu *pushMenu = [CCMenu menuWithItems:pushItem, nil];
  pushMenu.position = ccp(240,160);
  [self addChild:pushMenu];

  return self;
}

/* Push scene callback */
-(void) pushScene {
  CCScene* scene = [CCBReader sceneWithNodeGraphFromFile:@"scene.ccb"
owner:self];
  [[CCDirector sharedDirector] pushScene:scene];
```

```
}

/* Callback called from CocosBuilder scene */
-(void) back {
  [[CCDirector sharedDirector] popScene];
}

@end
```

How it works...

This recipe loads a CocosBuilder CCB scene along with its associated assets:

1. Installing CocosBuilder:

    First, we must download and install the **CocosBuilder** application. Go to `http://cocosbuilder.com/?page_id=11` and click on the **Download CocosBuilder Application** link. Drag the application to your `Applications` folder.

2. Starting out:

    CocosBuilder allows us to create a hierarchical layout of objects derived from `CCNode`. Available node types include `CCLayer`, `CCSprite`, `CCMenu`, and `CCParticleSystem`. The file assets for these nodes are expected to be in the same folder as the CCB file itself. So, before creating a new CCB file, we must create a folder and fill it with assets we'd like to use. When this is finished click **File | New**. Choose **CCNode** for the **root object type**. Save this file into the folder you created. If you would like to add more assets later, simple copy them into the folder and click **Object | Reload Assets**.

3. Adding objects:

    To add an object as a child of the root `CCNode` object, click on the root node and then click **Object | Add Object as Child**. Then click the object type you would like to add.

4. Adding a CCSprite object:

    In our example, we've added three `CCSprite` objects. Sprite objects are always added without a corresponding texture file. After adding a black sprite, choose your sprite file/sheet and corresponding sprite name on the right under the **CCSprite** heading.

5. Adding a CCMenuItemImage with callback:

    We also add a `CCMenu` object and a child `CCMenuItemImage`. On the `CCMenuItemImage` object we specify a callback. The method `back` will be called on the "Owner" object.

6. Loading our scene:

Inside of Cocos2d we use the following lines to load the scene file, set the scene's "owner", and to finally push the scene:

```
CCScene* scene = [CCBReader sceneWithNodeGraphFromFile:@"scene.ccb" owner:self];
[[CCDirector sharedDirector] pushScene:scene];
```

Clicking on the **Back** button in the scene calls the `back` method in our recipe file and the scene is then popped. Using these tools you can quickly mock up game menus and other stand-alone scenes.

Using Cocos2d-X

Cocos2d is not limited to iOS development. **Cocos2d-X** is a **C++** port of Cocos2d-iPhone. Using Cocos2d-X we can develop games for many platforms including Mac, PC, Linux, Android, and more. In this recipe, we will install Cocos2d-X XCode templates, create a simple Cocos2d-X application, and introduce the Cocos2d-X testbed.

Getting ready

Please refer to the project `Ch8_Cocos2d-X` for full working code of this recipe.

How to do it...

Execute the following code:

```
#include "HelloWorldScene.h"
#include "SimpleAudioEngine.h"

using namespace cocos2d;
using namespace CocosDenshion;

CCScene* HelloWorld::scene()
{
  //'scene' is an autorelease object
  CCScene *scene = CCScene::node();

  //'layer' is an autorelease object
  HelloWorld *layer = HelloWorld::node();

  //Add layer as a child to scene
  scene->addChild(layer);

  return scene;
}

// on "init" you need to initialize your instance
bool HelloWorld::init()
{
  //Super initialization
  if ( !CCLayer::init() )
  {
    return false;
  }

  //Add a menu item with "X" image, which is clicked to quit the
program. You may modify it.
  //Add a "close" icon to exit the progress. it's an autorelease
object
  CCMenuItemImage *pCloseItem = CCMenuItemImage::itemFromNormalImage("
CloseNormal.png", "CloseSelected.png", this, menu_selector(HelloWorld:
:menuCloseCallback) );
  pCloseItem->setPosition( ccp(CCDirector::sharedDirector()-
>getWinSize().width - 20, 20) );
```

```
  //Create menu, it's an autorelease object
  CCMenu* pMenu = CCMenu::menuWithItems(pCloseItem, NULL);
  pMenu->setPosition( CCPointZero );
  this->addChild(pMenu, 1);

  //Add a label shows "Hello World"
  // create and initialize a label
  CCLabelTTF* pLabel = CCLabelTTF::labelWithString("Hello World",
"Thonburi", 34);

  //Ask director the window size
  CCSize size = CCDirector::sharedDirector()->getWinSize();

  //Position the label on the center of the screen
  pLabel->setPosition( ccp(size.width / 2, size.height - 20) );

  //Add the label as a child to this layer
  this->addChild(pLabel, 1);

  //Add "HelloWorld" splash screen"
  CCSprite* pSprite = CCSprite::spriteWithFile("HelloWorld.png");

  //Position the sprite on the center of the screen
  pSprite->setPosition( ccp(size.width/2, size.height/2) );

  //Add the sprite as a child to this layer
  this->addChild(pSprite, 0);

  return true;
}

void HelloWorld::menuCloseCallback(CCObject* pSender)
{
  CCDirector::sharedDirector()->end();

#if (CC_TARGET_PLATFORM == CC_PLATFORM_IOS)
  exit(0);
#endif
}
```

How it works...

This recipe shows us a basic example of Cocos2d-X in action, which is done as follows:

1. Installing Cocos2d-X XCode templates:

   First, we must download the latest version of Cocos2d-X and install the XCode template. Go to `http://www.cocos2d-x.org/projects/cocos2d-x/wiki/Download` and download the latest source package. After unzipping the package you'll find tools to create projects for multiple development environments. To install the XCode templates, open the **Terminal**, navigate to the Cocos2d-X folder, and run the following command:

   ```
   sudo sh install-templates-xcode.sh
   ```

   This will install the templates.

2. Creating a Cocos2d-X project:

   To create a project with the newly installed XCode template click **File | New | New Project**. Under iOS you should see `cocos2d-x`. Under this there are a few templates for Box2D, Chipmunk, and Lua integration. Choose one of these.

3. Using Cocos2d-X:

   As you can see in the preceding code, `Cocos2d-X` is a full port of Cocos2d-iPhone to C++. For more information about `Cocos2d-X`, please consult the **Cocos2d-X | Doxygen** documentation located at `http://www.cocos2d-x.org/embedded/cocos2d-x/classes.html`.

4. The Cocos2d-X testbed:

   Inside the `tests` folder you will find a number of test projects for different operating systems. In the `test.ios` folder open the project `test.xcodeproj`. This is a thorough port of the Cocos2d testbed with the addition of a simple menu system to make navigation between the examples much easier.

Using Cocos3d

Cocos2d is such a versatile framework that it has even been ported and extended into a **3D game engine** appropriately titled **Cocos3d**. In this recipe we will install Cocos3d XCode templates, create a sample Cocos3d application, and introduce the Cocos3d demo `mash-up` project.

Getting ready

Please refer to the project Ch8_Cocos3d for full working code of this recipe.

How to do it...

Execute the following code:

```
#import "Ch8_Cocos3dWorld.h"
#import "CC3PODResourceNode.h"
#import "CC3ActionInterval.h"
#import "CC3MeshNode.h"
#import "CC3Camera.h"
#import "CC3Light.h"

@implementation Ch8_Cocos3dWorld

-(void) dealloc {
  [super dealloc];
}

-(void) initializeWorld {
  //Create the camera, place it back a bit, and add it to the world
  CC3Camera* cam = [CC3Camera nodeWithName: @"Camera"];
  cam.location = cc3v( 0.0, 0.0, 6.0 );
  [self addChild: cam];
```

```
    //Create a light, place it back and to the left at a specific
position (not just directional lighting), and add it to the world
    CC3Light* lamp = [CC3Light nodeWithName: @"Lamp"];
    lamp.location = cc3v( -2.0, 0.0, 0.0 );
    lamp.isDirectionalOnly = NO;
    [cam addChild: lamp];


    //This is the simplest way to load a POD resource file and add the
nodes to the CC3World, if no customized resource subclass is needed.
    [self addContentFromPODResourceFile: @"hello-world.pod"];


    //Create OpenGL ES buffers for the vertex arrays to keep things fast
and efficient, and to save memory, release the vertex data in main
memory because it is now redundant.
    [self createGLBuffers];
    [self releaseRedundantData];


    //That's it! The model world is now constructed and is good to go.


    //But to add some dynamism, we'll animate the 'hello, world' message
using a couple of cocos2d actions...


    //Fetch the 'hello, world' 3D text object that was loaded from the
POD file and start it rotating
    CC3MeshNode* helloTxt = (CC3MeshNode*)[self getNodeNamed: @"Hello"];
    CCActionInterval* partialRot = [CC3RotateBy actionWithDuration: 1.0
rotateBy: cc3v(0.0, 30.0, 0.0)];
    [helloTxt runAction: [CCRepeatForever actionWithAction:
partialRot]];


    //To make things a bit more appealing, set up a repeating up/down
cycle to change the color of the text from the original red to blue,
and back again.
    GLfloat tintTime = 8.0f;
    ccColor3B startColor = helloTxt.color;
    ccColor3B endColor = { 50, 0, 200 };
    CCActionInterval* tintDown = [CCTintTo actionWithDuration: tintTime
red: endColor.r green: endColor.g blue: endColor.b];
    CCActionInterval* tintUp = [CCTintTo actionWithDuration: tintTime
red: startColor.r green: startColor.g blue: startColor.b];
    CCActionInterval* tintCycle = [CCSequence actionOne: tintDown two:
tintUp];
    [helloTxt runAction: [CCRepeatForever actionWithAction: tintCycle]];
}
```

```
/* This template method is invoked periodically whenever the 3D nodes
are to be updated. */
-(void) updateBeforeTransform: (CC3NodeUpdatingVisitor*) visitor {}

/* This template method is invoked periodically whenever the 3D nodes
are to be updated. */
-(void) updateAfterTransform: (CC3NodeUpdatingVisitor*) visitor {}

@end
```

How it works...

This recipe shows us a basic example of Cocos3d in action.

1. Installing Cocos3d XCode templates:

    First, we must download the latest version of Cocos3d and install the XCode template. Go to `http://brenwill.com/cocos3d/`. On the right hand side you should see the latest Cocos3d source package. Download and unzip the package. To install the XCode templates, open the Terminal, navigate to the recently unzipped Cocos3d folder, and run the following command:

    `sudo sh install-cocos3d.sh`

    This will install the templates.

2. Creating a Cocos3d project:

    To create a project with the newly installed XCode template click **File | New | New Project**. Under iOS you should see `cocos3d`. Under this choose **cocos3d Application**.

3. Using Cocos3d:

    In the simple example we created we see a 3D font rendering that reads **"hello, world"**. This 3D model is a PowerVR POD file created in either Maya or 3DS Max and exported using PVRGeoPOD. For more information about Cocos3d, please consult the Cocos3d documentation located (as of this writing) at `http://brenwill.com/docs/cocos3d/0.6.0-sp/api/`.

4. CC3DemoMashUp:

    Inside the source package you will find the XCode workspace file `cocos3d.xcworkspace`. Open this and you will find the `CC3DemoMashUp` target. The mash-up contains a number of advanced examples using mesh models, cameras, lights, bump mapping, animation, and more.

Releasing your app

When you are finally finished creating your app it's time to release it on Apple's App Store. In this recipe we will go through this process.

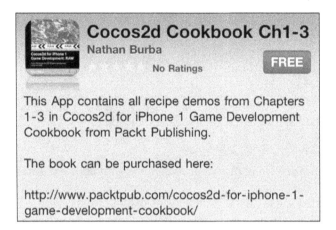

Getting ready

The scope of this recipe is rather large. Because of this we will provide a rough process outline along with supporting documentation, to help you publish your app to the App Store. These steps are mainly based on the guide in the **Distribution** section of the **iOS Provisioning Portal**. You need a valid **iOS Developer account** to access this guide. Another great guide can be found here (with a valid iOS Developer account): `http://adcdownload.apple.com/ios/ios_developer_program_user_guide/ ios_developer_program_user_guide__standard_program_v2.7__final_9110.pdf`.

How to do it...

Once your application is complete, it's time to start preparing your app for the App Store:

1. iOS Provisioning Portal:

    The iOS Provisioning Portal is where development certificates and provisioning profiles are created and/or managed, often in conjunction with XCode. The portal can be found by going to `http://developer.apple.com/ios/manage/overview/index.action` or by going to `http://developer.apple.com/devcenter/ios/index.action` and clicking on iOS **Provisioning Portal**. Once you are there, go to the **App IDs** section of the portal.

2. Creating an explicit App ID:

   Up until this point you may have been provisioning your app onto a device using an **App ID** with an asterisk as the ID suffix. This wildcard allows easy ad hoc publishing of any app onto a registered device. However, if we want to publish our app to the App Store and have features like `Push Notification` enabled, we need to create an explicit App ID. Click **New App ID** and instead of entering a `*` under **App ID Suffix**, enter a proper reverse-domain name style string. An example of this would be `com.domainname.appname`. This is your **Bundle ID**. Once this is finished, go to the **Distribution** section of the iOS Provisioning Portal.

3. Obtaining your distribution certificate:

   This is where you must begin to follow the on-screen instructions carefully. Click **Obtaining your iOS Distribution Certificate** to show the first set of instructions. Here, you will be told to generate a **Certificate Signing Request** using the **Keychain Access** app on your Mac. This request will then be submitted online. Once approved you can then download and install your distribution certificate.

4. Creating a Distribution Provisioning Profile:

   Next, we must create a new "provisioning profile" specifically for distribution on the App Store. This is handled under the **Provisioning** tab in the iOS Provisioning Portal. Remember that this profile will not allow you to push your app onto a device directly. For that, look into **Ad Hoc Distribution**.

5. Building your app for distribution:

   Once your **Distribution Provisioning Profile** is installed you must create a new **Build Configuration** for distribution in XCode. This configuration specifies the necessary certificate and provisioning profile as well as the specific **Bundle ID** created earlier. This step also takes you through setting up your `Entitlements.plist` file. Finally, you build your application and zip it up for transport.

6. Adding your application in iTunes Connect:

   As we've discussed previously, **iTunes Connect** is a set of tools that help developers publish their apps and manage app information. You can log into iTunes Connect by going to `http://itunesconnect.apple.com/`. Once you've logged into iTunes Connect you need to click on **Manage Your Applications**. Then, click **Add New App** in the top-left to begin adding a new application. Follow the on-screen instructions. This will include uploading an app icon, images, and description. When you are finished, go back to the **Manage Your Apps** page and select the app you just created. Finally, click **Ready to Upload Binary** and fill out any more necessary information. Your app should now show the **Waiting for Upload** state.

7. Using Application Loader:

   Now it is time to upload your application using **Application Loader**. Application Loader is a separate Mac application designed to handle the uploading of apps. Application Loader can be downloaded at `http://itunesconnect.apple.com/apploader/ApplicationLoader_1.3.dmg`. Once you've installed Application Loader, open it up and begin uploading the application we zipped up previously. For more information about using Application Loader, please consult the documentation found here: `https://itunesconnect.apple.com/docs/UsingApplicationLoader.pdf`.

8. The App Store Approval Process:

   Once your app has been uploaded it gets placed in a queue to await approval from Apple. This process can take upwards of one week, so be patient. Once your app has been approved, you will see a small green light and the app state will say **Ready for Sale**. Give Apple another 24-48 hours and your app should be on the App Store! For more information about the App Store review guidelines, please refer to this page: `http://developer.apple.com/appstore/guidelines.html`.

Index

touches variable 106
triangulation 49
type property 168

U

UIAcceleration variable 101
UIAlertViewDelegate protocol 256
UIApplication singleton 312
UIButton class 259
UIKit
  UIButton class 259
  UIScrollView class 259
  wrapping 256, 259
UIKit alert dialogs
  about 254, 255
  buttonIndex variable 256
  UIAlertViewDelegate protocol 256
UIScrollView class 259

V

variable time step 162
vehicle
  b2_maxPolygonVertices 207
  camera 207
  car, creating 207
  creating 202-206
  curved road, creating 207
  driving 207
  revolute joints, using 207

Vertex Buffer Object OpenGL extension 25
vertical sliding menu grid
  creating 265, 267
  SlidingMenuGrid class 267
video files
  movie file format 29
  MPMoviePlayerController, using 29
  Objective-C observers, using 29
  observer pattern 29
  playing 26-29
VRope class 221

W

world Step method 162
WYSIWYG editor
  about 410

X

XML data files
  processing 124
  reading 118-124

Z

Zwoptex application
  URL, for downloading 395
Zwoptex Texture Packer
  about 395
  used, for packing textures 395, 396

 **Thank you for buying
Cocos2d for iPhone 1 Game
Development Cookbook**

About Packt Publishing

Packt, pronounced 'packed', published its first book "*Mastering phpMyAdmin for Effective MySQL Management*" in April 2004 and subsequently continued to specialize in publishing highly focused books on specific technologies and solutions.

Our books and publications share the experiences of your fellow IT professionals in adapting and customizing today's systems, applications, and frameworks. Our solution based books give you the knowledge and power to customize the software and technologies you're using to get the job done. Packt books are more specific and less general than the IT books you have seen in the past. Our unique business model allows us to bring you more focused information, giving you more of what you need to know, and less of what you don't.

Packt is a modern, yet unique publishing company, which focuses on producing quality, cutting-edge books for communities of developers, administrators, and newbies alike. For more information, please visit our website: www.packtpub.com.

Writing for Packt

We welcome all inquiries from people who are interested in authoring. Book proposals should be sent to author@packtpub.com. If your book idea is still at an early stage and you would like to discuss it first before writing a formal book proposal, contact us; one of our commissioning editors will get in touch with you.

We're not just looking for published authors; if you have strong technical skills but no writing experience, our experienced editors can help you develop a writing career, or simply get some additional reward for your expertise.

Cocos2d for iPhone 0.99 Beginner's Guide

ISBN: 978-1-84951-316-6   Paperback: 368 pages

Make mind-blowing 2D games for iPhone with this fast, flexible, and easy-to-use framework!

1. A cool guide to learning cocos2d with iPhone to get you into the iPhone game industry quickly

2. Learn all the aspects of cocos2d while building three different games

3. Add a lot of trendy features such as particles and tilemaps to your games to captivate your players

4. Full of illustrations, diagrams, and tips for building iPhone games, with clear step-by-step instructions and practical examples

PhoneGap Beginner's Guide

ISBN: 978-1-84951-536-8   Paperback: 328 pages

Build cross-platform mobile applications with the PhoneGap open source development framework

1. Learn how to use the PhoneGap mobile application framework

2. Develop cross-platform code for iOS, Android, BlackBerry, and more

3. Write robust and extensible JavaScript code

4. Master new HTML5 and CSS3 APIs

5. Full of practical tutorials to get you writing code right away

Please check **www.PacktPub.com** for information on our titles

Sencha Touch 1.0 Mobile JavaScript Framework

ISBN: 978-1-84951-510-8   Paperback: 300 pages

Build web applications for Apple iOS and Google Android touchscreen devices with this first HTML5 mobile framework

1. Learn to develop web applications that look and feel native on Apple iOS and Google Android touchscreen devices using Sencha Touch through examples

2. Design resolution-independent and graphical representations like buttons, icons, and tabs of unparalleled flexibility

3. Add custom events like tap, double tap, swipe, tap and hold, pinch, and rotate

jQuery Mobile First Look

ISBN: 978-1-84951-590-0   Paperback: 216 pages

Discover the endless possibilities offered by jQuery Mobile for rapid Mobile Web Development

1. Easily create your mobile web applications from scratch with jQuery Mobile

2. Learn the important elements of the framework and mobile web development best practices

3. Customize elements and widgets to match your desired style

4. Step-by-step instructions on how to use jQuery Mobile

Please check **www.PacktPub.com** for information on our titles

www.ingramcontent.com/pod-product-compliance
Lightning Source LLC
Chambersburg PA
CBHW080142060326
40689CB00018B/3824